D1713094

In the Shadow of KINZUA

The Iroquois and Their Neighbors
Christopher Vecsey, *Series Editor*

In the Shadow of
KINZUA

The Seneca Nation of Indians
since World War II

LAURENCE MARC HAUPTMAN

SYRACUSE UNIVERSITY PRESS

For a listing of books published and distributed by Syracuse University Press, visit our
website at www.SyracuseUniversityPress.syr.edu.

ISBN: 978-0-8156-3328-0 (cloth)   978-0-8156-5238-0 (e-book)

Library of Congress Cataloging-in-Publication Data
Hauptman, Laurence Marc.
    In the shadow of Kinzua : the Seneca nation of indians since World War II / Laurence
Marc Hauptman.
        pages cm. — (Iroquois and their neighbors)
    Includes bibliographical references and index.
    ISBN 978-0-8156-3328-0 (cloth : alk. paper) — ISBN 978-0-8156-5238-0 (e-book) 1. Seneca
Indians—History—20th century.   2. Seneca Indians—Government relations.   3. Seneca
Indians—Land tenure.   4. Kinzua Dam (Pa.)—Environmental conditions.   I. Title.
    E99.S3H35 2014
    974.7004'975546—dc23   2013042648

To the elders of the Seneca Nation of Indians

Laurence Marc Hauptman is Distinguished Professor Emeritus of History at State University of New York, New Paltz, where he taught courses on Native American history, New York history, and Civil War history for forty years. On October 25, 2011, Dr. John B. King Jr., the New York State commissioner of education, awarded Hauptman the State Archives Lifetime Achievement Award for his research and publications on the Empire State. Professor Hauptman is the author, coauthor, or coeditor of seventeen books on the Iroquois and other Native Americans. He has testified as an expert witness before committees of both houses of Congress and in the federal courts and has served as a historical consultant for the Wisconsin Oneidas, the Cayugas, the Mashantucket Pequots, and the Senecas. Over the past two decades, he has been honored by the New York State Board of Regents, the New York Academy of History, the New York State Historical Association, the Pennsylvania Historical Association, the Wisconsin Historical Society, the New York Academy of History, and Mohonk Consultations for his writings about Native Americans. In 1987 and again in 1998, he was the recipient of the Peter Doctor Indian Memorial Foundation Award from the Six Nations for his scholarship and applied work on behalf of Native Americans in eastern North America.

Contents

Part IV. Conclusion

Illustrations

Maps and Chart

Preface

HISTORIANS ARE OFTEN captives of their times, affected by both the documents available during the era in which they write and their own limited learning curve in making sense of the records left behind. Sometimes, however, historians get lucky and live long enough to rewrite what they had previously published decades earlier. Such is the case with *In the Shadow of Kinzua: The Seneca Nation of Indians since World War II.* I started my research on Seneca history more than forty years ago. I arrived in Seneca Territory only six years after the Kinzua Dam had been dedicated in 1966. From the time of my first encounter with the Senecas, I tried to ascertain how and why this dam came about; however, I recently began to question my earlier conclusions. I had previously pointed out numerous reasons for the dam and its origins, including the Cold War climate; the longtime push for flood control along the Allegheny River by Pennsylvania politicians, Pittsburgh industrialists, the US Army Corps of Engineers, a key presidential adviser in the Eisenhower White House, and pork-barrel politics in Washington, DC, and Harrisburg.[1] In hindsight, what was missing from my narrative was how federal, Pennsylvania, and New York State interests intersected and complemented each other as well as how Kinzua became a hydroelectric project.

In the Shadow of Kinzua is far different from my previous writings. As in the past, I have made use of materials collected in my archival research and conducted extensive interviews with Senecas and non-Indians involved in policy decisions. However, this report is in part a memoir. I have personally witnessed the dramatic changes in the Seneca Nation since 1972 and have observed how these Native peoples have dealt with this crisis over

1. Kinzua Dam. Photograph by David G. Kanzeg. Used with permission of David G. Kanzeg.

the past four decades. I have been frequently invited to participate and speak at community events and commemorations held on the two Seneca residential territories, the Allegany and Cattaraugus Indian Reservations. In 1990, I worked with Congressman Amory Houghton's office and testified at two congressional hearings that led up to the Seneca Nation Settlement Act, which is discussed in chapter 10. In order to have full disclosure here before presenting material in this book, I should mention that after my congressional testimony I started to do contract research in the late 1990s, serving as a historical researcher and expert witness for the Seneca Nation and its attorneys in litigation in federal courts (described in chapter 9). Moreover, many of the Senecas mentioned in this book are not merely individuals mentioned in archival documents and in transcripts of state and federal hearings, but people I have known over these many years. Thus, I have borne witness to how the Senecas have dealt with the crisis and have rebuilt their nation. I have seen the Senecas' remarkable adaptability to overcome the devastation and the psychological hurt that is still caused by the dam.

The building of the $125 million Kinzua Dam between 1960 and 1965, dedicated officially in 1966, broke the federal Six Nations Treaty of Canandaigua of 1794; flooded approximately ten thousand acres of Seneca lands—all acreage below 1,365 feet elevation, including the entire Cornplanter Tract (Grant); destroyed homes, schools, churches, and the old Coldspring Longhouse, the ceremonial center of Allegany Seneca traditional life; caused the removal of more than 130 families and 600 persons from the take area; and resulted in the relocation of these same families from widely spaced rural surroundings to two suburban-styled housing clusters, one at Steamburg and the other at Jimersontown, adjacent to the city of Salamanca. The Senecas were forced to grant a "flowage easement" that resulted in the creation of the Allegheny Reservoir. The result has been devastating to the Senecas, and it is impossible to put a price tag on what was lost. The river itself had substantially helped shape Seneca existence—religion, worldview, residential patterns, subsistence fishing, hunting, logging, trapping, and travel from Killbuck to well beyond the Cornplanter Tract. This dam project not only took extensive acreage of Seneca lands but destroyed a way of life along the river, changing the whole ecosystem below and above the Seneca Pumped Storage Generating Station up to 1,365 feet elevation. Gone was the paddlefish as well as much of the wildlife that feed along the river. Gone was the Senecas' ability to collect traditional medicines along the banks.[2]

From its opening to the present day, the dam has cast a long shadow on events and politics within the Seneca Nation of Indians, a federally recognized Native American nation in what non-Indians would refer to as southwestern New York State. On February 24, 2011, I attended a Federal Energy Regulatory Commission hearing held at Salamanca High School on the Seneca Nation's Allegany Indian Reservation. In more than two hours of testimony, Senecas explained to the commissioners what the Kinzua Dam meant to themselves, their families, and their communities. Some of the most moving testimony was given by Senecas who had been

children, teenagers, and young adults during the troubling times in which
the dam was built. After introductory remarks made by then Seneca president Robert Odawi Porter, Salamanca High School students sang a song of
remembrance. A representative of the high school's Model United Nations
program, citing the Treaty of Canandaigua and the United Nations Declaration of the Rights of Indigenous Peoples, then urged the commissioners
to seriously consider giving the license for hydropower production at the
Kinzua Dam to the Seneca Nation.[3] Shane Titus, conservation officer and
fisheries manager for the Seneca Nation, described the disastrous changes
caused by the Kinzua Dam and the Seneca Pumped Storage Generating
Station in Warren, Pennsylvania, which produces hydroelectric power. The
Seneca wildlife biologist maintained that there had been a "steady decline"
of the Senecas' "fish habitat, fish diversity, and the shoreline," which has
"eroded to the point that our trees, grasses, and bushes can no longer take
root." Silt and sediment buildup that has accumulated for nearly fifty years
now occupy "areas that once harbored gravel beds, natural structures, and
habitats such as tree stumps." He added: "The water is now shallower at
the northern end of the [lower] reservoir, causing waters to heat faster during the summer time, spawning algae blooms, early algae blooms, forcing
fish to seek deeper waters, colder waters, more hospitable waters which are
unfortunately usually on the Pennsylvania border and into Pennsylvania
[behind the Kinzua Dam leading to fish kills]. The water fluctuation has
also had an adverse effect on some of the spring reproductive cycles . . .
of wildlife species, both fish, insects, and amphibians." Titus mentioned
three species listed as "critical, concerned, or endangered": paddlefish, hell
benders, and ray bean, a freshwater mussel.[4]

Other Senecas, women and men, recounted their personal remem-
brances of what they faced during the Kinzua crisis. Rebecca Bowen,
whose family was removed from the Senecas' Red House community,
which now no longer exists, to the Jimersontown relocation area, stated
that the river was "integral to my childhood experience." She indicated
that she would never forget the changes wrought:

> Like an occupation force, an army of construction companies invaded
> our homeland. . . . I remember putting the chair outside the front door of

2. Kinzua Dam and upper and lower Allegheny Reservoir, 1993. Photograph by Margaret Luzier, 1993. Courtesy of the US Army Corps of Engineers.

our house and watching as the earth movers removed the entire face of the hill that stood in front of our home. I remember shouting the angriest things a child could think of. At night, the piles of trees and brush would burn. The land was cleared right up to the river banks. One day moving men showed up and said they would be back in four hours to move us to a new home. Our lives were changed forever. The waters that generate the power [of today's Kinzua Dam] flows over our old homesteads where the Longhouse once stood, the foundations of our churches, our school, our old ballfields, even the graves of Senecas.[5]

Much of the Seneca anger then and now has focused on the Army Corps of Engineers because it was put in charge of the flooding that created the Allegheny Reservoir and contracted for the destruction of Seneca homes, schools, churches, and the longhouse; for the reburial of graves; and for the forced relocation of tribal members. The Army Corps presented the project, claiming that it was the Senecas' patriotic duty to abandon their lands for the good of their fellow Americans threatened by periodic floods down the Allegheny River! The incongruity of its logic was very apparent to the Senecas. The late George Heron, the most prominent tribal leader during this crisis and a veteran of the Pacific Theater during World War II, and numerous other Senecas who had served in combat during World War II and Korea now witnessed the same military taking their most sacred of all Seneca lands.[6]

The dam's full impact on the Senecas was first brought home to me in 1984. In September of that year, I participated in the first Remember the Removal Day, a commemoration that has become an annual event on the Allegany Indian Reservation. I have continued to attend this commemoration over the years and have presented several history talks at the event. The first commemoration, as is true of the others that followed, was a somber event. It included a prayer given by Richard Johnnyjohn of the Coldspring Longhouse; a brief statement by George Heron, the president of the Seneca Nation during the Kinzua crisis; and the tossing of a wreath tied with a black ribbon into the Allegheny River. It was then followed by a six-and-a-half-mile walk to symbolize the Kinzua removal of the Senecas in 1964, along old Route 17 from the bridge at Red House to the Steamburg Community Building. In 1984, as an invited guest, I had the privilege of walking with Merrill Bowen, a spokesman for the Cornplanter Heirs during the Kinzua crisis, who was being accompanied on the walk by Walter Taylor, the major community organizer sent by the Philadelphia Yearly Meeting of Friends to help the Senecas in the Kinzua crisis. Taylor also served the Senecas as a planner and a major publicist and lobbyist in securing monetary compensation from Congress. On display at the community building were photographs, maps, and documents related to life before the dam and what was lost forever by the creation of the Allegheny Reservoir. At the end of the walk, there were speeches, followed by a luncheon provided by the Seneca Nation.

Two years later Syracuse University Press published my book *The Iroquois Struggle for Survival: World War II to Red Power*. In it, I traced the history of the Kinzua Dam project, outlining Pennsylvania's concerns about flood control from the time of the Johnstown Flood of 1888. I described the major push for the project in the mid- and late 1950s by President

Eisenhower's Office of Public Works Planning, the US Army Corps of Engineers, as well as US representatives and Pennsylvania state officials intent on promoting pork-barrel projects.[7] From the early 1970s onward, my initial thinking about the dam had been shaped by listening to Seneca elders talk about the dam as well as about life before and after it was built. They were still in shock after their removal from the take area. These same elders frequently posed the question: Why was it so necessary to destroy a way of life along the upper Allegheny? After all, they frequently noted that, despite the Army Corps' flood control rationale for the dam, this objective had not been fully accomplished, pointing out to me that Hurricane Agnes in 1972 produced severe flooding within the region.

In the summer of 2009, I was contacted by attorneys from the firm Sonnenschein Nath and Rosenthal, now N. R. Denton, which at the time was representing the Seneca Nation of Indians. I was informed that the Senecas were seeking the federal license for hydropower generation at the Kinzua Dam, which for nearly fifty years had been operated by the Pennsylvania Electric Company, now a subsidiary of FirstEnergy Corporation. I was asked to do new research on the project's development and impact, visit libraries and archives to copy needed documents not available to me in the 1970s and early 1980s, attend meetings at the Seneca Nation as well as Federal Energy Regulatory Commission hearings, comment on drafts for accuracy, and write periodic reports. I quickly accepted the offer.

The Seneca Nation of Indians, Onöndowa'ga:', the "People of the Big Hill," one of the original nations of the Iroquois Confederacy, is a federally recognized Indian nation that has had a government-to-government relationship with the United States since the period 1784–94. No longer a nation of chiefs or a formal member of the Iroquois Confederacy's Grand Council at Onondaga, it has had an elected system of government since 1848. Today, the Seneca Nation of Indians' president, treasurer, clerk, and sixteen tribal councilors—eight each from the Allegany and Cattaraugus Territories—are elected for two-year terms. The offices of president, treasurer, and clerk are alternated every two years between Senecas residing on these two territories. The Seneca Constitution allows these three elected leaders to serve multiple but not consecutive terms. It should be noted that a separate community of Senecas, the Tonawanda Band, who occupy a reservation halfway between Rochester and Buffalo, broke away from the Seneca Nation in the years between 1838 and 1857; they maintain their own form of government, a council of chiefs chosen by clan mothers.

In the post–World War II era, the Seneca Nation of Indians' land base included four tribal territories: Allegany (Ohi:yo´), Cattaraugus (Ga´dägësgëö´), Cornplanter (Jonöhsade:gëh), and Oil Spring (Ga:no´s). The Allegany Territory is located along the upper Allegheny River from Vandalia, New York, to the Pennsylvania border in Cattaraugus County, New York; the Cattaraugus Territory is approximately thirty-five miles southwest of Buffalo in Cattaraugus and Erie counties, New York; and the Oil Spring Territory, a one-mile square nonresidential land base, is at the border of Allegany and Cattaraugus counties in Cuba, New York. A fourth territory, the Cornplanter Tract in Warren County, Pennsylvania, a state land grant awarded to Chief Cornplanter and his heirs from 1791 to 1796, was flooded by the Kinzua Dam construction between 1960 and 1965; only a few acres, largely inaccessible, remain of this territory today. Besides the Allegany Seneca Casino in Salamanca, the Seneca Gaming Corporation operates the Seneca Niagara Falls Casino on thirty acres of land in Niagara Falls and a smaller casino on nine acres of land in downtown Buffalo on its Indian restricted-fee lands.

Anthropologists have long recognized the importance of locality in shaping Iroquoia.[8] Today the Seneca Nation is a confederated reality of two major residential territories—the Allegany and Cattaraugus Indian Reservations—that are separated by thirty miles. They have common concerns, but also distinct ones as well as different histories. In each of these reservations—which Senecas now refer to as "territories"—there are distinct neighborhoods. For example, Allegany includes Killbuck, Salamanca, Shongo or Jimersontown (West Salamanca), and Steamburg today as well as others that were inundated by the Kinzua Dam construction in the early 1960s—Coldspring, Onoville, Quaker Bridge, Red House, Tunesassa. At the larger Cattaraugus Territory, there are numerous

Map 1. Eastern Iroquoia today. Map by Joe Stoll. Courtesy of Joe Stoll. There are three Seneca Nation casinos—two of which are off the Allegany and Cattaraugus Territories, in Buffalo and Niagara Falls. The casinos are not shown on this map.

neighborhoods—Bucktown, Burning Springs, Cayuga Road, Eleven Acres, Four Corners, Four Mile Level, Indian Hill, Newtown, Pinewoods, Plank Road, Sulfur Springs, and Taylor Hollow. The great diversity of Seneca existence is evident in other areas as well. Senecas attend church services at Mormon, Methodist, Presbyterian, Episcopal, and other Christian houses of worship. Others follow the Gaiwi:yoh, the Longhouse religion. Even the two Seneca longhouses at Allegany (Coldspring) and Cattaraugus (Newtown) are distinct from each other, in history as well as in their relationship with other Hodinöhsö:ni´ (People of the Extended Lodge/ Longhouse) territories. Although over the years residents of the Allegany and Cattaraugus territories have intermarried and married Hodinöhsö:ni´ from other communities as well as other Native Americans and non-Indians, there still remains a uniqueness to each Seneca territory.

Hence, the first theme of this book is that the Seneca Nation of Indians is a diverse cultural reality, with competing pulls under one umbrella, a federated political structure. In this fragile system, it is important to note that several major factors force compromise. The residents of these two Seneca territories are well aware of the unfortunate schism that led to the separation of their kin, the Tonawanda Band, after the Buffalo Creek Treaty of 1838.[9] Quite significantly, Allegany and Cattaraugus residents are brought together by the constant threats from the outside. Since the establishment of New York State and the United States in the revolutionary era, the Senecas have devoted much of their energies to maintaining their inherent sovereignty, one they say was given to them by the Creator and not assigned to them by outside governments. They have struggled to maintain it in the face of major land losses, attempts at removal, and policies designed to end their separate tribal political and cultural existence. Hence, as we will see, mostly strong male leadership in council and powerful women, "mothers of the nation," at the community level have kept this diverse federation together since major land losses in the 1950s and 1960s. To overcome internal tensions, Seneca leadership at times successfully shifts hostility outward toward officials and their policies in Albany, Harrisburg, and Washington, DC, thereby promoting the common goals of their two remaining residential territories.

Outsiders with little understanding of this nation's history or of its members' great diversity often misinterpret Seneca politics. As a result, the Seneca world is portrayed in simplistic, mostly negative terms in the *Buffalo News*, the newspaper with the largest circulation in the region. Reporters covering Seneca news stories are generally unaware of historical factors—namely, that at least since the time of the federal Treaty at Big Tree in 1797, these Native peoples have been distrustful of authority, frequently challenging their own leaders by questioning their abilities, strategies, and even honesty. Although it is true that Seneca politics is often combative, which makes for good headlines and sales of newspapers, accounts overemphasize Senecas' inability to cooperate with each other and do not recognize the great diversity of expression within this nation. They minimize Seneca successes in balancing these countervailing forces to maintain their fragile federated governing structure.[10] Reporters too often generalize and fail to realize the uniqueness of what they are observing or to credit the Senecas when they succeed. After all, it should be pointed out, the Seneca Nation of Indians has lasted longer than Czechoslovakia, the Soviet Union, and Yugoslavia. Its elected system of government, older than many nations of the world, was formally established in 1848, 165 years ago!

Scholars themselves are also too quick to label divisions within the Native American world as "factionalism" and to associate it with failures of leadership. They categorize divisions between Christian and Longhouse or between so-called progressive and traditional elements as "factionalism." I consciously avoid the latter term because to me it connotes a temporary political state rather than a permanent condition of shifting alliances based on kinship, locality, and other factors.[11] Indeed, the Senecas' political behavior within their territories is not simply a carbon copy of how Western democracies function. Anthropologist Bernard Cohn perceptively noted in early 1980 that the "historian needs the direct experience of another culture by undertaking systematic fieldwork. It is not just the idea of the exotic, but the sense one gets that there are such things as cultural logics, that there is as much rationality in other societies as in their own, even though they flow from other principles."[12] In combining fieldwork with archival research over the past forty years, I have come to realize that Seneca diversity of expression is as much a strength as a weakness.[13]

The Senecas have demonstrated great ability to adapt to change in order to survive as a distinct people, which has been apparent beyond the post–World War II period. This point is the book's second overall theme. In the past, the Seneca Nation had to deal with great challenges to its existence—the Sullivan–Clinton campaign, the nefarious machinations of the Holland and Ogden land companies, Jacksonian Indian removal, federal termination policies, state transportation development, and Kinzua—just to mention the major crises since the revolutionary era. In his classic *Apologies to the Iroquois*, excerpted in *The New Yorker* in 1959 and published as a book in 1960, Edmund Wilson, the legendary writer and literary critic, observed: "One finds thus at the core of the Seneca people an intelligence and a practical ability a kind of irreducible morale, which, in the course of their difficult relations with the whites, has always in the long run retrieved them from the disasters inflicted upon them and the results of their own vices."[14] Anthropologist Anthony F. C. Wallace, in his classic *The Death and Rebirth of the Seneca*, wrote about how the Senecas faced a terrible crisis that threatened their very existence following the American Revolution and adapted to change in order to survive.[15] Wallace was not the only scholar to recognize the Senecas' great adaptability. In 1965, during the Kinzua crisis, William N. Fenton, whose major works were centered on ceremonialism at the Coldspring and Tonawanda Longhouses, noted this adaptability as an Iroquoian quality, found not just among the Senecas. Fenton insisted: "If anthropologists have discovered anything important about the Iroquois or Iroquois culture, it is significant that it has refused to go away. In each generation and in each century, it has managed to adapt itself to the contemporary stream of events so that it has managed to survive."[16] Hence, this book clearly confirms Fenton's interpretation—namely, that one of the strengths of the Seneca Nation is its ability to adapt to change when faced with crisis.

In 1998, Joy Bilharz, an anthropologist from the State University of New York at Fredonia, also recognized the Senecas' great resilience in her work *The Allegany Senecas and Kinzua Dam: Relocation through Two Generations*. A theoretical work, it is based largely on her fieldwork among the Allegany and Cornplanter Senecas, testing a model put forth by Thayer Scudder and Elizabeth Colson from their fieldwork in Zambia in the 1950s. Bilharz made valuable contributions by describing some of the affects of the dam from the 1960s to the early 1990s. The present study differs significantly from her ahistorical monograph. It is a straightforward, less theoretical work based on extensive archival research—federal, state, and tribal—not used by or not available to Bilharz. It also is based on my participation as an expert witness and a historical consultant in some of the events described in several of the chapters. Bilharz's focus was on Allegany and Cornplanter, whereas this book treats Cattaraugus as well. Unlike her study, I deal with both sides of the divide. It is both a policy study—namely, how and why Washington, Harrisburg, and Albany came up with the project to build the dam—as well as a community study of the Seneca Nation in the post–World War II era.

To be fair to Bilharz, who sympathetically described the trauma faced by Senecas and made a significant contribution, as noted in my favorable review of her book, her fieldwork was done largely from 1980 to the mid-1990s, before the vast economic transformation of the Seneca Nation occurred, which is described in chapter 11 of this book.[17] Indeed, events happening in the past two decades have revealed much more about the origins and impact of Kinzua. Moreover, in contrast to Bilharz's work, my book sees the glass as being half full—that the Seneca governmental structure and intense politics, although openly criticized by most tribal members themselves, have actually benefited the nation in certain ways not recognized or acknowledged in her work. Indeed, the Seneca Nation's federated governmental structure has lasted since 1848, no mean achievement when faced with warding off the Dawes General Allotment Act and federal termination policies or with rebuilding after the Kinzua Dam crisis. As a consequence of these factors, I treat topics not dealt with in Bilharz's book, including health care, library and museum development, land claims, a major lease settlement act, and the establishment of three Seneca casinos.

The present Seneca Nation billion-dollar economy obscures the realities of what its communities were like at the time of Kinzua.[18] In the 1950s, the Seneca Nation's government did not operate as it does today. There were no full-time employees of the nation before the Kinzua crisis. The Tribal Council met mostly in a member's garage twice a year. Much of its focus was devoted to approving or renewing agreements for oil and natural gas exploration. As was true about most if not all federally recognized American Indian nations, the Senecas were nearly totally dependent on Washington—for travel moneys to go to federal hearings right down to basic office supplies. Their attorneys were approved by Albany, and New York State by law paid the attorneys' salaries until 1957. Indeed, a quasi-colonial relationship existed.

When I first visited the Seneca Nation territories in 1972, the Senecas were reeling from their greatest modern tragedy, the building of the Kinzua Dam. Only a handful of Seneca students went beyond high school to further vocational or college coursework, and more than one-third of the nation was unemployed. Health conditions were scandalous, mismanaged by culturally insensitive bureaucrats more than 250 miles away in Albany. The housing stock on both the Allegany and Cattaraugus Indian Territories, except for two neighborhoods of new homes for the hundreds of relocatees flooded out by the Kinzua Dam, included leftover trailers from the project and numerous homes in desperate need of repair.

Racism toward the Senecas was rampant both on and off the two reservation communities. Gowanda, a "border town" just off the Cattaraugus Indian Reservation, had a long reputation for intolerance. Even into the early 1970s, Salamanca, a small city on the Allegany Indian Reservation that was leased from the Seneca Nation and had a sizable white population, had separate Indian stores, bars, and other businesses owned by non-Indians. Until the early 1960s, the major hotel in town had a long-standing policy of not serving Indians.[19] Senecas would advise me not to frequent certain stores in Salamanca because "the owners don't like us."[20] When I first arrived in Salamanca and experienced its caste system, at times I thought I was in Mississippi during the civil rights movement!

Before tribal bingo operations and casinos, a tribal governmental infrastructure had to be built. The immediate crisis was for the Seneca Nation to find ways to provide housing for relocatees from the Kinzua Dam's flooding of tribal lands. For two decades, the Senecas also had to contend with New York State's efforts to secure an easement for the Southern Tier Expressway on Seneca lands that was directly tied to the Kinzua Dam crisis. Some problems that had preceded dam construction had to be dealt with and settled as well. Until the mid-1970s, Seneca medical care was a disaster caused by the poor services provided by New York State's Department of Health.

After an introductory section, this book is divided into three additional parts: Kinzua's origins, its impact on the Seneca Nation, and a concluding chapter. In part II, I clearly show that in studying the origins of the Kinzua crisis, it is necessary to go beyond examining policies emanating from Harrisburg or Pittsburgh. Pennsylvania officials' policies with respect to the dam clearly cannot and should not be separated from decisions emanating from Washington, DC, and Albany in the post–World

War II era. In parts III and IV, the last eight chapters, I focus on Kinzua's effects on Seneca existence right down to the present time. Chapters 5 through 7 describe the remarkable spirit of cooperation and volunteerism undertaken by the Senecas at both Allegany and Cattaraugus to recover from Kinzua. Chapters 8 through 11 focus on the effects of Kinzua on Seneca existence to the present time. In chapter 8, I discuss one of the more immediate results of the Kinzua crisis—how New York State's Southern Tier Expressway was a direct result of the building of the dam, facilitated by a sweetheart deal that the New York State Department of Public Works made with the US Army Corps of Engineers. This treatment is followed by two chapters in which I show that major issues—the filing of land claims litigation and the resolution of thousands of severely undervalued leases on the Senecas' Allegany Territory—had to be delayed because of immediate, more pressing concerns caused by Kinzua. In chapter 11, I discuss the individual and tribal initiatives to overcome the economic problems facing the Seneca Nation after Kinzua. Besides summarizing in the conclusion, I also try to put the crisis in perspective, comparing it with serious challenges facing the Seneca Nation today.

In the Shadow of Kinzua clearly shows that the Native peoples of the Kinzua era were truly heroes and heroines who faced problems head on and devoted their energies for tribal survival. Without adequate financial resources or college diplomas, they left legacies in many areas, including two community centers, a health-delivery system, two libraries, and a museum. Moneys allocated in a compensation bill passed by the US Congress in August 1964 produced a generation of college-educated Senecas, some of whom now work in tribal government making major contributions to the nation's present and future. Facing impossible odds and forces hidden from view, the Seneca leaders motivated a cadre of volunteers to help rebuild their devastated nation. Although their strategies did not stop the dam and their economic planning was largely ineffective, they did lay the groundwork for a tribal governing structure and major improvements in many other areas, needed for what followed from the 1980s to the present.

Three points relating to style must be clarified. First, I have employed the term *territory* wherever possible instead of *reservation* because the former term is more frequently used today by Senecas themselves. Second, there are variations in spelling the place-name "Allegany/Allegheny." The river, the valley, the state forest, the national forest, and the upper and lower reservoir created by the Kinzua Dam project are spelled "Allegheny," whereas Seneca territory and the nearby New York State Park are spelled "Allegany." Third, I have relied on Phyllis Bardeau's *Definitive Seneca: It's in the Word*, edited by Jaré Cardinal and published by the Seneca-Iroquois National Museum in 2011, for preferred spelling of Seneca names and place-names.

January 1, 2013
New Paltz, New York

Acknowledgments

I THANK ROBERT ODAWI PORTER, president of the Seneca Nation from 2010 to 2012, and the Seneca Nation Tribal Council for encouraging me to undertake this project. I especially acknowledge the help of Wendy Huff, the former executive director of the Seneca Nation of Indians' Kinzua Dam Relicensing Commission; Rovena Abrams, the editor of the *Seneca Nation of Indians' Official Newsletter*; Diane Kennedy Murth, the Seneca Nation's clerk; and Randy John, professor emeritus of sociology at St. Bonaventure University and now curator at the Seneca-Iroquois National Museum. Many other Allegany and Cattaraugus Senecas have contributed to this project, including Bruce Abrams, Caleb Abrams, Marilyn Jemison Anderson, Arlene Bova, Dave Bova, Becky Bowen, Pam Bowen, Ethel Bray, Tyler Heron, Rick Jemison, Marlene Johnson, Fred Kennedy, Norma Kennedy, David and Mark Kimelberg, Maurice "Mo" John Sr., Jean Loret, Lori Quigley, Lana Redeye, Cyrus Schindler Sr., Michael Schindler, Martin Seneca Jr., Penny Seneca, Anita Lillian Taylor, Marsha Thompson, and Merle Watt Sr. A special acknowledgment must go out to Caleb Abrams, an extraordinary young gifted Seneca filmmaker. My early Seneca teachers—Cornelius Abrams Jr., Duwayne "Duce" Bowen, George Heron, Jeanne Marie Jemison, Calvin "Kelly" John, Wini Kettle, and Pauline Lay Seneca, a remarkable Cayuga schoolteacher married to the late President Cornelius Seneca—are no longer here to correct their pupil to see if he "got it right." The late Carole Moses, artist, Peacemaker judge, and my former student, kindly introduced me to many Senecas and taught me more than I taught her about her people's history.

I was also aided in my understanding of Seneca history by my involvement in the events leading up to the passage of the Seneca Nation Settlement Act of 1990, when I worked with Congressman Amory Houghton's office and a group of extraordinary Senecas, including Marlene Johnson and two outstanding tribal attorneys, Loretta Seneca Crane and Douglas Endreson. My education was also furthered by my discussions with Arlinda Locklear and Jeanne Whiteing, two Native American attorneys who have served the Seneca Nation and other communities so well.

Over the years, I have had the privilege of speaking at the Seneca-Iroquois National Museum and working with its four directors since its opening more than thirty-five years ago: George H. J. Abrams, its first director; the late Judy Greene and Midge Dean Stock; and Jaré Cardinal, the present director. I also thank Sue Grey of the Seneca-Iroquois National Museum for her help in locating photographs for this book, and Stephanie Crowley, assistant editor of the *Seneca Nation of Indians' Official Newsletter*, who allowed me to use her photographs of Seneca leaders. While working at the State University of New York's Rockefeller Institute in Albany in 1985 and 1986, I had the opportunity to learn from Hazel Dean John, the noted Seneca linguist and educator, about her people and how they viewed Albany policies and policymakers.

Others have substantially aided me in this effort. Shannon O'Loughlin, attorney for the Seneca Nation of Indians' Kinzua Dam Relicensing Commission, added to my understanding of legal matters. Woldezion Mesghinna, the president and principal engineer of Natural Resources Consulting, Inc., of Fort Collins, Colorado, and his assistant engineer, Jordan Lanini, educated me about the science and impact of the Seneca Pumped Storage Generating Station at the Kinzua Dam. My friend Donald Quigley accompanied me on a major research trip to the Pennsylvania State Archives at Harrisburg, providing helpful assistance that led to mining valuable records. Kwinn Doran assisted me in retracing my earlier research steps at the Eisenhower Library. I have depended on the expertise of Andrew Arpy, James Folts, and William Gorman at the New York State Archives as well as of Nancy Horan, Paul Mercer, and Vicki Weiss, manuscript librarians at the New York State Library, who opened new doors in my reexamination of Seneca history.

Several of my neighbors in the mid–Hudson Valley and colleagues at the State University of New York at New Paltz aided me in my work. Corinne Nyquist and Joseph Stoeker of the interlibrary loan division of the Sojourner Truth Library helped me acquire essential materials for my research. David Krikun provided insights about the push by public and private interests for hydroelectric power development from the 1930s onward. I frequently traveled with Heriberto "Airy" Dixon, a scholar who has taught me much about the people, both Native American and non-Indian, of western New York, where he was born and raised. David Jaman, formerly of Gardiner, New York, and now resident of The Villages in Florida, provided technical assistance as well as good cheer.

Most important, my wife, Ruth, has always encouraged my research and excused my obsession with deadlines. She has also tolerated my inexcusable habit of cluttering up every nook and cranny of our home with documents and drafts of chapters. The love of my life is truly the one who anchors me in the present while I search for Truth in the past.

Abbreviations

BIA	US Bureau of Indian Affairs
DOT	New York State Department of Transportation
DPW	New York State Department of Public Works
FERC	Federal Energy Regulatory Commission
FPC	Federal Power Commission
ICC	Indian Claims Commission
IGRA	Indian Gaming Regulatory Act of 1988
IHS	Indian Health Service
KDRC	Kinzua Dam Relicensing Commission
PACT Act	Prevent All Cigarette Trafficking Act
Penelec	Pennsylvania Electric Company
SCOUT	Salamanca Coalition of United Taxpayers
SUNY	State University of New York
TAMS	Tippetts-Abbet-McCarthy
TVA	Tennessee Valley Authority
USET	United South and Eastern Tribes

PART I |||| *Introduction*

1

The Seneca Nation of Indians

Diversity and Adaptation

FROM 1972 TO 1985, I spent most of my research time doing fieldwork, interviewing and learning from Senecas at the Cattaraugus Territory (Ga´dägësgëö´). I would visit the reservation in June at the Strawberry Festival and in September during the annual fall festival, where I would be in the company of many of the elders affiliated with the United Mission Church, also known as the Wright Memorial Church. Besides the wonderful stories told to me by the elders, I relished the delicious pies prepared by the church ladies, which I brought home from the festival and shared with my wife. Since 1985, however, I have been more focused on the Allegany Territory (Ohi:yo´), doing applied historical research for the Seneca Nation of Indians on several projects, interviewing and learning from the elders and tribal officials there.

In reflecting on these experiences, I recalled something that the late Myrtle Peterson, a Seneca language teacher from the Allegany Territory, said to me while I was attending a conference at Cherokee, North Carolina, in 1978 that focused on Six Nations–Cherokee connections. After Peterson gave a presentation in the Seneca language to an audience composed of Cherokees and non-Native academics, I had the opportunity to interview her. In the course of the interview, she revealed something that I did not fully comprehend at the time. She stated that the Cattaraugus Senecas "speak differently there."[1] Four decades later, after numerous interviews and frequent visits to archival repositories, Peterson's remark finally made sense to me. I realized that she was commenting on more than the Seneca language and how Indian words were and are spoken differently at Allegany and Cattaraugus. Although under one very broad cultural umbrella and tied by kinship, the Seneca Nation of Indians today is a multicultural reality. It has a federated political system composed of two distinct communities containing diverse reservation populations with different origins, histories, political behavior, and problems.

The present political system of the Seneca Nation is not new; it dates back to the decade from 1838 to 1848. In 1838, in a federal treaty at Buffalo Creek, the Seneca Nation ceded its remaining residential territories to the Ogden Land Company in one of the more outright frauds in American Indian history.[2] Four years later, at another federal treaty at Buffalo Creek, only two of four reservations—Allegany and Cattaraugus—were returned to the Seneca Nation, although Buffalo Creek was permanently lost, and part of Tonawanda, which had separated from the Seneca Nation, had to be repurchased by these Indians after much struggle between 1857 and 1861.[3] Much of the blame for the permanent loss of Buffalo Creek, fairly and unfairly, went to the Seneca chiefs. Prompted by the Society of Friends to transform its government away from the operations of the traditional council of chiefs, the Senecas in convention on the Cattaraugus Indian Reservation on December 4, 1848, adopted a written constitution and a republic with an elected system of government.[4] Now, the Seneca Nation of Indians has an elected president, treasurer, and clerk, with an arrangement requiring the tribe to alternate the offices of president, clerk, and treasurer at every election. An equal number of elected tribal councilors—eight today from each of the two territories—makes up the sixteen-member Tribal Council, the legislative branch of government. A third branch of government, the judiciary, comprises elected Seneca peacemakers from each community to mediate tribal legal disputes in the traditional way; Surrogate Court judges at both Allegany and Cattaraugus to handle probate matters; and a Court of Appeals made up of six judges who hear appeals from both the Peacemakers and Surrogate courts. In another example of Seneca Nation adaptation, within the two-decade period after this Seneca revolution of 1848, the displaced chiefs accepted the existence of the new form of government, established their own political party, and ran for political offices, in contrast to what happened in the other Six Nations communities. In 1898, the Seneca Constitution was modified, changing the presidential term from one to two years.[5] In 1964, Seneca women, who had operated so effectively behind the scenes, were allowed to vote, and in 1966, they were for the first time allowed to hold tribal offices.[6]

Even though there is a major population imbalance between the Cattaraugus and Allegany Reservations—with the latter constituting half of the former—the 1848 compromise has held up. In many ways, the Seneca Nation government is unique for Hodinöhsö:ni´ (Iroquois) communities in New York State, both historically and at the present time. By the 1860s, the "Old Chiefs," by then a political party, accepted the existence of the elected Seneca tribal government and participated in the electoral process, a far different choice from that of the other Iroquois communities. Although frequently challenged, the practical settlement that was worked out during the crisis years 1838 to 1848 has worked to the present day.

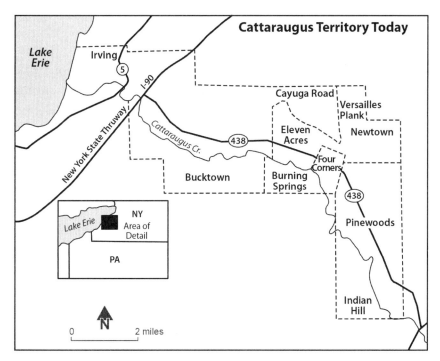

Map 2. Cattaraugus Territory today. Map by Joe Stoll. Courtesy of Joe Stoll.

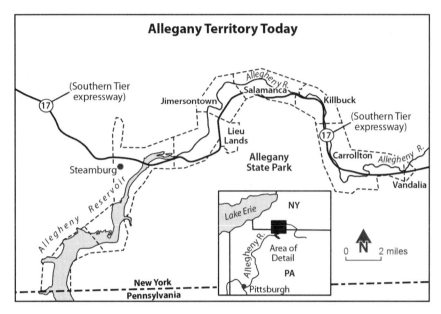

Map 3. Allegany Territory today. Map by Joe Stoll. Courtesy of Joe Stoll.

At times described as "factionalism," the Seneca polity since 1848 has been much more sophisticated than that word implies.[7] The Seneca Nation has a complex political system based on kinship and locale. It frequently shifts and morphs into new parties raising issues that rouse the electorate, be they reform challenges for better tribal government and ethical conduct, the pursuit of land claims, or protests against state road building or the imposition of state sales taxes. The political system has always been shaped by fears that outsiders want Seneca lands and resources. Seneca politics has been intense, and tribal officials are frequently blamed, rightly or wrongly, for decisions made. At times, the politics of blame leads to paralysis in implementing needed policies. In order to maintain equilibrium, politicians on one territory have to raise issues relevant to voters in the other Seneca territory, which leads to a tightrope-balancing act to keep the nation from splitting apart as it did in the period from 1838 to 1848. The fear of schism is always present, but it also forces practical compromises. Today, for example, every construction project and job-creation effort in one territory has to have a reciprocal project in the other. This practicality has kept the Seneca Nation afloat for more than 160 years, a major achievement when contrasted with the greater instability of some other Hodinöhsö:ni´ Mohawk and Oneida communities and the schisms and decline of the Cayuga Nation in New York State.

The Seneca Nation of Indians is clearly a federation. The word *federation* indicates that it is an alliance, an axis, a bloc, a coalition, or a confederation and that it is formed by an "act of uniting in a league by agreement of each member to subordinate its power to that of a central authority in common affairs."[8] Political scientist Chad Rector maintains that the term is "a description of the merger of states, and can refer both to the process of merging and to the political system resulting from the merger." Although Rector's focus is on international relations, he makes key points about the operations of federations, some of which apply to the Seneca Nation of Indians. Rector insists that federations are not necessarily created out of affection for one another, but more likely out of mistrust and mutual fears. This underlying threat requires a party system to maintain stability and work together for protection or prosperity or both. He maintains that cooperation in a federated state requires entities "to bargain with one another to divide among them the gains they reap by cooperating." Federations can benefit by cooperation, "but cooperation requires unequal levels of relationship-specific investments." Yet the more the separate entities within a federation cooperate, "the more they have to lose if cooperation fails." Thus, to maintain the continued operation of a federation, a high level of brokering is required that often leads to raised political tensions and at times acrimonious debate.[9]

Although the Senecas on the Allegany and Cattaraugus Territories are culturally Onöndowa´ga:´ (People of the Great/Big Hill), Rector's analysis does fit the way their political system works, in the past or now. I finally came to understand the very nature of the Seneca Nation federation when re-reading the Seneca periodicals published in the 1970s. Until the establishment of the *Seneca Nation of Indians' Official Newsletter* in 1994, which Rovena Abrams has edited for the past nineteen years, there was no long-standing official organ for this Indian nation. After the Kinzua crisis, the Senecas began publishing two reservation newsletters— *O He Yoh Noh* (People along the beautiful river), founded and edited by

Gertrude Claflin, Shirley Printup Vanetta, and Marlene Johnson and later edited by Thelma Ledsome with the help Janice Bowen, Alvina Cooper, Nellie Jack, and Gladys Jimerson; and *Si Wong Geh* (Have you heard about it?) at Cattaraugus, founded and edited by Wini Kettle, with the help of Alyssa Jemison, Marilyn Jemison Anderson, and Mary Snow.[10] Quite evident in each of the two publications were notices of Seneca eligibility for federal grants. Among these grants were the Comprehensive Employment Training Assistance grants and a variety of US Department of Education grants. To the impoverished Senecas, as was true of federally recognized Native American nations nationwide, this sudden infusion of millions of dollars had an enormous impact, not all of it beneficial (see chapter 11 for a full discussion of Seneca efforts to overcome economic dependence).

Each of the two newsletters covered social events, recognized personal achievements, and printed obituaries of reservation residents. Nevertheless, the differences between these two publications were striking and reflected the clear divergence of Seneca life, politics, and thought between the Allegany and Cattaraugus Senecas. The pages of *O He Yoh Noh* contained excerpts from works of anthropologists such as Anthony F. C. Wallace's *Death and Rebirth of the Seneca*, Arthur C. Parker's *Seneca Myths and Folktales*, and Edmund Wilson's *Apologies to the Iroquois*. Unlike *Si Wong Geh*, the Allegany newsletter frequently made reference to inspirational religious messages. It also covered Seneca Tribal Council meetings and its tribal resolutions less frequently and less specifically. *O He Yoh Noh* was more conservative and somewhat harsher in its criticism of Indian Red Power activism that was arising at the time. It was also much more supportive of economic development projects and tribal efforts supported by Robert "Bob" Hoag, an Allegany Seneca from Salamanca and dominant political leader of the era. Its articles also focused more on Seneca language and culture, with information about the meaning of Indian names as well as about the uses and functions of wampum in Iroquoian culture. In contrast, *Si Wong Geh* was filled with political news, devoting more attention to tribal council meetings and resolutions passed. It dealt more fully with controversial subjects such as the acrimonious debate over the possible siting of a Fisher-Price toy factory at Cattaraugus as well as legal challenges to it in state court. It allowed opposing opinions on this and other issues, including Red Power activism. Unlike *O He Yoh Noh*, issues of *Si Wong Geh* frequently contained columns sponsored by the Seneca Health Action Group, largely comprising Cattaraugus Seneca and Cayuga women, about ways to combat illness and maintain good health. The Health Action Group wrote of its determined efforts to improve Seneca health care by securing medical care, facilities, and funding from the US Indian Health Service. Seneca language efforts were less emphasized. On occasion, *Si Wong Geh* had brief articles on famous Senecas, treaties, and places associated with tribal history.

The differences in these two newsletters reflect the long-standing divisions between Allegany and Cattaraugus Senecas that are rooted in history. At the time of European contact, the Senecas lived between Canandaigua Lake and the Genesee River. Their villages were divided into two major settlement regions: the east region, slightly northwest of Canandaigua Lake, included the long-known Boughton Hill and Fort Hill sites near today's Ganondagan State Park at Victor, New York; and the western region, lands on the east side of the Genesee River and mostly south of today's city of Rochester, including the well-investigated Adams, Culbertson, Dann, and Dutch Hollow sites.[11] From 1638 to 1680, the Senecas fought a series of wars against the Eries, the Hurons, the Neutrals, the Susquehannocks, and the Wenros, and they incorporated numerous captives into their communities.[12] Moreover, close association and alliance with neighboring Cayugas, especially after the French invasion of Seneca territory in 1687, led to historic ties and intermarriage between these two Iroquoian peoples that remains to this very day. Throughout the eighteenth century, the Senecas adopted war captives into their population mix, including Cherokees, Catawbas, Ojibwes, as well as whites. They also allowed refugee nations to settle within their territory. These nations included significant populations of Mesquakies and Munsees. Highly adaptable, the Seneca villages by the eighteenth century were smaller and more dispersed, with large numbers of adoptees living among the Seneca.[13] Moreover, by the American Revolution, other Iroquoian peoples—Oneidas and Tuscaroras—had established villages within the Senecas' Genesee Valley lands. Thus, long before the formal establishment of eleven reservations in the period 1797–1801, the Senecas were a multicultural reality.[14]

With the federal treaty between the US government and the Six Nations in 1794 at Canandaigua, known to elders as the "Pickering Treaty," the US government and the Senecas were to establish a permanent peace and alliance after the great tensions, hostilities, and violence during the American Revolution.[15] Three years later, in the federal Treaty of Big Tree, ten land parcels totaling some 200,000 acres, or 311 square miles, in western New York—Allegany, Big Tree, Buffalo Creek, Caneadea, Canadaway, Canawaugus, Cattaraugus, Gardeau, Squawky Hill, and Tonawanda— were reserved for the Seneca Nation; an eleventh parcel, Oil Spring, was added in 1801.[16] However, in federal treaties from 1802 to 1842, all but three reservations—Allegany, Cattaraugus, and Oil Spring—were taken from the Seneca Nation. The Tonawanda Band of Senecas permanently separated from the Seneca Nation of Indians during this period; they were eventually able to sign a new federal treaty in 1857 and repurchase a small part of their territory from 1859 to 1861.[17]

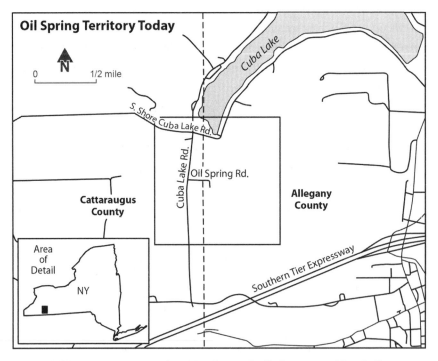

Map 4. Oil Spring Territory today. Map by Joe Stoll. Courtesy of Joe Stoll.

After the American Revolution, the world at Buffalo Creek, the Seneca Nation's largest and most populated community, was a multicultural reality far different from other Seneca communities until dispossession in two federal Buffalo Creek treaties in 1838 and 1842. It was at the center of Six Nations life in New York from 1784 to the mid-1840s. This Seneca territory became the major haven for displaced peoples, much like Iroquoia in the upper Susquehanna region, the Chenango Valley, had been a half-century earlier for other Iroquoian and non-Iroquoian tribes: Tuscarora, Tutelo, Conoy, Munsee, Nanticoke, and so on. Indeed, the Great Peace and Power, the Iroquois League, had from the seventeenth century operated in this manner to provide protection, secure adoptees and military allies, and establish a buffer against white settlement pressures.[18] While Joseph Brant was resurrecting the Iroquois Confederacy under Mohawk aegis at the Haldimand Patent along the Grand River in Lower Canada, the Senecas became protectors of the League tradition in New York. At Buffalo Creek, the Confederacy's council fire was maintained throughout much of this period largely by Captain Cold (Ut-ha-wah), an Onondaga sachem residing there. Importantly, Buffalo Creek became the ritual center of Iroquoian ceremonialism where the sacred wampum belts from the Onondagas were housed for their protection after "the Whirlwind," the Seneca designation for what befell them in the American Revolution.[19] Hence, the Senecas from Buffalo Creek were historically more closely tied to the Iroquois Grand Council and remained so even after being forcibly removed to Cattaraugus in the 1840s. They were never able to secure back their lands. Although they agreed, unlike the Tonawandas, to come under the rubric of the new Seneca Nation Republic in 1848, their underlying resentment about the loss of Buffalo Creek remained, especially at a time when the Allegany Senecas received back their lands. This factor has haunted Seneca politics ever since. Even today, one Seneca family, descendants of the last migrants from Buffalo Creek, refuses to recognize the existence of the Seneca Nation government established in 1848.[20]

The refugees, mostly Senecas but including Cayugas and Munsees from Buffalo Creek, rebuilt their lives at the Cattaraugus Indian Reservation. This territory, surveyed and laid out after the Treaty of Big Tree, was originally fifty square miles, extending fourteen miles in length along the south shore of Lake Erie and extending northward to eight miles from the city limits of Buffalo. In federal treaties in 1802 and 1826, Cattaraugus Reservation lands were reduced.[21] Today, this territory, which is in the three-county area of Cattaraugus, Chautauqua, and Erie Counties, is nine and a half miles in length from east to west along Cattaraugus Creek. At its widest, it is only three miles in length.[22]

The Cattaraugus Indian Reservation population, unlike the Senecas at Allegany and Cornplanter, were not led by Chief Cornplanter; they had their own diverse leadership. Moreover, because of long-standing ties between Senecas and the other member nations of the Iroquois Confederacy who had resided at Buffalo Creek, the Cattaraugus Senecas' Newtown Longhouse from the 1840s to the present has been tied more to the Iroquois Grand Council of Chiefs. Despite this traditional focus, the presence of missionary societies, which had also been so prevalent at Buffalo Creek, continued after the relocation to Cattaraugus. Presbyterians, Baptists, Episcopalians, Quakers, and, in more recent times, Mormons sought to convert Senecas there. It was no accident that the Thomas Institute for Orphan and Destitute Indians, later renamed the Thomas Indian School, was established here in 1855, founded by leading Baltimore Quaker Philip Thomas, the president of the Pennsylvania Railroad and Chesapeake and Ohio Canal, in an effort to transform these Indians into "productive" Christian taxpaying citizens.[23]

The geographical proximity of Cattaraugus to the city of Buffalo— thirty miles by the major New York State Thruway built in the 1950s— also has shaped the contemporary Cattaraugus community (see chapter 3). Despite the strong protest about this superhighway, it provided greater access to employment, especially in Lackawanna steel mills and construction, until the rapid economic decline of western New York. It also provided greater access to educational opportunities and facilitated connections to other Iroquois communities for religious ceremonies, for discussions of Six Nations politics, and for lacrosse, the Hodinöhsö:ni´ national sport. The latter, lacrosse, also separated the Cattaraugus from the Allegany Senecas. Until recently, the Allegany Senecas had no lacrosse facility, and the sport was more associated with Cattaraugus. An indoor arena was opened at Newtown in the mid-1970s during the Bob Hoag presidency, but the Cattaraugus Senecas had had a long tradition as participants in the sport even before that time. In the 1930s, Cattaraugus Senecas excelled as players and coaches in the professional leagues.[24] To this day, Cattaraugus Senecas are actively involved in the Iroquois National Team, strengthening ties across Six Nations lines. Besides lacrosse, the residents of the Cattaraugus Reservation, being less isolated from Iroquoia and from urban areas such as Buffalo and Niagara Falls, were also more affected by social movements such as Red Power and Black Power. Iroquois activism erupted at Tuscarora in the late 1950s, and Black Power activism in the urban areas of Buffalo, Niagara Falls, and Rochester in the 1960s and early 1970s.[25] Although many Seneca reservation residents, especially at Allegany, shunned these movements, Red Power activism became especially noticeable at Cattaraugus. Much like what happened throughout Indian Country in the early 1970s, a group of Cattaraugus Senecas challenged the legitimacy of the Seneca elected government and attempted to overthrow and replace it with what they considered the traditional "Seneka Nation" (see chapter 8).

Prior to the building of the Kinzua Dam, the upper Allegany River valley contained the 30,469-acre Allegany Indian Reservation and the 780-acre Cornplanter Tract (Jonöhsade:gëh). Both lands were associated with the life and leadership of Gayëntwahgöh (the Cornplanter). Both Seneca territories, as well as Oil Spring in the lower Genesee Valley, were also associated with the life and visions of Sga:nyodai:yoh (Handsome Lake), the Seneca prophet, and as a consequence these lands have deep religious meaning to all Senecas, be they Allegany or Cattaraugus residents, who follow the Gaiwi:yoh, the spiritual teachings of this Seneca prophet.[26] In the mid-1940s, anthropologist William N. Fenton described the Senecas' upper Allegheny lands in the following way: "Here are heaps of earth, hills, rising upwards of 2,100 feet, that they [Seneca Indians] say the Creator had left over when he finished making the earth."[27]

The flooding of one-third of the Seneca territory in the upper Allegheny River valley and the forced relocation of the Onöndowa´ga:´ from this sacred region—a landscape associated with rituals and traditional medicine gathering, place-names and storytelling, and even smells in the air—were therefore to have profound effects. As anthropologist Keith Basso has perceptively pointed out, one must understand a people's sense of place and how they fit into a landscape as much as their spoken words to really understand them. To Basso, "the past lies embedded in features of the earth . . . which together endow their lands with multiple forms of significance that reach into their lives and shape the way they think." He adds: "Knowledge of places is therefore closely linked to the knowledge of self, to grasping one's position in the larger scheme of things, including one's own community, and to securing a confident sense of who one is as a person."[28]

These Senecas' lands in the upper Allegheny River valley were largely isolated and with few white settlers until the completion of the New York and Erie Railroad in 1851. Before dam construction, the Allegany Indian Reservation stretched thirty-five miles in length on both sides of the Allegheny River. This Seneca territory varied in width from one to two and a half miles.[29] The federal government formally recognized these lands as part of the Seneca Nation of Indians in the Pickering Treaty of 1794. The reservation's boundaries were set under the federal Treaty of Big Tree in 1797 and the surveys that followed this agreement.[30]

The second Seneca territory in the upper Allegheny River valley was the Cornplanter Tract. From 1791 to 1796, the Pennsylvania State Legislature, at the behest of Governor Thomas Mifflin, granted Chief Cornplanter several parcels of land in gratitude for his part in ending hostilities and encouraging negotiations with the Americans after the Revolutionary War. The grants totaled 1,500 acres and included Hickey Town (West Hickey or Richland), the Oil City grant, and the Cornplanter Tract, which encompassed Planter's Field, Liberality Island, and Donation Island. All but the 780-acre Cornplanter Tract were sold off in questionable deals. Lands here, unlike at Allegany and Cattaraugus, were owned in fee-simple title by Cornplanter and later by his heirs, who included Cayugas, Onondagas, and non-Indians as well as Senecas. Unlike Allegany and Cattaraugus, the Cornplanter Tract was not federal Indian treaty land because the parcel had been set aside by Pennsylvania state action. Although Senecas at Cornplanter identified with their kin at Allegany and at times participated in the government of the Seneca Nation, the community's multiethnic nature and its separate land status set it apart.[31]

From the 1850s onward, the Allegany Senecas faced increasing challenges that slowly broke down their isolation from the outside. Although the Quakers had established a presence there since the 1790s and had funded a school at Tunesassa, the Senecas were off the beaten path until the completion of the New York and Erie Railroad in 1851. Non-Indians began to come onto the reservation at Allegany, and numerous questionable leasing arrangements were consummated. By 1900, approximately eight thousand non-Indians had settled on Indian lands, many of whom had come as railroad workers or in-service industry workers for rail operations. The federal government confirmed these leases for ninety-nine years at infinitesimal rates in 1890 (see chapter 9).[32]

The large presence of non-Indians at Allegany, especially in the city of Salamanca, has had a major impact on Seneca life, separating these tribal members from their Cattaraugus counterparts. For more than one hundred years, Allegany Senecas had to live with and adjust to these newcomers. Right through the mid-1980s, the white leadership of the city of Salamanca sought to gain title to the lands they rented from the Seneca Nation and frequently lobbied legislators in both Albany and Washington to buy out the Indians.[33] Southwestern New York State politicians promoted the development of Allegany State Park after World War I, which impinged on Seneca life within the region by bringing more outsiders to the region. They also supported the creation of Cuba Lake State Park and challenged every Seneca effort to regain part of this territory (see chapter 10). They promoted efforts to divide and allot tribal lands, build the Southern Tier Expressway through Seneca lands, extend state jurisdiction over fishing and hunting on reservation lands, and prosecute Indians for all crimes on tribal lands in state instead of federal courts.[34]

Indeed, Allegany Senecas were in a quasi-colonial relationship with their white neighbors as well as with Albany. As part of northern Appalachia, they were dependent on Salamanca's powerful white families—the Dowds, Fanchers, and Vreelands—for employment opportunities in the railyards, furniture factory, and homes of the city's elite. As a consequence, they were somewhat less assertive than their kin at Cattaraugus until the Kinzua Dam era. They learned early on to broker and make deals to survive within the impoverished upper Allegheny River valley. From the 1880s to the late 1920s, the master of this Allegany Seneca broker politics was Willie C. Hoag. Although he was suspect in some of his questionable dealings with southwestern New York politicians, he and his ally Frank Patterson of Cattaraugus did manage to prevent Congress from allotting tribal lands in the age of the Dawes General Allotment Act. This was no small accomplishment.[35] His type of leadership at times operated as a well-oiled political machine that rewarded certain families. Hoag did succeed in keeping the diverse Seneca Nation and its distinct communities together. Allegany broker politics continued until the mid-1980s with Willie Hoag's descendant Bob Hoag as president. After that, a more combative style of politics was to emerge.[36] As a result, for the past quarter-century Senecas have more vociferously challenged decisions affecting them made by outsiders in Albany.

In the post–World War II era, the Seneca Nation faced termination policies that attempted to end their treaty status; the transfer of criminal and civil jurisdiction to New York State; massive road-building efforts promoted by Albany through both the Allegany and Cattaraugus Indian Reservations; the flooding of their lands by the Army Corps of Engineers that resulted in the loss of approximately 10,000 acres and forced relocation of numerous families; as well as repeated state attempts to apply sales taxes to tribal lands. These threats first arose at a time when Senecas were returning home from military service in the war. Approximately five hundred Senecas (including Allegany, Cattaraugus, Cornplanter, and Tonawanda Senecas) had served in the war in every branch of the military and in every theater of the conflict. Although opposed to conscription, most of these Senecas volunteered for service, thus reaffirming in their minds their separate Indian nationhood and the alliance with the United States consummated in the Pickering Treaty at Canandaigua in November 1794. Unlike African Americans, they fought in integrated fighting units. Some, such as Kenneth Parker and Arnold White, never made it home, giving their lives to protect their homeland. Parker, who enlisted in the US Marines at sixteen in 1943, was killed at Iwo Jima on February 19, 1945, and White, who served in the navy for five years, was killed during the Battle of Okinawa on March 27, 1945, when a Japanese kamikaze flew into his ship, the USS *O'Brien*.[37]

Although these Senecas faced open discrimination in the city of Salamanca and towns such as Gowanda that bordered the Cattaraugus Reservation, they had encountered less open racial hostility in military service. Yes, they were stereotyped—nearly every Seneca was dubbed "chief" by his white comrades and assigned more often than not to the most difficult work as scouts on reconnoitering duty—but they bonded with their band of brothers, including white servicemen in their units who recognized their abilities and bravery. These Seneca soldiers, sailors, and airmen were extremely proud of their contributions to winning the war in Europe and the Pacific.[38]

When they returned to their territories, they associated with their fellow veterans residing at Cornplanter, Allegany, and Cattaraugus and participated in events that strengthened the connections between the diverse Seneca communities. These veterans were welcomed back and integrated into the very fabric of their communities. Charles E. Congdon, a prominent white Salamanca attorney and keen observer of Seneca culture, described the scene at the Coldspring Longhouse when the soldiers returned for Midwinter Ceremony in early 1946. Congdon indicated that, unlike the war years, it "was a time for general rejoicing and there was a crowd most every day." He then noted:

> There were a dozen soldiers of this war present, but none of them sang *Adowa*. The chants belong to the clans and are handed on from one man to another. Sometimes a man makes up his own. The ex-soldiers were on hand for *Ganeowe*. That came next. They had fine new suits with beads and shells for ornaments. The trousers were wide and had decorated bands down the outside. The head-dresses [*gustoweh*] were full with feathers. One young fellow back from the army had a beautiful new suit with real black-tipped feathers. His brother got it out West. Their jackets and head bands were covered with beadwork. One of the new suits was yellow cloth like buckskin and the feathers in the head-dress were yellow. There never were so many beads and feathers in this long house.

People were coming from all directions. The house was full of men and women, boys and girls and many babies.[39]

At Coldspring, Senecas from Cattaraugus, Tonawanda, and as far away as Grand River were there to welcome the soldiers back. Congdon added that after the Great Feather Dance was performed at the longhouse,

[t]he soldiers boys just home from Europe and the South Seas were there. All glad to be safe home. One boy stepped on a mine when they took Remagen Bridge. It took off his foot, but he was glad to be back in the long house. They thought about the three [Allegany Senecas] who did not come back and danced all the harder for them. Round and round they went. Every one joined in. Women and girls, feeble old men, little boys, some of them with fine new suits and little feather head pieces. The men carried their babies so that they would get the benefit of the song. It is good for everyone.[40]

Soon thereafter, the Seneca Nation Tribal Council paid for and erected a panel made by Dwight Jimerson, the Senecas' Surrogate Court judge, and prominently displayed it in the court house at Jimersontown.[41] The commemorative panel contained the names of all the veterans from Allegany who had served in the war effort. Meanwhile at Cattaraugus, the veterans founded the first all-Indian American Legion post in the United States.[42]

In November 1946, World War II veterans swept into power and were elected to most of the Seneca Nation's political offices. These same veterans were to dominate Seneca politics into the early 1970s. Almost immediately after the election in 1946, these battle-tested young men were faced with a series of crises—the worst since the removal era in the 1830s. These challenges came from three directions—Washington, DC; Albany, New York; and Harrisburg, Pennsylvania.

PART II |||| *Origins*

2

Federal Policies

Termination

CALVIN "KELLY" JOHN, a highly decorated war hero who received two Bronze Stars, was one of those Senecas who returned home from the war in 1945. A year later, this twenty-five-year-old battle-tested veteran from Allegany ran for the presidency of the Seneca Nation of Indians at the urging of Cornelius Seneca, a Cattaraugus ironworker and longtime political leader. John, a soft-spoken person with great diplomatic skills, was elected president of the Seneca Nation for a two-year term in November 1946 and was subsequently elected three more times, serving from 1950 to 1952, 1966 to 1968, and finally 1990 to 1992.[1]

From 1974 to just before his death in 2004, I would see John every year on the Allegany Reservation or at the annual Peter Doctor Indian Education Scholarship Foundation dinner, at which time the elders of the nation would give small grants to Hodinöhsö:ni´ young men and women who were planning to continue with their schooling after graduating from high school.[2] Because he was the most knowledgeable community historian, we had many discussions about different aspects of his people's past. He greatly influenced the direction of my research and writing over a thirty-year period. We talked about the Seneca treaty era, 1784 to 1857, and the activities of the Holland Land Company and its agent Joseph Ellicott, whom he referred to in the Seneca language as "the mosquito." I was told that Ellicott had an appropriate Seneca name because he was always buzzing around, annoying the Indians, stinging them, and finally sucking their blood. John took pride in recounting the story of his personal hero, Governor Blacksnake, the Allegany chief and nephew of Sga:nyodai:yoh, who had saved the one-mile-square Oil Spring Reservation from land speculators.[3]

John was especially descriptive of the problems he faced when he first entered politics. He had assumed office at the very time of a major effort by New York officials to lobby Congress for criminal and civil jurisdiction over the Iroquois communities in the state. Albany policymakers were also making postwar plans for highway development through Seneca Country. These state plans, which also involved related park and power development, coincided with a major shift in national Indian policy, commonly known as "termination," that was to seriously affect the Senecas. Cornelius Seneca, the previous president, had educated John about events that had transpired on the home front while the young Seneca was away in military service. In 1942, with the help of the US Department of Justice, the Senecas won a federal Court of Appeals case, *United States v. Forness*, that centered on the Seneca Nation's right to cancel delinquent leases in the City of Salamanca and called into question whether New York State laws could be applied on Seneca lands. The federal decision recognized "the long struggle by the Indians to enforce their economic rights" as well as the federal government's trust responsibility as guardians to protect their interests.[4] The following year, angered by the cancellation of these leases and the court's dismissal of state jurisdiction on Iroquois reservations, the New York State Legislature created its Joint Legislative Committee on Indian Affairs, headed by legislators from the southwestern part of the state.[5]

From 1943 to 1945, the committee held hearings, took testimony, and began an intensive campaign to get Congress to transfer criminal and civil jurisdiction from the federal government to the state. Its most outspoken opponent was Cornelius Seneca, a well-respected ironworker who had served as president of the Seneca Nation twice and as its treasurer three times. He was elected treasurer during World War II and then president in the latter stages of the war. At the state hearings held in Salamanca, Seneca questioned the motives behind the creation of the Joint Legislative Committee, referring to Albany officials' past failures to recognize Iroquois land claims and treaty rights. He saw the committee's work as a backlash against the Senecas for canceling delinquent leases.[6]

By 1945, the Joint Legislative Committee had drafted two transfer bills that it recommended Congress to consider. In its 1945 report, the committee also called for a congressional act to allow the three thousand non-Indian leaseholders in the city of Salamanca the right to obtain title by purchasing their rentals from the Seneca Nation, an idea universally opposed by the Indians.[7]

Previously the US Senate had signaled the beginning of a change in national Indian policies.[8] In 1944, Commissioner of Indian Affairs John Collier, finally realizing that his New Deal Indian program was at an end and was now threatened with severe budget cuts from Congress, recommended relieving federal supervision over some Indian tribes, including the Senecas and other members of Six Nations in New York and Wisconsin.[9] By the late summer of 1946, Acting Commissioner William Brophy Jr. indicated that his agency, the Bureau of Indian Affairs (BIA), should set a time limit within which it would cease to exist.[10] In 1947, William Zimmerman Jr., BIA acting commissioner, testified before the Senate Civil Service Committee. The senators on the committee had demanded that he provide a list of Indian nations ready for "release" from federal supervision. In his first category—those he labeled "predominantly acculturated population"—Zimmerman put ten groups, including the Seneca Nation of Indians and other Iroquois in New York, whom he claimed could be immediately removed from federal supervision.[11]

Thus, by the late 1940s Washington policymakers in Congress and in the Department of the Interior had become more assertive in pushing for termination—namely, federal withdrawal from Indian affairs and a shift of responsibilities to state governments. In actuality, termination was both a philosophy and a specific legislation applied to the Indians. As a philosophy, the movement encouraged assimilation of Indians as individuals into the mainstream of American society and advocated the end of the federal government's responsibility for Indian affairs. To accomplish these objectives, legislation fell into four general categories: (1) the end of federal treaty relationships and trust responsibilities with certain specified Indian nations by means of lump-sum cash commutations of annuities or Indian claims; (2) the repeal of federal laws that set Indians apart from other American citizens; (3) the removal of restrictions of federal guardianship and supervision over certain individual Indians; and (4) the transfer of services provided by the BIA to the states and their localities or to other federal agencies, such as the Department of Health, Education, and Welfare.[12]

The termination laws of the Truman and Eisenhower administrations ended federally recognized status for approximately one hundred Indian tribes, bands, and *rancherías*, totaling 13,263 individuals owning 1,365,801 acres of land.[13] Other laws established relocation programs to encourage Indian out-migrations from reservations to urban areas. Even the creation of the Indian Claims Commission (ICC) in 1946 became tied to congressional efforts at "getting the United States out of the Indian business." Moreover, in the postwar years, both Democrat and Republican congressmen sought to promote parks, dams, and other projects that impinged on Indian tribal rights and land holdings. The policies they formulated, with the Interior Department's reluctant, tacit, or open support, led to so-called termination legislation.[14]

In Congress, these efforts were led by Arthur V. Watkins, a senator from Utah and the head of the Subcommittee on Indian Affairs of the Senate Committee on Interior and Insular Affairs. He advocated the buying out of federal treaty obligations, the elimination of the separate legal status of federally recognized American Indian nations, and the closing down of the inefficient and costly operations of the BIA, a historically mismanaged division of the Interior Department. He referred to termination as Indian "emancipation," a policy that would eliminate dependency and rapidly integrate the Indian into mainstream American life.[15] Watkins gained support from key colleagues, including Hugh Butler of Nebraska, the chairman of the Senate Interior and Insular Affairs Committee, and Daniel Reed, a thirteen-term representative from Seneca Country (comprising the forty-third and later forty-fifth district) of southwestern New York. Reed, who had been in Congress since 1919, later served as chairman of the powerful House Ways and Means Committee during President Eisenhower's first term in office. In 1947, these congressmen called for the shift of federal responsibilities from the BIA to the states, beginning importantly with jurisdictional change. Prompted by New York State's Joint

Legislative Committee on Indian Affairs, Congressman Reed and Senator Butler introduced bills in 1948 to 1950 to accomplish this objective.[16]

In May 1948, Watkins's Senate Subcommittee on Indian Affairs held a hearing on versions of Butler's transfer bills.[17] Both Watkins and Butler hammered away at the numerous official Seneca delegates and other individual Senecas giving testimony. Indeed, more Senecas from Cattaraugus and Allegany attended this hearing and voiced their opposition than Natives from any other Iroquois community in New York State. A four-man official delegation represented the Seneca Nation: President Calvin "Kelly" John, Clerk Wayne Printup, as well as two future presidents of the Seneca Nation—Treasurer Dean Williams and Tribal Councilor George Heron.[18] From the beginning, President John, hoping to win favor at the hearing, testified that his administration was led by veterans of the US Armed Services who had come home from the war and entered tribal politics, motivated to help their people by initiating needed reforms. The Seneca delegation had to sit through the hearing and calmly listen to senators and officials from New York State besmirch their people's reputation.[19] Although the transcript of the hearings does not reveal the Senecas' emotions, in two personal interviews, both war hero John and Heron, a World War II Navy veteran who had been at the Battle of Leyte Gulf and in the bloody invasion of Okinawa, indicated that the delegates had to contain themselves when misinformation and slanderous testimony was presented about the Senecas and their government. The delegates, who were fuming, had to "hold their tongues" when New York officials claimed that there was a lack of law and order on the reservations and that the situation could only be corrected by transferring responsibilities to state police and state courts.[20]

When Senecas Heron and Printup testified that racism toward the Indians existed in southwestern New York and that they feared that the transfer of jurisdiction to local state courts would jeopardize their right to fair trials, Watkins quickly dismissed this point.[21] Reacting to the official Seneca delegation's condemnation of the bills for jurisdictional transfer, Watkins indicated that his overall goal was to amalgamate the Indian population as quickly as possible and close down the BIA. He lectured the

Senecas on what he deemed was their future—namely, to end the Indians' special status because he believed that they had been in "the melting pot long enough to be assimilated with the rest of the population" and were now "able to live under the same laws as the rest of us do, get the benefits and take on the responsibilities."[22] Watkins also insulted the Senecas, who follow matrilineal descent for tribal enrollment, when he asked each one about the quantity of their "Indian blood." When Heron, then a structural bridgeman working at Bethlehem Steel, indicated that his father was an Irishman, the Utah senator believed he was proving his case about the melting pot. It was apparent from Watkins's questioning that he believed that the Senecas were not "real Indians" anymore and thus that they did not need a separate legal status, treaty guarantees, or an agency, the BIA, to administer their affairs. To him, they were just like all other Americans and should be treated as such.[23]

Other Senecas, all from Cattaraugus, gave oral testimony at this hearing, attempting to counter the movement for jurisdictional transfer. They heard federal and state representatives announce plans to buy out federal obligations under the Treaty of Canandaigua of 1794, the most important federal commitment to the Six Nations. In response, Cornelius Seneca described the Seneca Nation's governmental structure, including its court structure, attempting to counter the false image that lawlessness reigned on the reservations and that New York State courts and law enforcement were needed there. Seneca, the most prominent political leader of his generation, made it clear that he feared jurisdictional transfer to New York State courts, reiterating the point made by the Seneca Nation's official delegation that the switch would lead to prejudicial decisions against the Indians and insensitivity toward long-held Native customs. He blamed the New York State Joint Legislative Committee on Indian Affairs, composed of southwestern New York interests at odds with the Senecas over the *Forness* decision, for the transfer bills before Congress. Seneca indicated that he was the only Indian allowed to speak at a hearing of the Joint Legislative Committee held in Salamanca, whereas fifteen of the city's white residents had given testimony.[24] Watkins responded by insisting that his subcommittee members "think the Indians of the State of New

York are grown up, and they do not need the United States anymore, just like the rest of the citizens."[25]

Five other Cattaraugus Senecas testified at the hearing. The most well known was Alice Lee Jemison, the longtime Seneca activist who had been one of the major opponents of the Indian Reorganization Act of 1934 and Commissioner John Collier's Indian New Deal programs. Jemison, a journalist and activist from Cattaraugus, was Cornelius Seneca's niece and had been a critic of the BIA since the early 1930s, believing the agency needed to be abolished altogether. This commitment to the BIA's abolition unfortunately fed into Watkins's agenda of emancipation, or federal withdrawal from Indian affairs.[26] At the hearing, however, Jemison gave a historical overview of Seneca history, explained the importance of keeping the promises made in the Pickering Treaty, and indicated that five hundred Senecas had served as American allies in World War II. She tried to educate the subcommittee members about the treaty's meaning to the Senecas—that receiving a yard and a half of calico each November from the United States was a symbolic reaffirmation of an alliance, not a mere token.[27] Senator Butler, imitating Watkins's offensive style, questioned Jemison's "Indianness" because, although enrolled within the tribe and a descendant of the prominent Tandy lineage, she was one-quarter Seneca and thirty-second Cherokee and was residing in Washington, DC, working for the federal government.[28] Although her adult life was spent attempting to close down the BIA's operations, Jemison testified that she was opposed to Butler's transfer bills. In her typical virulent, anti-Communist rhetoric, she mentioned her long crusade against the Indian Reorganization Act and emphasized the importance of maintaining treaty rights without the BIA's oppressive administration. She concluded her testimony by pointing out that "we come under the supervision of our own nation and we are not injuring the people of the United States by so doing. We are keeping our side of the treaties, and we fought by your side in every war to preserve the union."[29]

Cornelius and Nellie Plummer, Lafayette Williams, and John Snyder also testified, opposing the bills and bringing other grievances to the attention of the subcommittee. Nellie Plummer, a Cornplanter Heir living at Cattaraugus, had been designated by the Seneca women to bring their formal protest to the congressional hearing. Reacting to the ignorant statements made by Watkins and Butler, she tried to explain to the uninformed subcommittee members that, according to Seneca custom, women and their children are the "sole owners of the Allegany and Cattaraugus Indian Reservations." She added that a "child born to an Indian woman, no matter whether the father was a white man or an Indian, they are full-blooded Indians." She questioned state officials' motivation behind the pending legislation and insisted that New York State owed her people millions of dollars for allowing the Erie Railroad and various electric transmission, telephone, and pipelines the "right" to come across the Allegany and Cattaraugus Reservations.[30] Cornelius Plummer pointed out that the state had not recognized the legitimacy of Iroquois land claims assertions and that there was a great need for better Indian health care services.[31] Lafayette Kennedy, a farmer who also ran a fruit market on the eastern end of the Cattaraugus Reservation, questioned why New York officials were so concerned about obtaining jurisdiction over the Indians when its employees in the state's Department of Social Welfare had always complained about spending too much money for Indian needs. He, like others at the hearing, also asserted that the state's courts discriminated against the Indians. Kennedy saw the motivation behind this transfer legislation as a state ruse, a sneaky effort to impose taxation on the Indians. He insisted that treaty rights had to be respected and that Congress be hesitant in passing new legislation because most Senecas had opposed the state's efforts in the past.[32] John Snyder, a Seneca attorney, brought a petition containing the names of hundreds of Senecas opposed to the Butler bills. These Seneca petitioners pointed out that the pending legislation violated the Pickering and other treaties. The signatories to the petition insisted that those forefathers who had designed the treaty relationship between the United States and the Senecas believed that those accords could not simply be overturned by the actions of one of the parties to these agreement. Like Cornelius Seneca and Lafayette Kennedy, Snyder saw that there were other motivations behind the state's attempt to assume jurisdiction. He countered arguments about Albany officials' generosity in providing moneys, a total of $400,000 annually, for its services to reservation communities statewide: "It is a fact that in this day and age in history, after collecting taxes within a territory it does not have jurisdiction, the State of New York now seeks at the hands of Congress to be granted the necessary jurisdiction. Approximately half of the tax money so collected are [sic] retained." Snyder then went on to note that Cattaraugus and Erie Counties had also collected tax moneys that "grow and accrue within the boundaries of the Allegany and Cattaraugus Indian Reservations of the Seneca Nation of Indians' territory." He listed them as "five town sites, a city, railroads, pipelines, telephone, telegraph, oil, gas wells, and other small business enterprises, and electric-powerlines." Snyder estimated that this tax totaled approximately $800,000 each year for the two counties, among all kinds of taxes in which Albany "shared proportionately."[33]

Despite the unanimous condemnation of the Butler bills by diverse voices within the Seneca Nation, Congress passed the legislation, transferring criminal jurisdiction over all the Iroquois communities to New York State in 1948. Two years later Congress transferred civil jurisdiction over the Indians to New York State.[34] In the same period, the BIA closed its New York Agency office as part of federal withdrawal policies. Congress also passed an act allowing rental moneys in Salamanca to be collected by city officials, who would then turn over these moneys to the Seneca Nation. Although this process facilitated payment and replaced the role of collection undertaken in the past by the BIA Indian agent, the legislation created the false impression that the non-Indian officials of the city, 85 percent of which is on the Senecas' Allegany Indian Reservation and has a significant number of non-Indian residents, had paramount authority over all of its residents, Indian and non-Indian (see chapter 9).

In 1949, the Special Presidential Commission on the Organization of the Executive Branch of the Government, better known as the Hoover Commission, filed a task force report on Indian affairs that, among other suggestions, advocated the transfer of federal programs to the states, urged policies that would encourage and assist Indians to leave the reservation and enter the mainstream of American life, and called for the "ending of tax exemption and of privileged status for Indian owned land and the payment of the taxes at the same rates as for other property in the area."[35] A year later, President Truman appointed Dillon S. Myer as the new BIA commissioner. Myer, a career administrator who had served in numerous posts in the Department of Agriculture, had headed the War Relocation Authority from 1942 to 1944 and had been a commissioner of the Federal Housing Authority since 1946. As head of the War Relocation Authority, he had supervised the tragic removal and detention of tens of thousands of Japanese Americans at special camps, some of which were located on Indian reservations. Almost immediately on assuming office, Myer focused attention on the step-by-step transfer of BIA functions to other federal agencies.[36]

On August 1, 1953, the Eighty-Third Congress passed House Resolution 108, declaring that Washington's policy was to abolish federal supervision over tribes as quickly as possible and subject the Indians to the same laws, privileges, and responsibilities as other citizens of the United States. The resolution specifically mentioned New York State, declaring that it was "the sense of Congress that at the earliest time, all of the tribes and the individual members located within the following states of California, Florida, New York, and Texas should be freed from federal control and from all disabilities and limitations specially applicable to Indians."[37] Even well-respected liberals in the US Senate, such as Herbert Lehman, the former governor of New York who had long-standing ties to Senecas, did not question termination policies but insisted that they be modified to ensure that the Indians be protected.[38]

Importantly, in January 1954, Assistant Secretary of the Interior Orme Lewis spelled out federal policies toward the Senecas in a letter and report sent to President Eisenhower. In response to House Concurrent Resolution 108 outlining termination as national policy, the Eisenhower administration drafted two proposed bills for consideration by Congress—the first "[t]o provide for the capitalization of the treaty annuity paid to the Six Nations of Indians, and for other purposes," and the second "[t]o provide for the distribution of funds belonging to the Seneca Nation and the Tonawanda Band of Senecas, and for other purposes." After outlining federal treaty obligations to both the Seneca Nation of Indians and the Tonawanda Band of Senecas, Lewis indicated that a lump-sum payout of federal treaty obligations "to each group will be made only with the consent of the group." He pointed out that at that time "capitalization of this annuity" was "vigorously opposed by the Indian recipients, who place a high symbolic value on the continued affirmation of their historic treaties with the United States." Lewis added: "In New York, the Indians further consider the presentation of the [treaty] cloth by the Federal Government as a continuing Federal recognition of their land rights."[39]

Lewis indicated that since 1951 the BIA had been trying unsuccessfully "to negotiate a settlement of the treaty annuity," which the Senecas had rejected in meetings. Despite these setbacks, federal officials, according to Lewis, believed that the 1954 bills would "provide an orderly procedure under which this obligation can be terminated in an equitable manner, and will constitute a firm standing offer to each Indian group if the prevailing attitude should change." The assistant secretary informed the president that the bill removed unnecessary "restrictive measures" on "leases, contracts and other actions by the tribal bodies." He stressed that these bills would not interfere with the recent federal transfer of criminal and civil jurisdiction to states or with the "application of state game and fish laws on some of the reservations."[40]

With reference to the second bill aimed specifically at the Seneca Nation of Indians and the Tonawanda Senecas, Lewis pointed out that "they [the Senecas] will strongly oppose disposition [sic] of their funds if the proposal is tied to any measures affecting the treaties between the United States and the Six Nations, which include the Senecas." This second bill, one favored by New York State officials, would "result in the distribution of the funds in an equitable manner, and in desirable administrative economies." To the assistant secretary, the bill was a logical follow-up to the closing of the BIA's New York Agency in 1949 and transfer of responsibilities to the State of New York.[41] Six months after Lewis's analysis, Senator Butler died in office. The congressional push for termination turned away from New York State to focus more on Wisconsin and points west. The Menominees of Wisconsin, the Klamath of Oregon, Native *rancherías* in California, and the smaller northeastern Oklahoma Indian communities soon became the focus of congressional terminationists. Efforts to fully terminate the Iroquois in New York were set back when its major proponents left Congress. Daniel Reed died in office in 1959. In the same year, Watkins left the Senate to work for Secretary of the Interior Fred Seaton. The next year President Eisenhower rewarded Watkins with an appointment to head the ICC, where he served for the next seven years adjudicating tribal grievances and claims against the United States.[42]

The threat to the Senecas had slowed down; however, it did not end when these three men departed Congress. Other congressman, all from western states and from both political parties, were to take up the banner in the 1960s. Republican senator Clinton Anderson of New Mexico, who was to head the Senate Subcommittee on Indian Affairs, joined in with his fellow Republican Peter Dominick of Colorado. Democrat Frank Church of Idaho, who later served as chair of the Senate Subcommittee on Indian Affairs, and his fellow Democrat the powerful Henry "Scoop" Jackson of Washington State were to push the terminationist agenda well into the 1960s.[43] Led by Anderson, these men held the Senecas hostage, forcing their tribal leadership to agree to prepare a formal plan for federal withdrawal before Congress would release money to help them relocate and rebuild from areas flooded by the Kinzua Dam. These senators put this requirement into section 18 of the 1964 act "compensating" the Senecas.[44] As late as 1967, a bill was introduced into Congress to complete the termination of the Seneca Nation.[45] However, on July 8, 1970, President Nixon, in one of the more extraordinary and important policy statements ever made dealing with Native Americans, formally ended the era of termination.[46] Nevertheless, the policy, even well after its demise, had a long-term psychological impact on the Senecas, affecting their politics well into the 1970s and 1980s.[47]

Thus, the federal government's actions after World War II—jurisdictional transfer, the closing of the BIA's New York Agency, and attempts to buy out treaty obligations—forced the Seneca Nation to the brink. The federal government's abandonment of the Senecas in this period impelled them to act alone in a weakened condition against an increasingly aggressive leadership in New York State, led by public-works czar Robert Moses and his protégé Bertram D. Tallamy. These two men, with the cooperation and support of three-term governor Thomas Dewey, the powerful Republican and former presidential candidate in 1944 and 1948, pushed land acquisition, public power projects, and highway construction, all of which negatively affected the Senecas. In an era before Red Power activism and faced with constant efforts to end the Seneca Nation's treaty status, the Seneca leadership, which included some of the more respected council members of the age, were forced to give way under these unrelenting pressures. Having few financial resources, high unemployment, and limited educational opportunities, and facing racism in western New York, they had no leverage to fight back against Albany. Already reeling from postwar events transpiring in Washington, the Seneca Nation now had to contend with Albany's planned take of Cattaraugus lands to build the New York State Thruway.

3

Empire State Policies

The Thruway

IN THE MID-1970S, I would visit the Cattaraugus Indian Reservation several times a year and stay over at the home of the late Pauline Lay Seneca, a well-respected Cayuga elder who lived along State Road 438, which traverses this Seneca community. Because numerous Cayugas had Seneca spouses, Mrs. Seneca would introduce me to her many Seneca relatives, the Campbell, Hewitt, Jemison, Kettle, and Lay families on and off the reservation. Francis Kettle, a former president of the Seneca Nation in the mid-1950s, was one of Mrs. Seneca's relatives. A star lacrosse player and coach in Rochester in western New York's professional leagues in the 1930s, Kettle would accompany me to the newly opened Newtown Arena to watch Senecas play teams from Akwesasne, Grand River, and Onondaga. Sitting in the Newtown Arena on the reservation, he would point out some of the finer elements of this rough game to me, a nonathlete from the streets of Brooklyn who had never before seen this sport live.[1]

I had no idea then that the Seneca elder who was sitting beside me had been the president of the Seneca Nation of Indians in the mid-1950s, precisely the time when New York State officials forced these Indians to surrender some of their lands for the completion of the New York State Thruway. Thirty years after my visits, long after Kettle had died, I undertook contract research from the Seneca Nation about the thruway. In the process, I finally realized that I had missed an opportunity to hear from him about a continuing sore—namely, the thruway take of 1954—that festers to this day at Cattaraugus. This take was to occur just after New York

34

State obtained civil and criminal jurisdiction over the Six Nations and just prior to the push by Pennsylvania for an upper Allegheny River dam.

Major state roads built exclusively by the state such as Route 17 (now Interstate 86) and the New York State Thruway (now Interstate 90) and less traveled state roads such as Route 438 traverse Seneca Country. As early as the United States–Six Nations Treaty negotiations at Canandaigua in 1794, road building became a point of contention between the Senecas and the non-Indian world.[2] At other times, New York plans for transportation development brought the Senecas into conflict directly with Albany officials. Although the New York State Thruway take in 1954 was infinitesimal compared to the lands condemned by the federal government in the later Kinzua project, the state's acquisition of Seneca lands at Cattaraugus has shaped Seneca society, politics, and relationship with Albany right down to the present day.

In August 1954, more than two-thirds of the New York State Thruway had been laid out, and construction completed. It was at this time that state officials arrived in Seneca territory to "negotiate" with the Senecas for acquisition of the 3.6-mile easement. Yet this "acquisition" was already a fait accompli. Nothing could now stop the massive road construction equipment that was in place just a few miles from the reservation or prevent the Senecas from being steamrolled. The federal government had abandoned these Indians in the years following World War II. By October 1954, the Senecas were forced to give way to American progress, this time in the form of the construction of the New York State Thruway. This massive highway project, as was true of the building of the Erie Canal,[3] which had led to massive Iroquois dispossession in the first decades of the nineteenth century, was built in several stages with no federal moneys. Funding was secured by the state's issuing of securities until the thruway was federalized into the Eisenhower interstate highway system in 1957.

Thomas E. Dewey's governorship of New York State from 1942 to 1954 occurred at precisely the same time as the origins and development of federal termination legislation. Despite lobbying by Louis R. Bruce Jr., who later served as US commissioner of Indian affairs from 1969 to 1972, the governor never met with tribal leaders during his three terms in office. Finally in 1952, at Bruce's urging, Dewey established the Interdepartmental

Committee on Indian Affairs, which proved totally ineffective.[4] During his three terms, the governor left the direction of Indian policy in the state to the New York State Legislature's Joint Legislative Committee on Indian Affairs and its counsel, Leighton Wade. Attorney Wade was from Olean, less than twenty miles from two of the Senecas' territories—the Allegany and Oil Spring Reservations. He had previously joined in with a group of southwestern state legislators whom the Senecas strongly resented because they had pushed for state jurisdiction over the Indians.[5]

At a Buffalo news conference on August 26, 1954, Dewey lauded his own accomplishments in promoting highway building and announced his administration's plans to extend New York State Thruway construction south from Buffalo to Erie, Pennsylvania, which would carve a path through Seneca Territory at Cattaraugus. The news conference occurred merely two days before negotiations were to begin with the Seneca Nation of Indians' Tribal Council. The governor never bothered before or after his Buffalo announcement to make face-to-face contact with Senecas on the state's acquisition of an easement through tribal lands.[6]

During Dewey's three-term administration, no single state official had more influence in shaping public policies than Robert Moses, who served as chairman of the New York State Council of Parks and later as chairman of the New York State Power Authority. Whether over expansion of state parks, highway construction projects, or public power development, Moses's incredible energy, abilities, and actions helped reshape the New York State landscape. Studies of his role in affecting Indian policy have focused for the most part on his tenure as chairman of the New York State Power Authority and its appropriation of Mohawk-claimed lands at Barnhart Island, the industrialization of the St. Lawrence River valley and its environmental impact, and his high-handed actions in creating the Niagara Power Project, which took a substantial part of the Tuscarora Reservation.[7] Yet Moses's hand was both in the acquisition of the 3.6-mile easement through the Cattaraugus Reservation as well in the early development of the Kinzua Dam.

On January 3, 1945, Governor Dewey announced his Essential Postwar Building Program. He had requested the New York State Department of Public Works (DPW), to prepare a postwar plan for highway improvements, which he claimed had been neglected for fifteen years. He made an $800 million commitment to build new highways and improve older highways, which he deemed essential for the expansion of tourism and the Empire State's overall economic growth.[8] By February 1945, Moses followed up Dewey's message, corresponding with Alfred P. Sloan Jr., the chairman of the board of General Motors, and other automobile executives about the needs of the postwar nation, which Moses had always defined in terms of highway construction and improvements. He continued to correspond with General Motors executives about highway planning right through 1954.[9]

Dewey's three-term governorship also coincided with the beginnings of a national push for superhighway construction. The completion of the Pennsylvania Turnpike by 1942 had motivated New York State public officials and businessmen to contemplate the building of the Empire State's own superhighway system; however, wartime necessities delayed the project in New York. In the winter of 1946, without gaining Seneca permission beforehand, A. R. Lane, employed by the New York State DPW, went onto the Cattaraugus Indian Reservation and began making a survey. He soon found himself lectured to by President Cornelius Seneca. On January 15, 1946, C. R. Waters, district engineer of the New York State DPW, wrote to President Seneca explaining to him that Lane was doing essential work because it was necessary "to make a careful survey, locating buildings, property lines and general topography." Without apologizing for Lane's unannounced intrusion, Waters added that in order to design the bridge over Cattaraugus Creek, Lane had to make water borings, study the subsurface soils, and determine the elevation of hard strata. Waters maintained: "We are doing this work now, and where the Thruway crosses the Reservation at Irving it will be necessary to cover quite an extensive area. The first contract will probably extend about six miles south of Cattaraugus Creek, but we are endeavoring to work out the highway plan as far as the northerly Reservation Line and decide on the land which will be needed to build the road." He then asked permission to proceed in finishing the survey at Cattaraugus "to know what lands will be needed for the new road." Whether the Indians agreed to the take or not, Waters insisted, "[t]he proposed Thruway is a State matter and the road will be obtained by the State." Without any concern for cultural sensitivities, he offered the Senecas the privilege of visiting his Buffalo office to "talk over the studies we have made of the proposed road location."[10]

When no response was forthcoming from President Seneca and the Seneca Tribal Council, in the early spring of 1946 both Waters and J. Frank O'Marah, director of the Bureau of Rights-of-Way and Claims of the New York State DPW, wrote to the BIA New York Agency asking for help in arranging a sit-down with the Senecas. Waters included Lane's completed survey as well as a map indicating the lands involved. By June, the matter reached the US Department of the Interior in Washington.[11] O'Marah claimed that President Seneca insisted that any agreement provide compensation for damages both to the tribe as a whole and to individual Senecas. Acting Interior Secretary Oscar Chapman agreed with the Senecas' position, responding that before any construction work was commenced, consent of both the individual Indians and the Tribal Council had to be obtained, and payment of the damages had to be made to both.[12] State officials were to find that no Senecas were willing to cede land. In the age of termination, the Senecas were left to face off against state officials in the latter's renewed efforts to push for this superhighway.

Although other officials, especially Governor Dewey, have been credited with the construction of the New York State Thruway project, Moses was its political architect. Bertram D. Tallamy, Moses's protégé from the mid-1920s onward, carried forth with the idea of building this massive project and selling the idea for its inclusion in the federal interstate highway system created in 1956. A graduate of Rensselaer Polytechnic Institute, Tallamy spent his earlier career in Buffalo working for a private engineering firm. He later served as deputy chief engineer for the Niagara Frontier Board and directed the planning of the Buffalo–Niagara Falls section of the thruway, including the twin Grand Island bridges that traverse the Senecas' traditional territory. Tallamy, a civil engineer, headed the New York State DPW from 1948 to 1950, was appointed by Governor Dewey as first director of the New York State Thruway Authority in 1950, and was named by President Eisenhower to serve as the first full-time federal highway commissioner, taking office in 1957.[13]

Moses, as chairman of the New York State Power Authority from 1952 onward, combined his earlier park interests with new concerns for public power development, seaway transport, and heavy industry. He promoted a series of state parks and parkways for tourist and recreational purposes, while providing special low electric rates, which countered any local opposition to his projects. By improving the state's total economic picture, he would satisfy the public utilities' quest for increased profit margins. By sacrificing Indian lands—Tuscarora (560 acres) and Akwesasne Mohawk (130 acres)—or those that were claimed by Indians, powerless and largely outside of the American electoral process, he would not alienate white voters and their political representatives.[14] Moses saw reservation life as antiquated and the Indians residing there as living off the state's generosity. To him, reservations were ghettos; only the Indians who did not live there were worthy and hard-working individuals. Moses believed that Indians needed to leave the reservation behind and enter the mainstream of American society.[15] Although historians in recent days have tried to rehabilitate Moses's reputation, there was no place for American Indians in his idea of progress.[16]

Moses's connection to the thruway project is less well known. As chairman of the Triborough Bridge Authority and head of the New York State Council of Parks, Moses wrote articles during World War II on postwar planning. In one, he praised the General Motors exhibit at the 1939 World's Fair that predicted sixteen-lane roads in the future. He maintained: "Out of all the welter of controversy about postwar public works, one fact is emerging. The average citizen is enthusiastic about highway improvements."[17]

In 1952, Moses was appointed chairman of the New York State Power Authority. He continued to push for parks and parkways as well as for public power development from the Niagara frontier region to Long Island. His cronies—namely, the key contacts in the engineering profession, business community, and government who depended on him for work, contracts, investment opportunities, and re-election based on the successful projects he could deliver—provided a formidable lobbyist network for his massive construction efforts. As a consequence, this human dynamo steamrolled over opponents by skillfully networking, by delivering projects on time, and by bringing economic benefits to both organized labor and Wall Street investors. Taking advantage of the Cold War climate with its fears of Soviet domination, Moses's power as czar of public-works projects in New York State reached its height by the early 1950s.

By 1953, both the governor's office and the Thruway Authority were being bombarded with petitions to extend the thruway south from Buffalo to Erie, Pennsylvania. On April 7, 1954, Governor Dewey signed a bill passed by the New York State Legislature enabling the Thruway Authority to finance the construction of its Erie section from the city of Buffalo to the Pennsylvania border as well as to Niagara Falls. In his message accompanying the signing, Dewey insisted that "the magnitude of the Thruway project is difficult to comprehend," far exceeding other state highway projects. Asserting that the completed project would be "the greatest highway in the nation," the governor justified it by indicating that it was not going to lead to higher taxes, but that "fees paid by users of the Thruway will cover the cost of its construction and operation." He concluded by referring to this massive project as "one of the greatest engineering accomplishments of our times. It will yield immeasurable benefit to hundreds of communities along its route and many hundreds of others close to it. It will improve highway safety, provide the basis for a truly modern highway system, reduce transportation costs and strengthen greatly the economy and competitive position of the State."[18]

Among the lobbyists for the thruway route from Buffalo to Erie, Pennsylvania, were Greyhound Bus Lines, Buffalo banks, the United Florists of Western New York, the Chautauqua County Grange, and various western New York chambers of commerce.[19] Yet behind the governor's office push were Moses and Tallamy, who were encouraging the project. Moses's efforts in promoting the state's and the nation's massive road-building efforts were aided by powerful forces. These forces included Harlow Curtice, the president of General Motors.[20] After all, more highways meant more automobiles on the road. Because both Moses and Tallamy envisioned the thruway as a major part of a national effort in massive highway construction, they spent much of the year 1954 in Washington lobbying before congressional committees and meeting with Eisenhower's staff, most notably Sherman Adams, the president's chief of staff, and General John Bragdon, former deputy chief of the US Army Corps of Engineers, and father of the Interstate Highway Act of 1956, who would also later be a major White House proponent of the Kinzua Dam.[21] In April 1954, at a meeting with Moses and Tallamy in attendance, the Eisenhower administration established a federal advisory committee to further federal–state cooperation, coordinate road construction planning, and work out details about how interstate construction could be financed. Moses, who now had a new responsibility added to his full plate in being appointed New York City construction coordinator, and Tallamy subsequently submitted a report promoting their highway agenda to the US Conference of Mayors. Moreover, as early as May 4, 1954, they had sent Adams and Bragdon a draft bill of what in 1956 became the Interstate Highway Act.[22] Thus, by 1954, Moses and Tallamy had become chief lobbyists for the construction of a national highway system; however, the federalizing of the New York State Thruway was not yet a reality in late August 1954, when New York State officials, not federal representatives, made their way to Cattaraugus to negotiate with the Senecas.

Initially undertaken by the New York State DPW, the New York State's postwar superhighway expansion project was shifted to the New York State Thruway Authority when that agency was created in 1950.[23] By the late summer of 1954, two of the major sections of the New York State Thruway had been completed. Hailing the progress of thruway construction and announcing plans for its final stage southward from Buffalo, Governor Dewey made his August 26 announcement.[24] Two days later state representatives formally met with the Seneca Nation Tribal Council on the Cattaraugus Reservation. P. G. Baldwin, director of the Bureau of Rights-of-Way and Claims for the New York State DPW, later filed a report of this meeting with the Seneca Nation Tribal Council on August 28, 1954, held at the Thomas Indian School. In two separate sessions that day, the conferees concerned themselves "with acquisition of rights of way within the Reservation lands as required for Subdivision 5, Erie Section of the Thruway." Seneca representatives in attendance were Francis Kettle, president; Ernest Sutton, treasurer; John Van Aernam Jr., a substitute for the clerk;

"about fifteen councilmen"; and Seneca attorney Edward E. O'Neill.[25] O'Neill was a Jamestown, New York, resident and former US Department of Justice lawyer who had worked at the Nuremberg Trials. He later was the Seneca Nation's initial attorney in federal court cases attempting to stop the Kinzua Dam. Importantly, it should be noted that until 1957 the State of New York paid for Seneca legal services. Yet just before the meeting with the state representatives on August 28, the Senecas, not trusting their state attorney, quickly hired O'Neill, the first lawyer independently hired in their long history.[26] At the request of President Kettle, O'Neill attempted to explain and clarify the nature of an easement agreement. O'Neill made it clear from the beginning of the meeting onward that the Seneca Nation as a whole and tribal members affected by the project had to receive equitable compensation.[27]

Baldwin was the major state negotiator at the August 28 meeting. He was accompanied by three of his junior colleagues—Roswell Hall, W. H. Kerr, and Ed McCord—as well as by Ali D. Good, title attorney for the New York State Department of Law. No representative from the US Department of the Interior was present to monitor the proceedings. Baldwin's account of the August 28 meeting is quite revealing. Perhaps trying to win points with Tallamy and others in Albany or misreading the entire situation, Baldwin claimed that there "did not seem to be any opposition to the Thruway as a project, nor did anyone clearly intimate that the Seneca Nation would resist the acquisition of rights of way." The Seneca Nation Tribal Council, through their attorney, O'Neill, responded that their Indian nation should receive a percentage of the tolls collected for the "3.6 more or less miles of Thruway" that would cross their reservation. Baldwin quickly labeled this idea "highly improbable."[28]

The state negotiator hoped to cut a deal right away, but doing so went against the traditional Hodinöhsö:ni´ way of conducting diplomacy. He was impatient with the Senecas' style of negotiating, unaware that the Indians had used this deliberate style since before colonial times. Disappointed by the Indians' failure to accept immediately what was proposed, Baldwin wrote in his minutes of the August 28 meeting that the only commitment he could obtain from the Senecas was the council's appointment of a committee to discuss this matter further with the state's representatives.[29] Because Governor Dewey had already gone on record announcing phase three of thruway construction south from Buffalo, and construction equipment was now in place just off the reservation, any delay would prove costly to the state. The Seneca Nation Tribal Council passed a resolution that day insisting that their committee "be guided by the present opinion of the council" and that "the negotiations and agreement with that state authorities be based upon the following general principles":

a. That the fee to the land will be reserved in the Nation;

b. That the individual Seneca Indian landowner be fully compensated for their lands and damage thereto;

c. That any present or future loss of revenue to the Nation, resulting from loss of gravel sites, etc., be fully compensated at the time permission is granted;

d. That the Nation be compensated one-third (⅓) of the gross income received by the Thruway Authority from tolls or otherwise, from the Thruway lands within the Reservation.[30]

On August 29, O'Neill notified Ali D. Good that the Seneca Nation's Tribal Council had appointed a committee of three—Alton Van Aernam, Leo Cooper, and Frank Goode—to work with President Kettle, Clerk John Van Aernam Jr., and Treasurer Ernest Sutton—as the Seneca Nation negotiating committee. The attorney for the Seneca Nation requested a copy of the letter from the Thruway Authority to individual contractors advising them "that construction was to be withheld pending clearance with the Nation of the right of way permission." O'Neill added to his note to Good that it was "the desire of the Council to cooperate fully with the Thruway Commission in the granting of this right of way," but that the Tribal Council had the overall responsibility and duty to protect the rights of the Seneca Nation, "a duty with which I believe the State is in full accord. With the exception of 'opinion d' [monetary compensation], I believe little or no controversy exists between your office and the [Seneca] Nation."[31]

President Kettle, the Tribal Council, the Indian negotiating committee, and O'Neill were well aware of the Senecas' weak position and that their claim for a share of thruway tolls would be rejected outright. They knew that they could not turn to Washington for help in the post–World War II climate of termination. Moreover, the Senecas were not the only Hodinöhsö:ni´ faced with land loss in 1954. That summer the United States and Canada were constructing the massive St. Lawrence Seaway Project, which appropriated Mohawk lands at Akwesasne and Kahnawake and seriously disrupted tribal life. Without doubt, this take affected the Senecas' apparent acquiescence to the New York State Thruway's acquisition of the 3.6-mile easement through the Cattaraugus Reservation. In an age before Red Power activism, the Senecas' position and its insistence on one-third of the thruway tolls was an attempt to delay the inevitable. It was also a way to express the Senecas' collective anger at yet another state action limiting their sovereignty. After all, the thruway was a fait accompli.

On September 17, representatives of the Seneca Nation of Indians held a negotiating session in Buffalo. No report of this second meeting has been located; however, the next day, the Seneca Nation of Indians Tribal Council held a meeting at the Allegany Courthouse, with Baldwin once again in attendance. At the afternoon session, Councilor Leo Cooper, a well-respected Seneca voice of this era, introduced a motion before the council to grant the thruway easement. The motion was seconded by Watson Pierce and then carried by an eleven to one vote.[32] Two days later Baldwin glowingly announced that a deal had been struck. With great satisfaction, he wrote to thruway chairman Tallamy that instead of coughing up what he feared was one-third of the revenues from thruway tolls, or an estimated half-million dollars, to the Seneca Nation, the state negotiators acquired the lands for $75,000, "much lower than any of us expected to acquire these lands for." Pleased with the accord, Baldwin maintained:

> I am pleased to advise that I have been able to work out a deal with the Seneca Nation of Indians which I believe will be satisfactory to all concerned. You will recall from my previous memorandum that the Indian representatives had demanded, among other things, one-third of the revenue received from toll collections over that portion of the Thruway passing through the Indian reservation. Although no figures were mentioned at that time, our calculations in this item alone indicated that the

Indian nation might be seeking as much as one-half million dollars for the right to pass through their lands. It required several hours of very frank talk to convince them that we would not entertain any proposition based upon revenues received from the operation of the Thruway. Our appraisal of the rights of the nation in the 300 acres of land required for the Thruway was estimated to be some figure between $50,000.00 and $100,000.00. We finally got the Indian representatives to come out with an asking of $150,000.00, which we finally hammered down to a settlement of $75,000.00 [$69,500 to the Senecas and $5,500 to attorney O'Neill]. This is much lower than any of us expected to acquire these lands for, but I believe that such a figure represents a very fair settlement for all concerned.[33]

Baldwin's reference to "several hours of very frank talk" is not very difficult to interpret, considering that the future existence of the Seneca Nation of Indians hung in the balance in 1954. Congressional bills introduced that year aimed to end the Seneca Nation's treaty status as a federally recognized nation. Could the Seneca Nation, with its limited financial resources and single attorney, legally challenge and delay the massive New York State Thruway project? Did the Seneca Nation have the power and influence to stymie Governor Dewey, a leading Republican in the nation and twice the presidential nominee of his party? Could the Seneca Nation of Indians win outside support to resist when highway development and improvements were very popular with the American public at large? The answer to all these questions was *no*, and the Seneca Nation of Indians Tribal Council understood the tenor of the times and power realities that existed.

By the accord, the Seneca Nation reserved the legal title to the land given to the state for the right-of-way. The easement would not exceed the 300 acres of land ceded by the Seneca Nation. Individual Senecas affected by the project would be compensated, and a list of the rightful landholders disturbed would be designated by the Seneca Nation Tribal Council. Although local newspapers indicated that $100,000 was promised to individual Senecas affected by the project, the signed agreement did not list the amount that the state had to compensate these individual

Senecas.[34] Instead, New York State was to pay the Seneca Nation $75,000. Out of this sum, $1,500 was to be set aside for the expenses incurred by the Seneca Nation Tribal Council, and attorney O'Neill was to be paid $5,000, thus leaving $68,500 to be distributed per capita. Another sore point was that the Seneca Nation would have to grant rights-of-way to those public utilities affected by thruway construction, although the New York State Authority did agree to pay all the costs for relocation of these public utilities.[35]

On October 5, 1954, at the formal closing on this conveyance, New York State officials delivered a check to Ernest Sutton, treasurer of the Seneca Nation of Indians, at the Statler Hotel in Buffalo and then filed the legal conveyance of the easement in the Erie County Clerk's Office.[36] Although New York State had paid out $75,000 on that day, compensation for individual Senecas whose homes and barns were affected by the construction did not happen right away and led to extensive appeals. One Cattaraugus Seneca, Merwin Pierce, had to wait for eighteen years to be reimbursed for property damages caused by thruway construction.[37] Nevertheless, once the deal was consummated, the New York State DPW immediately moved onto Seneca territory. On October 13, just eight days after the conveyance of the easement, Governor Dewey officially broke ground on a thirteen-mile stretch of the planned thruway route that included the easement obtained from the Senecas.[38] By August 21, 1957, the Buffalo–Erie section of the thruway was completed. The same year, the New York State Thruway, later renamed after Governor Dewey, became an integral part of the interstate highway system.[39]

If you divide $68,500 by the population of the Senecas in 1954, the amount per capita would be less than $11 per person. If you calculate based on the acreage obtained by New York State for the easement, 300 acres, the cost of the right-of-way was $231.67 per acre. These extremely low figures should not be a surprise in that the 1954 accord was hardly an agreement between equals. After World War II, the Senecas had been deserted by Washington officials, and the federal government had failed to exercise its trust responsibilities. Between the original negotiations of August 28 and the filed conveyance of October 5, 1954, no federal official oversaw the process. At a time of aggressive New York State policies directed at land acquisition and extending jurisdiction over the Indians, the federal government had withdrawn from the scene. Congress had even turned hostile to Seneca interests and was seriously considering full-scale termination.

Because of the federal government's actions after World War II—termination policies, jurisdictional transfer, the closing of the BIA's New York Agency, and attempts to buy out treaty obligations—the Seneca Nation of Indians was forced to act alone against a aggressive leadership in New York State, led by public-works czar Robert Moses and his protégé Bertram D. Tallamy, pushing land acquisition, public power projects, and highway construction, all of which negatively affected the Senecas. The model for financing this massive public-works project was clearly the Erie Canal—built in sections without federal moneys—which had led significantly to the dispossession of the Senecas in western New York in the first half of the nineteenth century.

Red Power activism in New York was born only later in the 1950s during the Tuscaroras' unsuccessful fight to stop another of Robert Moses's plans, this time for a reservoir on tribal lands for the Niagara Power Project.[40] The Seneca thruway easement came seventeen years before the Onondagas sat down on Interstate 81 to protest road construction on their lands and thirty-one years before the Senecas themselves did the same to protest the Southern Tier Expressway easement through the Allegany Indian Reservation (described in chapter 8).[41] Faced with constant efforts to end Seneca treaty status, the nation's councilors, including some of the more respected Senecas of the age, conceded to the easement. Having to deal with high unemployment, limited educational opportunities, and outright racism in western New York (Gowanda and Salamanca), they made the best deal they could at the time. No level playing field existed in the era of termination. State officials presented the easement as a "done deal," and the Senecas had no leverage except to annoy the negotiators and delay the conveyance of the easement for six weeks.

The thruway take is still a sore point for Senecas today.[42] On two separate occasions in the past two decades, the Senecas at Cattaraugus have brought traffic on the New York State Thruway temporarily to a halt in large protests against Albany's insistence on collecting the state sales tax from the Indians on their lands.[43] It is important to note that one of the Cattaraugus Senecas most affected by the thruway easement was Cyrus Schindler Sr., whose family's farm was sacrificed in the name of progress in 1954. Thus, it was no coincidence that Schindler entered the world of Seneca politics in the 1990s, at a time when his nation was suing the Thruway Authority. The Senecas' tribal land claim to Grand Island initiated in 1994, discussed in chapter 10, was in part directed at the New York State Thruway Authority because it built and maintains the roads and bridges to territory claimed by the Senecas. Schindler was later elected to the presidency of the Seneca Nation and was to sign the New York State–Seneca Gaming Compact of 2002.[44] Moreover, in 2007 Seneca president Maurice "Mo" John Sr. threatened to put a toll booth on thruway lands taken from the Senecas in 1954. He also sent a bill to the state comptroller demanding payment of $2.6 million for all the vehicular traffic through Seneca territory—namely, the easement lands between thruway exit 57 (Eden/Angola) and exit 58 (Silver Creek).[45] Enraged over the state's efforts to collect sales taxes on Indian sales of cigarettes and gasoline, the Seneca Tribal Council unilaterally rescinded the easement conveyance in 2007.[46] Although the Seneca abrogation of the state accord of 1954 is mostly symbolic and may not have legal standing in court, it is significant nevertheless in that it shows that the past is a present reality to Senecas, shaping their politics and worldview.

The residents of Cattaraugus Territory were not the only Senecas faced with crisis in the postwar years. Allegany Territory and the Cornplanter Tract were about to be threatened as well. Three years after the thruway crisis, the Senecas were to face off against a far greater threat, this time pushed by Pennsylvania politicians and private power interests in the state, the US Army Corps of Engineers, and advisers to two presidents—all intent on building a dam on the upper Allegheny River.

4

Keystone State Policies

Power Trip

THE KINZUA DAM was the third crisis that the Seneca Nation of Indians faced in the post–World War II era. Although Pennsylvania politicians and corporate leaders were directly behind this effort to construct the dam, both federal and New York State officials were to play significant roles in helping the Keystone State achieve this objective. Despite the extensive literature on Kinzua and its origins, no previous scholar has examined how and why the dam became transformed into a hydropower project. Indeed, scholars have ignored this motive behind the building of the dam, swayed by the rhetoric of the dam's proponents. They have not examined it in the context of federal Indian and energy policies in the post–World War II era and of Pennsylvania's energy concerns and needs for industrial development in the western part of the state, a region of northern Appalachia.

In one of the better treatments on the origins of the dam, Paul C. Rosier of Villanova University focuses his attention on Pittsburgh's civic and business leadership and their lobbying efforts. Rosier insists that the project was pushed to treat low-flow regulation and pollution abatement rather than flood control because the former "were of paramount importance to Pittsburgh and Ohio Valley industries; they were essential elements in a plan of industrial expansion to be built, in part, at public expense."[1] He traces the lobbying efforts by the Allegheny Conference on Community Development founded by moguls Richard King Mellon and H. J. Heinz as well as by other lesser-known magnates. Mellon alone had controlling interests in Gulf Oil, ALCOA, Pittsburgh Consolidated Coal, Keppers Utility, and major banks across the nation. Although the leaders of the Allegheny Conference on Community Development were Republicans, these powerbrokers worked closely with and supported Pittsburgh's powerful Democrat mayor David Lawrence, later governor of Pennsylvania and a major promoter of the Kinzua Dam, in his efforts to revitalize his city.[2]

What Rosier and others fail to bring to attention is the issue that industrial development in western Pennsylvania required harnessing energy. Although Pennsylvania is an energy-rich state, more coal production—even to Mellon, who owned a major coal company—meant greater problems. The sulfurous drainage from the coal mines along the Allegheny and Monongahela Rivers were rusting boilers in the city's steel mills, affecting the hulls of ships at Pittsburgh, and running into the Ohio River.[3] Before the nuclear option, the answer to the power issue by the mid-1950s was the promotion of hydropower. Envious of New York's massive Niagara project, whose power production the Empire State refused to share with its neighbors, Pennsylvania officials began to focus on ways to harness more hydropower.

My interest in how hydropower came about at the Kinzua Dam and its impact on Seneca life was whetted by my attendance at six Federal Energy Regulatory Commission (FERC) hearings. On November 30, 2010, at a news conference held at the sparkling new administration building at the Allegany Indian Reservation, Seneca president Robert Odawi Porter announced that his nation was seeking the federal license to run the hydropower-generating facility—the Seneca Pumped Storage Generating Station—at the Kinzua Dam, now held by FirstEnergy Corporation and set to expire in December 2015. Porter recounted that for fifty years the Seneca Nation and its people had borne the burdens of this development, while the US government, Pennsylvania communities downstream of the dam, and a private power company holding the Federal Power Commission (FPC) license for the Seneca Pumped Storage Generating Station, as well as its shareholders and its customers, had reaped significant benefits, financial and otherwise. He noted that not only had the Senecas, who had lost their most productive as well as sacred lands, suffered economic losses, but the trauma inflicted by the project had caused psychological damage to his people. The Seneca president insisted that his tribal government had never been included in discussions about power development when the license was granted by the FPC in 1965, nor were his people ever compensated financially for the use of its waters for hydroelectric power generation. Time and time again federal officials, from the White House to the district engineers of the Army Corps of Engineers in Pittsburgh, had told them that their lands were needed for Allegheny River valley flood control. Porter, a Harvard Law School graduate and law professor at Syracuse University, maintained that now, in 2010, the Seneca Nation had the capacity—both an educated populace and financial resources—to receive the license and copartner with an energy company of its choosing to administer and run the hydroelectric power of the Kinzua Dam for the next fifty years. Taking their cue from the Confederated Tribes of Warm Springs in Oregon and the Confederated Salish and Kootenai Tribes of the Flathead Nation in Montana, both of whom were severely affected by massive dam projects and who much later secured profitable FERC licenses to run hydropower projects, the Seneca Nation of Indians became determined to pursue a similar course. Thus, for the Senecas, the past had once more become a present reality, one that required adaptation by combining the pursuit of justice with the realities of economic survival.[4]

What President Porter was referring to specifically was the Seneca (Kinzua) Pumped Storage Generating Station, a hydropower-generating facility housed at the dam that can produce 400,000 kilowatts of electricity per hour at peak capacity and is able to service 266,400 homes each year. It makes use of the Kinzua Dam, a lower Allegheny Reservoir comprising Seneca lands flooded between 1961 and 1965, and an upper reservoir situated in the US Department of Agriculture's Allegheny National Forest. It employs two pump-turbine generator units, one conventional turbine-generator unit; associated water intakes, conduits, and discharge facilities; a powerhouse; and transmission lines.[5]

Today the Seneca Pumped Storage Generating Station is run by FirstEnergy Corporation, a conglomerate of ten electricity-distribution companies, including Pennsylvania Electric Corporation (Penelec) and Cleveland Electric Illuminating Company, which received the FPC license

3. Seneca Pumped Storage Generating Station at the Kinzua Dam. From the Seneca Pumped Storage Project website at http://www.senecaproject.com/lfigs.html.

on December 28, 1965, to run operations for fifty years. Based in Akron, Ohio, FirstEnergy has paid the federal government rental fees at the dam and has made hundreds of millions of dollars for it and its shareholders since the Seneca Pumped Storage Generating Station went online in 1970. FirstEnergy has large holdings in coal, natural gas, nuclear (including Three Mile Island), and pumped storage hydroelectric divisions and is the nation's largest privately owned electricity-transmission system in the United States. Stretching from the Ohio–Indiana border to the Jersey shore, FirstEnergy supplies 23,000 megawatts of power in its 20,000 miles of high voltage transmission lines to millions of customers in six states—Maryland, New Jersey, Ohio, Pennsylvania, Virginia, and West Virginia. It has 17,000 employees and $48 billion in assets and has made $18 billion in revenues in 2010.[6]

Flood control along the Allegheny River had always been a concern as far back as the historic Johnstown Flood of 1888, but by the 1950s this rationale obscured the energy-producing motive for the dam. After a destructive flood in 1907, the Pittsburgh Chamber of Commerce established a commission to lobby for flood-control measures. In 1928, the Army Corps of Engineers issued a report on Allegheny River flood control, which it soon rejected because there was little enthusiasm for the proposed project at that time. On St. Patrick's Day in 1936, a flood at the Golden Triangle, the confluence of the Allegheny and Monongahela Rivers in the downtown commercial district of Pittsburgh, killed forty-seven people and caused $5 million in property damage.[7]

In part as a result of this disaster and earlier major floods along the Allegheny and Ohio Rivers, Congress passed the Copeland Omnibus Flood Control Act in 1936, which called for the Army Corps of Engineers to develop a comprehensive flood-control plan. It should be pointed out that utilities companies also lobbied for passage of the act. In another flood-control act in 1938, Congress authorized the Army Corps of Engineers to develop a plan for thirty-nine reservoirs, nine of them above Pittsburgh along the Allegheny River, including the future Kinzua Dam in the vicinity of Warren, Pennsylvania. The act also placed the Army Corps in charge of the design and implementation of future flood-control projects but gave the FPC an equal voice in determining future projects. Of the nine proposed plans for the Allegheny, only one—*not* the proposed Kinzua project near Warren—included hydropower production. The 1938 act, however, also had the following provision in section 4: "That penstocks or other similar facilities adapted to possible future use in the development of hydroelectric power shall be installed in any dam herein authorized when approved by the Secretary of War upon the recommendation of the Chief of Engineers and of the Federal Power Commission." A third congressional act in 1941 authorized a modification of the original

plan for the Ohio River basin to take into account the interests of pollution abatement and stream-flow regulation for navigation. No specific
funds were allocated for dam projects because of foreign crises, military-
preparedness needs, and opposition from the Roosevelt administration.[8]
It should be noted that from 1936 to 1940 Senecas as well as the US Department of the Interior officially protested plans for the dam.[9] After World
War II, the Interior Department was to abandon the Senecas in the era of
termination, instead promoting the expansion of hydropower for industrial growth required in Cold War America.

In August 1938 at Congress's behest, the Army Corps of Engineers
filed a major study, the Covell report, that specifically discussed the possibility of the condemnation of Seneca Indian lands for the Kinzua Dam
project.[10] The report's author, William E. R. Covell, concluded that the
Kinzua project was needed for flood control and pollution abatement, but
he also brought up the possibility of configuring the proposed dam for
future hydropower production. He recommended a "combined development of the reservoir featuring flood control, pollution abatement, and
water power development" and that the "Allegheny River Reservoir Dam
should be constructed at a site in the general vicinity of Kinzua, Pa., the
exact location to be determined at the time of construction." The report
discussed the need to acquire lands at the Cornplanter Tract and the Allegany Indian Reservation, both of which would eventually be affected by the
proposed reservoir. Covell described the legal procedures for acquiring
these lands, pointing out the different histories and legal status of these
two Seneca parcels as well as the preemptive claim of the Ogden Land
Company to Seneca lands. Importantly, Covell, an Army Corps colonel
and engineer, noted, "It is obvious that any agreement entered into by the
Seneca Nation would of necessity contain provisions making it incumbent
upon the United States to provide lands in New York State for said nation
to replace those." Covell went on to suggest that New York State's Allegany State Park could be affected by the proposed dam and that the United
States had the power to condemn state property by eminent domain. He
maintained that he believed there would be no difficulty in negotiating
with Albany and western New York officials to work out legislation. Too

optimistic and perhaps unaware of the poor history of state–Iroquois relations, Covell stated that the Senecas could possibly obtain other lands, suggesting an exchange of a part of New York State's third-largest park— Allegany State Park—for those lands flooded by the proposed dam.[11]

Covell's solution was to be rejected outright by powerful New Yorkers inside and outside state government who were unwilling to trade off park acreage or highway development for Indian cultural survival. Robert Moses himself—then the chairman of the New York State Parks system and head of the New York State Council of Parks and in the 1950s chairman of the New York State Power Authority—was to be the driving force behind rejecting the idea of exchanging park lands for reservation lands. In a 1964 interview conducted by anthropologist William N. Fenton, Charles E. Congdon, former head of the Allegany State Park Commission, revealed much about the hidden history of the Kinzua Dam project. According to Congdon, Robert Moses had been a consultant for Pittsburgh after the serious flooding in the city in 1936. At the time, he headed a planning firm in New York City. Federal officials had contracted with him for $100,000 to prepare a plan redesigning highway and rail access to Pittsburgh. His consulting experience in Pittsburgh led him to discussions with the Army Corps of Engineers' district office in the city. Moses later sent his assistant, hydraulic engineer William Chapin, to Pittsburgh "to see what effect the [proposed] Kinzua Dam would have on Allegany State Park [ASP]." As result of his visit to the Army Corps of Engineers district office, "Chapin got the idea that ASP would get a lake [Allegheny Reservoir] at government expense out of the reservoir, by putting a dam at the mouth of Quaker Run." According to Congdon, this arrangement was a quid pro quo: Moses would get the lake (the reservoir) for tourist development of the adjacent Allegany State Park and for not opposing Kinzua. Pittsburgh and the corps took Moses and Chapin into their camp. Congdon added: "Ever since the State of New York has tended to sympathize [with the Senecas' plight], but always the State people [in Albany] have taken Moses' advice on the benefit that ASP [would get] from the reservoir, when the real reason is Moses' obligation to the U.S. Corps of Engineers[,] who hired him to make the plan in the first instance."[12] Because of

World War II, further consideration of the Kinzua Dam was postponed; however, even before the war ended, the Kinzua Dam project once again received official attention, and the Senecas petitioned against it.[13]

In January 1946, the New York State Council of Parks commissioners met in New York City to discuss postwar planning. They considered a study made by Chapin analyzing a plan for a dam based on a report by Colonel W. E. Lorence, assigned to the Army Corps of Engineers' Pittsburgh district. Lorence had recommended a joint federal–state development of an Allegany reservoir. He offered two separate alternatives. The first, rejected by Moses and the New York State Council of Parks, "was based on federal acquisition of only flowage and clearing rights for the parts of the Allegany reservation which would be subject to flooding." It "would leave the Indians in possession of their present land, but their homes would be liable to flooding whenever operation of the dam required the reservoir to be filled." The second plan, enthusiastically endorsed by Moses and the New York State Council of Parks, called for the "elimination of the Allegany Indian reservation, relocation of the Indians and joint federal–state development of the Allegheny River Valley as a recreational area." This second proposal stated: "In addition to taking over all the reservation, including that part of Salamanca, which is on Indian land, the War Department would purchase all privately-owned land, on tributaries of the river, necessary for flood control or recreation."[14]

Moses's past work for the Army Corps of Engineers in consulting on the Kinzua Dam project and his New York State Parks Council policy statement in 1946 suggests a cozy relationship between the Army Corps' Pittsburgh District and Empire State officials. Some Senecas believed that Pennsylvania and New York State officials had made some sort of a deal related to the Kinzua project, a guess that appears to be correct. In 1961, at a hearing before the New York State Joint Legislative Committee in Indian Affairs, one Cattaraugus Seneca suggested in his testimony that he saw a conspiracy at work: "The Kinzua Dam problem is not a flood control dam. . . . It consists of a few other things and that is a reservoir for commercial uses of water" for Pittsburgh. "They want to store water in the State of New York—flood out the Indian reservation for their benefit." The

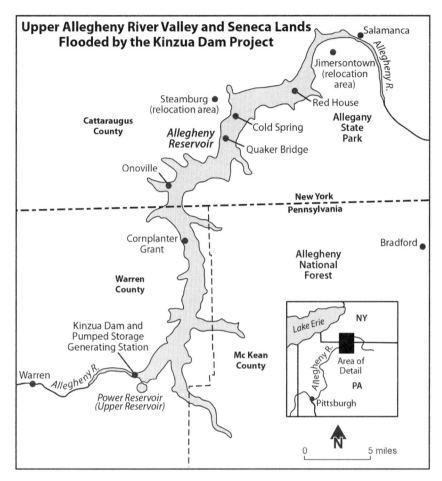

Map 5. Upper Allegheny River valley, showing Kinzua Dam, upper and lower Allegheny Reservoir, Allegheny National Forest, Allegany Reservation, and local and state boundaries. Map by Joe Stoll. Courtesy of Joe Stoll.

Seneca claimed that New York State's Allegany State Park would benefit in return. "On the other hand, the recreational purposes is where the State of New York comes in."[15]

While Robert Moses's efforts were designed to promote economic development by building highways, encouraging tourism and greater park use, and at the same time ensuring the continued viability of Allegany State Park, New York State's third-largest park, his counterpart in

Pennsylvania, Maurice Goddard, had much the same agenda. Goddard was the Keystone State's secretary of forests and waters and had served five separate governors from the late 1940s through the late 1960s. His role was especially important during the administrations of George Leader (1954–58) and David Lawrence (1959–63).[16] A former professor of forestry at Pennsylvania State University, Goddard served as a major proponent of the Kinzua Dam from his Harrisburg office. With the postwar decline of coal mining in the state, he and many influential Pennsylvania officials saw the Kinzua project not only for flood control, but also as a spur for economic development. In May 1957, writing to Congressman Clarence Cannon, the powerful chairman of the powerful House Appropriations Committee, Goddard maintained that the dam was necessary "for the safeguarding of our economy and way of life." He insisted that the dam was required for "transportation, water supply, flood control, conservation of natural resources, and national welfare and defense." To Goddard, Native Americans were US citizens and, as such, had "to give up their homes and lands, in accordance with law, for the common good of the great majority." In words that echoed nineteenth-century expansionist Thomas Hart Benton, he concluded that "in the march of civilization and progress, there must be sacrifice of a few for the protection and well-being of many."[17] Goddard, along with Senator Joseph S. Clark of Pennsylvania, later chair of the US Senate Subcommittee on Public Works, and Congressman Leon Gavin, allies of the powerful Lawrence machine of Pittsburgh, continued to push for the dam in congressional committees and hearings throughout the late 1950s and early 1960s.[18]

Goddard was directly affected by Moses's actions as well as by his inactions. By the 1950s, Moses, now chairman of the New York State Power Authority and an advocate of public power development, was unwilling for his state to sell power to Pennsylvania or Ohio. In the late 1950s, New York State expanded its Niagara hydropower operations after the collapse of the Schellekopf Power Station. The United States and Canada made a treaty, pushed by Moses, giving New York State the exclusive right to control the hydropower produced at Niagara. After receiving a license from the FPC for the Niagara Power Project, the New York State Power Authority was to condemn one-sixth of the Tuscarora Indian Reservation.[19]

Moses, as chairman of the New York State Power Authority, then refused Pennsylvania's and Ohio's repeated requests to share in this bonanza. Yet, it is clear, he never objected to allowing these two states to develop their own sources of power on their own. Goddard's role changed from simply promoting Kinzua as a flood-control project, a shift made in response to Robert Moses's actions in New York State. Governor Leader's administration failed in its efforts to secure a sale of Niagara hydroelectric power from New York State to Pennsylvania's electric rural distribution cooperatives, an idea pushed by William Wenner, then manager and chief lobbyist for the Northwestern Rural Electric Cooperative Association.[20]

Wenner used the argument that by acquiring a share of Niagara hydropower, Pennsylvania would have access to cheap electricity, which would result in expansion of needed industry.[21] Goddard became convinced of the need for greater availability of hydropower; nevertheless, throughout the late 1950s he had to carefully walk a tight rope in the bitter rivalry between public and private power interests, the latter of which dominated the electric industry in the Keystone State. When Moses refused to share Niagara hydropower with Pennsylvania and Ohio and a recession hit the United States hard late in 1957, Goddard became more determined in his push to have hydropower at the Kinzua Dam. After David Lawrence was elected governor in November 1958, Goddard in his correspondence began openly to mention hydropower as a reason for supporting the Kinzua Dam project.[22]

In January 1958, Colonel H. E. Sprague of the Army Corps of Engineers sent a report to the governor's office summarizing the Pittsburgh's district office's extensive activities in Pennsylvania and its plans for the future. He did not mention hydropower development at the Kinzua Dam. In the report, he did focus on the need to create a $101 million storage reservoir on the upper Allegheny River between Warren, Pennsylvania, and Salamanca, New York, for the specific purpose of flood control and "low-water regulation for domestic water supply and for pollution abatement."[23] Despite this report, the Army Corps and Pennsylvania officials were already planning for future hydropower development at Kinzua. In May 1959, Goddard wrote to William Wenner, now coordinator of the Allegheny Electric Corporation:

We have checked with the Corps of Engineers regarding any proposed plans for the inclusion of hydro electric power facilities in the structure [Kinzua Dam], and have been informed that, as a result of recent negotiations between that agency and the Federal Power Commission, the question is under discussion, *and it is quite probable that penstocks for the future production of power will be included.* There is still a difference of opinion to be received as to the exact elevation of the penstocks. *In light of this recent development, it would appear that even though plans did not include power generation, this question is now being taken into consideration by the Corps.*[24]

In the late 1950s and early 1960s, Goddard corresponded with and attended planning sessions held by the Army Corps of Engineers for the Kinzua Dam. Because of his expertise in forestry management, he also met with representatives of both the US Interior Department and the US Agriculture Department, which administered the Allegheny National Forest, to develop recreational sites for tourism in the upper Allegheny River valley. Goddard also worked closely with Senator Joseph Clark. Although a highly respected liberal Democrat with a strong commitment to civil rights, Clark never seemed to see the moral dilemma in his position in favor of the Kinzua Dam. In a statement prepared in May 1957 for presentation at a congressional hearing focusing on public-works appropriations for 1958, Clark criticized the delay in building a dam whose merits had been debated for twenty years, He, like Goddard, viewed the loss of Indian lands as essential: "While we are all sympathetic with the problems of the American Indians and while they certainly deserve just and fair treatment by our Government, in cases such as this one, their interests, like those of any other citizens affected, are subordinate to the interests of the entire region."[25] Clark praised the expertise of the Army Corps of Engineers and, with Hugh Scott, his Republican colleague in the House, worked the floor for key votes to get approval each time the project came to a vote in the late 1950s. To be fair to Clark and Scott, their two New York Republican colleagues in Congress—Senators Jacob Javits and Kenneth Keating—never testified against the Kinzua project before its construction, although they, as well as Clark and Scott, later supported the proposal that monetary compensation be awarded to the Senecas.[26]

A renewed push for the Kinzua Dam began in March 1956 when another disastrous flood struck the upper Allegheny River valley, seriously affecting the area around Warren. Pennsylvania proponents of the dam began to resurrect the Army Corps of Engineers' plans for a Kinzua dam from the late 1930s. When the Army Corps of Engineers initiated condemnation proceedings in January 1957, the Seneca Nation immediately protested and hired Dr. Arthur E. Morgan, the eminent civil engineer who was then president of Antioch College. Morgan was to provide an alternative to Kinzua, the Conewango–Cattaraugus plan, intended to prevent the loss of Seneca territory.[27]

During the New Deal, Morgan, a largely self-educated genius in the civil engineering community, had helped write the bill creating the Tennessee Valley Authority (TVA), which had excluded Army Corps Engineers from planning, chairing, or being the chief engineers of the massive project. As head of the TVA from 1933 to 1937, he was an outspoken critic of the Army Corps as well as of politicians seeking pork-barrel projects who did not question the corps' faulty plans or bloated budgets. TVA was initially designed to build dams along the Tennessee River to provide impoverished rural communities with cheap electricity in order to create industry, produce employment opportunities, give flood-control protection, and reclaim land. In sharp contrast, David E. Lilienthal, Morgan's chief foe at TVA, viewed southern Appalachian communities as backward, needing to be brought into full modernity, and assumed that industrial opportunity would follow. A first-rate scholar of rural sociology, Morgan empathized with residents of small communities, such as the Senecas, who were faced with what he called the great "American inquisition."[28] Morgan was a utopian planner with little skill or interest in politics. In 1937, President Roosevelt fired him because of his political insolence, uncompromising manner, and battles with David Lilienthal, the Army Corps of Engineers, congressmen, and even the president himself and his staff.[29] During the economic crisis of the New Deal, Morgan, unlike Lilienthal, did not oppose private power companies partnering with the federal government. However, he did fear their political influence because, as he stated in one speech, the "aims of some powerful leaders in the private electric utility industry commonly have been to ruthlessly destroy public ownership by every possible means." Perhaps naively, he insisted that the ultimate goal was to eliminate abuses by private power companies, "while preserving the right of the people to acquire their own power service by public ownership if they choose."[30]

With respect to the Kinzua Dam project, instead of seeing private power interests behind the Army Corps' work on the project, Morgan spent his years battling the corps itself, his long-standing enemy. He developed an alternative to the corps' Kinzua project, the Conewango–Cattaraugus plan, which the corps and the White House systematically rejected at every turn.[31] On May 10, 1957, President Cornelius Seneca, attorney O'Neill, Morgan, as well as representatives of Quaker and reform organizations and conservation groups appeared before a subcommittee of the House of Representatives Committee on Appropriations. President Seneca testified that his people were not against progress, but that they were opposed to Kinzua and the taking of Indian lands based on the federal government's breaking of the Pickering Treaty of 1794. He insisted that Morgan had an alternative plan and that it should be studied before Congress went ahead and overturned Seneca Nation treaty rights and removed his people from their ancestral lands.[32] President Seneca, O'Neill, and Morgan would repeat their testimony ten days later before the Senate Subcommittee on Public Works Appropriations. It should be noted that in this second hearing the National Rural Electric Cooperative Association submitted a resolution in favor of Kinzua Dam construction.[33] Despite the Senecas' and their supporters' efforts, Congress was eventually to pass the Omnibus Public Works Act of 1958, which allocated $1 million to the Army Corps of Engineers to undertake a feasibility study about its Kinzua Dam project. However, Congress restricted releasing this specific appropriation until the Seneca legal fight against the dam based on their Pickering Treaty argument was heard and determined in the federal courts. While congressmen were still discussing this bill, President Cornelius Seneca and the Seneca Nation Tribal Council were trying to slow down the push for the dam. Seneca directly appealed to President Eisenhower. He once again used the argument that the US government had a moral and legal commitment to the Senecas based on the Pickering Treaty of 1794: "Under the terms of the treaty, which my fellow tribesmen have faithfully abided by for the past 163 years, the United States Government solemnly promised never to 'claim this land, nor disturb the Seneca Nation' in its 'free use and enjoyment thereof.' The construction of this Kinzua Dam with this resulting artificial lake will be in direct violation of these treaty rights."[34]

In order to silence Morgan and his vocal supporters, John S. Bragdon, the White House director of Public Works Planning who had been the former deputy chief of the Army Corps of Engineers, met with Army Corps officials and agreed to hire an "independent" consulting firm to evaluate the Conewango–Cattaraugus plan. They then employed the Ohio firm of Tippetts-Abbett-McCarthy (TAMS) to evaluate the cost and feasibility of Morgan's alternative. TAMS included former Army Corps personnel. Retired General James H. Stratton, a partner in the firm, had been director of civil works for the Army Corps before his retirement and had been in charge of engineering in the construction of the Dennison Dam, another project that had involved condemning Indian lands. Not surprisingly, the TAMS report, issued in 1958, concluded that Morgan's plan would cost 25–38 percent more, would require 108 percent more land, and would dislocate 150–180 percent more people than the one proposed by the Army Corps.[35]

Although Morgan realized that the Army Corps had stacked the deck, he was unwilling to accept the situation as being hopeless. He challenged TAMS's findings and questioned the firm's impartiality.[36] He continued to push this alternative, working closely with George Heron, who succeeded Cornelius Seneca as president of the Seneca Nation of Indians in 1958, and later with Basil Williams, who was elected to the presidency in 1960. They drew support from a diverse coalition of reform organizations and religious societies. Among their major supporters were the Society of Friends, Brooks Atkinson, and Edmund Wilson.[37] Despite the extensive campaign waged to stop the dam, the Senecas were fighting a losing battle from the start. Native Americans simply didn't count in federal policy circles or with most of the public at large in the two decades after World War II. Although there were efforts to help impoverished Navajos during the Truman years and to overhaul operations of the Indian Health Service during the Eisenhower years, Indian lands became sacrifice areas in massive flood-control and hydroelectric projects deemed essential in America's Cold War climate. Most Americans viewed Indians as just another racial minority, not sovereign nations with treaty rights. Their reservations were seen as impoverished enclaves, rural ghettos alien to mainstream American values.

On January 11, 1958, the federal District Court for the Western District of New York held that despite the 1794 treaty the United States had the right to condemn any land essential for the purpose of the Kinzua project. To federal Judge Joseph McGarraghy, moneys ($1 million) for the dam project had been provided in the Public Works Appropriation Act of 1958, which had passed in 1957. He maintained that this act was sufficient congressional intent to set aside the commitments made in 1794 because federal Indian treaties could not rise above the power of Congress to legislate. He maintained that the Indian lands were subject to the power of eminent domain, just as are all lands privately held in the United States. On November 25, 1958, in what proved to be the last major rendering on the legality of the Kinzua Dam involving Seneca lands, the three justices of the US Court of Appeals for the District of Columbia unanimously affirmed the lower court's decision. In June 1959, the US Supreme Court denied a writ of certiorari and refused to hear further on the issue.[38] The same year, after this final judicial determination, the House Appropriations Committee and the House–Senate Conference Committee agreed to a massive 1960 bill for public works; however, in responding to this exorbitant pork-barrel legislation, President Eisenhower, although he and his staff favored going ahead with the dam, vetoed the entire bill, which had included a $1.4 million appropriation for Kinzua. With bipartisan support, Congress nevertheless overrode the president's veto.[39]

By mid-1959, when the US Supreme Court refused to hear their case, the Senecas had already lost in Congress with the Public Works Appropriation Act of 1958, in two lower federal court decisions rendered in 1958, and in the conclusions presented in the TAMS report. On August 24, 1959, Bragdon wrote to President Eisenhower about Kinzua. He insisted that the "controversial aspects of this project have received extensive review and have been resolved by the decision of the Courts and by congressional action." He added that there "is no reason why this project should not proceed subject to budgetary considerations," adding that "the situation concerning the project has developed sufficiently that you may consider the matter closed." Bragdon and his staff members of the Office of Public Works Planning had repeatedly defended the Kinzua Dam project, suggesting that it was a reasonably priced dam, but that some compensation—substitute lands—be considered for the Senecas. Until the end of Eisenhower's presidency, Bragdon continued to support the dam's construction. As a result, President Eisenhower's appropriations request for the 1961 budget included an added $4,530,000 for the Kinzua Dam project.[40]

Both the Eisenhower and later the Kennedy administration's handling of Kinzua is hardly surprising given the way federal officials treated other Native Americans and their lands in the twenty-year period after World War II. The rationale for the taking of Indian lands for flood-control, water, and hydro projects after World War II was common throughout the country. The US government built numerous dams by flooding Indian lands and encouraging water projects and power development in the American West in this period. Ironically, a department—Interior—that was supposedly committed to carrying out the government's trust responsibility to federally recognized American Indian nations was instead increasingly working with the Army Corps of Engineers and private and public power interests and sacrificing tribal lands in a concerted effort to develop hydropower. Among these western projects were the Big Bend, Bonneville, Boyson, Cochiti, Dalles, Fort Peck, Fort Randall, Garrison, Glen Canyon, Grand Coulee, Oahe, Roosevelt, and Yellowtail Dams. All were devastating to Native peoples.[41] During the height of the Cold War, the Interior Department's Bureau of Reclamation viewed flooding Indian lands as a necessity required for the production of electricity needed for industrial growth, a national goal to meet the Soviet challenge. By 1958, the Bureau of Reclamation had constructed thirty-four power plants, producing more than 5 million kilowatts of electricity; by 1966, it had put an additional nine more power plants into operation.[42] The Interior Department hailed its accomplishments as multipurpose projects "undertaken with the aim of obtaining the greatest benefit from the standpoint of irrigation, flood control, hydropower, municipal water, recreation, fish and wildlife resources, and sediment control."[43] Protecting Native peoples—their lands, their cultures, their traditional subsistence—was never seen as part of the equation.

By far the worst disaster affecting Native communities was the building of four dams along the Missouri River. One of them, the Garrison Dam, permanently shattered the lives of the Three Affiliated Tribes (Arikara, Hidatsa, and Mandan) at Fort Berthold Indian Reservation. This 210-foot dam, constructed between 1947 and 1953, cost $299 million, led to the flooding of 152,360 acres, thus reducing the reservation's agricultural output by 94 percent and inundating most of the commercial timber, wildlife habitats, and coal that the Indians had previously used for fuel; segmented the land base into five water-bound sections separating Indians from their kin, in some instances by hundreds of miles; and led to the relocation of 325 families, dislocating 1,700 people, or 80 percent of the population. These Arikara, Hidatsa, and Mandan Indians faced the difficult adjustment of relocation and resettlement, precisely the same problems that the Senecas were to experience. After much delay and years of lobbying, the Fort Berthold community received $12,605,625 in federal compensation, far less per acre than the Senecas were to receive later.[44]

The Eisenhower administration actively promoted the development of America's energy resources. His Atoms for Peace program initiated the start of constructing nuclear-driven plants. Leasing of federal dam projects to private power companies was encouraged to meet the challenges faced by the United States in the Cold War. In 1953, Secretary of the Interior Douglas McKay addressed the forty-sixth meeting of the Pennsylvania Electric Association in Philadelphia. A year later Jerome K. Kuykendall, the FPC chairman who was later appointed to the ICC, recommended greater cooperation between two rival governmental agencies—the Army Corps of Engineers and the Bureau of Reclamation—and collaboration with the Association of Edison Illuminating Companies interested in power development along the Ohio River.[45] Yet, at the time, Interior Department secretaries as well as personnel at nearly every level gave little priority to tribal concerns. When the Senecas asked for a meeting to explain personally to President Eisenhower their opposition to the Kinzua Dam, they were denied and referred to the secretary of the interior. Secretary Fred Seaton did not give the Senecas any support to challenge dam construction; instead, he met with President Seneca and recommended that these Indians be given some lands in return for the large acreage to be flooded out.[46] Both he and O. Hatfield Chilson, later interim secretary of the interior, "washed their hands" of the controversy by insisting that the "proposed flood control project is entirely a Corps of Engineers project *with which we have no connection.*"[47]

One should not be surprised by the Eisenhower administration's and later the Kennedy administration's callous treatment of the Senecas. The same department that was mandated to protect the nation's natural resources and allow for planned energy use and development to secure the country's future was also in charge of administering Indian affairs. Within the Department of the Interior, there were major conflicts of interest. Until 1974, when the Nixon administration established the separate Department of Energy, the Interior Department was supposed to help the Indians manage their lands, minerals, timber, and water resources. Yet, as indicated in the department's briefing books, Native Americans and their concerns had less standing in the department than energy, land reclamation, national parks, and water and wildlife management.[48]

During the two terms of Eisenhower's presidency, there were increasing concerns about environmental issues as well as questions about the Interior Department's role in promoting private power projects, especially in its making of sweetheart deals with these companies at federally operated dam sites.[49] In Eisenhower's second term, outspoken environmentalist Republican John Saylor of southwestern Pennsylvania actively came to the Senecas' defense, and Congressman James Haley from Florida, the fiscal conservative chairman of the Subcommittee on Indian Affairs of the House Committee on Interior and Insular Affairs, was soon to become the great defender of the Senecas in Congress (see chapter 5). Both men suspected that flood control was not the only reason behind the push for the Kinzua Dam project. As early as 1961, Haley had written to President Kennedy insisting that there was more to the project than flood control and that powerful interests were pushing it. Later, in 1963, the Congressman maintained that the impetus for the dam came from powerful Pittsburgh industrialists concerned about alleviating water pollution caused by extensive coal mining in southwestern Pennsylvania that was affecting their factories. It appears from his congressional testimony that Haley was misled by information that the Army Corps and the Interior Department had provided to his subcommittee about the Kinzua Dam's hydroelectric potential.[50]

On October 22, 1960, with Army Corps officials and local politicians in attendance, Pennsylvania governor David Lawrence held a ground-breaking ceremony outside of Warren, Pennsylvania, to initiate construction of the Kinzua Dam.[51] Despite promises made by candidate John Kennedy during the election campaign of 1960 to evaluate the merits of the dam, the president, once elected, refused to break with his Democratic ally, Governor Lawrence, who had helped him win the presidency. Kennedy did not impound funds to stop the project and indicated that the issue had been resolved by federal court decisions. Three weeks after Kennedy's inaugural, Secretary of the Interior Stewart Udall announced a new national energy policy.[52] In an internal memorandum to his staff, Udall told his staff that the "Department of the Interior is committed to the full development and maximum utilization of the natural resources of the country" and required the full cooperation of utility systems of all kinds to service a dynamic economy, stimulate economic growth, and defend the nation.[53]

Udall's point man, Kenneth Holum, assistant secretary of the interior for water and power, was to carry out Udall's policy statement with little or no concern for the Senecas and other Indians. His records at the National Archives reveal much about the push for hydroelectric generation in Pennsylvania from 1961 to 1965. Holum's office staff gathered statistical information, did extensive reports, and met with Army Corps officials and corporate power-development executives from the Keystone State. Through his engineering assistant, Knoland J. Peterson, Holum followed the application licensing progress, keeping informed of the FPC's work and the applications before it, including the one related to hydropower in the Kinzua project.[54]

In the late winter and spring of 1960, several energy companies had issued news releases about their plans to lease the proposed Kinzua Dam facility administered by the Army Corps of Engineers to install turbines and produce electricity.[55] On September 28, 1960, perhaps attempting to soften the criticisms cast at private power development in the mid- and late 1950s, Penelec, based in Johnstown, Pennsylvania, and largely having coal-driven operations, and Warren Electric Cooperative announced that they were allying in filing an application for a permit to run a power-generating facility at the dam. In a joint statement, Louis H. Roddis Jr., president of Penelec, and Maxwell D. Rhodes, general manager of Warren Electric Cooperative, insisted that by joining together to unite investor-owned and government-financed electrical companies in the project, they were creating a model for future development.[56] By 1962, however, Penelec's partnership with Warren Electric had ended. Penelec soon faced the challenge issued by Allegheny Electric Cooperative to secure the permit to run the hydropower operations at the Kinzua Dam. By 1964, Penelec had received financial backing from major banks such as Morgan Guarantee, Bankers Trust, and Chemical Bank. In the same year, it copartnered with the Cleveland Electric Illuminating Company, a much larger private corporation with more significant capital, pushing for the fifty-year permit to operate hydroelectric production at the Kinzua Dam. Unlike the partnership with Warren Electric Cooperative, a small public regional power operation, the bigger combination of Penelec and Cleveland Electric Illuminating had now set its sights on larger horizons—namely, power transmission across state lines.[57]

On October 31, 1960, Penelec filed with the FPC its preliminary permit application under the provisions of the Federal Power Act for a proposed water power project, the "Kinzua Pumped Storage Project," "to be located on the Allegheny River, affecting a Government dam authorized for construction by the U.S. Corps of Engineers, in the Townships of Kinzua and Glade, Warren County, Pennsylvania, and affecting lands of the United States within the Allegheny National Forest and lands acquired for the Allegheny River Reservoir."[58] On May 3, 1961, Chairman Jerome K. Kuykendall announced that the FPC would grant a twelve-month preliminary permit to Penelec. Kuykendall, it may be recalled, had seven years earlier addressed the need for greater cooperation among the Army Corps of Engineers, the Interior Department, and private power companies on

Army Corps projects in the Ohio River valley. In his announcement, he acknowledged that the Army Corps did not oppose the Penelec power project as long as it didn't interfere with flood control and flow regulations and the power companies would reimburse the federal government at a "reasonable annual charge."[59]

The FPC's initial findings indicated that there were some concerns about wildlife habitats in the Department of Agriculture's Allegheny National Forest project area, but that the Interior Department claimed that the project would not significantly affect fishery resources and that archaeological surveys had been undertaken. Nowhere did these two cabinet-level departments or the FPC consider living Indians and their communities, and they appeared to be more concerned about ones long deceased.[60] Thus, from 1960 to 1965 the FPC permit process never considered the Senecas, consulted with the tribal leaders, or even had thoughts about the impact of the proposed hydropower project on the Indians' lands, lifeways, and subsistence patterns, even though the water in the Allegheny Reservoir created by the project was to be affected by the future Seneca Pumped Storage Generating Station.

On October 31, 1961, Penelec filed a preliminary report with the FPC indicating that it had started its core-drilling program, having sunk sixteen test pits at the planned dam site. It had undertaken a geological survey and had contracted with the Carnegie Museum in Pittsburgh to do salvage archaeological work. Nowhere in the report was there a mention of Allegany Senecas living within the Army Corps' take area for the creation of the Allegheny Reservoir, and no living Indians appear to have been consulted, even though the design of the project was to prevent the free flow of the river through the Seneca Nation and to impound water on one-third of the tribe's upper Allegheny River valley homeland.[61] Well into the licensing process, the Seneca Nation Tribal Council was finally informed of Penelec's efforts to secure a permit when the Indians' attorney, Arthur Lazarus Jr., happened to read an FPC press release in February 1962.[62] At that time, the Senecas were busy making plans to relocate hundreds of people from the area affected by the Kinzua Dam construction. The Senecas had neither financial means nor trained personnel within their community to challenge Penelec or question the FPC process.

In 1963 and 1964, a spokesman for the Army Corps of Engineers, obviously knowing full well of the FPC's granting of Penelec's preliminary license at Kinzua and the company's continuing efforts to obtain a permanent one, clearly mislead two congressional committees by minimizing the dam's power production in testimony before them. On July 15, 1963, at a hearing of the House Subcommittee on Indian Affairs held on Capitol Hill, Congressman Compton I. White of Idaho asked Colonel Bert de Melker of the Pittsburgh District of the Army Corps of Engineers, about the dam's overall purpose:

> WHITE: I am not completely familiar with the project, and I think it would help me a great deal if I knew exactly the purpose of this project— whether it is for power production, flood control, or what?
>
> DE MELKER: Yes, sir. The project was authorized in the comprehensive plan for the Ohio River Basin for flood control and other purposes. *It is a multipurpose reservoir for flood control and low flow augmentation.*
>
> WHITE: *Has it any power production connected with it?*
>
> DE MELKER: *There is no hydropower as such.* We are studying pump power, which is a system whereby they pump water from the reservoir to a higher elevation and let the water run from the higher elevation back to the reservoir.[63]

In March 1964, Idaho senator Frank Church questioned Colonel de Melker before the Senate Subcommittee on Indian Affairs about whether the dam would generate hydropower. Even though turbines to produce electricity were eventually installed at Kinzua, de Melker obfuscated his answer at this point:

> CHURCH: Will power be generated at this dam?
>
> DE MELKER: We had studied the power in the Allegheny Reservoir and find it economically not feasible. It is feasible, however, depending upon the system that ties into produced pump power. Now, pump power is not production power, it is merely a strong battery type of thing. You take water from the reservoir, pump it up on the canal, during peak hours bring it back down. We are making provisions in the construction of the dam to put in turnstiles.

CHURCH: But no turbines are anticipated at this time?

DE MELKER: We find that there is a small amount of power that could be produced by making the regular releases that we need to make of downstream water and our water supply regulation of that stream, so if you are going to run it anyway, you could produce a small amount of power.[64]

Thus, it is not surprising that nowhere in the printed congressional hearings and reports or in the internal minutes of meetings of Congressman Haley's House Subcommittee on Indian Affairs is there any discussion of compensation to the Senecas for hydropower development. Even Congressman Haley, a true advocate for the Senecas, was clearly misled. The Army Corps' testimony and reports gave Haley the impression that power interests were less important at Kinzua than they were for western projects pushed by the Interior Department's Bureau of Reclamation. Although a conservative Democrat from Florida and generally supportive of private power development, Haley was a strong critic of wasteful government spending and giveaways to private power interests.[65] As a consequence of this obfuscation, the Senecas never received any moneys, were never compensated for their flowage easement, and were never granted a reduction in their electrical costs even though their lands and water resources were essential for the production of electricity at the Kinzua Dam. Indeed, the US Treasury, not the Senecas, has received substantial lease payments from Penelec and its successor, FirstEnergy Corporation, since 1970, the time power production went on line.

Facing increased competition when Allegheny Electrical Cooperative intervened to seek the fifty-year lease, Penelec aggressively pursued its hydroelectric project plan. In 1963 and again in 1965, Penelec and the US Department of Agriculture, which administers the Allegheny National Forest, agreed to a Memorandum of Understanding about Penelec's use and occupancy of the Allegheny National Forest land for power purposes. In this lengthy agreement, neither party acknowledged the local Senecas or described how the upper Allegheny Reservoir, hidden away on high ground in the national forest, would affect the Indians, their subsistence, their water rights, their way of life.[66]

Even before the FPC finalized Penelec and Cleveland Illuminating's joint license, work at the dam was already under way on preparations for the construction of hydropower facilities. The *Warren County Observer* viewed this preparation as a positive development that would encourage industry to locate in the region. It noted that an expansion of electricity would be required to handle new recreational facilities as well and that "the use of water which is pumped to a hilltop [the upper Allegheny Reservoir in the Allegheny National Forest] during low production can prove a very economical procedure." Never mentioning the Senecas, the article, however, did point out that there was some concern that the water temperature would rise significantly when the water was returned from the hilltop reservoir to the waters below. The anonymous author concluded that he or she had confidence in the engineers "to solve the problem and determine whether the water would go back into the lake [Allegheny Reservoir] or directly into the river."[67]

On December 28, 1965, the FPC granted Penelec, copartnering with Cleveland Electric Illuminating Company, the much larger private power-producing company with substantial capital, a license for fifty years to build and operate the hydroelectric storage facility at the Kinzua Dam.[68] According to its annual report for 1965, Penelec was to own 20 percent and Cleveland Electric Illuminating Company 80 percent of this $30 million project, which was ironically to be named the "Seneca Pumped Storage Generating Station," even though the Indians were once again never consulted on it.[69]

Governor William W. Scranton of Pennsylvania dedicated the Kinzua Dam before an audience of two to three thousand people on September 16, 1966.[70] In his speech, Native Americans were once again depicted as obstacles to progress of the state and the nation. He praised the cooperation between the Army Corps of Engineers, the US Forest Service, and the Commonwealth of Pennsylvania in promoting a "new spirit of conservation." The governor traced the project's long history. He stated that the dam was "conceived as a flood control project in 1936 after a disastrous Pittsburgh flood " but was transformed into a major tourist attraction, "despite congressional plodding, political haggling, and opposition from the Seneca Indian Nation." Importantly, Scranton pointed out that the Kinzua

Dam would "serve as a source of hydroelectric power. The Pennsylvania Electric Company and the Cleveland Illuminating Company, are building a hydroelectric power station on this northwestern Pennsylvania site."[71]

In late 1969, the $30 million Seneca Pumped Storage Generating Station at the Kinzua Dam was completed, and in the following year, hydropower and electrical transmission began. The sale of electricity by these two companies, now part of FirstEnergy Corporation, has resulted in an estimated $13 million dollars a year in profits and upward of hundreds of million dollars to shareholders. FirstEnergy pays $340,000 a year to the federal government for the right to produce electricity for profit at the dam.[72] Without the sacrifice of Seneca lands, burial grounds, churches, farms, homes, longhouse, and schools, which are now under the waters of the Allegheny Reservoir, the dam could never have produced this electricity.

Historian Thomas Clarkin has suggested that the Kennedy and early Johnson administrations were faced with great resistance on American Indian policies from conservative congressmen, such as Senator Clinton Anderson of New Mexico, who were totally committed to termination. Although Stewart Udall, as a progressive congressman from Arizona, had opposed these forces in the 1950s, he and other members of the Kennedy and Johnson administrations, according to Clarkin, were restricted by Anderson's chairmanship of the Senate Subcommittee on Indian Affairs until 1964. The same year Anderson added a termination clause in the federal Seneca "compensation" act passed by Congress. As Clarkin points out, Secretary Udall began to focus more on Indian issues after 1965, when Anderson was out of the picture, when Native voices spoke louder, and when Joseph Califano of the Office of Economic Opportunity and Sargent Shriver of VISTA began focusing their programs on reservation Indian populations.[73] Yet there was more to the decision for power development at Kinzua than stonewalling terminationist congressmen and the pressures they exerted. The final pieces to the Kinzua hydropower puzzle are to be found in the inner workings of the Kennedy administration and in Secretary Udall's leadership of and policy directives for the Interior Department.

If concerns for the protection of Indian resources were so minimally important to government officials in the 1950s and early 1960s, helping the Senecas keep their lands was hardly on the radar of American political leadership, even during the Kennedy administration. After all, since 1950, these Native peoples had been under state criminal and civil jurisdiction, and the BIA had closed down operations in New York State. Plans were under way for full termination, and the Interior Department had been encouraging Native peoples to relocate to urban areas since the early 1950s. To policymakers in Washington, the Seneca Nation and all of the Six Nations in New York State were already quasi-terminated.

On January 23, 1961, Secretary Udall, two days after his own confirmation by the US Senate, established a task force to examine federal Indian policies. He appointed W. W. Keeler, the prominent western Cherokee and Phillips 66 oil executive, as chair of the task force, which also included BIA commissioner Philleo Nash; former acting commissioner William Zimmerman Jr., the author of the major termination report of 1947; and anthropologist James Officer. Much of this task force's focus was on improving reservation economies. It is important to note that its final report did not repudiate federal Indian termination policies, nor did it address the current Kinzua crisis. It did call into question some of the BIA's past policies, making a vague commitment to protect Indian water rights and insisting that the agency had "a heavy responsibility to be at all time a vigorous defender and developer of what is perhaps the most valuable of all resources."[74] Yet from 1961 onward this stated goal in the report was ignored. Flood control was somewhat mitigated but not permanently solved along the Allegheny River after the Kinzua Dam was completed. A private power company, its officers, employees, and stockholders benefited. Certain downstream communities as far as Pittsburgh also benefited economically, and water quality improved to some degree in areas contaminated by coal production. However, the task force statement was not applied to help the Senecas protect their lands and water; the federal government gave away the Senecas' resources without providing compensation—replacement lands, money, or free electricity—for the use of these resources.

In order to satisfy diverse and oftentimes competing interests within government agencies such as the Interior Department, to win political support from powerful governors such as David Lawrence, and to get their legislative agenda through Congress, Udall and the Kennedy administration made compromises that sacrificed the interests of Native peoples. American Indians, as was true during the previous two-term Eisenhower presidency, still didn't count. When tribal representatives who had attended the American Indian Chicago Conference in 1961 aimed to bring attention to Indian concerns, including the Kinzua Dam project, President Kennedy politely accepted their Declaration of Indian Purpose in a brief Rose Garden photo opportunity—and then ignored the Native Americans' appeal(see chapter 5).[75] It may surprise people that American liberalism failed the Senecas at the time when the civil rights movement was gaining strength in the country. As late as 1962, Michael Harrington's classic *The Other America: Poverty in the United States*, which influenced President Johnson's later War on Poverty, had substantial coverage of urban and rural blacks, Hispanic migrant farmworkers, and the white Appalachian poor, but *not one word* on American Indians.[76]

A final push for hydropower at Kinzua came from liberal Democrats. The Kennedy and Johnson administrations had looked for ways to prop up the declining coal economy and to promote industry and jobs in Appalachia. By supporting a variety of energy plans for industrial development and job creation in the region, they were not averse to working with private power companies and public power cooperatives. Because the concerns of Appalachia had come to the fore during Kennedy's primary battle with Hubert Humphrey in 1960, there was impetus for power generation within the region, which was eventually to include southwestern New York and much of western Pennsylvania. Despite the environmental activism of Congressman Saylor, Pennsylvania's and West Virginia's focus was on industrial capacity and job opportunities, which were equated with power development. Once again the Senecas were not included in the conversation.

Although Secretary Udall was a nationally admired conservationist, his Interior Department had a hand in promoting power-development projects, such as Kinzua, that negatively affected Native Americans and despoiled certain areas such as the pristine environment of the upper Allegheny River valley. It should be noted, in fairness, that Udall did not initiate the Kinzua project and had to manage a federal bureaucracy of competing interests, work with Congress, and meet a young president's expectations. On the one hand, Udall tried and failed to reconcile the contradictions of conservation and pork-barrel, special-interest politics. On the other hand, he and his agency had to make compromises to satisfy other constituencies within his hodge-podge department—including reclamation, national parks, power, and water. Yet Udall, an Arizonan with little affinity for or knowledge of eastern Native Americans, was a loyal supporter of two presidents and was well aware of Capitol Hill politics— namely, that twenty-nine out of thirty Pennsylvania congressmen (Saylor excluded) of both parties supported the initial dam project and that Kennedy was beholden to Governor David Lawrence for delivering Pennsylvania to the Democrats in the election of 1960. It is interesting to note that later, in 1965, Secretary Udall sponsored Robert L. Bennett, a Wisconsin Oneida, the first American Indian to be named BIA commissioner of Indian affairs since Reconstruction.[77]

Udall and other social-minded Democrats envisioned a new TVA to bolster industry and jobs for impoverished white and black Appalachian folk. Holum and Udall pushed for the creation of the Appalachian Regional Commission, whose mandate was to improve the economic, educational, health, and social conditions of the region, which was to include Pennsylvania and later southwestern New York State. Not surprisingly, their ally was Franklin D. Roosevelt Jr., whose father had received accolades for the original TVA project, ironically conceived of and directed by Arthur E. Morgan. On March 27, 1964, armed with the endorsement of another Roosevelt, Udall lauded electric expansion plans to aid Appalachia. Once again the Interior Department had failed the Indians, sacrificing their ecological niche in the name of American progress.[78]

While a private corporation and the federal government profited financially by their partnership, the Allegany Senecas' old way of life— their fishery, their areas for hunting and gathering medicinal plants, their holy lands and sacred sites—were all lost forever. At every stage of the history of power generation in the upper Allegheny—from the 1930s to

2010—their voices were not heard. The FPC hydropower licensing process for the Kinzua project from 1960 to 1965 totally ignored the Seneca Nation as if it did not exist. Even though Seneca lands and water resources were essential for hydropower, these Native peoples were never consulted and never compensated for the electricity produced once turbines began operating in 1970. Unfortunately, despite the Senecas' and the Six Nations' treaties with the federal government and their loyal military service to the United States since 1812, they were the forgotten Americans. Ironically, during the fertile years of the civil rights movement, the Senecas just didn't count.

Early in 1963, recognizing the utility companies' incredible power, Howard Morgan, an FPC commissioner, wrote to President Kennedy. In his formal letter resigning from the FPC, Morgan outlined the immense pressures on his commission and on other regulatory agencies. Emphasizing the important contributions made by Progressive Era statesmen George Norris, Hiram Johnson, and Gifford Pinchot in creating federal regulatory agencies, Morgan indicated that the pressures on the commissioners were great, but not in outright attempts to bribe. The commissioner insisted that there were more subtle pressures. Morgan concluded that faced with making hundreds of decisions each year, an FPC commissioner in his self-interest "can find it very wary to consider whether his vote might arouse an industry campaign against his reaffirmation by the Senate, and even easier to convince himself that no such thought ever crossed his mind."[79]

PART III ||||| *The Impact of Kinzua*

5

George Heron, the Kinzua Planning Committee, and the Haley Act

ON MAY 26, 2011, George Heron, the Allegany Seneca who twice served as president of the Seneca Nation during the Kinzua crisis, died at the age of ninety-two. Heron had also served as the chairman of the Kinzua Planning Committee, which had helped rebuild the Seneca Nation of Indians during the crisis. Looking back at the work of the Kinzua Planning Committee, one cannot fully comprehend the myriad problems it had to face. Although it was not successful in certain areas such as in economic planning, its contributions to the survival of the Seneca Nation were no small accomplishments. At a time when tribal survival as a federally recognized Indian nation was in doubt, the Senecas had to face the threat of termination pushed by powerful voices in Congress and supported by the Department of the Interior. It had also to contend with state officials in Pennsylvania and New York pushing their own agendas, especially for hydropower and expressway development. At Heron's passing, Seneca president Robert Odawi Porter issued an official press release, praising this major figure in contemporary tribal history: "He was our leader during a critical time in the 1960s when the atrocities associated with the Kinzua watershed and dam hit our nation." Porter added that the present government of the Seneca Nation was committed to pursuing what Heron had stood for all his life. "We have his legacy of protecting our nation during such adverse times by fighting today to protect our sovereignty, treaties, and lands and pursuing the Kinzua hydropower re-licensing."[1]

I first formally met Heron in 1983 at a conference on Native Americans at Westchester State College sponsored by Bonnie and John Witthoft, two anthropologists with long ties to the Senecas. I had previously known Heron only in his capacity as one of the vendors selling corn soup at the Cattaraugus Fall Festival that I attended in the 1970s and early 1980s! At the recommendation of Tuscarora chief Edison Perry Mt. Pleasant, my mentor in the study of Iroquoian culinary arts, I had sampled Heron's Seneca corn soup at his stand. Now in 1983, Heron was sitting at a table with George H. J. Abrams, then director of the Seneca-Iroquois National Museum. I finally had a chance to listen to his life experiences. I heard the former president of the Seneca Nation reflect on the Kinzua crisis and the federal government's breaking of the Treaty of Canandaigua, what he called the "Pickering Treaty." In a remark that has remained with me for the past three decades, Heron, in his characteristically pithy way, stated: "How long is forever?" Heron, who had just retired from his long career as a bridge structural and ornamental iron worker, was clearly making a point, succinctly stating that federal officials' commitments to respect the sanctity of Indian treaty rights were hollow promises that could be overturned by congressional action at any time, as it had done during Kinzua.

Heron had succeeded the well-respected Cornelius Seneca as president in November 1958, being elected to office just at the time the federal courts were deciding against the Senecas in the Kinzua issue. For the next two years, Heron the political realist understood that Kinzua could not be stopped. He tried his best to delay it, an old Indian strategy, by continuing to talk about Arthur Morgan's alternative plan and frequently going on the road and speaking to diverse audiences to try to change public opinion. What little hope the Senecas had ended in early in 1961. At a news conference on March 8, President Kennedy was asked a question about the planned dam and Morgan's alternative to Kinzua. The president indicated that the matter was a dead issue, having been already settled by the federal courts.[2]

In the summer of 1961, Lee White, Kennedy's White House counsel, indicated that the president would not impound funds for the project because the federal government's right to expropriate Seneca lands had already been determined; however, the counsel added that the White

House would explore the possibility of securing other lands contiguous with the Senecas' remaining land base as an exchange. He also indicated that federal officials were not opposed to assessing damages in order to compensate Senecas affected by the project. White claimed that the president favored assistance for economic development, believing that there was recreational potential for the flooded lands, and supported counseling efforts to help those Senecas affected psychologically by being relocated.[3] President Kennedy also personally gave assurance to the Seneca leadership that the federal government would provide planning, financial assistance, and social services; however, both men's promises were never fully met.[4] The Interior Department merely planned a study and sent Sidney Carney, a Choctaw working for the agency, as its representative to the Allegany Indian Reservation, and the Kennedy administration gave little priority to and support for a compensation bill that finally passed Congress in 1964.[5] Yet before, during, and after this act was passed, the BIA supported the full termination of the Seneca Nation. On September 19, 1964, a month after Congress passed the Seneca Nation Compensation Act, Commissioner Philleo Nash addressed the Seneca Tribal Council:

> The Congress as is authorized this program of rehabilitation [H.R. 1794: Seneca Nation Compensation Act] concluded that it offered so much hope of economic self-sufficiency and self-determination that we all ought to look forward, actively and affirmatively, to an end of the special Federal–tribal relationship. Accordingly, the Congress directed the Secretary of the Interior in consultation with the Seneca Nation to submit plans within a period of three years from the passage of the act looking toward an eventual withdrawal of Federal services and supervision over Seneca affairs.[6]

Thus, while faced with rebuilding their nation, the Seneca leadership had to contend with the very real threat of termination and the end of their status as a federally recognized Indian nation that dated back to the period 1784 to 1794. To senators, such as Clinton Anderson of New Mexico and Peter Dominick of Colorado, pushing termination had greater priority than funding projects to aid poor, displaced Native Americans flooded out by federal dam building.[7] When Merrill Bowen wrote an angry article in the

Kinzua Planning Newsletter attacking the Senate subcommittee for holding up the compensation bill for the Senecas and labeling its members "John Bircher" extremists, both senators forced Bowen to apologize formally.[8]

Indeed, today one can hardly comprehend the full extent of the crisis. After the BIA closed its office in New York in 1949 as part of federal withdrawal, the total federal expenditures for the Senecas was only $6,000 a year as well as $4,500 in treaty cloth distribution. In 1961, the Seneca Nation's tribal income was infinitesimal, less than $100,000 a year. Much of it was derived from rights-of-way easements given to public utilities, natural gas leases, land rentals, and more than three thousand ridiculously undervalued leases in Salamanca and the other congressionally established villages. These congressional leases together totaled only between $13,000 and $15,000 a year.[9] Despite their impoverished state, the Seneca Nation spent more than $40,000 in engineering studies to counter the Army Corps of Engineers' plans to flood one-third of the Allegany Indian Reservation.[10] A BIA socioeconomic study undertaken in 1962 and released the next year stated that the median cash income in 1959 for all husband–wife families with two or more children in Cattaraugus County, part of the depressed northern Appalachian area, was $5,600 a year. In contrast, Senecas in the same category in the take area had a cash income of only $3,900.[11] Moreover, only 1.03 percent of Senecas forty-one years of age or older—the age of almost all the tribal councilors at the time— had four years of high school education. Less than 3 percent of Senecas enrolled in high school went on to attend institutions of higher learning, whether technical/vocational or college.[12]

In response to the promises made by federal officials in 1961, Heron and Taylor encouraged the slow restructuring of Seneca government. At the time of President Kennedy's news conference denying support for the Senecas, Basil Williams, the president of the Seneca Nation from 1960 to 1962, was working in the tribal business office, which "consisted of a single large room and a single salaried full-time employee who had the title of deputy clerk but also was responsible for performing the necessary clerical duties."[13] Hence, the formation of the Kinzua Planning Committee in the second half of 1961 was determined to meet the challenges put forth by this crisis. Importantly, the committee and its work became the later basis of departments within the Seneca Nation government. It had subcommittees on cemeteries, economic development, education, housing and relocation, lieu lands and land acquisition, public facilities, tangibles and intangibles, and recreational development. Many Senecas were directly involved, and they came from diverse backgrounds—women and men; Longhouse and Christian; Allegany, Cattaraugus, and Cornplanter. They included Cornelius Abrams Jr. and Rovena Abrams; DeForrest Billy; Leslie and Merrill Bowen; Nora Crouse; Delbert and Shirley Crowe; Hazel Dean (John); Calvin, Coleman, and Franklin John; Russell King; Maribel Printup and Wayne Printup; Clifton Rice; Theodore Snow; Dema Crouse Stouffer; Maxwell Thompson; and Harry Watt.[14]

Walter Taylor, head of the American Friends Service Midwestern Indian Committee, came to Salamanca in 1961 as a community organizer to help Heron deal with the crisis. A man well respected by all the Senecas, Taylor was employed by the Philadelphia Yearly Meeting of Friends. He served as the key adviser to Heron, worked in community planning efforts at relocating Senecas displaced by the Kinzua Dam, and along with Heron and attorney Arthur Lazarus Jr. worked tirelessly as a lobbyist before Congress in efforts to seek federal compensation. In October 1961, Taylor helped establish the *Kinzua Planning Newsletter*, which was funded by the Philadelphia Yearly Meeting of Friends and kept community members informed about the Army Corps of Engineers' construction schedules, the progress on the congressional compensation bill, and deadlines to seek housing applications. The newsletter's advisory committee included Rovena Abrams (the current editor of the *Seneca Nation of Indians' Official Newsletter*), DeForrest Billy, George Heron, and Basil Williams. The newsletter was first edited by Jack Preston, my former colleague at the State University of New York (SUNY), New Paltz, who had grown up in Salamanca and who was well versed in the Seneca language and lifeways; however, within a few months, Taylor took up the reins as editor. In 1963, when lobbying efforts for congressional compensation intensified, requiring more of Taylor's time, he resigned as editor but maintained his presence in Salamanca with a small staff of Seneca volunteers, including Hazel Dean (John). Merrill Bowen, the Cornplanter spokesman, became editor in 1963 until the publication's demise in 1965.[15]

The Senecas were determined to survive and rebuild their nation as best as they could under the trying circumstances of the Kinzua Dam crisis. They had done so in the past when a massive French military force and their Indian allies invaded Seneca territory in 1687. They had survived "the Whirlwind," the American Revolution, in which George Washington, known to them as "the Town Destroyer," had sent his generals, James Clinton and John Sullivan, to burn the Indians' villages. After the revolution, they had to contend with being dispossessed of millions of acres of their homeland as well as removal pressures from the Empire State. While numerous Native communities were shattered by federal allotment policies that followed in the wake of the Dawes Act of 1887, the Senecas resisted these efforts as well. Now, with the final realization that Kinzua Dam construction could not be stopped, the Senecas began a major effort to rebuild their community.

In their planning process, Heron and the Kinzua Planning Committee were to transform the Senecas' governmental structure; construct two buildings to house administrative offices and serve as community centers; plan, develop, and complete two major residential building projects at Allegany—one at Steamburg and the other at Jimersontown—to house the hundreds of Senecas displaced by dam construction; establish the Seneca Housing Authority to provide some new housing at Cattaraugus; lobby for a replacement school for one condemned at Cold Spring with the building of the dam; and establish the Seneca Educational Foundation, which provided Senecas with some money for higher education, until the funds ran out two decades later. Yet the presidents during these crisis years from 1956 to 1966—Cornelius Seneca, Basil Williams, George Heron, and Martin Seneca Sr.—also faced criticism from within. Although leaders made mistakes, especially in the area of economic planning, they were too often unfairly blamed for the actions or the inactions of federal and state officials. They were also accused of favoring one Seneca community over another or for dispensing patronage based on familial ties. This criticism only added to the already existing long-standing contentious politics within the Seneca Nation.[16]

Heron's great skill was in publicizing the crisis and in networking. He coordinated his efforts with Walter Taylor.[17] Heron also worked closely with Arthur Lazarus Jr., the Washington, DC, attorney for the Seneca Nation, in the major lobbying effort on Capitol Hill to secure compensation in a bill that was to be passed by Congress in August 1964.[18] However, Heron's primary duties were chairing the Kinzua Planning Committee; educating the public at large about the Senecas' crisis; and attending regional events, state and federal hearings, as well as the annual meetings of the National Congress of American Indians.

Heron was especially adept in working with the scholarly community. He and tribal councilor Lafayette Williams were the official Seneca representatives at the American Indian Chicago Conference in 1961, organized by anthropologists Sol Tax and Nancy Lurie. Heron served as a member of the conference's Steering Committee. The conferees drafted the Declaration of Indian Purpose.[19] Each one of the Native representatives of the Indian communities in attendance in Chicago received a copy of the Society of Friends booklet *The Kinzua Dam Controversy: A Practical Solution—without Shame.*[20] It was no coincidence that the conference's Declaration of Indian Purpose contained a major statement supporting the Seneca efforts to stop the Kinzua Dam and favoring Arthur Morgan's alternative plan.[21] In 1962, the Declaration of Indian Purpose was presented to President Kennedy at a White House ceremony. Yet, by that time, Heron's appearance at these and other events was more geared to winning popular support to convince Congress to aid the Senecas by allocating federal moneys for relocation, housing, and rehabilitation because he, unlike Morgan and many of Morgan's Quaker supporters, was well aware that the dam project no longer could be stopped.

In order to get support for the Seneca Nation compensation bill, Heron and attorney Lazarus presented a memorandum drafted by anthropologists—acknowledged experts on Seneca mores—and entered it into the official record at the US Senate hearing on March 2, 1964. The statement was written by three prominent scholars: William N. Fenton, William Sturtevant of the Bureau of Ethnology at the Smithsonian Institution, and Stanley Diamond of Syracuse University. In their appeal, the three scholars identified themselves as anthropologists "with special knowledge of and experience among the Allegany Senecas." The anthropologists' hope was that "Congress award just compensation to the Indians [not just the

Senecas] displaced by Government owned, operated, or subsidized hydro-electric or industrial projects." They attempted to educate congressmen and their staffs about Native peoples. The three anthropologists insisted that the issue was not just a moral one conditioned by the breaking of the Canandaigua Treaty of 1794. They eloquently stated that the fundamental criterion of American Indian policies should be cultural—namely, "that reservation lands were directly tied to Indian identity," which to them was the "most tangible symbol of Indianness, both for those tribal members living on and off reservations." The scholars stressed the great adaptability of Native peoples and their cultures, pointing out that an Indian reservation should not be viewed as a "repository of a dwindling heritage." They urged Congress to grant the Senecas "the resources to construct what is in effect, a new reservation," not necessarily simply an allocation of a new tract of land, but "community facilities, new housing, and sufficient natural resources to make the reservation an attractive substitute for the flooded lands." The anthropologists maintained that "no Indian in recent years has volunteered to sell his reservation, either as an individual or as a member of a community. That in itself helps illustrate a critical distinction in values between Indians' and other citizens' culturally inherited values which are a proud part of our American heritage."[22]

Heron was a realist, a pragmatic Seneca politician. He had no illusions, no false hopes that outsiders would somehow swoop in and rescue his people. He left those utopian thoughts to his many Quaker friends and supporters. As a consequence, the cool-headed Heron was less concerned about taking a firm stand in pushing tribal sovereignty and more concerned with the immediate survival of his Indian nation. Thus, he was willing to negotiate with state officials and ask them for financial support.[23] Unlike other Senecas such as Merrill Bowen, Heron carefully chose his words and never presented himself as combative or radical. After all, he had to find ways to build housing, to find parcels and housing sites to relocate families, and to lobby to get Congress to pay for the removal. A proud navy veteran of World War II and active member of the Veterans of Foreign Wars, he had to negotiate with high-ranking and less than culturally sensitive officers of the Army Corps of Engineers about the reinternment of graves and location of new cemetery parcels to replace older ones, while these same officers, without consultation with the Senecas, were negotiating with New York's transportation officials about replacement roads and the state's future plan to construct the Southern Tier Expressway through the Allegany Reservation. Heron also had to ingratiate himself to state officials to find ways to secure state support to replace the Allegany school condemned in the Kinzua Dam project. Adding to his problems, he had to deal with the realities of the Senecas' own combative politics. He was criticized for being less concerned over issues of sovereignty when he dealt with the state in efforts to build replacement housing units at Cattaraugus and for being more concerned about his own Allegany Senecas than for the Cornplanters. During this period, he supported the push for women's suffrage, which came about in 1964, and he appointed highly respected women to important Kinzua Planning Committee posts to help him rebuild the modern Seneca Nation.[24]

Heron's astute political skills were noticeable in other areas as well. In one instance that illustrates his approach, in 1962 Heron and his Seneca Hawk Clan helped organize the adoption of Nelson Rockefeller. On several occasions, the New York State governor had refused to grant the Senecas an audience to plead their case for state assistance during the Kinzua crisis; however, Heron the savvy politician did not abandon hope. He used the old Seneca ploy of adopting powerful white politicians. He understood that politicos from Calvin Coolidge on had relished photo opportunities with "real chiefs." In 1962, Rockefeller's adoption ceremony gave the Senecas, including Heron, the opportunity to have an audience with the governor.[25] Although the Senecas had to wait nearly three years for the school because of bureaucratic delay, the state eventually came through at the last possible moment in 1965.[26] In the same year as Rockefeller's adoption ceremony, Heron was once again elected president of the Seneca Nation but continued to chair the Kinzua Planning Committee.

On March 13, 1963, Seneca Nation clerk DeForrest Billy outlined the changes in tribal government that had already taken place as a result of the work of the Kinzua Planning Committee. Writing to Congressman Wayne Aspinall, chair of the House Committee on Interior and Insular

Affairs, he referred to what had already occurred: the expansion of the tribal office; the founding of the *Kinzua Planning Newsletter* to keep the Senecas informed about dam construction and the Army Corps of Engineers' plans; the creation of the Seneca Housing Authority; and the selection of two resettlement sites for the Kinzua relocatees. The Seneca clerk indicated that his nation's Tribal Council now met monthly instead of holding biannual meetings and that it was about to hire expert appraisers to evaluate individual, family, and tribal losses caused by dam construction. The Tribal Council had also sent a formal request for BIA moneys to conduct a survey of the recreational and industrial potential of remaining Seneca lands at both Allegany and Cattaraugus. Billy then described the creation of the Kinzua Planning Committee by the Seneca Tribal Council "from both within and without its membership to work on programs for the future and concern themselves with diverse subjects: relocation, lieu lands, cemetery relocations, recreational development, housing, tangible and intangible damages."[27]

Billy also brought to Aspinall's attention some of the problems that the Senecas faced, indicating to the congressman that not everything was working so smoothly. He blamed the Army Corps of Engineers: "the Corps has been inexplicably slow, while in other cases, such as the relocation of Route 17, a state highway, the Corps has made final decisions without even consulting the Nation."[28] Using the Kinzua crisis as a smoke screen, the New York State DPW had secretly negotiated an agreement with Army Corps officials for the corps to condemn Seneca lands to provide enough acreage for a future four-lane state expressway through the Allegany Indian Reservation. In November 1963, Heron testified about the same matter at a hearing of the New York State Legislature Committee on Indian Affairs held at the Tonawanda Indian Community House. Anxious about the state's delay in providing funds for a replacement school for the one about to be condemned in the dam project, Heron also brought up his people's concerns about the proposed Southern Tier Expressway, which would dissect the remaining lands at Allegany:

> There is also one other specific point I would like to speak on today and that is the matter of the Southern Tier Expressway. . . . The State of New

York proposes to construct a four-lane, limited access highway through our Reservation, which will cut it the other way. In other words, there will be a concrete wall. A person will not be able to go across this highway. It followed the pattern of the New York State Thruway. There are now three bridges existing on the Reservation, which will be torn down. The State of New York will replace those with one bridge. A person will not be able to walk across the bridge because it is in the status of a limited access bridge or highway. So, no member of the Nation will have any method of cross other than boat. He cannot walk across the bridge. He cannot walk across the highway. We will be divided into two distinct communities and to get from one community to the other one, with one on each side of the river, we will have no choice but go by automobile. If he doesn't have a car, he'd have to go out on the road and hitch-hike his way to Salamanca and then to the other community.[29]

Heron saw a cabal formed by the Army Corps of Engineers and New York State transportation planners, accusing them of plotting to take tribal lands for the expressway. To Heron, they were working behind the Senecas' backs at a time when the Indians' desperate housing needs had not been met by federal and state officials. As will be shown in chapter 8, the Senecas brought suit in federal courts regarding the Army Corps' right during the Kinzua crisis to appropriate tribal lands for the future state expressway, but they were to lose the decision. The Southern Tier Expressway was to remain a contentious issue between the Senecas and the state as well as internally in tribal politics into the 1980s.

The most ambitious as well as the most important part of the Kinzua Planning Committee's work was the establishment of two new housing settlements at Steamburg and Jimersontown. In June 1962, the committee chose these sites. They also established the Seneca Nation Housing Authority to provide public housing for the relocatees at Allegany and Cattaraugus. In addition, several churches, the Coldspring Longhouse, and the Allegany Schoolhouse had to be replaced after the condemnation for the Kinzua project. However, until Congress's passage of the Seneca Compensation Act in August 1964, there was no assurance that federal moneys would be allocated for the relocatees.[30] This delay stands in marked contrast to $20 million in federal compensation paid immediately to the Pennsylvania Railroad for ceding its right-of-way, which was affected by the creation of the Allegheny Reservoir.[31] The Senecas did not receive funding until September 4, 1965, just four months before the Army Corps of Engineers' deadline for Senecas to leave the take area.[32]

As these events were happening, William N. Fenton accurately observed that the Senecas' ability to work under these pressures and establish housing in two relocation areas was truly "a remarkable one." Even before the Senecas received federal moneys, Fenton noted, they had done more than select the two relocation sites. They had employed Lloyd Barnwell, a Seneca construction worker, to oversee the building projects, hired a Seneca workforce, and established the Seneca Nation Housing Enterprises, taking the risk that they would secure federal funding. Fenton described the process:

> The size of the [new] house [for the relocatees] was governed by the number of bedrooms required for each family. The value of their recent home was then prorated in terms of the appraisal value as set by the Corps of Engineers against a schedule of subsidies, to a maximum of $15,000. For example, Nettie Watt's four bedroom frame and clapboard house appraised at $7,500; but her family agreed to accept three bedrooms, for which the subsidy was $7,600. Those who had the least to trade stood to gain the most. There have been some bitter complaints, ending in lawsuits, and there are one or two cases of ingenious speculation. At least two houses in the take area that were owned by non-resident Senecas were purchased on speculation for a fraction of their appraisal and trade-in value. One was in the path of a bridge approach, and netted the new purchases almost the entire subsidy for a new house. Final approval of these subsidies rested with the Council, and it would be naive to assume that political considerations did not enter into the decision. But these few cases of questionable ethics do not negate the overall accomplishment, which is impressive.[33]

At the federal level, Heron, Taylor, and Lazarus were quite effective as lobbyists, working closely with Congressmen Haley and Saylor. In studying the two congressmen's backgrounds, one would never guess that they would work together and become the major advocates for the Senecas. Yet as early as 1957 Saylor had come to the aid of President Cornelius Seneca and his people. Saylor was from Johnstown, the corporate headquarters of Penelec. He had previously worked with Penelec to promote the building of three dams in his congressional district and supported the local coal, steel, and utility industries so vital to his own district. However, Thomas G. Smith, his recent biographer, has concluded that Saylor was hardly "a shill" for these interests and was one of the founders of the modern environmental movement. The congressman spoke out against strip mining and nuclear power plants, supported the Water Quality Act of 1965 and the Air Pollution Control Act of 1967, and worked with the Sierra Club in efforts to save California's giant sequoias and to preserve wilderness areas and scenic rivers.[34]

Congressman Haley was a fiscal conservative and a states-rights southern Democrat. He supported segregationist policies and opposed the Civil Rights Acts of 1964 and 1965. An Alabamian and an accountant by profession, he had married Aubrey Black Ringling, the widow of Richard Ringling, the president of the Ringling Brothers Circus based in Sarasota. He eventually rose from business manager to vice president. In 1944, as a result of the Ringling Brothers Hartford Circus fire that took the lives of at least 167 people, including numerous children, Haley was convicted of involuntary manslaughter and sent to prison. After serving eight months, he returned to the circus's home base in Sarasota. His actions in assuming fault had saved the circus, a vital part of central Florida's cultural, economic, and philanthropic scene, and was soon made president of the newly reorganized Ringling Brothers, Barnum and Bailey Circus. He and his wife later sold their interest in circus operations.[35]

In 1952, Haley was elected to Congress. From 1953 to 1977, as chair of the House Subcommittee on Indian Affairs and later chair of the House Committee on Interior and Insular Affairs, he was a major figure in reshaping policies. The Florida congressman was a frequent critic of the Interior Department and the wasteful spending of its BIA. According to Vine Deloria Jr. and Clifford Lytle, Haley did real service for Native Americans and insisted on more equitable treatment for them, especially in his monitoring of lease arrangements. He was especially critical of Secretary Stewart Udall: "Had Haley not stood firm against the policies of [his own] Democratic Administrations, there might be few Indian reservations today in the hands of Indians."[36] The Florida congressman was the sponsor of and guided the Seneca compensation bill, H.R. 1794, identical to the Senate version, S. 1836, through both houses of Congress in 1964. Although the amount of moneys awarded by Congress appears to be infinitesimal compared with later settlements, in 1964 it was much higher per capita compared with compensation awarded during the same period to Missouri River tribes affected by the construction of dams.[37]

Haley was the major advocate for the Senecas in both houses of Congress. In 1960, he unsuccessfully tried to have the Kinzua project delayed until Morgan's alternative was fully considered. In August 1961, Haley attacked his colleagues in Congress for their past support of what he saw as the Kinzua boondoggle, "the most underhanded method of taking land away from the Indians, and violating a treaty that has ever been witnessed in this country." Haley questioned the congressional approval process for the Kinzua project because it bypassed consideration by his Subcommittee on Indian Affairs.[38] On more than one occasion, he insisted that "treaty lands" were not "something to be treated like ordinary real estate." He added that the United States had a "special and peculiar responsibility to its Indian wards. . . . This [the Kinzua project] is not the first time—nor will it be the last time I fear—that Indians have seen their land taken in a ruthless manner for the benefit of persons other than themselves."[39] Because of his unwavering commitment to aid the Senecas, they adopted him in 1963 as "Chief of Twenty Canoes."[40]

President Heron educated Haley about Seneca history, especially about treaties. It was no coincidence that Haley's bill in Congress was numbered H.R. 1794. The congressman later explained the reasons for this number to Hugh Downs, the television personality who had become sympathetic to the Seneca cause. Haley sent Downs a copy of his bill, indicating that "1794 is the year in which the Seneca Nation entered into a treaty with the United States, a treaty signed by our first president,

George Washington [it was actually signed by US Six Nations commissioner Timothy Pickering]. Because I wanted to obtain this number, the bill was quickly drawn."[41] Although Haley was not opposed in the long run to the end of the federal government's administration of Indian affairs and initially favored termination policies, he was wary of forcing the issue. He also clearly believed that the interests of the Seneca Nation of Indians, *his tribe*, had not been protected by the Interior Department and had been treated poorly by the Army Corps of Engineers.[42] In order to deflect northern criticism of his segregationist position, Haley pointed out to his Florida constituents that his stand against Kinzua differed from positions held by pro–civil rights liberals such as his Democrat colleague Senator Joseph Clark of Pennsylvania, a major proponent of the Kinzua Dam project, and Republican Senator Jacob Javits of New York, who had never spoken up in an effort to stop it. It should be pointed out that only after the dam was a "done deal" did these two senators support Haley's efforts at compensation for the Senecas.[43]

In 1963, in order to push his bill, Haley held a House Subcommittee on Indian Affairs hearing. Importantly, in order to gather firsthand testimony, he made an on-site visit and held several sessions at Salamanca High School on the Allegany Indian Reservation.[44] President Heron invited members of the subcommittee to Allegany for an inspection of proposed relocation sites. In his testimony at the hearing, Heron indicated that the Kinzua Planning Committee had "been working hard these past two years. We have borrowed a page from Congress and appointed various committees to make a detailed study of our needs." He proudly pointed out to the subcommittee that Kinzua Planning Committee members—working on lieu lands, tangible and intangible damages, education, housing, and relocation—had served "without compensation and devote a great deal of their time looking forward to the betterment of the Senecas." The president added that the Senecas were "going to take advantage of the new programs offered by Congress." Haley then responded, praising Heron:

Mr. Heron has been to Washington several times. I have had the pleasure of working with him on some of your problems. I intend to continue to work with him. I think he is sincerely interested in your problems which, after all, became the problems of the committee and the nation. And I think you are fortunate in having a man of his stature, this caliber, to be participating in what I think is a very important time in the history of your nation. He is to be commended because, undoubtedly, I think his actions speak louder than words.[45]

At the same hearing, former Seneca president Basil Williams described the desperate situation facing the people of the Allegany Indian Reservation. He pointed out that although the reservation had contained 30,469 acres, the Kinzua Dam took 10,210 acres; six congressionally established villages leased to non-Indians contained another 10,000 acres, and 2,000 acres were used as rights-of-way, leaving only 8,459 acres, much of it hilly and inaccessible. Williams insisted that the Senecas' deepest concern was a need for more land: "We have little land left on the Allegany Reservation and what land we have left is not suitable for relocation on a basis that the Indians are accustomed to." The Senecas needed replacement lands for those taken in the Kinzua project because the Allegheny Reservoir created in the project was "taking the heart of the [Allegheny] valley and leaving us hillsides and isolated parcels of the reservation, not connected in any way."[46] Despite the hope that extra lands or moneys for purchase would be provided, local Cattaraugus County non-Indian residents torpedoed the idea because they opposed adding lands to the Allegany Indian Reservation, arguing that the move would further erode the already weak county tax base. Haley, showing that he leaned toward helping the Senecas, then called into question why no Indians were represented on the Cattaraugus County Planning Board.[47]

At the same May 1963 hearing at Allegany, Dema Stouffer, who headed the Kinzua Planning Committee's housing and relocation project, made the case for federal subsidies for housing. She testified that she and six other Senecas had been working in a crisis mode for six months, dealing with problems caused by the planned forced relocation of families from the take area. Stouffer welcomed Haley's subcommittee to Allegany and hoped that in their brief visit its members "will see and understand our problems." She prefaced her remarks to the Florida congressman and his subcommittee by teaching them something of traditional Seneca ways: "In times past, it was considered not proper for an Indian woman to speak at a public meeting, usually a chief was chosen to speak for the women, but we have come a long way."[48]

Stouffer then explained that the Senecas were giving up their "beautiful valleys and streams and the woods, a real Indian country . . . a way of life," and that her people were "filled with fears and anxieties." She indicated that moneys for their old modest homes would be insufficient to rebuild their new homes. She requested a congressional grant for Senecas in the take area because her committee believed that these relocatees should not be forced "to rent or go into debt to have suitable homes after the dam is built."[49] For nearly three more years, Stouffer worked with more than 130 families forced to relocate on the final details of their new homes, including heating systems, porches, window and door styles, siding, and fireplaces. She helped draw up contracts detailing specifications and guaranteeing payment.[50] She and the Kinzua Planning Committee had to contend with the slow bureaucratic process of securing funding. However, even as late as January 1966, with the dam's dedication ceremony fast approaching, thirty-seven families still had not been provided for.[51]

Maribel Printup then testified about how the Seneca's Kinzua Planning Committee had developed a plan to use funding provided in the proposed federal legislation being considered at the hearing. Early in 1963, its education subcommittee had pushed for the establishment of an education trust fund of $2.3 million and a board of trustees from Allegany and Cattaraugus. The proposal received approval from the Tribal Council. The subcommittee developed a questionnaire and surveyed students in the four school districts serving the Allegany and Cattaraugus Reservations about their interest in pursuing an education following graduation from high school. In 1963, only seven Seneca students were in college, and five were in postgraduate vocational training. Printup presented a twenty-year plan to encourage post–high school education. If $2.3 million were to be provided in the Seneca compensation bill, she predicted that with 4 percent interest added per annum, eighty Seneca students would be in college and thirty-five would seek vocational training by 1983.[52]

After moneys were provided with passage of the Seneca Nation Compensation Act of 1964, the Seneca Educational Foundation was established, with Printup as chair. The foundation included an equal number of male and female representatives from Allegany and Cattaraugus Territories, the school superintendents from the Salamanca and Gowanda School Districts, as well as the principal of the Silver Creek Central School. Printup's prediction was quite accurate: moneys were made available for two decades until the fund ran dry in the 1980s.[53] One former councilor, Merle Watt Sr., who is Maribel Printup's brother, later called this provision of education the "greatest positive legacy of the Kinzua disaster for the Senecas."[54] It is important to note that the president of the Seneca Nation in 2010, his assistant for social policies, the executive director of the Kinzua Dam Relicensing Commission, and the acting head of the Seneca Archives had received financial support from the Seneca Educational Foundation to go on to college.[55]

The Kinzua Planning Committee was also faced with a crisis caused by having to remove Senecas interred in more than forty graveyards within the take area. Despite Seneca concerns, the Army Corps of Engineers waited until late in the summer of 1964 to award the Grant Irwin Company of Honesdale, Pennsylvania, a contract for the relocation and reinterment.[56] Because of the lack of sensitivity displayed by some Army Corps engineers, the issue was not resolved quickly. It was further complicated when an offer of private lands by a local prominent non-Indian family had to be withdrawn because it was determined that these same lands were also in the take area.[57] Three thousand bodies at a cost of $14.40 per grave were eventually reinterred in two new cemeteries.[58]

On August 31, 1964, President Johnson signed H.R. 1794, which became Public Law 88-533, designed "to provide for the relocation, rehabilitation, social, and economic development of the members of the Seneca Nation."[59] The Seneca Nation Compensation Act provided $1,289,060 for "Direct Damages," namely for land and improvements; $945,573 for "Indirect Damages," relocation, loss of timber wildlife, and so forth; $387,023 for "Cemetery Relocation"; $250,000 to reimburse the Senecas for appraisal and legal fees; and $12,128,917 for "Rehabilitation," to be used for programs to benefit the Seneca Nation. Quite significantly, as a result of attorney Lazarus's lobbying efforts and Congressman Haley's political dealings, the Seneca Nation was to receive federal funds, nearly $1 million, to construct two community buildings, the first of their kind at Allegany and Cattaraugus, which were to serve their people well for the next forty years. However, in section 18 of the act, the legislation required that the Seneca Nation of Indians develop a plan for termination within three years. In order to satisfy Senators Clifford Anderson, Frank Church, Peter Dominick, and Henry Jackson of the Senate Subcommittee, the Senecas, despite Heron's, Lazarus's, and Taylor's efforts to remove this section, reluctantly accepted this provision to get the federal funds the Senecas desperately needed.

On October 31, 1964, President Heron wrote Haley: "Indeed, for the Senecas, Public Law 88-533 is truly the 'Haley Act.' Were it not for the strong and previously determined position which you took on our side, I know that this legislation at best would have been far less generous and at worst might never have reached enactment." Heron added that with this fund his people could "rebuild our reservation community and establish for the Seneca people a higher level of education and an improved standard of living." However, Heron expressed a great fear of termination based on section 18 in the act and beseeched the Florida congressman to come to the aid of the Seneca Nation because he feared further "alienation under state law."[60] Despite this provision, the Senecas had a friendly congressman monitoring their concerns about termination on Capitol Hill. Well after Haley's sponsorship of the Compensation Act, he continued to support the Senecas in their efforts for tribal rebuilding and opposed the withdrawal of federal services. The Senecas honored Haley and Saylor for their support during the Kinzua crisis by naming new tribal administration buildings after the two men in 1966 during Martin Seneca Sr.'s presidency.[61] That same year Harry Watt, a leading Seneca voice in the Coldspring Longhouse, concerned about section 18 of the Compensation Act, wrote Haley about this fear. He thanked him for his many efforts on behalf of the Seneca people. He added that he felt secure because he had Haley "like a big brother at Washington, D.C.," watching over things.[62] The Seneca leadership continued to correspond with Haley in an effort to kill a bill that had been introduced by Democratic Senator Henry Jackson of Washington intended to terminate the Senecas.[63] Jackson's effort went nowhere, but lingering fears of termination continued to reverberate within the Seneca world into the mid-1970s, well after President Richard Nixon had formally ended the policy in July 1970 (see chapter 8).

In his State of the Seneca Nation Address in January 1966, President Martin Seneca Sr. outlined the many changes that had come about as a result of the Kinzua Dam crisis. He focused mainly on the positive achievements by George Heron and the Kinzua Planning Committee. In reference to dealing with the immediate needs of Senecas displaced by the dam, President Seneca noted that 75 percent of the "relocation homes" had been completed, that the rest would be finished in the spring, and that the newly created Seneca Housing Authority had rented all thirty-five of its homes at Cattaraugus. He indicated that two new community buildings, later named for Congressman Haley at Allegany and Congressman Saylor at Cattaraugus, would soon be completed and that they would serve as community centers housing a gymnasium and providing cultural and educational programs. He pointed out that the Seneca Educational Foundation, established during the crisis, was already assisting fifty-three students in a "wide range of schools and business colleges to four-year colleges." President Seneca informed his people that his nation was continuing to pursue its claims before the ICC for monetary compensation "for lands improperly acquired [from the Senecas by the United States] in the nineteenth century." He emphasized the scope of the changes instituted when he noted that for the very first time in its history the Seneca Nation had formally prepared a budget, which was now required to handle "the increasing volume of business transactions from our various programs as a result of Public Law 88-533." After expressing his hope for establishing a monthly Seneca newspaper "to carry on where the *Kinzua Planning Newsletter* left off," the president then maintained that his people had "confronted many roadblocks, contradictions and other problems" in their "major effort to recast our community life following its disruption by the Kinzua Dam. The true test of our ability to *survive* will now lie in what we do with what we have accomplished so far." Quite aware of the divisive, intense, and often combative politics within his confederated nation, he added that he hoped that every Seneca would "do his best to make his own community a better place to live in," expressing confidence that his people would join together and cooperate fully to "overcome all obstacles." He concluded: "Let us all strive to build and not destroy—our success or failure lies with our own people."[64]

In one major area, economic development, the Seneca's efforts proved ineffective. Haley encouraged the Seneca leadership to push more in this area. Even before H.R. 1794 was passed, Haley—a successful business-man—notified George Heron that he had been contacted by the president of Pal Precision Products, who had expressed interest in establishing a plant and employing between twenty and a hundred people in Seneca Territory.[65] In December 1964, the Seneca Nation Tribal Council estab-lished the Industrial Development Committee, composed of former Sen-eca Nation president Basil Williams, Cornelius Abrams Jr., Delbert Crowe, and Howard Maybee. Fruit of the Loom and eight other corporations began negotiations with President Heron and BIA representative Sid Car-ney about the possibility of establishing a factory on one of the Senecas' reservations. With the Senecas shaken by the Kinzua crisis and with little tribal infrastructure, capital, or management expertise, these ventures were to go nowhere. In January 1966, President Seneca announced that the nation, at the recommendation of its Industrial Development Com-mittee, had formed the First Seneca Corporation, in its goal to develop a fifty-two-acre industrial park on Route 5 at the western end of the Cat-taraugus Indian Reservation and eventually employ 100 to 150 Senecas in manufacturing "pillows and other related items" for the United States Pil-low Corporation. In July 1966, at Congressman Haley's recommendation, the Senecas received a matching grant of $373,000 from the Department of Commerce's Economic Development Corporation to build a factory on one of two sites that it had demarcated for potential industrial develop-ment at Cattaraugus.[66]

In July 1966, Senator Robert Kennedy, whose brother most Senecas blamed for going ahead with the Kinzua Dam construction, dedicated the factory project at a groundbreaking ceremony at Cattaraugus. Although sixty Senecas were hired, within five years the First Seneca Corpora-tion went bankrupt and was liquidated. Its collapse left a bad taste for later efforts at economic development and called into question both the capabilities and the honesty of certain tribal officials associated with the First Seneca Corporation, known as "Seneca, Inc.," and contributed substantially to popular distrust of the nation's leadership, especially during the later controversy over siting a Fisher-Price factory at Cattaraugus.

Other efforts at stimulating the Seneca economy also fell flat. More modest efforts during those years—the American Urethane Sole Company's employment of the Senecas to manufacture one-piece molded soles for shoes and the United Fiber Corporation's employment of thirty Senecas in manufacturing cellulose insulation—proved fleeting and did not contribute to long-term economic growth or to more permanent employment.[67] Moreover, the Senecas' important efforts to promote tourism, described in the next chapter, had only a limited economic impact, although they did have a major educational and cultural impact on Seneca life in the long run.

Subsistence at Allegany was seriously undermined by the dam, and the Senecas became more dependent on government grants for employment and welfare for economic survival. According to anthropologist Joy Bilharz, the "most obvious legacy of the dam" was the creation of an "institutionalized bureaucracy." She added that although the number of jobs increased, "so has political patronage and its inherent evils."[68] Yet by the late 1970s the Seneca Nation had only 165 employees, a mere fraction of its tribal workforce today.[69] Moreover, the growth of Seneca dependence on federal programs in the 1960s and 1970s was not unique; it was nearly universal throughout Indian Country. Great Society programs, through the Johnson administration's Office of Economic Opportunity, were extended to impoverished reservation Indian communities. The passage of the Comprehensive Employment and Training Act during President Nixon's administration continued and even expanded programs aimed at helping Native communities.[70]

The work of George Heron's Kinzua Planning Committee permanently transformed the governmental structure of the Seneca Nation of Indians and did meet the immediate challenges of tribal survival brought on by the Kinzua crisis. Importantly, in April 1966, Seneca women, who had played a vital role in working as volunteers for the Kinzua Planning Committee and who had received suffrage in 1964, were now rewarded by being allowed the right to hold tribal office. In the immediate years that followed Kinzua, they were to play a much more open role in Seneca governmental operations and, as shown in chapter 7, were the driving force in establishing revolutionary changes in health care delivery.[71]

In November 1966, Heron stepped down from his post as head of the Kinzua Planning Committee. That month Calvin "Kelly" John was elected as the first full-time president of the Seneca Nation, receiving the modest sum of $6,500 per year.[72] John had to contend with finding ways to build a tribal economy and to fend off congressional efforts to terminate the Seneca Nation. He also had to deal with projects carried over from the work done by the Kinzua Planning Committee. One of the committee's proposed projects, whose plans were first drawn up in 1962, Iroquoia, described in chapter 6, is generally viewed as an abysmal failure. However, as we shall see, its planning laid the base for two important tribal educational institutions, the Seneca Nation libraries at Allegany and Cattaraugus and the Seneca-Iroquois National Museum, which continue to this day to serve the nation so well.

6

The Iroquoia Project and Its Legacies

Failure?

WHEN COMING TO SOUTHWESTERN NEW YORK, I made it a point to stop by the tribal offices in the Plummer building on the Allegany Indian Reservation and pay a visit to Rovena Abrams, the longtime public-affairs officer who has served as editor of the *Seneca Nation of Indians' Official Newsletter*. Mrs. Abrams has worked for the Seneca Nation government since 1962, longer than any other employee, although she frequently reminds me that there were brief lapses in her tenure in office. I first met her, a member of the prominent Watt family from Cold Spring, while I was working in the early 1980s doing research on the Salamanca lease controversy. I would also see her at every community event, with her camera ready to create a record of what transpired. Mrs. Abrams still comes every day to her office on the second floor of the new Seneca Allegany Administration Building on Ohi:yo´ Way in Salamanca, where she spends her time working on editing and publishing the newsletter, whose operations and distribution have significantly expanded over the years.

This publication is a vastly different from the previous newsletters *O He Yo Noh* and *Si Wong Geh*, in both its improved quality and content. By presenting news of both communities, Cattaraugus and Allegany, the *Seneca Nation of Indians' Official Newsletter* purposefully attempts to create more unity within the nation to bridge the gulf between Allegany and Cattaraugus Reservation residents. Today, this newsletter presents the nation's policy statements on important issues and features a column by the Seneca president in every issue, information about Tribal Council discussions and resolutions, community news of all kinds, as well as job and grant notices.[1]

Rovena Abrams's personal story as well as that of her sister, Maribel Printup, are directly tied to the Senecas' rebuilding efforts after Kinzua. Both women were relocates and were directly involved in the inner workings of the Kinzua Planning Committee, directed by George Heron beginning in 1962. It is no coincidence that the future editor of the *Seneca Nation of Indians' Official Newsletter* and her sister contributed their time and articles to the *Kinzua Planning Newsletter*, edited by Jack Preston, Walter Taylor, and Merrill Bowen from 1962 through 1965. Moreover, during this crisis both women were directly involved in the creation of two Seneca Nation libraries, the Seneca-Iroquois National Museum, and the Seneca Nation Highbanks Campground enterprise, which grew out of discussions for a massive tourist undertaking known as "Iroquoia," a largely misinterpreted effort seen as a major failure.[2] Although Iroquoia as an elaborate economic development project originally conceptualized by outsiders never came to fruition, the Senecas modified this plan, and in the mid- to late 1970s, several positive components of the plan lived on in other forms at Allegany and Cattaraugus.[3]

The initial project, known as "Iroquoia," was to develop a tourism industry to help generate a tribal economy after the Kinzua disaster. It entailed developing a parcel, Hotchkiss Hollow Plateau, on the western shoreline of the Allegheny Reservoir, newly created by the flooding of Indian lands. It involved at least four sets of consultants from 1962 to 1969: Brill Engineering; Childs and Waters; Johnson, Horrigan, and Yeaple Engineers and Architects; and Neilan Engineers in collaboration with Development International. These consulting firms produced nine separate drafts of the project during these years.[4] Although the Senecas kept acquiring new federal planning moneys for the proposed project until at least 1974, the plan was basically on life support by 1969.[5]

In 1962, BIA officials recommended that the Senecas contract with Brill Engineering Corporation for a master plan; however, the company was ill suited for the project. Brill specialized in building superhighways and constructing factories and suburban housing units. It had no experience in tourism and recreational projects. This firm soon envisioned the creation of a massive project, an Indian Williamsburg, to spur Seneca economic development and create jobs by establishing a tourist industry at Allegany.[6] On September 29, 1962, the Seneca Nation Council passed two resolutions recommending that two feasibility studies be conducted on the Allegany Indian Reservation—one regarding the possibility of recreational development and the other regarding economic development.[7] Some Senecas expressed concern about the plan to establish a tourist-driven industry out of the Kinzua tragedy. They also thought that the tribal leaders' limited education and management training would restrict their ability to develop and manage this massive undertaking.[8] Nevertheless, George Heron, Wayne Printup, and other members of the Kinzua Planning Committee pushed the plan forward.

On February 20, 1963, with a grant of $1 million provided by the BIA and with the Interior Department's formal approval, Brill's engineers were requested to develop plans and evaluate "the feasibility of commercial recreation and tourist facilities at the Allegany Reservation and industrial parks at Allegany and Cattaraugus Reservations, NY." Although in their reports the Brill engineers concerned themselves with a need for a $4,379,000 investment to attract industry to the Cattaraugus industrial park, they nevertheless largely focused most of their attention on the Allegany Reservation.[9]

The Brill firm considered two plans: (1) a water-oriented marina–motel complex on the west side of the Allegany Reservation at the Pennsylvania–New York state line; and (2) a "Williamsburg type, historical Indian exhibit," more of a theme park, at Hotchkiss Plateau, fifteen miles upstream from the marina–motel complex, on the west side of the reservoir that would be created by the construction of the Kinzua Dam (remember, these plans were being formulated before the dam was completed).[10] In a Capitol Hill hearing before Congressman Haley's Subcommittee on Indian Affairs in August 1963, Brill representatives proposed the creation of a "nonprofit historical and educational institution" for the "purpose of increasing the understanding and appreciation of our Nation's rich Indian heritage." To accommodate visitors, an operating corporation would be developed for the purpose of providing the necessary lodging, restaurant, and recreational facilities.[11]

In testimony before the subcommittee, Peter Stark and Ralph Anoushian of Brill Engineering first described the second part of the project, indicating that it would be divided into seven sections to draw tourists for two days to learn about Native peoples. It would include a reception and administration area, lodging, an Indian village, a "living nature museum," and three other sections covering the Indian heritage of the United States, Great Britain and British Canada, France and French Canada. Connected to the main exhibit area would be corridors containing administrative offices, a cafeteria, an auditorium to house and show orientation films, and a library for research on Indian life. Stark, an assistant to the president of Brill, described the project's five objectives:

1. To preserve the Senecas' culture, traditions, language, and way of life.

2. To educate the American public as to its Indian heritage and how the Indian tribes of the Northeast influenced America's history and culture. The Indian influence on Canadian, British, and French history would also be developed.

3. To improve the economy of the Seneca Nation by providing a wide range of new employment opportunities.

4. To do the above on a self-sustaining basis, the project would be designed to provide funds to enable it to grow and expand to take care of the educational need of a growing visitor population and to increase job opportunity for a growing population of Senecas.

5. To provide income to the Seneca Nation through rental of land occupied by the project.[12]

When Stark indicated up front that a successful venture of this type could "not be financed through normal commercial channels" and needed an infusion of federal moneys, members of the congressional subcommittee immediately questioned the feasibility of the project on economic grounds.[13] In their testimony, Brill representatives indicated that nearly $90 million were needed to successfully accomplish the company's goal, including an outright federal grant of $29 million, a long-term commitment of $59 million financed through issuing private bonds or directly funded by US Treasury financing, and an additional $1,095,900 to relocate roads.[14]

In response, Haley, the fiscally conservative chairman of the House Sub-committee on Indian Affairs, and Congressman Ed Edmondson of Oklahoma recommended that private financing be raised for the project. After all, Edmondson pointed out, in the case of the Williamsburg restoration project, John D. Rockefeller Jr. had donated $61 million of his family fortune to its development.[15]

Members of the House Subcommittee on Indian Affairs challenged the Brill engineers' testimony in other areas as well. Brill's proposal included the construction of a marina, motel, and parking lot that required the acquisition of an additional 860 to 1,370 acres of land. In defending this future land acquisition, Stark claimed that when the Iroquoia project was fully completed over the ten-year period, it would eventually produce between 3,300 and 5,000 jobs, a figure that he and his firm later substantially reduced in its final report.[16] According to testimony presented before the subcommittee, the firm also unrealistically assumed that state officials would provide lieu lands for the Iroquoia project. The engineers also believed that, to further the project, the Army Corps of Engineers would be willing to condemn additional lands, including those held by private non-Indian landowners, by eminent domain in the same manner it took land from the Senecas for the creation of the Allegany Reservoir. They incorrectly assumed that lands could be acquired through negotiations between the Army Corps, Cattaraugus County, and the Seneca Nation.[17] Subcommittee members quickly shot down all of the engineers' assumptions as false hopes. Moreover, the Brill engineers did not win favor with the Senecas themselves because part of their plan for Iroquoia took into account the building of the future Southern Tier Expressway, which the Senecas themselves were challenging at that time.[18]

The final Brill report, issued in September 1963, indicated that the marina–motel operation would be too seasonal, operating only four months a year and seeing too much competition downstream in Pennsylvania. Nevertheless, it pushed Brill's plan for an Indian version of Williamsburg even though the firm never made an attempt to interview the Senecas themselves about their culture, history, and thoughts about the direction of the project. Instead, Brill Engineering submitted a slickly packaged report in which it envisioned creating a large-scale tourist industry over a ten-year period, but one now reduced from nearly $90 million to $72 million. The report claimed that a thousand jobs would be created. The firm estimated that the Iroquoia project could attract two hundred thousand visitors in its first year in operation and could grow annually to as many as one million admissions. Not surprisingly, the Seneca Tribal Council dubbed the Brill Engineering report "grandiose" and "colossal" and immediately rejected it.[19]

Childs and Waters, a second consulting firm recommended by the BIA, had been brought in to work with Brill in 1963. It was a museum design team out of New York City whose staff knew tourism but did not know the first thing about Native Americans and their mores. They initially copartnered with Brill, appearing jointly at the House Subcommittee on Indian Affairs hearings in August 1963, but soon replaced the engineering firm as lead consultants on the project. In October 1965, Childs and Waters issued its fourth and final report, in which it modified the Brill report, significantly reducing the size and cost of the project. Forty-three Senecas were to be hired full-time, 259 for half of the year and 83 for a four-month period during peak tourism in the late spring and summer. According to the firm's estimates, at least 165,000 people would likely visit Iroquoia in its first year of operation; Childs and Waters estimated that by the third year attendance would reach 190,000. The overall cost of the project was substantially reduced to $9.5 million. However, there were major problems with the plan. The firm conceived that Iroquoia would be a historical theme park and would include a cultural center, a motel, and a restaurant complex; however, although its report indicated that Iroquoia would produce a favorable rate of return, that would happen only after several years of being in the red.[20]

In the same year that Childs and Waters submitted its report, the Seneca Nation created an expanded committee to evaluate the Iroquoia project. In January 1965, William N. Fenton, the director of the New York State Museum, was chosen as the temporary chair and served until his formal resignation in December that year.[21] Other members of the Provisional Committee on Iroquoia included four prominent Senecas—George Heron, Martin Seneca Sr., Merrill Bowen, and Wayne Printup. Other members included Sid Carney, a Choctaw, the resident BIA representative during the Kinzua crisis; Water Taylor of the Society of Friends; Arthur Lazarus Jr., the Seneca Nation's attorney; and Somerset Waters of Child and Waters. Maribel Printup, John Abramson, and Elisabeth Tooker, a consulting anthropologist, were later added to the committee.[22]

In appointing Fenton, President Martin Seneca Sr. stated that the aim was to create a viable tourism industry at Allegany and that Fenton, "a long-time friend of Seneca Indians and noted Iroquois scholar," had agreed to serve, subject to approval by the Tribal Council, as temporary chairman of a provisional planning committee for Iroquoia, the proposed "high-quality educational, historic and cultural portrayal of the Indian contribution to American society during the past 500 years."[23] Prior to his appointment, Fenton had provided valuable service to the Seneca Nation. He had recruited well-known writers to their cause—Carl Carmer, Brooks Atkinson, and especially Edmund Wilson. In 1957 and 1958, Fenton worked closely with Seneca attorney Edward O'Neill, answering O'Neill's inquiries, tutoring him on Seneca history and treaties, and reviewing his writings and briefs for accuracy. The anthropologist also began a massive study of the Canandaigua Treaty of 1794 for O'Neill to use in the Senecas' defense in federal courts.[24] When the Senecas fired O'Neill after his inability to win in federal court, Arthur Lazarus Jr., an attorney with the Washington, DC, law firm Strasser, Spiegelberg, Fried, and Frank, was hired to replace him. From 1959 to 1964, Fenton, Heron, and Lazarus collaborated in several areas, including on testimony before congressional committees. The anthropologist sent the attorney information about historic sites and cemeteries threatened by the dam's construction and submitted testimony to congressional committees recommending monetary compensation for the Senecas for their efforts to recover from the dam's devastating effects.[25]

Now, because of his twenty-five years of experience as a museologist at the Smithsonian Institution, Fenton was to volunteer his time to help the same Seneca families who had taught him so much in his fieldwork experiences along the Allegheny in the 1930s. The anthropologist worked closely with George Heron, Walter Taylor, and especially Wayne Printup, the Seneca Tribal Council's official liaison on the Iroquoia project.[26] Moreover, upon Fenton's resignation as chairman of the Provisional Committee on Iroquoia, he nominated Printup as his successor.[27]

Throughout his tenure as Provisional Committee chairman, Fenton recommended greater Seneca participation in the development of the Iroquoia project, including the hiring of respected Coldspring Longhouse members as well as a chief from Tonawanda. As early as January 1965, he believed that knowledgeable Senecas should be tapped for their expertise and employed in this effort. He wrote: "I am concerned that we get someone like Harry Watt [highly respected Coldspring Longhouse preacher] into the planning early. We need someone who is in touch with the grassroots Seneca culture, who knows where to look for it, and how to marshal it."[28] Seeing the great possibilities of promoting Iroquoian art, somewhat like Arthur C. Parker's Seneca Arts Project during the New Deal, Fenton wrote Taylor that Watt, Richard JohnnyJohn, and Coleman John of the Seneca Nation, accompanied by Chief Everett Parker of Tonawanda, could be helpful. Fenton suggested that they could be employed as part of the Iroquoia project by having them visit Seneca collections at the Rochester Museum and Science Center, the Museum of the American Indian, the Buffalo Museum of Science, and the Buffalo and Erie County Historical Society and create an inventory of Seneca objects. They could make a checklist of items, indicating the artist of each item and whether the artist who had made it was still alive. Then they could have the museum photographer provide copies of the art for the Iroquoia project.[29]

The Iroquoia committee strongly reacted to the Childs and Waters final report. In a detailed critique, Wayne Printup pointed out that the tourism industry was seasonal in southwestern New York, that environmental factors such as heavy snows and insect infestation were not considered for outdoor exhibits, that repairs and maintenance and overall upkeep would make the plan prohibitively expensive, and that few Senecas were trained in business management to run the proposed complex effectively.[30] Fenton objected to the design script written by Alan Forbes—with beliefs presented as hard facts, historical inaccuracies, and failure to treat Seneca history from the American Revolution to the twentieth century.[31] Taylor feared that the whole project could lead to commercialism and exploitation of the Senecas. He and his Quaker supporters also believed that the script should have had more focus on Seneca religious beliefs; that the script's graphic treatment of Iroquoian warfare and scalping had to be modified and be put in comparative context with other societies' tendencies toward violence; and that Native values, especially Iroquoian views about the environment, had to be stressed to teach greater lessons needed in the world.[32]

At the core of the Provisional Committee's vision, not the poor draft produced by Childs and Waters, was a living museum with contemporary Senecas employed in a full-scale replica of a seventeenth-century village. In this setting, various craftsmen would be at work, while the women would tend gardens and prepare foods in the old-time way. Included in the core would be relevant materials—as are now present in the Seneca-Iroquois National Museum—explaining the nature of the League of the Iroquois as well as tribal governments. Iroquois community members could be hired as paid employees to bring their expertise to teach tracking, lacrosse, archery, and canoeing. School groups, the Boy Scouts, as well as children summer campers could be attracted by these programs. Native and local regional cuisine could be served in a restaurant facility. Instead of building and promoting a low-end motel full of "cheap gimmicks" to attract tourists, which would be "totally unworthy of the Iroquois," the committee considered promoting "beautiful campsites and the most attractive cabins in the woods in the United States." A theater complex could host Seneca cultural programs and attract Native American actors, choreographers, playwrights, filmmakers, and speakers on a wide variety of subjects.[33] However, the Senecas themselves were concerned about how the invasion of swarming tourists would affect ceremonies at the Coldspring Longhouse. Fenton recommended that, to insulate themselves, the Senecas enact parts of ceremonies at Iroquoia's theater complex "to satisfy the curiosity of visitors and prevent them from invading the privacy of the real Longhouse."[34]

Knowing that in the eastern region of the United States the public was less informed about Native art traditions, committee members hoped to encourage a greater awareness by museum displays, special exhibits, and artists in residence giving presentations and demonstrations, all of which twelve years later became featured in programming at the Seneca-Iroquois National Museum. Although the Iroquois core remained the centerpiece of the project, Iroquoia also aimed to educate the public about

Native peoples on a more widely geographic basis—from South America to the Arctic. Importantly, at the heart of the committee's own thinking was a planned library/museum research center that would be run by Senecas themselves. It would be open to scholars as well as to community people, all who had a real desire to further their knowledge about the Senecas and other Iroquois.[35]

In the end, the committee agreed that the project as designed by Childs and Waters was worthwhile because the firm's report indicated that Iroquoia would lead to the hiring of 43 Senecas for full-time employment, 259 for half-year work, and 83 for twelve weeks during the heavy tourist season in the summer.[36] However, the committee did not endorse the project designed by Childs and Waters. Its own report maintained: "We therefore cannot recommend this total project. . . . It calls for more money than the [Seneca] Nation has available; financing the total project would raise the overhead costs and increase the probability that the project would be an uneconomical venture; when its success would be marginal at best."[37] By the first days in 1966, the Seneca Nation Tribal Council had changed the committee's name to the "Recreational Development Committee" and, although retaining Wayne Printup as chairman, had reconstituted the committee to include six tribal councilors and four advisers.[38]

The Senecas' reluctance to go along with the Childs and Waters proposal or with subsequent plans put forth by Johnson, Horrigan and Yeaple in 1967 or with those developed by Neilan Engineers in collaboration with Development International in 1969 is not surprising. Although there was definite need to rebuild the nation, many Senecas, poor to begin with and traumatized by the effects of the Kinzua Dam crisis, rejected this course of action. The timing of this proposal seemed wrong as well. Inviting tourists to Allegany at this sad time was incongruous: white politicians in Washington were breaking the most solemn of the Senecas' federal treaties, thus condemning Indian lands and uprooting and relocating families.

The Iroquoia project continued to be brought up in council in the early 1970s, but after the Neilan Engineers' report of 1969, few Senecas saw it as a realistic possibility. However, the planning done in the 1960s paid off later. Senecas themselves, including Wayne and Maribel Printup and Rovena Abrams, pushed for certain points outlined and emphasized in the drafts. These points included a Seneca enterprise—the Highbanks Campground—along the reservoir created by the building of the Kinzua Dam, and the construction of the Seneca-Iroquois National Museum and two Seneca Nation libraries. As in the past, it took the organizational ability of Seneca women, "keepers of the kettle," to achieve success in getting things moving in this direction in the 1970s. It was no accident that the trustees of the two tribal libraries and museum established in the 1970s had on its board the same three Senecas—Maribel Printup, Wayne Printup, and Rovena Abrams—who had worked on the Iroquoia project planning committee.[39]

Some of the ideas put forth in the Iroquoia project were to come to fruition in the 1970s. The final creation of the Seneca Nation libraries and the Seneca-Iroquois National Museum must be understood in the context of this decade. The New York State Department of Education had ignored securing federal Johnson-O'Malley funds for nearly forty years, losing millions of dollars that could have been used for the improvement of Indian education. The department's policy was not to encourage the teaching of Native American history, culture, and languages. With the rise of Red Power activism in the late 1960s and early 1970s, however, the department was forced to reconsider its historic educational policies vis-à-vis American Indians. As a result of two major protests—by the Mohawks in 1968 and by the Onondagas in 1971—that led to temporary boycotts of the public schools attended by Indian youth, the New York State Education Department and the New York State Board of Regents were forced to respond.[40]

The determined efforts by Ann Lewis of the Native American Indian Education Unit within the US Department of Education and the annual Iroquois Conference, a gathering of concerned Native Americans held throughout the decade of the 1970s, helped women throughout Iroquoia to organize. Women came and went from these annual conference gatherings, first held at St. Lawrence University in 1971 under the auspices of Dean Robert Wells as well as Lloyd Elm and Minerva White, two key Iroquois educators and advocates. Seneca women involved in this initial gathering included museum trustee Maribel Printup and Arliss Barse, whose mother, Reva, was the most vocal advocate of Seneca women's suffrage. Many prominent Seneca and Cayuga women from the Cattaraugus and Allegany Reservations attended these meetings and learned of Minerva White's and Margaret Jacobs's determined efforts to establish a Mohawk Nation Library at the Akwesasne Cultural Center, which had opened in 1973.[41]

Women formed committees on both the Allegany and Cattaraugus Reservations. Besides Rovena Abrams and Maribel Printup, who had been involved in the earlier Iroquoia planning, others joined in on the effort: Alberta Austin, Dorothy Cox, Marjorie Curry, Hazel Dean John, Marjorie Farmer, Grace John, Wini Kettle, Marlene Johnson, Myrtle Peterson, Pauline Seneca, Tessie Snow, Virginia Snow, Dena Stouffer, and Alice Waterman. Lana Redeye, hired as head of the Seneca Education Committee, served as liaison to the Seneca Nation Tribal Council and reported on these women's efforts. She also served as the major contact person from the Seneca Nation government to the New York State Education Department's Office of Library Development in Albany. Rae Snyder, the Seneca Nation's director for Comprehensive Employment and Training Act concerns, was also directly involved in the planning and hiring of Peggy Bray, Eleanor Bowen, Dorothy Cox, and Merrill Bowen as library staff. George Abrams, Martha Symmes, and others helped push for the present Allegany Library's location, drew up the necessary legal incorporation, planned the inner and outer design of the library, and coordinated the later essential effort of making the two libraries part of the Cattaraugus–Chautauqua Library network.[42]

The women of the Seneca communities at Allegany and Cattaraugus and their ally Ramona Charles at Tonawanda carefully cultivated a relationship with Laura Chodos, member of the New York State Board of Regents; Joseph Schubert, assistant commissioner of Education and head of the New York State Library, who had formerly lived at North Collins, New York, near the Cattaraugus Indian Reservation; and Department of Education personnel such as Bernard Finney of the New York State Library's Office of Library Development. Both Schubert and Finney visited the reservations, at which time the community women helped sell the idea for two libraries.[43] These women took advantage of the spade work done by the Mohawks as well as by Lotsee Patterson, a librarian of Chickasaw–Comanche ancestry at the University of Oklahoma,[44] and by Charles Townley, a librarian at the University of Minnesota who had received a major four-year federal grant to promote Indian libraries nationwide. Both Patterson and Townley were associated with the American Library Association and the National Indian Education Association and accomplished much in their push for Indian tribal libraries.

Exploiting the tenor of the times with its call to provide access to library services, these women also secured the support of the New York State Library Association. They won over Dadie Perlov, its director, who wrote to Governor Hugh Carey that "this service [library access to American Indians] is still part of the unfinished business of this state [New York]" and that the lack of such access "is an embarrassment at a time when the country's conscience has been raised about the legitimate grievance of its native [sic] Americans." She emphasized that this "piece of progressive legislation will begin to redress a very old problem."[45]

By the mid-1970s, the New York State Board of Regents had finally recognized that there had been failures in providing for the educational needs of American Indians. Led by Regent Laura Chodos, the board took several steps to remedy the situation. First, in 1975 the regents announced a position paper, *Native American Education*, which significantly altered the Education Department's past educational policies with respect to American Indians in New York State. This position paper, number twenty-two in the Board of Regents series, maintained that it now finally recognized that Native Americans preferred "to retain their specific tribal cultural identities and life styles and that they wish to exercise the prerogatives of adopting only those components of the dominant American culture that meet their needs."[46] Second, Chodos lobbied for the establishment of a tribal library system. She convinced State senator James Donovan, an ultraconservative legislator from Utica, to sponsor an "Indian library bill." Donovan, who had a background in the building construction trades, was approached by Mohawks with a similar background. He reached out in this fashion because he and his district were beset with the Eagle Bay (Ganienkeh) takeover and sought a way out of this Indian–white confrontation. The bill passed with only one dissenting vote in both houses of the New York State Legislature. The

New York State American Indian Library Act of 1977 helped create an Indian public-library system, the first of its kind in the United States, and initially appropriated $175,000 for its operations. The act provided tribal libraries the means of acquiring and accepting surplus library books, a specific formula of apportionment of state aid to Indian libraries—100 percent reimbursement compared to 10 percent for off-reservation community libraries—and a mechanism for distribution of state aid to either the Indian library board of trustees or directly to the tribal government for a contract for library services.[47]

The Senecas still faced the real problem of finding a community member trained to administer their new library program. They were able to find a most capable one—Ethel Peggy Bray, a Cattaraugus Seneca—who was to serve for the next fifteen years and help build the collections and community services of the two reservation libraries. Because of the Comprehensive Employment Training Act, a federal program initiated and passed by Congress during the Nixon administration, Bray had been hired in the Role Model Program of the federal government's Title IV-C. Importantly, she had been placed in the Silver Creek Junior-Senior High School library and had worked there for five years after her children had grown up. Although Bray was not a certified librarian, her work experience and abilities qualified her to serve as the first Seneca Nation librarian, and she was formally hired in the spring of 1979 to administer her staff, who included Merrill Bowen, Eleanor Bowen, and Dorothy Cox.[48]

The Seneca Nation libraries and Seneca-Iroquois National Museum were finally established in 1977, and the proximity of the two facilities today is no accident. Although there was opposition to placing the library on Salamanca's main commercial thoroughfare, and there was talk of placing the library building behind the Haley Building, the library board and its supporters pushed for the present location of the library next door to the museum. According to members of the library committee, it was placed on the main thoroughfare intentionally to "show *all* that the city was on Indian land."[49]

The creation of the Seneca-Iroquois National Museum was similar to the establishment of the two Seneca libraries in other ways. The idea for the museum came in planning discussions for the Iroquoia project.

The museum's first director, George Abrams, had even been nominated in 1965 as a potential director of the project.[50] As in the creation of the libraries, the Senecas took advantage of the tenor of the times to push for a tribal museum. During the decade of the 1970s, twelve new tribal museums were built on reservations in the United States. In sharp contrast, only eight tribal museums had been built from 1932 to 1969. Much like the grandiose thinking in the original concept design of Iroquoia made by Brill and later by Childs and Waters, Washington policymakers in the Departments of the Interior and Commerce saw tribal museums as one way of attacking the problems faced by impoverished Indian communities. They unrealistically saw tourism as the answer, even though most Native communities were in rural areas isolated at great distances from major population centers. Nevertheless, by the mid-1970s, federal moneys from the Economic Development Administration flowed into Indian Country in this new government experiment.[51]

The result was the funding and construction of the Seneca-Iroquois National Museum, a 6,400-square-foot facility that opened in 1977. George Abrams and the museum committee chose Carson Waterman, the most accomplished Seneca artist of the time, to design the exterior of the building—a wampum belt design—tying the museum back to its historic Iroquoian roots. Besides a longhouse and exhibits dealing with the Seneca past, the museum includes displays of contemporary Seneca arts. On the walls are complementary leaflets explaining Seneca government then and now, clan structure, wampum, and other aspects of Iroquoian culture. The museum sponsors educational programs and speakers in an open area in the museum's center, promotes Hodinöhsö:ni´ artists, has a permanent exhibit on Seneca life before Kinzua and after, and has historical exhibits dealing with a wide variety of subjects ranging from Seneca boarding school days to sports.[52] By re-reading the critiques of the Iroquoia project made by Senecas, Walter Taylor, and anthropologists William N. Fenton and Elisabeth Tooker, one can easily conclude that at least some of what the Seneca-Iroquois National Museum has done since 1977 was rooted earlier.[53]

The museum has had four able but very different directors since its founding: George Abrams, Judy Greene, Midge Dean Stock, and Jaré

Cardinal. Abrams had the longest tenure as director, serving for thirteen years in that capacity. Trained in anthropology at the University of Arizona under Edward Spicer's tutelage and in archaeology at the State University of New York at Buffalo by Marian White, Abrams, a Cornplanter Seneca, gave up a career in academia to plan the building of and administer the new Seneca museum. His mother, Cordelia, and the much revered elder Genevieve Plummer had worked during the Kinzua crisis in the Buffalo office of the Army Corps of Engineers, where they had helped acquire inside information about plans the federal government had for the Senecas. George Abrams himself had been directly involved in Kinzua planning, helping the Seneca Nation as a trained archaeologist with the sensitive relocation of graves that were threatened by the land take and dam construction flooding. The late Judy Greene, an Allegany Seneca, was an accomplished artist trained in ceramic design at Alfred University and was very much concerned with promoting Hodinöhsö:ni´ artists and Iroquoian art traditions. Midge Dean Stock—a Cornplanter Seneca and the daughter of Hazel Dean John, who, in working with Walter Taylor, had played a major role in the Senecas' Kinzua crisis planning efforts—served for a brief time as the museum's director. A gifted musical performer, she was educated at St. Bonaventure in educational studies, and her focus was on teaching Seneca youngsters about their past. She was especially concerned about the need to remember what had happened in the Kinzua crisis. The present director is Jaré Cardinal, a non-Seneca who is a historian trained at Bowling Green University. She wrote her master's thesis on the Kinzua Dam crisis and later worked for twenty-five years as an educator at the Rochester Museum and Science Center, which houses one of the largest and finest Seneca collections in the world.[54]

The Seneca-Iroquois National Museum, much like other tribal museums, is quite distinct from what federal bureaucrats envisioned in the 1970s. In 2002, George Abrams undertook a major study of tribal museums for the Association of State and Local History, a revealing one that analyzes their roles and evaluates their importance. He found that the roles played by tribal museums were very similar in all locations and that their first priority was to promote the "cultural retention of the tribal group and service to the local community." Of much less importance were tourism, economic development, public relations, and education of non-tribal members. Instead of being seen as profit-making ventures, museum administrators saw museums as a way of teaching their own people, in particular the younger people, about their culture.[55]

Over the past decade, the Seneca Nation has greatly expanded its efforts to promote greater protection of its historical records, cultural artifacts, ritual objects, and sacred sites. In 2000, it established the Tribal Historic Preservation Office, which works under the provisions of the National Historic Preservation Act of 1966 and the Native American Graves Protection Act of 1991 to ensure that any federal project affecting historic properties, cultural resources, or funerary sites will include consultation with the Senecas to develop plans for mitigation. In 2003, the Seneca Nation Archives Department was founded under the leadership of David George-Shongo Jr.[56] Unlike in the past, when records were improperly stored and ruined, carted away by past tribal leaders, or simply thrown out, official documents and visual records now have a safe storage facility within the nation. It is to be hoped that researchers will no longer have to repeat collecting the same documents, as they did in the past.

In the 1960s, the Senecas faced the challenges of tribal survival in the termination era as well as problems directly and indirectly caused by the Kinzua crisis. Although during this difficult period they were never able to achieve economic self-sufficiency, they, like so many other Native communities, were not averse to accepting federal grants and job programs as temporary lifejackets to keep them afloat. Prior to Indian casinos and gaming, most federally recognized Native nations had little choice but to look to Washington for War on Poverty moneys under President Johnson's Economic Opportunity Act and later under President Nixon's Comprehensive Employment and Training Act program. One result was the beginning of a tribal bureaucracy, a phenomenon that was not just happening on New York State's reservations. It was a nationwide trend in the late 1960s and 1970s. Although this bureaucracy perpetuated dependence, Native communities also used it to develop new institutions such as libraries and museums that benefited their peoples—no small achievements.

Despite the pressures caused by the Kinzua crisis, the fragile federated structure of Seneca government held together. Although the crisis centered largely on Allegany and Cornplanter, Senecas at Cattaraugus joined in to help rebuild the nation. This united effort was especially noticeable in the area of health care, where an extraordinary group of Cattaraugus Seneca women, working with an Allegany Seneca tribal councilor, set out to establish a health care program for the tribe.

4. New Coldspring Longhouse, Allegany Territory, 2012. As a result of the building of the Kinzua Dam and the flooding of Seneca lands to create the lower Allegheny Reservoir, the old Coldspring Longhouse was torn down and a new one at Steamburg was constructed. Photograph by Caleb Abrams. Courtesy of Caleb Abrams.

5. Newtown Longhouse, Cattaraugus Territory, 2012. Photograph by Caleb Abrams. Courtesy of Caleb Abrams.

6. Wright Memorial Church (United Mission Church), Cattaraugus Territory, 2012. This Presbyterian church was first established by missionary Reverend Asher Wright at Buffalo Creek and then reestablished at Cattaraugus Territory after the removal of the Senecas under the provision of the Buffalo Creek Treaty of 1838. Photograph by Caleb Abrams. Courtesy of Caleb Abrams.

7. Thomas Indian School (originally the Thomas Institute for Orphan and Destitute Indians, established in 1855, closed in 1957), Cattaraugus Territory, c. 1950s. The controversial educational institution with an assimilationist focus administered by New York State after 1875 was both a day school and boarding institution for Native Americans. Courtesy of the Seneca-Iroquois National Museum.

8. Calvin "Kelly" John, c. 1990, Seneca Nation president 1946–48, 1950–52, 1966–68, 1990–92. Courtesy of Marilyn John George.

9. Cornelius V. Seneca, c. 1950, Seneca Nation president 1940–42, 1944–46, 1956–58. Courtesy of the Seneca-Iroquois National Museum.

10. Seven Seneca "mothers of the nation," c. mid-1950s. *Left to right*: Nettie Watt, Hattie Cooper, Sadie Butler, Effie Johnson, and Danny Jimerson (little boy in front). *Back row, left to right*: Colleen JohnnyJohn, Dorothy Jimerson, and Reva Jacobs. In 1956, these prominent Seneca women sent a formal protest to Washington expressing their united opposition to the building of the Kinzua Dam. Courtesy of the Seneca-Iroquois National Museum.

11. Arthur E. Morgan, president of Antioch College and engineering consultant for the Senecas in the Kinzua crisis, c. 1960. Photograph by Dr. Theodore Hetzel. Author's collection.

12. George Heron, c. 1961, Seneca Nation president 1958–60 and 1962–64; chairman of the Kinzua Planning Committee 1961–66. Photograph by Dr. Theodore Hetzel. Author's collection.

13. Walter Taylor and George Heron discussing Kinzua planning, early 1960s. Walter Taylor, a community organizer for the American Friends Service in the Midwest, was the representative of the Philadelphia Yearly Meeting of Friends sent to help the Senecas in the Kinzua crisis. Courtesy of the Seneca-Iroquois National Museum.

14. Congressman James A. Haley, 1964. Haley was the major congressional advocate for the Seneca Nation during the Kinzua crisis and afterward. The Florida congressman's actions aided the Senecas in securing the passage of a bill, House Resolution 1794, that helped these Native Americans rebuild. Courtesy of the State Archives of Florida.

15. President Martin Seneca Sr. and most of the Seneca Nation of Indians Tribal Council, c. 1965. *Front row, left to right*: DeForest Billy, George Heron, Martin Seneca Sr., and Basil Williams. *Back row, left to right*: Dale Crouse, Elwin Watt, Virgil Halftown, Cornelius Abrams Jr., Delbert Crowe, Quinton Biscup, Merrill Bowen. Courtesy of the Seneca-Iroquois National Museum.

16. Rovena Watt Abrams and Maribel Watt Printup, 2012. These two sisters were directly involved in rebuilding the Seneca Nation as members of the Kinzua Planning Committee and helped establish the Seneca-Iroquois National Museum and the two Seneca Nation libraries. Printup was the director of the Seneca Nation Educational Foundation, which successfully promoted postsecondary educational opportunities, and Rovena Abrams has been editor in chief of the *Seneca Nation of Indians' Official Newsletter* for several decades. Photograph by Caleb Abrams. Courtesy of Caleb Abrams.

17. Ed Curry and Harry Watt, c. early 1960s. Watt was a leading voice in the Coldspring Longhouse. Courtesy of the Seneca-Iroquois National Museum.

18. Ramona (Norma) W. Charles, Laurence M. Hauptman, Jeanne Marie Jemison, and Ruth Hauptman at the 1987 Peter Doctor Memorial Indian Foundation Dinner, May 2, 1987, Allegany Territory. The late Ramona Charles, a Tonawanda Seneca, was the longtime president of this educational foundation, which since 1941 has provided small grants to Iroquois students seeking postsecondary education. The late Jeanne Marie Jemison, a Cattaraugus Seneca, was a Surrogate Court judge of the Seneca Nation of Indians and the daughter of activist Alice Lee Jemison. Author's collection.

19. Cattaraugus Library, 2012. Photograph by Caleb Abrams. Courtesy of Caleb Abrams.

20. Allegany Library, 2012. Photograph by Caleb Abrams. Courtesy of Caleb Abrams.

21. Seneca-Iroquois National Museum, Allegany Territory, 2012. Photograph by Caleb Abrams. Courtesy of Caleb Abrams.

22. Lionel R. John, c. early 1980s, Seneca Nation president 1982–84 and health care advocate. Courtesy of the Seneca-Iroquois National Museum.

23. Winifred "Wini" Kettle, the first woman elected as a Seneca Nation clerk; director of the Women, Infants, and Children Clinic; and major health care advocate. Courtesy of the Seneca-Iroquois National Museum.

24. Lionel R. John Health Center, 2012. Photograph by Caleb Abrams. Courtesy of Caleb Abrams.

25. Robert "Bob" Hoag, c. mid-1970s, Seneca Nation president 1974–76, 1978–80, 1986–88. Courtesy of the Seneca-Iroquois National Museum.

26. Congressman Amory Houghton, Laurence M. Hauptman, and Seneca Nation president Dennis Lay, September 13, 1990, at the US House of Representatives Committee on Interior and Insular Affairs hearing on the Salamanca leases, Capitol Hill. Photograph by Rovena Abrams. Author's collection.

27. Marlene Bennett Johnson, n.d., former tribal councilor and member of the Seneca Nation Salamanca Lease Negotiation Committee. Johnson was also the former chair of the National Advisory Committee on Indian Education and head of the Higher Education Opportunity Program at St. Bonaventure University. In September 1990, she gave testimony before two committees of Congress helping to resolve the Salamanca lease controversy. Courtesy of Lori Johnson Quigley.

28. Seneca Nation president Maurice "Mo" John Sr., 2007, Seneca Nation president 2006–8. Photograph by Maurice John Jr. Courtesy of the *Seneca Nation of Indians' Official Newsletter.*

29. Three Seneca Nation presidents, 2011: Michael Schindler, 1996–98; Calvin Lay Jr., 1976–78, 1984–86; and Robert Odawi Porter, 2010–12. Photograph by Stephanie Crowley. Courtesy of the *Seneca Nation of Indians' Official Newsletter.*

30. Seneca Nation president Cyrus Schindler Sr. and Governor George Pataki signing the Nation–State Gaming Compact, August 18, 2002. Photograph by Rovena Abrams. Courtesy of the *Seneca Nation of Indians' Official Newsletter.*

31. Arlene Bova, tribal councilor and chair of the Seneca Nation Land Claims Committee, and attorney Jeanne Whiteing, 2005, after the return of fifty-one acres of Cuba Lake to the Seneca Nation. Courtesy of Arlene Bova.

32. Seneca Allegany Hotel and Casino complex, Allegany Territory, 2012. Photograph by Caleb Abrams. Courtesy of Caleb Abrams.

33. Seneca Niagara Falls Casino and Resort, Niagara Falls, New York, 2012. Photograph by Caleb Abrams. Courtesy of Caleb Abrams.

34. Seneca Allegany Administration Building, Allegany Territory, 2012. Photograph by Caleb Abrams. Courtesy of Caleb Abrams.

35. Wendy Huff, former tribal councilor and former executive director of the Seneca Nation Kinzua Dam Relicensing Commission, 2012. Photograph by Caleb Abrams. Courtesy of Caleb Abrams.

36. Lana Redeye, member of the Seneca Nation Kinzua Dam Relicensing Commission and former longtime director of the Seneca Nation Education Department, 2012. Photograph by Caleb Abrams. Courtesy of Caleb Abrams.

37. Former Seneca Nation clerk Diane Kennedy Murth and her mother, Norma Kennedy, 2012. Kennedy Murth worked for Florida congressman James Haley, an advocate for the Senecas during the Kinzua crisis. Both women also worked many years for the BIA. Photograph by Stephanie Crowley. Courtesy of the *Seneca Nation of Indians' Official Newsletter*.

38. Robert Odawi Porter, Seneca Nation president 2010–12. Photograph by Stephanie Crowley. Courtesy of the *Seneca Nation of Indians' Official Newsletter*.

39. The inauguration of Barry E. Snyder Sr. as president of the Seneca Nation of Indians, November 13, 2012. Geraldine Huff, the newly elected clerk of the Seneca Nation, is administering the oath of office to Snyder, who was elected for the fifth time. Photograph by Stephanie Crowley. Courtesy of the *Seneca Nation of Indians' Official Newsletter.*

7

The Health Action Group

Lionel John and the Power of Women

THE SENECAS' SUCCESS in improving health care came about during the era of Robert "Bob" Hoag, who was elected president of the Seneca Nation in 1974, 1978, and 1986 and treasurer in 1976, 1980, and 1988. Lionel R. John, who had been one of the Seneca Nation's tribal councilors, was given free rein to work with the newly formed Health Action Group, composed of about a dozen women volunteers mostly from Cattaraugus Territory, to develop a proposal for federal Indian Health Service (IHS) medical and dental care. The experience these women had gained as volunteers working on behalf of Seneca survival during the Kinzua crisis directly affected their involvement in improving health services. It was no coincidence that Wini Kettle, the first woman to be elected clerk of the Seneca Nation in November 1967, was a leader of this important reform. Until the mid-1970s, IHS did not provide these services in New York State. According to William Millar, the former director of the Tribal Health Division at IHS's eastern regional headquarters in Nashville, Tennessee, these Seneca women and their designee, Lionel John, were to transform health care within their communities and create a model for other Native Americans in the Northeast.[1] Their achievement also led to John's election to the presidency of the Seneca Nation in 1982.

The two-decade period of the 1970s and 1980s can be labeled the "Hoag era" in Seneca history. Bob Hoag first came to prominence during the Kinzua crisis when he was elected treasurer in 1964. His ancestor Willie Hoag had controlled the politics of the Seneca Nation from the

1880s to the late 1920s, ruling with an iron hand. Bob Hoag followed this firm style of leadership, but his administrations nevertheless achieved some remarkable results. During his tenure, the Senecas received funding to build, open, and operate two tribal libraries and the Seneca-Iroquois National Museum and to construct the Newtown Arena for hockey and lacrosse, Seneca Lanes Bowling Alley, and Highbanks, a campgrounds enterprise. By far, the greatest achievements of Hoag's long tenure were the vast improvements in medical and dental care and the establishment of two IHS-funded facilities.[2] Although the Senecas still face major challenges in improving the tribe's health, especially in combating the diabetes and substance abuse epidemics, in the 1970s and 1980s they were quite successful in overcoming major problems in the delivery of medical and dental services.

At the time of my arrival in Seneca Country in 1972, approximately 1,200 hundred Indians lived at Allegany, and 2,400 resided at Cattaraugus. The unemployment rate was 35 percent, and the median family income was $1,500 per annum on each reservation.[3] I was to visit the Cattaraugus clinic, an abysmal health care facility that operated on a limited basis for medical treatment of the Indians. Coming from a family of physicians, I was shocked by what I saw and heard from the Senecas as well as from western New York health experts. Upon my visit to Cattaraugus, I was also informed that the situation at Allegany was even worse because no clinic existed there.

The poorly financed state-operated clinic at Cattaraugus was housed in a three-story, dilapidated building that was not easily accessible to the elderly or physically challenged. It was located in the ruins of the Thomas Indian School complex at the center of the reservation. This medical facility had been housed in this building since it was constructed in 1932 and had been administered until the mid-1950s by the New York State Department of Social Welfare, formerly the Board of Charities, the lead agency in administering Indian affairs in New York State.[4] Upon its opening in the Great Depression, its mission was described as the following: "1. Weekly Dispensary Service; 2. Syphilogy Clinic (V.D.); 3. Dental Clinic; 4. Ophthalmology Clinic (eye care); 5. Tonsil Clinic; 6. Minor Surgery and Fracture Service; 7. X-ray Services; 8. Diabetes Treatment."[5] Thus, nowhere in its initial mission did it state that its responsibilities included neonatal care or combating two scourges wreaking havoc in Indian country: tuberculosis and alcoholism.

Despite efforts by President Cornelius Seneca to convert the Thomas Indian School into an Indian junior college modeled on Haskell, the institution closed its doors forever in June 1957.[6] Nevertheless, its so-called hospital continued to function as a part-time clinic for residents of Cattaraugus. Yet the clinic's location on the old school grounds was to limit its efficacy. The Thomas Indian School had had both day and resident students, and pupils' experiences there had varied widely. As was true of Native Americans nationwide who were resident students at such institutions, many Senecas, but not all, had horror stories about their time as pupils there. Now as adults with families of their own, some avoided paying needed visits to the clinic in the old school building because they still had bad memories of being humiliated or even abused there.[7]

The New York State Department of Health had assumed supervisory control of Indian health care in 1955, when medical services were transferred from the Department of Social Welfare following a recommendation by the New York State Interdepartmental Committee on Indian Affairs. The philosophy of Indian health and medical delivery in New York State at the time of transfer in the mid-1950s was succinctly put by the director of local health services in the Department of Health. He insisted that although his short-term focus was to raise Indian health and medical services to the level of the general state population, his "long term objectives" for "Indians residing on the reservations was to assist them in achieving complete social and economic integration and the eventual elimination of any special projects or programs on their behalf."[8] This assimilationist thinking reflected much of the tenor of governmental Indian policy at both the state and federal levels in the period.

In 1971, a report by the New York State Assembly Subcommittee on Indian Affairs outlined the state's responsibilities to its Native American communities. It indicated that the state Health Department was responsible for reimbursing counties for operating and maintaining general health clinics on the reservations. The department's associate commissioner was supposed "to coordinate health services at a State level, and delegates direct coordinating responsibility to the Regional Health Director, particularly those in Buffalo, Syracuse, and Albany." The department also had the responsibility to hire physicians from the surrounding communities on a part-time basis and other personnel—nurses, clerks, "sanitarians," and sanitation engineers—as well. The subcommittee reported that the Indian clinics operated for "a total of six hours or less weekly in one or two sessions." "[C]hild health care clinics, tuberculosis control clinics, and dental clinics were conducted" only occasionally on some reservations.[9]

At the time this report was issued, the New York State Department of Health, in cooperation with Erie County Department of Health, administered only one medical facility within the territory of the Seneca Nation of Indians—the clinic at the abandoned Thomas Indian School at the Cattaraugus Indian Reservation. There had been one at Steamburg on the Allegany Indian Reservation before the Kinzua Dam construction, which had provided services to only a small clientele largely because of its location away from the center of Seneca population. By the mid-1960s, no medical or pediatric clinic operated there, and Senecas at Allegany frequently complained about the lack of emergency care.[10]

At Cattaraugus in the late 1960s and early 1970s, two part-time doctors worked alternate weeks in the general medical clinic. Although there was a pediatric clinic, it was open for only four hours on Thursday mornings to deal with the needs of children. New York State's Interdepartmental Committee on Indian Affairs also noted in its 1968–69 report the lack of resident physicians near the reservation to handle the Indians' medical needs when the clinic was closed. Moreover, at that time, Albany's total funding for Seneca services—educational, health, and social services at Cattaraugus—was $137,592 per year out of a paltry budget of $769,765 for all of the reservation communities in the state.[11] Two years later, in 1971, in response to a major series of hearings by the New York State Assembly Subcommittee on Indian Affairs, the funding at Cattaraugus increased to $222,588, and state funding to all Indian reservations increased to $1,079,982.[12] As late as 1973, the total expenditure by Erie County and New York State Health Departments for medical services at Cattaraugus was merely $42,386.38 per year. The clinic saw approximately three thousand patients that year, so the administrative costs came to about $14 per patient.[13]

The Cattaraugus clinic was less than a quarter-mile from Cattaraugus Creek, a heavily polluted waterway. The Senecas had complained at least since the mid-1930s about the contamination in the creek, where many of their children swam and fished. The creek supplied the water for many home wells, resulting in a health danger to the community. Neither the Moench Tannery nor the adjacent village of Gowanda nor the Gowanda State Hospital had an adequate water-treatment plant, resulting in the pollution of Cattaraugus Creek, which flows through the reservation.[14] To make things even more dangerous for groundwater wells and recreation on the Cattaraugus reservation, nearby Little Valley, New York, was the site of the first commercial nuclear waste reprocessing plant in the United States, opening in 1966. Until 1972, when the plant was shut down, it was managed by Nuclear Fuel Services on a 3,345-acre site. In its six years of operation, the company had stored six hundred thousand gallons of radioactive waste on its property. The plant's operators were subsequently cited for carelessly releasing radioactive emissions into the area and causing seepage of stored radioactive wastes into nearby waterways, including Cattaraugus Creek. After the Nuclear Fuel Services ended its operations, New York State acquired the contaminated site. In 1980, Congress passed the West Valley Demonstration Project Act and over the past thirty years has spent hundreds of millions of dollars in an attempt to monitor the site and ameliorate the contamination.[15] Right down to the present time, the West Valley site has not been cleaned up, and Seneca Nation officials have repeatedly brought up their concerns at federal and state hearings.[16]

Importantly, in 1970 and 1971 the Subcommittee on Indian Affairs of the New York State Assembly Standing Committee on Government Operations, co-chaired by Joseph Reilly and Joseph Lisa, two assemblymen from downstate, held hearings and took extensive testimony at Native American communities from Niagara to Suffolk Counties, including at the Cattaraugus Indian Reservation. On August 28, 1970, the subcommittee held a hearing in the Saylor Building in the center of the reservation. More than two hundred Senecas attended, and official testimony was taken from tribal leaders. The subcommittee heard from the audience a number of long-standing complaints against the state, including on topics such as failure to properly educate Seneca children and to recognize

Indian fishing and hunting rights, land claims, and taxation. Importantly, the Senecas also brought up their environmental problems, including the state's inability to mitigate the contamination of Cattaraugus Creek.[17]

In interviews with Subcommittee on Indian Affairs staffers John Hudacs and Fred DiMaggio, I was informed that Assemblyman Reilly and other members of the subcommittee hoped to build trust with leaders within Indian communities and head off some of the tensions that had already begun to erupt in Iroquois Country. Although successful in a few areas, the subcommittee could never completely overcome the Indians' anger about the way state and local officials historically viewed and treated Hodinöhsö:ni´ communities.[18] In its groundbreaking final report issued in 1971, the subcommittee described the poor health care provided to the Indians by the state. The report pointed out that the state clinics' service hours were "too short"; that facilities were outdated, unheated, and not accessible to aged and physically challenged patients; that the clinics provided limited patient privacy; that medical supplies were inadequate and were too often not packaged; that physicians did not keep to their scheduled times; and that transportation to and from the clinics was a "serious problem" for tribal elders and the infirm because physicians did not make home visits.[19] It recommended that the state Health Department make a determined commitment to focus its attention on meeting with tribal representatives to establish a survey of reservation communities' sanitation needs. To ensure that the state would follow up on these recommendations, the subcommittee report advised the Indians themselves to monitor the responses to the survey and to conduct a survey of their own to determine their needs for added services.[20]

Winifred "Wini" Kettle, a politically savvy Seneca, was in attendance at this hearing, as were several other members of the future Seneca Health Action Group. Her father, Francis Kettle, had been president of the Seneca Nation during the thruway take in 1954. Wini Kettle had been elected to the important post of Seneca Nation clerk for 1968 and 1969. She was subsequently returned to that post in the tribal election of November 1971. Kettle was also the editor of the newsletter *Si Wong Geh*. All of these factors made her a formidable voice and leader on the Cattaraugus Indian Reservation. Seneca women's involvement in tribal issues and their efforts to lead the way were hardly new in 1970. Although women in the Seneca Nation did not receive the right to vote or hold elected political office between 1964 and 1966, their role in Seneca society was historically exerted behind the scenes as keepers of the kettle or mothers of the nation, often coming to the fore in times of crisis. Their traditional responsibility in Iroquoian culture was to maintain community, to ensure survival for seven generations to come.[21] A cadre of women who were mostly from Cattaraugus was soon focused on improving health care.

These women's timing turned out to be perfect. From 1968 to 1974, New York State–Iroquois relations were in turmoil. In 1968 and again in 1971, Iroquois Indians at the Akwesasne Mohawk and Onondaga Indian Reservations led major protests against New York State and local school district educational policies, leading to boycotts. In 1971, the Onondagas sat down on Interstate 81 south of Syracuse to protest state plans to widen the route and impinge on their tribal lands. In 1974, the Oneidas won a US Supreme Court case that for the first time allowed all eastern federally recognized Indian nations to sue in federal courts for the return of lands allegedly taken in violation of federal law. In the same year, a group of armed Mohawks from the Kahnawake Reserve took over an abandoned Girl Scouts camp in the Adirondacks at Eagle Bay, historic Oneida Territory, and proclaimed it Ganienkeh, Mohawk Territory. Although Seneca health advocates did not employ the tactics used by the Mohawks at Ganienkeh or those employed by the American Indian Movement at Wounded Knee in 1973, they were clearly aided by these actions because state as well as federal officials were now put on the defensive in dealing with Native American communities, which would lead to concessions in certain areas.[22]

Wini Kettle and Roseine Mohawk were the driving forces behind the Health Action Group's work in addressing the need for improved health services for Senecas. In 1972, Kettle was to receive a $1,500 grant from the national Presbyterian Church in her efforts to help organize the effort.[23] She and the other women in the group were to make use of the Assembly Subcommittee on Indian Affairs' report, which documented the insensitivity of medical personnel working on Iroquois reservations and recommended the establishment of a health aide program. This recommendation eventually resulted in the state Health Department employing Roseine

150THE IMPACT OF KINZUA

Mohawk as a health aide to monitor care and to ensure that Native Americans at the Thomas Indian School clinic received proper respect and satisfactory medical attention.[24]

By the summer of 1973, the Health Action Group announced a meeting in which Roseine Mohawk and Karen Kalaijian, a sympathetic public-health educator at the Buffalo office of the New York State Department of Health, would speak. The meeting's stated aim was to launch a major campaign to form a community coalition of Seneca and Cayuga residents to deal with health problems at Cattaraugus. The group announced the meeting and its objectives in *Si Wong Geh*: "Many people who are concerned with our health services have been deeply involved in trying to bring about changes—but it is up to the consumer of health services to make known his complaints and needs. It is up to the people on our reservation to establish self-help programs which can benefit all of the people. Let's *do* something instead of just talking about doing something."[25]

Nearly every issue of *Si Wong Geh*, the newsletter that Wini Kettle edited and distributed in the 1970s with the help of younger Senecas such as Marilyn Jemison Anderson and Mary Snow, announced the times and locations of the Health Action Group's community meetings, its long-term plans to improve health care, and its sponsored visits to health facilities off the reservation.[26] In *Si Wong Geh*, the Health Action Group attempted to educate reservation residents about how to maintain a healthy diet and ways to mitigate the effects of debilitating diseases such as diabetes and hypertension. Their columns gave information about how to recognize the symptoms of mumps and rubella and to lessen the incidence of strokes, heart attacks, diabetes, and venereal disease.[27]

After a year of being formally organized, the Health Action Group summarized its accomplishments in the pages of *Si Wong Geh*:

> [The Health Action Group has] renovated an unused room at the clinic to be used as a waiting room, provided free coffee for clinic consumers, insured [sic] the consumers' right to privacy while being interviewed, formed a clinic auxiliary to aid the clinic staff in non-professional routine tasks, requested a pharmacist for the clinic, had the WIC [Women, Infants, and Children] nutrition program extended to the reservation,

established a Family Life Clinic at our clinic, provided free Hematocrit screening, provided educational programs on cancer, human growth and development, respiratory diseases, communicable diseases, taken tours of various health facilities including Roswell Park Institute and Buffalo General Hospital, provided diabetic screening, sponsored a free chest x-ray day and helped make students aware of the role Indians can play in health care.[28]

These Cattaraugus women were clearly advocates pushing for health services that Native Americans by state law were entitled to but were not receiving.[29] In their activism, they presented the Health Action Group as an Indian rights organization, constantly referring to patients using clinical services as "consumers." They insisted: "Most importantly they serve as a means by which clinic consumers can make their complaints made known to the clinic staff."[30]

Because of her past service as the Seneca Nation's clerk and her great knowledge of the inner workings of Seneca government and state policies, Kettle remained a central figure in the group until she was later appointed director of the newly created Women, Infants, and Children Clinic at Cattaraugus. Her Health Action Group responsibilities were taken over by Roseine Mohawk, who was chosen as the group's coordinator, especially in its major effort—the collection of health data for a Seneca proposal submitted to IHS. *Si Wong Geh* described Kettle and Mohawk as the group's "watchdogs," who kept "their eyes and ears open for new programs" that pertained to health matters.[31] Both women recruited Senecas, Cayugas, and Seneca-Cayugas living on the reservation, including Marilyn Jemison Anderson, Jane Jackson, Alyssa Jemison, Maxine Jimerson, Betty Nephew, Faith Nephew, Olive Nephew, Edna Parker, Doris Patterson, Connie Pierce, Rhoda Pierce, Vicky Seneca, Pauline Seneca, Mary Snow, Virginia Snow, Fleta Twoguns, and Dodie White.[32] Although these Cattaraugus women and Lionel John drove the health initiative, the Health Action group also later included two Cattaraugus men—Ron Patterson and Gene Brooks—as well as Steamburg residents Nettie Watt and Anita Lillian Taylor, who supported the effort because the Allegany Reservation's health care delivery system was nonexistent at the time.[33]

In traditional Seneca society, women designated the chief of their clan to speak for them in council. Even though the Seneca Nation of Indians had replaced their chiefs with elected officials in 1848, the women of the Health Action Group employed that very traditional model. Lionel R. John, a former tribal councilor from the Allegany Indian Reservation, soon became their voice in tribal meetings. John, a physically imposing man, provided a bridge between the group and Bob Hoag, who had recently been elected president of the Seneca Nation. On June 8, 1974, the Seneca Nation Tribal Council formally designated the Health Action Group its official health advocacy committee. The council appointed Lionel John as health project director and assigned him to establish a health care delivery system at Allegany, allocating $15,000 for the effort.[34] Even before its official designation, the Health Action Group had already made some inroads in lobbying outside of the nation. Because of this lobbying effort, besides creating a state Indian health aide program, the state started dental services three times a week; initiated a family planning and immunization clinic; and extended clinic hours, including evening hours at Cattaraugus. Other changes followed a year after the council's designation of the Health Action Group and with John's able leadership. On April 5, 1975, the state opened a small clinic at Steamburg on the Allegany Indian Reservation. As a result, by 1975–76 state expenditures per annum for Seneca health care had risen well more than 200 percent since 1973: $42,851 at Cattaraugus, $42,851 for the new Allegany clinic, and a separate allocation of $8,087 total for two Indian aides at the clinics.[35]

Unlike earlier health reports that had been undertaken with little or no support from the Seneca Nation Tribal Council and had created significant backlash regarding "studying the Indians,"[36] one study conducted by two physicians at Myer Children's Hospital in Buffalo and Strong Memorial Hospital in Rochester, respectively, collected valuable data from 1968 to 1973. Dr. Henry Staub of the Myer Memorial Hospital and the Department of Pediatrics of the State University of New York at Buffalo had volunteered at the New York State pediatric clinic held on Thursday mornings at the Cattaraugus Indian Reservation. In 1973, working with Dr. Robert Hoekelman of the Department of Pediatrics at the University of Rochester

School of Medicine and Dentistry, Staub and two of his medical students collected additional health data at Cattaraugus. The 1973 study, made available to the Senecas, was funded by the American Academy of Pediatrics and Wyeth Laboratories and was later published in the journal *Clinical Pediatrics* in 1976. The physicians' report concluded that pediatric health care at Cattaraugus was no better than in big-city slum areas in Rochester and New York City because the Indian children were not receiving, among other things, their complete set of immunizations, and 56 percent of them were receiving poor care. They noted that raw sewage flowed directly into Cattaraugus Creek because of a downed sewage facility and that 30 percent of the homes on the reservation had no running water.[37]

From June 1974 on, Lionel John and the Health Action Group met with state health officials at the Saylor Building on the Cattaraugus Reservation, in Health Department offices in Buffalo, and at the New York State governor's satellite office in Manhattan. In hearing and studying officials' responses, the group's members came to the realization that the state Health Department's failures could not be fixed easily. Although they initially attempted to work with Albany officials, they soon understood that they were dealing largely with bureaucrats who were totally misinformed about the Hodinöhsö:ni´, their culture, and their health needs. Top administrators in the state health commissioner's office were totally ignorant about the Seneca Nation's legal status, not even aware that the Senecas were a federally recognized Indian nation.[38]

Although state expenditures for Indian health care rose, they were still far from being adequate. An internal memo circulated in the state Department of Health in 1975 frankly admitted major past failures. It listed four areas in need of remediation, the four C's: "communication; credibility, cooperation; and coordination."[39] To make matters even worse, the New York State Department of Health actually challenged Senecas' efforts at improving the conditions in which they lived. When the Senecas initiated a much needed housing project funded by the US Department of Housing and Urban Development in the mid-1970s, Robert Whelan, New York State commissioner of health, challenged their right to do so without abiding by his department's regulations. New York State attorney general

Louis Lefkowitz quickly dismissed Whelan's insistence on state jurisdiction, however, and acknowledged that Senecas were subject to federal laws in this regard, not to state departmental regulations.[40]

Despite this objection, the Senecas received support in their efforts from two regional employees of the New York State Department of Health at Buffalo—Karen Kalaijian and Anthony Golda, who complemented the Health Action Group's data-gathering efforts. Kalaijian and Golda prepared a report to Albany further documenting conditions and worked off state time to help the Senecas prepare their comprehensive health plan for IHS. Kalaijian and Golda submitted their detailed report to the health commissioner's office in Albany in June 1975. In the report, the two attempted to clarify state and federal health policies and responsibilities; provided a socioeconomic portrait of the reservation populations at Allegany, Cattaraugus, Tonawanda, and Tuscarora; described health care delivery systems on these four reservations; and made recommendations. Kalaijian and Golda were diplomatic in this report, stating the facts and never attacking past state Indian health policies. The report lauded the department's newly initiated effort in establishing the Indian Health Aide Program, which aimed to advance knowledge of reservation residents' health, and pointed out the opening of a new clinic at Steamburg. Importantly, the report praised the work of the Health Action Group and lauded the Seneca Nation's government for its formal establishment of a transportation program to make health services more accessible to the physically challenged and the elderly. Thus, the report gave support to the idea that the Senecas themselves could make their own decisions, run their own health program, and not have to depend on inefficient, culturally insensitive state officials.[41]

The Senecas chose to go another route to improve tribal health—namely, to seek federal funding. Once again the Senecas benefited by good timing. In 1955, the IHS, which had been administered poorly by the BIA in the Department of the Interior since the 1880s, had been transferred to the Public Health Service in the Department of Health, Education, and Welfare.[42] Even after this transfer, however, Native Americans still continued to have the worst health care in the nation and were increasingly bringing their complaints to legislators' attention. At congressional hearings, Native Americans called for reform of IHS policies, greater agency sensitivity to Indian cultures and needs, better medical facilities, and improved overall medical care delivery. Despite making significant strides in combating tuberculosis, IHS was substantially underfunded by Congress, and the medical services it did provide were housed in antiquated, subpar facilities. The Indian infant mortality rate in 1971 was 23.8 per 1,000, compared to 16.8 for whites. In 1972, the national mortality rate for Indians from bronchitis, emphysema, and asthma was 5.4 times higher than the national average.[43] By the early 1970s, IHS was also under attack because of its sterilization practices, which had a long and sordid history in certain areas of Indian Country.[44]

In 1974, a Senate subcommittee concluded that the IHS and United Southeastern Tribes (USET), a regional Native American organization based in Nashville, Tennessee, and founded in 1968, needed to work together to expand IHS's health care programs.[45] At the time, USET's member nations included only the Cherokee, Chitimacha, Choctaw, Coushatta, Miccosukee, and Seminole. Two years earlier, in the spring of 1972, Seneca president James George, accompanied by Allan Jemison and several youngsters, had attended one of this organization's conferences in Nashville. When George returned home, he had reported that the USET chair had indicated to him that the Seneca Nation would be welcomed into this association of Native American nations, one of whose objectives was to lobby for the improvement of Indian health care. Shortly thereafter, USET held a conference on alcohol abuse and treatment on the Allegany Indian Reservation, whereby its members became familiar with the Seneca tribal leadership and the very real health crises that existed in New York.[46] As a result of tribal councilor Lionel John's efforts, USET accepted the Seneca Nation as a formal member in 1974.[47] This southern-based organization was soon to formally change its name to "United South and Eastern Tribes."

From 1974 on, much of John's work was centered at USET in Nashville. John worked with USET personnel and William Millar, the newly appointed IHS–USET director of Tribal Health Programs. Millar, a pharmacist by profession and longtime IHS administrator who had been appointed to his post in response to congressional hearings of the previous year, befriended John.[48] He helped provide a health delivery road map to the Senecas that eventually allowed them to take advantage of the Indian Self-Determination and Educational Assistance Act of January 4, 1975, and later of the Indian Health Care Improvement Act signed into law on September 30, 1976.[49]

Dr. Emery Johnson, the head of IHS, had encouraged and advised Lionel John to undertake a thorough study of what was needed to meet the tribe's medical needs.[50] In 1974, Johnson recommended that Dr. David W. Kaplan of the Harvard University School of Public Health be hired as a consultant to administer a survey and develop a comprehensive health plan for the Seneca Nation. After Kaplan agreed to administer the study and help prepare a master plan, twenty-five women of the Health Action Group went door to door on the Cattaraugus Reservation in January 1975 to collect data about immunization, infant mortality, diabetes, and infectious diseases. In the winter months in frigid western, New York, they canvassed all ten distinct neighborhoods on the reservation: Irving, Bucktown, Ozarks, Four Corners, Plank Road, Newtown, Four Mile Level, Taylor Hollow, Pinewoods, and Indian Hill.[51] To win support for this survey and calm fears about data collection, the Health Action Group wrote about it in *Si Wong Geh*, clearly explaining to reservation residents the reasons it was to be undertaken. The group maintained that the survey was aimed at securing money for additional health services because the Allegany Reservation was without a clinic and the Cattaraugus Reservation had only four-hour clinic sessions two days a week. "The purpose of the survey is to determine what health services we need. Our Nation cannot be strong if its people are physically poor." The Health Action Group then announced that its direction would be not to look once again to Albany for help, but to seek assistance in Washington, DC: "The federal government has the obligation to all Indian people to provide health care and this is what is being attempted—to insure [sic] that we are getting proper services."[52]

The women were to reach 97 percent of all Cattaraugus residents. The information collected revealed the poor health conditions and the need to secure IHS funding in lieu of state Health Department support, which had obviously failed to come in the past. The survey revealed that 40 percent of Indian women had no prenatal care in the first trimester of their pregnancy; that 26.5 percent of every tribal member had diabetes, four times the rate in the general population; that *otitis media*, a swelling of the inner ear causing acute pain and hearing loss, was rampant in children on the reservation; that 18 percent of children had never had an eye examination or any dental care and had never been checked for anemia; that 50 percent of the children had never been immunized; that Seneca infant mortality was 41 deaths per 1,000 in the first year of life, twice the state average; and that Seneca life expectancy was only 51.1 years. The Health Action Group also reported that the Seneca unemployment rate in 1975, a year of a major state budget crisis, had risen to 68 percent. Unlike state bean counters, the Seneca women included those Cattaraugus residents who had given up seeking work, those unemployed for more than a year, and those infirm and unable to work.[53]

Now armed with this data, President Hoag went to Capitol Hill on May 13, 1975, and testified at a House Appropriations Committee hearing about the proposed 1976 federal budget. Among the items in the budget was a substantial increase in IHS funding. Two months later Lionel John formally presented the Seneca Nation's proposal for IHS services, with its attached supporting survey, to USET and IHS.[54] Again the Seneca timing was perfect. In 1975 and 1976, Congress passed two of the most important legislative changes regarding American Indian health care in the history of the United States:, the Indian Self-Determination and Educational Assistance Act of January 1975 and the Indian Health Care Improvement Act of September 1976. Having a detailed plan for health delivery and politically supported by two Republican congressmen from New York State—Representative Jack Kemp of Buffalo and Senator James Buckley—the Senecas were now in a position to take advantage of the provisions of these two major pieces of legislation.[55] By this time, state officials in Albany were willing to go along with the transfer of jurisdiction of Seneca health care to IHS. Of course, they could not ignore the damaging report by two of their employees, Karaijian and Golda. More to the point, the state was facing a major budgetary crisis. Commissioner Whelan of the state Health Department looked at the bottom line. In his communications, he never hid the budget-saving reason for his support of the transfer.[56]

Because of the groundwork done by Lionel John and the Health Action Group, the Seneca Nation was better positioned than most other federally recognized Native communities to take advantage of changes presented in the Indian Self-Determination and Educational Assistance Act and the Indian Health Care Improvement Act. Section 103 of the Indian Self-Determination and Educational Assistance Act directed the secretary of health, education, and welfare "to enter into a contract or contracts with any such Indian tribe to carry out any or all of its functions, authorities, and responsibilities." This section was to allow the Senecas to contract for IHS services for the first time. Equally important was section 104(b) of this act, which allowed the secretary of health, education, and welfare "to make grants to any Indian tribe or tribal organization for (1) the development, construction, operation, provision, or maintenance of adequate health facilities or services including the training of personnel for such work from funds appropriated to the Indian Health Service for Indian health services or Indian health facilities; or (2) planning, training, evaluation or other activities designed to improve the capacity of a tribal organization to enter into a contract."[57]

The next year, the Indian Health Care Improvement Act recognized past federal failures to provide adequate services to Native Americans, maintaining that "the unmet health needs of the American Indian people are severe and the health status of the Indians is far below that of the general population of the United States." It spelled out IHS's past major failures, including "inadequate, outdated, inefficient, and undermanned facilities"; personnel shortages; poor eye care and poor mental health, laboratory, inpatient, and outpatient hospital services; undeveloped or underdeveloped communication and transportation systems, which impeded access to health services; and deficient concern for public health in promoting better water and sewage systems. The result was the Indians' overall lack of confidence in IHS services. The act was aimed at providing incremental funding for improved health services and building new facilities or renovating old facilities over a seven-year period; it also provided moneys for training American Indians in the health professions.[58] In addition, IHS services were extended for the first time to off-reservation urban areas.[59]

Besides the Indian Health Care Improvement Act's general provisions, one specific section focused directly on the Iroquois. Section 303(a) gave "preference to any Indian or any enterprise, partnership, corporation, or other type of business organization owned and controlled by an Indian or Indians including former or currently federally recognized Indian tribes in the State of New York . . . in the construction and renovation of service facilities . . . and in the construction of safe water and sanitary waste disposal facilities."[60] Hence, not only were the Senecas awarded more money for improved health care, but any construction of IHS facilities would give preference to the Senecas' construction firms or those owned by other Hodinöhsö:ni´. Thus, the act both improved health care and infused construction money into an economically depressed northern Appalachian Indian community. The result was the building of a new Cattaraugus Indian health center that opened in 1977 and another at Allegany that opened four months later in 1978.

As a result of Lionel John's remarkable efforts, he was formally appointed Seneca Nation health director in 1976, serving in that capacity until he was elected president of the Seneca Nation of Indians. Over the next three decades, other tribal health directors—Marilyn Jemison Anderson, Patricia Canfield, John Hanley, Suzanne John, Thomas John, Rae Snyder Jones, Darlene Miller, Mark Reitnauer, Adrian Stevens, Anita Lillian Taylor, and Jay Toth—were to build on John's and the Health Action Group's achievements. Because of John and the determined women of the Health Action Group, Senecas were also encouraged to enter the health sciences. Several Iroquois women sought employment in this field after Rick Jemison helped establish a training program at Niagara University.[61]

When the US secretary of health, education, and welfare accepted the Seneca Nation's health delivery proposal sent to IHS, the Seneca Nation became the first to receive Public Law 638 status under the Indian Self-Determination and Educational Assistance Act, meaning that it was the first federally recognized tribe nationwide to contract its services with IHS, allowing it to hire medical personnel and implement training for staff.[62] Under the Indian Health Improvement Act, the Senecas received funding to construct two health facilities, one at Cattaraugus and the other at Allegany. In the early 1980s, each of the Seneca health centers was expanded. A new and expanded facility was opened in Jimersontown in 1992 and renamed the following year after Lionel John, who had died in February that year. In 1993, a second new and expanded health center opened at Cattaraugus. Both facilities were recently expanded, doubling their capacity.[63]

Today more than two hundred people are employed by the Seneca Nation Health Department to serve the needs of more than five thousand Native people in western New York State and northwestern Pennsylvania. Because of recent economic success, these Native Americans are no longer totally dependent on the IHS funding for tribal health needs and contribute approximately $12 million dollars to what Seneca president Robert Odawi Porter in 2011 called the "most significant program that provides services to the Seneca people."[64] The Seneca Nation contracts with physicians, pharmacists, clinical nurses, family nurse practitioners, and physician assistants in its efforts to manage and improve its overall health care. The current program is extensive. It is divided into three major areas: (1) clinical services—a wide range of medical, dental, and optical services; (2) community health—a women, infants, and children program as well as child and family services, environmental health, and health education and outreach; and (3) behavioral health—mental health and chemical dependency counseling as well as alcohol and substance abuse prevention. Besides operating two recently enlarged reservation health centers, the Health Department provides services to Senecas and Cayugas, some of whom reside in Allegany, Cattaraugus, Chautauqua, Erie (excluding the Tonawanda Seneca Reservation), and Niagara Counties in New York State and Warren County, Pennsylvania. A satellite office operates at the Millard Fillmore Hospital in Buffalo to attend to the needs of Senecas and Cayugas in this urban setting. The department provides transportation for Native Americans in need of chemotherapy and dialysis.[65]

Thus, the Senecas have substantially benefited from the changes in health services over the past four decades. No longer dependent on the poor and outdated health care facilities provided by New York State, they have built an infrastructure and a capable tribal management team to meet the needs of residents—children and adults—on both reservation communities as well as in the urban setting of Buffalo. In their quest for better services, a greater voice in decision making, and respect for their inherent sovereignty, the Senecas reacted to Albany's historic colonial relationship with Indians, which they considered debilitating, demeaning, and harmful for their survival. The result of their reaction was a model health program that has influenced those in other Native American communities. According to Marilyn Jemison Anderson, the Health Action Group member from the early 1970s who went on to become the director of the Seneca Health Department in the mid-1990s, "We wanted the Seneca people to be treated with compassion, dignity, and respect. We sought providers who were already seeing our community members and brought them to our facilities. . . . At that time we had the complete support of the [Seneca Nation] Tribal Council and IHS to develop our programs. New York State wasn't as happy as they didn't think that we knew how to establish such a program."[66]

Despite its successes in providing better health care to its people, the Seneca Nation is not without major health problems today. It has not succeeded in defeating two major health threats to the communities' welfare. Because of the epidemic of diabetes in Indian Country—Native Americans have the highest rates of Type 2 diabetes in the United States, and it is now common even among youth in Indian communities—the Seneca Nation established a special diabetes program in 1997 to face this scourge. The program works with tribal members to educate them about diet to stem obesity, a major factor in the onset of the disease; to promote exercise programs; and to monitor blood sugar. The IHS recently reported that these tribal programs, such as the one at the Seneca Nation, has had some moderate success—namely, a 10.4 percent decrease in blood sugar levels over the past thirteen years, resulting in an almost 40 percent reduction in diabetes-related complications.[67] In an attempt to prevent and fight off the debilitating effects of diabetes, Seneca president Maurice John Sr.'s administration in 2008 created the Health Incentive Program, which rewarded enrolled members who succeeded in changing their eating habits, committed themselves to healthy diets, and lost weight through a routine of regular exercise.[68]

The Seneca Nation of Indians, much like white and black communities in the United States, faces increasing health challenges. In a national study of alcohol and drug use published in 2005, Native Americans were found to have a higher rate of alcohol- and drug-use disorders than among any other racial group in the United States.[69] Random testing of four hundred

Seneca tribal employees recently found that 10 percent had illicit drugs in their system.[70] More disturbing, on December 23, 2011, President Porter reported that a recent study by the Seneca Nation Health Department found that 74 percent of all Seneca women who were receiving prenatal care at its centers had tested positive for drug use.[71] Hence, one of the greatest challenges to Seneca survival in the future is to find ways to combat diabetes and substance abuse.

The Senecas were to employ far different methods than lobbying when other problems came down the road. By the mid-1980s, any and all intrusions by the state government in Albany were to stir Seneca nationalism and lead residents of Allegany and Cattaraugus to coalesce and resist. In 1985, a Seneca battle line was to be drawn in front of the encroaching Southern Tier Expressway. Although the Senecas were to lose this battle, their stand at the barricades clearly changed tribal politics. No longer willing to accept the state's arbitrary hand in their nation's affairs, the Senecas were now going to push back forcefully.

8

Showdown on the Forbidden Path

THE KINZUA PROJECT had other affects on the Seneca Nation besides the large loss of Seneca lands in the upper Allegany River valley. The Senecas' immediate concern for tribal survival delayed the nation's filing of litigation on long-standing land claims. It also delayed tribal efforts to resolve the severely undervalued lease situation on the Allegany Indian Reservation. Importantly, the Army Corps of Engineers' condemnation of lands in the Kinzua project included more than the relocation of families who were displaced. Making a deal with the New York State DPW, without any approval or even consultation with Seneca officials, the Army Corps condemned additional tribal land for a planned four-lane state highway through the Allegany Reservation. This effort grew out of a plan by the New York State DPW, now known as the Department of Transportation (DOT), to improve, expand, and extend the 207-mile section of Route 17 that stretches from Binghamton, New York, to Erie, Pennsylvania, to establish the Southern Tier Expressway. The highway, soon to be included in the federal interstate highway system as Interstate 86, would traverse the entire length of the Seneca Nation's Allegany Indian Reservation. The take of a twelve- to thirteen-mile corridor between Steamburg and Salamanca during the Kinzua crisis and later the consummation of an easement agreement of nearly equal length from Seneca Junction west to Salamanca in 1976 have affected Seneca responses to New York State officials and their policies right down to the present day.

In colonial America, old Route 17 was part of a major trail from what is today's Tioga, New York, then well west along the Allegheny River valley, into Seneca Country. It was known as the "Forbidden Path." The Senecas' permission to travel westward along this major Indian trail was a prerequisite because they were quite protective of their isolation and their control of the region southwestward to the so-called Forks, where the Allegheny joins with the Monongahela to form the Ohio River. According to oral traditions, Munsee Indians were stationed along the Forbidden Path at Painted Post to warn their allies the Senecas about intruders traveling west along this route into the Ohio Country. One did not dare travel along this route without permission, or one might find oneself running the gauntlet in a Seneca village in an unlikely attempt to survive.[1]

More than two centuries after the French and Indian War, the Senecas were still protective of their territory; however, this time they were influenced by two additional factors: first, the land losses of the Kinzua and the New York State Thruway takes and, second, the activist politics in Indian Country, including in New York State, occurring at that time. In July and August 1985, Senecas sat down on a section of the Southern Tier Expressway that was being constructed through the Allegany Reservation, forcing a temporary closing of the highway. Although only a few Senecas participated in the actual occupation, and many Indians and non-Indians were highly critical of the action, the protest was to transform Senecas political behavior in dealing with Albany officials.

The Army Corps of Engineers' action to replace a two-lane highway with a four-lane expressway was tied to New York State road-building plans on the books since before the end of World War II. On January 3, 1945, Governor Thomas Dewey had requested the New York State DPW to prepare a postwar plan for highway improvements, which he claimed had been neglected for fifteen years. In 1953, he announced plans to construct four superhighways across the state to be connected to the thruway project. Soon thereafter, the westward connection of the Quickway, Route 17 from Harriman (the thruway nexus) to Binghamton was completed, and a new westward expressway along the southern tier of the state to Olean and beyond was planned (see chapter 3).

The issue of the Southern Tier Expressway lay dormant until the Kinzua Dam project began in earnest. Less than three months after the dam construction groundbreaking ceremony, a lobbyist for the Associated Industries of New York State advanced the idea of making Route

17 from Corning to Jamestown an expressway.[2] In February 1961, E. B. Hughes, the deputy superintendent of the New York State DPW, indicated that his agency had already made aerial photogrammetric and reconnaissance surveys of the route. Because the area had less traffic volume than the area eastward, he added that construction would not take place in the near future, but that "this will not keep us from going ahead with our planning and design work as rapidly as possible."[3] As early as March 2, 1961, just five days before President Kennedy's news conference in which he formally ended all speculation about halting Kinzua Dam construction, J. Burch McMorran, the New York State superintendent of public works, wrote US senator Kenneth Keating to discuss highway planning for the new and expanded Route 17 necessitated by Kinzua Dam construction. He informed Keating that his staff had attended a meeting with Colonel W. W. Smith Jr. of the Pittsburgh District of the Army Corps of Engineers as well as representatives of Cattaraugus County. No Senecas were in attendance.[4] It should be noted that the New York State DPW had a long-standing working relationship with Army Corps personnel on local improvements, especially those involving flood control.[5]

At the start of his long reign as governor in 1959, Nelson Rockefeller, taking his cue from his fellow Republican governor Dewey, announced an accelerated state highway program. In contrast to Governor Averell Harriman's tenure (1955–58), Rockefeller doubled highway construction in his first four years in office. In 1962 alone, New York State DPW highway construction contracts totaled $787,509,219 for 1,891.38 miles of roads, making the state first in the nation for awarding the biggest contracts.[6] In January 1963, Rockefeller announced his intention to expand the Southern Tier Expressway from Binghamton to Lake Erie and requested that the thoroughfare be made part of the federal interstate highway system: "New York has long been in the forefront of the states in its development of modern highway facilities. Its construction of the Thruway and other major parkways and expressways, both toll and toll-free, even before passage of the 1956 Federal Aid Highway Act, attests to its leadership in highway development. Furthermore, New York . . . has appropriated and obligated more funds for construction of highway and bridge facilities than in any previous corresponding period in its history."[7]

Although the federal government rejected Rockefeller's request for the state's inclusion in the interstate highway system and thus withheld federal funding, the governor nevertheless pushed on with the project. On February 14, 1962, a bill "to amend the highway law in relation to establishing state expressways on the state highway system" was introduced in the New York State Legislature. The bill provided that Route 17 would be converted into a modern expressway from the Broome–Tioga County line "through or in the vicinity of Jamestown and thence westerly to the New York–Pennsylvania border."[8] One of the concerns from the beginning was whether the state would maintain the old Route 17 and other access roads that would soon be bypassed once the expressway was completed. This concern was not voiced only by the Senecas.[9] In March 1962, Saul Corwin, the counsel for the New York State DPW, maintained that his department would not abandon the existing highways because they "serve as important feeders of the new controlled access highways and thus serve as a connection between the various smaller communities bypassed by the controlled access highway." He estimated that the annual cost of maintaining 210 miles of the new Southern Tier Expressway would be $1.25 million per year, a figure that included equipment and snow removal, but that an added $2.1 million would be needed annually for "personal [personnel] service and materials."[10]

Superintendent McMorran somewhat modified Corwin's commitment in April of the same year. Writing to the governor, McMorran insisted that his department believed "there is need in the Southern Tier Expressway for both Route 17 and the new expressway on the State highway system," but he added that the "abandonment of other sections of highway no longer needed" could be worked out with the "appropriate officers of the affected municipality."[11] Arthur Levitt, the state comptroller, and T. Norman Hurd, the budget director, supported the bill to amend the highway law; Louis Lefkowitz, the state attorney general, also supported the legislation, but he suggested that it be amended slightly in the future.[12] However, certain staffers in the Division of the Budget were more critical. Two of them questioned costs and whether existing state highways parallel to the expressway were to be maintained by the DPW once the new expressway was completed. They insisted that it was "difficult to rationalize State maintenance of two parallel highways."[13] Despite these concerns, the bill received substantial support in western New York. Lobbyists included the director of the Route 17 Association, the Chautauqua County Republican Party, the Allegany Board of Supervisors, as well as highway superintendents from Chautauqua and Allegany Counties. Interestingly, Amory Houghton Jr., then chief executive officer of Corning Glass and later a Republican congressman who aided the Senecas in their Salamanca lease controversy, wrote in support of the bill.[14]

After the state legislature's favorable action, Governor Rockefeller signed this bill into law on April 29, 1962. With its passage, the state still had to find ways to obtain the necessary lands for the expressway and at the same time to obtain rights-of-way from those to be affected, including the Senecas. By cooperating with the Army Corps of Engineers in the Kinzua crisis, state officials were to save money by finding a way to have the federal government lay out and pay for the costs of road building through the Allegany Indian Reservation corridor of the planned expressway. This joint effort was not something that suddenly occurred with the Kinzua Dam project; the Army Corps and the New York State DPW had been cooperating, especially on flood control, for decades in the Empire State.[15] From 1961 on, Army Corps representatives met with DPW officials as well as with various county leaders, including members of the Cattaraugus County Board of Supervisors, about expressway planning.[16] The Senecas were not invited to these meetings. In July 1962, the Army Corps of Engineers advised the Senecas "not to relocate where they would have to move again if the freeway [Southern Tier Expressway] should go through," thus indicating collaboration between the Army Corps and state officials. The Army Corps added that it would not build access roads "for two or three families who chose to move to an isolated area" cut off by the planned freeway.[17]

The same month, the cabal existing between Albany officials and the Corps of Engineers was exposed in an article by Brooks Atkinson in the *New York Times*. After conversations with George Heron and Basil Williams, Atkinson reported that although the state could not "condemn lands outside its jurisdiction, the Senecas fear that the state can secure them through the Army Corps of Engineers, which is building the [Kinzua] dam." The

New York Times drama critic observed that the planned expressway, violating the Senecas' treaty rights guaranteed by the United States, would use a wide strip of reservation land and destroy the Senecas' privacy, leaving the Allegany Senecas with mostly steep hills on their remaining lands, which they could not use for housing.[18]

On November 15, 1962, DPW representatives attended a public hearing at Salamanca High School called to discuss Indian and non-Indian concerns about the proposed Southern Tier Expressway. Attorney Arthur Lazarus Jr. cross-examined Edward W. Umiker, the state highway-planning engineer, about the project's impact on the Senecas. Lazarus asked Umiker whether the state would provide the necessary access roads, whether the state would collect tolls, whether the expressway would be fenced like the New York State Thruway, whether adequate underpasses would be provided to ensure the utilization of remaining reservation lands, whether more Indian land would be required for the extra lane and center mall, and whether the state would follow federal law that required Tribal Council approval for state use of reservation lands for highway purposes. Umiker replied that 102 acres would be required, 50 of which were in the Kinzua take area; that the construction would make use of federal funds and probably not be a toll road; that the highway would be fenced in; that his department could consider requests for underpasses as well as service roads into the resettlement areas; and that all legal issues and questions would be referred to the appropriate state agency.[19]

Attorney Lazarus brought the situation to the attention of Congressman James Haley's House Subcommittee on Indian Affairs in August 1963. When questioned by Congressman Wayne Aspinall about the Army Corps of Engineers' plan to condemn more Seneca land in the Kinzua project to facilitate the state's construction of the four-lane expressway, Lazarus responded: "I think this is a matter of principle that the Corps should not be stepping in as a volunteer to do for the state what the state otherwise has to negotiate with the Senecas and certainly the corps should not be asking this committee to give the authority to take additional Seneca land." He told the committee that he had been informed that representatives of the Army Corps of Engineers had met with the New York State DPW about the simplest way to acquire the right to obtain the needed lands, bypassing the Seneca Nation and its very real concerns. Lazarus noted that because the planned expanded expressway "cuts right through the reservation, there was no way a Seneca on one side can get to see a Seneca on the other side without going 5 miles down to Salamanca and 5 miles back." He questioned past promises made by both the Army Corps and state transportation officials. They promised crossovers, "but they have told us a lot of things that we never have got."[20] Lazarus also brought up that this land grab was in violation of existing federal law. Citing section 8 of the 1875 federal Lease Act, which established congressional villages on the Allegany Indian Reservation, the attorney pointed out "'that all laws of the State of New York now in force concerning the laying out, altering, discontinuing, and repairing [of] highways and bridges shall be in force within said villages, and may, *with the consent of the Seneca Nation in council*, extend to, and be in force beyond the villages in said reservations; Provided, nevertheless, that nothing in this section shall be construed to authorize the taxation of any Indian, or the property of any Indian not a citizen of the United States.'"[21]

Despite promises to hear Seneca concerns about underpasses and access roads, no outreach was forthcoming, leading the Seneca Nation to bring suit once again against the US Department of the Army. Five days after the congressional hearing, Lazarus filed a suit on the Senecas' behalf against the Department of the Army in federal district court in Buffalo. Representing the federal government in the case was US attorney for the Western District of New York, John T. Curtin, who was later appointed a federal judge and who was to play a major role in later decisions affecting the Senecas. Lazarus argued that the federal government's right to the land extended only to the same amount of land to duplicate and relocate the existing highway. Nevertheless, on December 31, 1963, federal judge John Henderson declared summary judgment against the Senecas, deciding that the secretary of the army had the authority to relocate Route 17 in the "Allegheny Reservoir project" and that the Corps of Engineers could take into consideration present state plans for a new and larger expressway. Henderson rationalized his decision by stating that it would produce savings by allowing for "a single acquisition and highway design to accommodate future improvement."[22]

The Seneca Nation appealed the decision, and the case was heard in the Federal Circuit Court of Appeals for the Second Circuit, but the three-judge panel ruled two to one against the Senecas. The court's majority opinion was written by Thurgood Marshall just before his appointment to the US Supreme Court. Marshall indicated that Congress had clearly given the secretary of the army the authority in the "reservoir project" so that no special enactment by it was necessary for each particular taking of Indian land and that Congress can "choose to delegate some of its authority in this regard to administrative offices and agencies" (that is, the Department of the Army and the Army Corps of Engineers). Thus, the secretary of the army acted within his authority. Showing a lack of understanding of the dimensions of the planned expressway project and of sensitivity to what the Senecas were facing with the Allegheny Reservoir and forced relocation, Marshall concluded: "It is hard to see how a four-lane road will interfere with communication among the Senecas so much more than a two-lane road." Judge Irving Kaufman concurred with Marshall, but Judge Leonard Moore dissented. Moore wrote: "Under the guise of a road of a higher standard, New York State is, in effect, promoting a public highway project quite independent of the water resources projects authorized by Congress." Noting the civil rights fervor of the times, Moore held that the federal government officials needed to become more sensitive to the rights of racial minorities, also pointing out that treaty commitments made by George Washington's administration to the Senecas should be respected.[23] Subsequently in 1964, the US Supreme Court denied the Senecas' writ of certiorari, thus ending the Senecas' effort to stop the Army Corps of Engineers from taking more tribal lands for the expanded thoroughfare.[24]

The construction of the expressway project was nevertheless to be delayed for a number of reasons. Even after the federal condemnation of land for the expressway, the state still had to officially obtain an easement agreement with the Seneca Nation, but none was forthcoming. Expressway development was on hold on until 1976. Instead, the New York State DOT, an agency carved out as a separate entity from the DPW in 1967, focused on other state projects, such as Interstate 88, as well as on building the expressway east and west of Seneca territory. Although the DOT frequently announced plans for the start of expressway construction in this corridor, published maps of the route, and held discussions with local non-Indian Cattaraugus County officials, they made no progress in winning over the Senecas.[25]

Highway expansion projects in other parts of the state and Native Americans' reaction to them were also to dramatically affect state–Seneca relations. In 1971, DOT implemented a plan to widen Interstate 81 south of Onondaga Reservation lands just south of Syracuse in order to provide an acceleration lane and improve highway safety. In 1952, the Onondagas had granted the state an easement over eighty-nine acres of their land for $31,500. The Onondagas argued that the easement agreement specified only repairs and improvements, not additions, and that in any case the agreement with the state was illegal because it was not approved in advance by the federal government. Thus, in August 1971, about one hundred Indians—mostly Onondagas but including Oneidas, Mohawks, and Tuscaroras—went to the road site and sat down to protest the construction project. From mid-August through the end of October, tensions built. By early September, more than two hundred Indians were sitting on the highway to make sure the construction was not resumed, and the situation appeared to be a stalemate.[26]

Governor Nelson Rockefeller met with the Iroquois Grand Council of Chiefs in late October to resolve differences, and a week later a six-point agreement was reached. The state agreed to abandon plans for the construction of an acceleration lane on Indian lands, to drop charges against Indians arrested, and to consult with the Council of Chiefs at all stages of the highway improvement project. In return, the Onondagas consented to allow the resumption of construction in order to provide a six-and-a-half-foot-wide highway shoulder, not a lane, with a three-foot wide gravel slope.[27] Thus, it was not surprising that in its final report Assemblyman Joseph Reilly's Subcommittee on Indian Affairs recommended that "semi-annual, informal meetings between tribal leaders and the [Transportation] Department's regional office representatives" be "conducted on the reservation."[28]

For the Senecas, the actions of the Iroquois Grand Council over Interstate 81 was not lost. Many, especially those Cattaraugus Senecas who remembered the New York State Thruway take of 1954, began to see that a similar protest action might help their nation stop future loss of tribal lands. A decade before the establishment of the American Indian Movement, a new activism among the Six Nations had slowly evolved. In New York in the late 1950s, it began with the Tuscaroras' failed attempts to thwart the New York State Power Authority from taking their lands for a reservoir for the Niagara Power Project. In 1968, Mohawks protested the denial of their Jay Treaty rights and Canada's policies of not recognizing Native Americans' free and unlimited passage across the United States–Canada boundary line. Moreover, from 1969 to 1973, Indian Country nationally was undergoing significant upheaval—the takeovers of Alcatraz, the seizure of the BIA office, and Wounded Knee—and the Hodinöhsö:ni´ were involved in all these events.[29]

By the early 1970s, the Southern Tier Expressway issue became intertwined with internal tribal politics. Those Senecas more closely allied to the Iroquois Confederacy's Grand Council at Onondaga—which included a significant number of members of the Newtown Longhouse as well as those longtime critics of the Seneca Nation's elected government and its operations, mostly the large Kennedy family at Cattaraugus—provided a constant and vociferous challenge to the Seneca leadership throughout the 1970s and 1980s. President Bob Hoag and his supporters frequently presented these critics as only one group of dissidents, largely unrepresentative of the majority of Senecas living at Allegany and Cattaraugus.[30] It is true that the disaffected elements within the Seneca Nation were but a small group in the mid-1970s; however, by the 1980s, they were joined by others on both reservations disenchanted with tribal leaders, especially with some of the policies and methods used by Hoag, who had dominated tribal government since the early 1970s. Their dissatisfaction was fueled by the continuing weakness of the tribal economy and the high unemployment on the two reservations. By the mid-1980s, these critics were also incensed by the Seneca leadership's outwardly friendly relationship with Albany (see chapter 11), whom many Senecas judged as the enemy.

In 1973, the New York State Legislature enacted chapter 31 of the New York State highway law authorizing state officials to acquire lands from the Seneca Nation of Indians "upon such terms and conditions as the Seneca Council shall deem reasonable" *and to obtain federal approval "if required by federal statute or treaty with the appropriate federal officials"* for the building of the Southern Tier Expressway. In exchange, the Senecas were to receive state lands in compensation for their land loss. The act stated that "in order to effect any such exchange the commissioner of transportation is hereby authorized to execute and deliver, in the name of the people of the state, a quitclaim of, or grant in and to, such property, to the Seneca Nation, involved to hold for the benefit of the Nation." Land acquired by the Senecas in this exchange were to be recognized by the state as reservation lands, "enjoying all the rights and privileges and subject to all the limitations which now or hereafter shall inhere in Indian reservation lands under law."[31]

Despite the passage of the bill, Attorney General Louis J. Lefkowitz objected strongly to the legislation, fearing its implications on pending Indian land claims litigation and in other New York State–Indian controversies. According to Lefkowitz, New York State's alleged power of eminent domain had been employed in Indian matters for almost two hundred years without approval by federal officials. To now include the formal provision in state legislation that federal permission was necessary before Indian land transactions with the state could be accomplished was to Lefkowitz a "serious admission" of state culpability in the past. He added that it would "surrender . . . the inherent sovereign powers of the State of New York." The state attorney general continued: "Existing laws of the State of New York provide whatever authority is needed to acquire Seneca Indian reservation land for highway purposes." He advocated that the governor seriously consider not signing the bill into law until "all present litigation on this subject has been finally judicially determined" because "it would be legally hazardous for this bill to be approved. It would recognize the necessity for federal approval of the exercise of the power of eminent domain over Seneca Indian reservation lands."[32]

The attorney general then concluded by maintaining that it "would be preferable that all the lands required for [the] Southern Tier Expressway be acquired by appropriation pursuant to the provisions of Section 30 of the Highway Law"—namely, through the state's alleged power of eminent domain.[33] Despite Lefkowitz's objections, Governor Rockefeller signed the bill into law as a result of pressures from DOT officials who had been lobbying for the route for decades and who were less concerned about any future legal fallout than was the Department of Law.

Although negotiations with the state resumed by 1973, the Seneca Nation was undergoing significant internal political upheaval in the early 1970s. No longer faced with fighting the thruway and the dam, the nation erupted in bitter divisions. There was even talk that the two communities would splinter apart, forming two governmental entities—an Allegany Seneca Nation and a Cattaraugus Seneca Nation—much like what had happened from 1838 to 1857 when the Tonawanda Band of Senecas separated themselves from the Seneca Nation. The two reservations had become increasingly divided, pulled apart by several specific issues, including whether to trust their leaders in dealing with the state on the Southern Tier Expressway issue. The Seneca Nation, as was true of tribal elected systems around the country, were also faced with open rebellion, including by Red Power activists who claimed that these governments were not legitimate and did not represent tribal traditionalists.

Tribal Council attempts to develop a viable tribal economy immediately after the Kinzua crisis failed, and high unemployment rates continued through the 1970s. The poor economic situation exacerbated the internal political situation. By 1972, the United States Pillow Corporation went into bankruptcy, and the constructed plant lay vacant at Cattaraugus. Soon thereafter, Fisher-Price, the leading manufacturer of children's toys, made a proposal to locate a $6 million factory on Cattaraugus. The Seneca Nation Tribal Council agreed to seek two grants totaling $5.4 million from the federal government, which would pay 55 percent of Fisher-Price's factory construction costs. Fisher-Price's corporate management had indicated that as many as a thousand jobs would be created at this new factory. Under the agreement with Fisher-Price, the Senecas would receive $40,000 in rent on fifty-five acres for twenty-five years, jobs for the Indians, and ownership of the constructed factory after twenty-five years.[34]

Despite the unanimous vote in the Seneca Nation Tribal Council, some Senecas challenged the council's actions and as the Constitutional Rights Committee even filed a federal suit to stop the lease.[35] About one-third of the Senecas in this organization were members of the Kennedy family, sovereignty-minded Indians who referred to themselves as traditional "Senekas." They were frequent critics of the elected Tribal Council and its creation of the First Seneca Corporation (Seneca, Inc.). Now, with the Tribal Council's approval of the Fisher-Price lease, Fred Kennedy and other family members began to question the legitimacy of the entire Seneca governmental structure as set forth in its original constitution of 1848. In criticizing the Seneca government, the Kennedys were joined by other longtime critics of state road building, such as the Van Aernam family.[36]

Other Senecas with close ties to the Six Nations Grand Council at Onondaga and critical of the Seneca Nation's elected system of government looked to the continued Seneca chieftain structure that still existed at Tonawanda and to the pronouncements of the Grand Council at Onondaga for inspiration. Although the Seneca Nation had been cast aside as a formal member of the Iroquois Confederacy when it deposed its chiefs and established an elected system in 1848, some of these critics hoped for rapprochement with the confederacy's sachems and a final acceptance back into the fold. They were greatly influenced by efforts in the late 1960s and early 1970s to bring Six Nations' communities together. At the time, unity meetings and gatherings were held at Tonawanda, Onondaga, and Grand River. Some Cattaraugus Senecas, such as John Mohawk, joined the White Roots of Peace, a group that had originated at Akwesasne and carried the message of unity and the teachings of the Iroquois Great Law of Peace to Native communities and universities throughout the United States. John Mohawk later became editor of the highly influential Mohawk newspaper *Akwesasne Notes*, which brought attention to Native peoples' problems and concerns around the globe and presented the Iroquois Confederacy at the forefront of correcting worldwide injustices toward indigenous peoples.[37] By October 1972, the Constitutional Rights Committee's case to void the Fisher-Price lease was quickly dismissed in federal district court on the grounds that no condemnation proceedings had yet occurred.[38]

The Fisher-Price lease became an issue in tribal politics throughout 1972. In November 1972, Dean Williams was elected president. An ironworker who had been involved in tribal government since the late 1940s, Williams had joined the Constitutional Rights Committee opposing the Fisher-Price project, calling the contract into question: "It would destroy our way of life. If you let someone on a reservation for twenty-five years they are likely to stay and stay and grow and grow."[39] He pointed to the Senecas' shrinking land base caused by the Kinzua Dam project, which resulted in restricted acreage for home lots.[40] One week after Williams's election, Fisher-Price, shying away from this politically divisive controversy, abandoned its plans and relocated to Kentucky.[41] Despite the end of the Fisher-Price project, Williams himself was soon faced with a growing challenge to his leadership.

Into this volatile setting came Meredith Quinn from Sisseton, South Dakota, an activist who claimed Santee Sioux heritage. At the time, the nine bands of Lakota, including the Santee, were litigating their Black Hills claim. Their attorney was Arthur Lazarus Jr., the very same longtime lawyer for the Seneca Nation. Many Lakotas, including Quinn, were opposed to a financial settlement of the Black Hills claim, which Lazarus and his firm favored. Quinn and a majority of Lakotas pushed instead for a return of land in the Black Hills. These activists considered a financial settlement a sellout of Lakota nationhood and the first step toward termination.

The timing of Quinn's appearance on the Seneca scene was no accident. In October 1972, activists had seized and occupied the BIA building in Washington, DC. In February 1973, the American Indian Movement occupied the hamlet of Wounded Knee on the Pine Ridge Reservation in South Dakota, challenging the elected system there and receiving worldwide news coverage. Senecas, influenced by the Grand Council at Onondaga, nostalgically looked back to the time when they had a council of chiefs, much like their relatives the Tonawandas, in a consensus-style government where clan mothers advised and sanctioned the appointment of new leaders.

With the high unemployment, the state knocking at the door for more Seneca lands for the Southern Tier Expressway, and lingering anger over the Tribal Council's vote in support of the much maligned Fisher-Price project, Senecas—even supporters of the elected system—began to question the council's effectiveness. In June 1973, the situation grew to crisis proportions when Quinn claimed that Senecas' reliance on their elected Tribal Council could ignite more Wounded Knees. At the annual Indian

Defense League dinner at the Sheraton Hotel in Niagara Falls, Ontario, he indicated that his mission was to expose the fictional nature of US Indian citizenship and assert Native American sovereignty under international law.[42]

The Seneca Nation Tribal Council's actions were now scrutinized more than ever. On September 12, 1973, the Tribal Council held an informational meeting about an ICC settlement award for the federal government's failure to carry out its trust responsibilities and for its improper acquisition of lands from the Senecas in the nineteenth century. A capacity crowd attended at the gymnasium at Saylor Building on the Cattaraugus Indian Reservation. Although no one openly voiced an opinion in favor of accepting a settlement award, others were vocal in condemning it, and without the Senecas' approval the council could not act. *Si Wong Geh*, the reservation newsletter, reported: "Some of the reasons against accepting the money revolved around fear of termination. Others stemmed from the fear of the individual not receiving his fair share, while some people may receive more than others." The crowd was further incensed by the Tribal Council's failure to plan adequately for the meeting. The newsletter indicated great dissatisfaction: "Poor acoustics, an insufficient number of information sheets, and the feeling that President Dean Williams and Councilors Gilbert Lay, Kenneth Waterman, and Floyd Bucktooth had provided an inadequate explanations of the bill, added to the confusion."[43]

Quinn, presenting himself as a traditionalist medicine man, and those Senecas he influenced began to challenge the Seneca Tribal Council at every turn. When the Tribal Council agreed to accept ICC settlement money, Quinn and his associates attacked the acceptance of the award as a sellout that would further federal efforts to terminate the Seneca Nation.[44] Presenting himself as an authority on Indian law, Quinn soon fed on this dissatisfaction, misinforming the Senecas that they had been terminated by accepting moneys from Congress in the Seneca Nation Compensation Act in 1964. On September 11, 1973, at the Newtown Longhouse, he called for the overthrow of the Seneca elective system and a return to a chiefs' council, the aboriginal system of the Seneca Nation. Responding to Quinn, highly respected Senecas including Calvin "Kelly" John, Harry Watt, and several faithkeepers of the Seneca Nation, countered Quinn's assertions that the Seneca leadership had favored being terminated by producing a letter addressed to former secretary of the interior Stewart Udall.[45] This response did not quell the unrest, and in early October there was an armed confrontation outside the Newtown Longhouse. Threats of violence spread throughout the Cattaraugus Reservation, with supporters of President Dean Williams on one side and those diverse opponents of the Tribal Council on the other.[46]

In April 1974, the Senecas voted 659 to 75 to accept $4.6 million as an award from the ICC for 4,395,000 acres of land lost between 1788 and 1842. The money was to be distributed equally—$810 per individual—and 20 percent of the award would be put into a separate fund for care of the elderly.[47] After the vote, in an effort to regain favor, the heavily criticized President Williams and his Tribal Council pledged themselves to fight any future attempts to reduce Seneca land holdings.[48] Criticisms of Quinn continued, and *Si Wong Geh* reported in August that even the American Indian Movement had disavowed him and his actions. Three weeks later the Seneca Nation Tribal Council refuted Quinn's statements and banned him from its territories.[49]

On a campaign focusing on law and order and tribal political stability, Bob Hoag was elected president of the Seneca Nation in November 1974. On his election, Hoag insisted that he "represented 99 percent of the 5,050 members of the Seneca Nation, and he maintained that the so-called traditionalists—he estimated their number to be only about twenty—"would stand up and realize that." He threatened that if Quinn returned, he would have the activist thrown off Seneca lands. He added that Senecas "live in the United States and in New York State. We want the services of both, and both have an obligation to perform some services for us on the reservation."[50]

In April 1975, the confident Hoag, an Allegany Seneca, announced that the Senecas had received federal moneys to build a hockey and box lacrosse rink at Cattaraugus as well as a bowling center at Allegany; other projects would soon follow, in-ground swimming pools and tennis facilities for both reservations, thus skillfully balancing the interests of Allegany and Cattaraugus Senecas.[51] Hoag announced that he and the Tribal Council were optimistic about negotiating with the state over the completion of the Southern Tier Expressway. He pointed out that state officials viewed the twelve-mile section of the Allegany Indian Reservation east of Salamanca as essential but that the Senecas would insist on three broad bargaining points if the state desired this easement. To the Seneca president, the state had to provide monetary compensation, replacement lands, and twenty-one fringe benefits. He also tied the Southern Tier Expressway project to plans for extending Route 219 southward, a move that he considered would promote Seneca tourism and economic development.[52]

In July 1975, the Seneca negotiating position was strengthened when John Curtin, now a judge in federal district court in Buffalo, held that the New York DOT's 1971 filing of maps under the state's highway law did not constitute extinguishment of Seneca title to the corridor sought by Albany for its completion of the Southern Tier Expressway. Curtin maintained that the plaintiff, the Seneca Nation, had unrestricted use and occupancy of these lands, citing the Oneida land claims case, and that the federal Indian Trade and Intercourse Act required a federal presence in all negotiations over tribal lands held by federally recognized Indian nations.[53]

Throughout 1975 and into early 1976, Hoag meet with Raymond Harding, Governor Hugh Carey's secretary; Raymond Schuler, commissioner of transportation; John Shaffer, assistant commissioner of transportation; and William Hennessy, the prime state negotiator with the Senecas for the Southern Tier Expressway easement, who had been involved in acquiring lands from the Senecas in the thruway take of 1954. Meanwhile, Hoag's opponents were attempting to stymie the effort, seeing any negotiations over land to be a sellout of Seneca sovereignty. Figuring that the Southern Tier Expressway negotiations were a good avenue to bring other outstanding issues to the attention of New York State government officials, Hoag met with regional and state administrators of the DOT. Both sides understood full well that the New York State Thruway take of 1954 and the Kinzua Dam project (1956–66) cast a heavy shadow on Seneca–DOT relations. Because of this history, several council members feared and expressed in council that the DOT was intent on acquiring title to Indian lands.[54]

Realizing the Senecas' sensitivity over loss of lands and fearing an Onondaga-style confrontation, DOT officials, in a highly irregular fashion, agreed to negotiate on a wider range of issues beyond the expansion of the Southern Tier Expressway. In the process, Schuler and his assistant Hennessy went beyond the legal limits of state authority and jurisdiction and federal law. Even after the Lefkowitz letter, Hennessy negotiated an easement land settlement with the Senecas without formal federal supervision under the provisions of the Trade and Intercourse Acts. State officials and the Senecas reached an accord only after Hennessy convinced the governor to pay the Senecas double compensation—money and land exchange—for the easement and only after Seneca president Bob Hoag was allowed to address the New York State Legislature. The Senecas, desperate for funding for economic development because of their high unemployment, desirous of tax relief, and pushing for the improvement of abysmal health facilities and conditions, approved both the agreement and the Memorandum of Understanding in July 1976. Although the Tribal Council approval vote was twelve to zero, four tribal councilors absented themselves from the vote—Maurice "Mo" John, Wayne Abrams, Francis George, and Gilbert Lay—a typical Seneca councilor strategy to express dissatisfaction and disagreement with the majority when outvoted, but to avoid appearing to be a recalcitrant and break consensus.[55]

State officials often incorrectly refer to the agreement over the Southern Tier Expressway easement as the "Lieu Lands Treaty," even though the state had no legal authority to make treaties with or without federal consent. Under this agreement, the Seneca Nation of Indians received $494,386 with interest at the rate of 6 percent from April 1, 1977. The Senecas also received 795 acres of lieu lands (out of the Allegany State Park) from New York State. In return, the Senecas granted to the state's DOT an easement for highway purposes only and agreed to the application of the New York State highway law for purposes of the agreement. In effect, the Lieu Lands Treaty facilitated the completion of the final uncompleted section of the Southern Tier Expressway in the environs of Salamanca. The agreement exclusively dealt with "the claim of the Seneca Nation of Indians for its tribal interest in the appropriated property" and was exclusive of any and "all claims of lessees and allottees." An original provision listing US interior secretary approval of the agreement was crossed out, so the only signatories to the Lieu Lands Treaty were Senecas Robert C. Hoag, Genevieve R. Plummer, and Calvin E. Lay Jr.; Commissioner Raymond T. Schuler of the DOT; and Gerald G. Hall of the New York State Department of Audit and Control.[56] It should also be noted that, separate from the "Lieu Lands Treaty," the DOT eventually allocated $1.3 million to be paid in the future to individual tribal members whose land was affected by the Southern Tier Expressway construction and to non-Indian lessees whose rental lands were also affected. The Allegany State Park Commission delayed the negotiations with its initial refusal to accede to the DOT's trade-off of park lands for Seneca tribal lands as compensation to the Indians.[57]

On the same day, the DOT and the Senecas signed a Memorandum of Understanding. It called for the DOT to construct and maintain two access roads of one-half mile each within the lieu lands, to maintain certain roads within the Cattaraugus Reservation, and to continue to maintain existing roads within the boundaries of the nation's reservation "in as good or better condition than other comparable roads in the state system of highways." The Memorandum of Understanding also conveyed a small triangular parcel in the Crick's Run area of Allegany State Park to the Seneca Nation, gave the Allegany Senecas preference in gravel contracts, and prevented building on a "buffer zone" area between Red House Road and the replacement acreage. It also dealt with a variety of issues that the Senecas believed had not been addressed by the New York State government in the past. DOT officials promised to support "legislation or administrative action" to exempt Senecas from state laws regulating hunting, fishing and trapping" as well as in transporting game on state roads beyond the reservations' boundaries; to support Seneca efforts at the state and federal levels to improve their medical facilities and health care delivery; to support the waiver of licensing fees for motor vehicles owned by Senecas; to support tourist development by recommending state funding; and to recommend state and federal funding for the development of a Seneca tribal minibus transportation system for the two reservations. Perhaps most important, the Memorandum of Understanding committed the DOT to "encourage and support legislation which, for the purpose of promoting and facilitating industrial development on the Nation's reservations, *provides relief from state taxes*, including corporation and excise taxes, for corporations and enterprises which commence commercial activities on the nation's reservations."[58] The state's failure to act on this last point continues as an open sore to this day in Seneca relations with Albany.

In stereotypical fashion, the DOT published a photograph in its annual report showing Hoag, Hennessy, and Richard JohnnyJohn wearing traditional regalia at the signing of the agreement. The hokey caption read: "Executive Deputy Commissioner William C. Hennessy was made 'blood brother' of the Seneca Indians and named 'Peacemaker' because of his five years of negotiation for Seneca land needed for the Southern Tier Expressway."[59] In news coverage, the Southern Tier Expressway agreement was inaccurately referred to as a "treaty" and hailed as a historic agreement between "equals," suggesting that both parties were especially pleased by the accord.[60] Nothing could be further from the truth. The drafting of the "Lieu Lands Treaty" led to problems almost immediately after it was consummated. As early as 1977, the state officials', President Hoag's, and the Tribal Council's actions were called into question, especially because the federal government had not been involved, as required by law to watch over and protect the Indians' interests. The signing of another easement allowing the state to use more tribal lands offended Cattaraugus Senecas, who recalled the thruway crisis of 1954, and Allegany Senecas were once again reminded of their flooded homeland taken for the Kinzua project. Indeed, the design of the Southern Tier Expressway stemmed directly out of the Kinzua Dam disaster. Despite the extensive positive media coverage, Albany officials also had some concerns about the agreement. In 1977, one year after the agreement was made, Lou Grumet, the special assistant to Secretary of State Mario M. Cuomo, expressed concern about this agreement because the US Department of the Interior had indicated in a letter that the accord had not been executed properly.[61] To complicate and intensify the growing crisis, the DOT began monetarily compensating non-Indian leaseholders for lands condemned for the expressway, to which many Senecas objected.[62]

Other Senecas, influenced by the actions of other Iroquois communities, questioned whether it would be wise to compromise at all with

Albany. They saw Oneidas, Cayugas, and Mohawks filing claims in federal court seeking lands back from the state (see chapter 9).[63] They witnessed an armed activist group of Mohawks win concessions from the state and secure lands known as "Ganienkeh" in Clinton County, near Plattsburgh, New York. By 1982, Seneca anger started to boil over when US representative Gary Lee and US senator Alphonse D'Amato of New York sponsored the Ancient Indian Land Claims Settlement Bill in Congress, which called for the extinguishment of all Indian land claims. Seneca President Barry Snyder Sr. immediately sent a tribal protest against the bill.[64]

Joy Bilharz has discussed how a post-Kinzua generation of Seneca women was emerging by the early 1980s. In 1984, they formed the Seneca Nation Women's Awareness Group, which planned and organized a commemoration of the Kinzua tragedy, calling it "Remember the Removal," to be held each year in September, reminding the younger generation of Senecas what their families went through during the 1950s and 1960s. This somber occasion would include a seven-mile walk from the bridge at Red House to the Seneca community building at Steamburg in remembrance of all those relocatees who gave up their lands, homes, and life along the Upper Allegheny. These same women were to play a major role in events that were to transpire on the Southern Tier Expressway.[65]

In February 1985, Senecas began their protests against the Southern Tier Expressway at the construction site along the planned link on the reservation. These demonstrations would reach a boiling point by July. On July 21, the protesters, numbering around thirty, set up a barricade and encampment, "Camp 17," at the construction site for one of the last links of the Southern Tier Expressway. They demanded the abolition of the state's right to take Seneca lands for the Southern Tier Expressway as well as for a future Route 219 project and the protection of ancient Seneca villages, burial sites, and artifacts threatened by road construction. They also charged the Seneca Nation Tribal Council, the BIA, and New York State officials with forming a "fraudulent conspiracy and colluding in dealing with Seneca lands." The protesters also accused the US Department of the Interior of ignoring its "trust responsibilities to the Seneca People."[66]

Although the Seneca Nation government and most individual Senecas had previously reached agreement with the New York State DOT, some Senecas continued to refuse to accede to the agreement. In the summer of 1985, the DOT had moved its road construction equipment near to and onto the property of these irreconcilable Senecas, leading to the July protest. Allegany Senecas such as Kenneth and Fred Van Aernam, whose family had done battle with construction efforts along old Route 17 since the early 1940s, and Floyd Redeye, who had refused to settle with the DOT's land acquisition personnel, led the protest. They were soon joined by Fred Kennedy and other Cattaraugus Senecas who had opposed the 1976 agreement with New York State and for years had challenged Bob Hoag's leadership as well as the legitimacy of the tribally elected government. Redeye insisted: "They [DOT officials] don't seem to understand the word 'no.' This is family land. I want to pass it on to my family. No amount of money attracts me."[67]

Despite the labeling of these protestors as "dissidents" by their Indian and non-Indian critics and dismissed as a fringe movement, numerous Senecas silently supported the effort, and others joined in the protest, including members of the Seneca Nation Women's Awareness Group, who had helped organize the Remember the Removal commemoration under the directorship of Brenda Pierce Deeghan.[68] College-educated women who had returned to the community after living in urban areas and being exposed to Indian activist politics of the early 1970s, such as Diane Beaver and Carole Moses, joined the movement. Moses was a Cornplanter Heir. Her grandmother, Martha Bucktooth, was one of the first women to serve in the Seneca tribal government. Moses and several other women who participated at the protest along the Southern Tier Expressway construction site near Salamanca had been children during the Kinzua crisis and had been relocated to Jimersontown as a result of the dam's construction. These young, largely idealistic women wanted the Seneca Nation leadership to become more assertive in defending tribal sovereignty and more protective of its treaty rights. They also aimed to strengthen the Seneca Nation's ties to the Iroquois Grand Council at Onondaga, which had been severed in 1848.[69]

The charismatic Maurice "Mo" John also joined the protests and soon formed, as Bilharz points out, the Sovereign Seneka Party. The anthropologist has accurately noted: "John was well known for his willingness to do battle with New York State and the City of Salamanca over issues of taxation and application of municipal building codes of Indian-owned properties." John's presence in Camp 17 was quite significant. Two decades later he would be elected president of the Seneca Nation of Indians, winning support for his strong stand against New York State's threatened imposition of its sales tax on the Senecas. His flair for the dramatic would include threatening to put up a Seneca toll booth on the portion of the New York State Thruway that crosses the Cattaraugus Indian Reservation and sending the New York State Comptroller's Office in Albany a bill for every car that crossed Seneca Territory.[70]

Because some of the protesters were individuals who had for years tried to overthrow the Seneca Nation's elected system of government, the Tribal Council did not openly support Camp 17. Indeed, Seneca government employees were threatened with dismissal if they joined the protest. The Six Nations' Grand Council at Onondaga refused to become involved in the demonstration, claiming it was an internal affair. Even some Senecas at Coldspring Longhouse looked askance at the protesters, who claimed they were traditionalists. Some questioned the protesters' commitment to the faith, and others who had lived through the Kinzua crisis saw the demonstrators' actions as naive as well as futile based on power realities.[71]

In early August, after seven months of protests along the Southern Tier Expressway, New York State Supreme Court justice Roger Cook issued a temporary restraining order prohibiting disruption of construction. Fred Van Aernam and others were arrested for trespass soon thereafter. On August 13, 1985, construction work was resumed on the Southern Tier Expressway from Seneca Junction to Salamanca; this section of the road was finally completed in 1989.[72]

The showdown on the Forbidden Path was no minor event in Seneca history. It had a short-term as well as a long-range impact on Seneca politics. To most Senecas, state officials had cast aside the promises they had made in the Memorandum of Understanding signed by the Indian nation in good faith in 1976. To them, Albany had not honored any part of the document—ignoring Seneca needs for economic development, minimizing Seneca fishing and hunting rights, and, above all, not taking seriously the Senecas' real concerns about taxation. Now was the time to become more assertive, and Senecas in both reservation communities, usually divided, were soon to express common opinions—namely, that there was a need by tribal leadership to take a harder line with state officials. It is little wonder that in the same year as the showdown along the Southern Tier Expressway, the Seneca Nation filed suit in federal court for other lands appropriated by the state, part of the Oil Spring Reservation, and began to focus on resolving a century-old inequitable leasing arrangement at Salamanca, New York.

9

One Win, One Loss

Seneca Land Claims

THE CRISIS over the Southern Tier Expressway from 1962 to 1985 was to push the Seneca Nation of Indians in another direction. It was to give impetus to its pursuit of land claims litigation in federal courts. The Senecas now sought the return of lands at Cuba Lake and on Grand Island, two territories that they believed had been fraudulently taken from them. By the 1980s, the Senecas tried to take advantage of a new climate favoring Native Americans and their rights in the federal judiciary, especially the US Supreme Court.

In the early and mid-1980s, I would visit an old schoolhouse building at Killbuck that housed the Seneca Nation's Maps and Boundaries Department to meet and discuss Seneca history with two remarkable Allegany Senecas, Cornelius Abrams Jr. and Duwayne "Duce" Bowen. Both men were to influence my research, writings, and applied work over the next thirty years. It is important to note that their families had been relocated to Jimersontown as a result of the building of the Kinzua Dam. Abrams, a member of the Coldspring Longhouse, had worked for years in Denver promoting tourism in Indian Country before his return to Allegany to head the Seneca Nation of Indians' Maps and Boundaries Department, where he and his assistant (Bowen) gathered, preserved, and analyzed cartographic records. Abrams and Calvin "Kelly" John, more than anyone I have met within the Seneca Nation, were the most historically knowledgeable tribal members. It was no coincidence that until his death in an automobile accident on the Southern Tier Expressway Abrams was a key adviser and researcher for President Bob Hoag. I always wondered why much of our conversations at Killbuck, at his home at Jimersontown, or on the telephone focused on the histories of the Oil Spring Reservation and on Seneca leasing. What I was not privy to was that the Seneca Nation leadership was beginning to focus more on these same two concerns.

The Senecas had long contemplated legal action to secure back some of their lost lands, but they had been stymied in the past by state and federal roadblocks. Until 1974, American Indian nations were precluded from suing states for the return of tribal lands because of the US Supreme Court's 1831 decision in *Cherokee v. Georgia*. Although they could seek monetary awards from the United States in the Court of Claims or from the ICC, they could not bring land claims suits against states in federal courts. On January 21, 1974, the Supreme Court unanimously overturned 143 years of American law. *Oneida Indian Nation of New York v. County of Oneida, et al.* allowed the Indian nation that had brought the suit as well as other federally recognized Indian nations access to federal courts in the pursuit of their land claims. This landmark decision held that the Federal Trade and Intercourse Acts (or Nonintercourse Acts, 1790–1834) were applicable to the original thirteen states. These acts regulated trade with the Indians and prohibited the unauthorized purchase of all land sales not approved by the federal government. They were designed to tighten the central government's control over Indian policy by requiring the presence and approval of a federally appointed commissioner at the treaty grounds when a state intended to extinguish Indian land rights. In addition, as was true of all treaties, before any cession of tribal lands could take place, the US Senate had to ratify the accord. On numerous occasions from the 1790s to the 1840s, officials of the State of New York, in clear violation of these acts, had ignored these requirements and had negotiated and "purchased" lands from the Oneidas and other Hodinöhsö:ni´. Justice Byron White wrote in *Oneida Indian Nation v. County of Oneida*: "The rudimentary propositions that Indian title is a matter of federal law and can be extinguished only with federal consent apply in all of the States, including the original 13." White added that the controversy arises under the laws of the United States sufficient to invoke the jurisdiction of federal courts. As a consequence, the Supreme Court reversed the lower-court decision and remanded the case to the Federal District Court for the Northern District of New York.[1]

As a result, several other Iroquois nations besides the Oneidas—Cayugas, Mohawks, as well as Senecas—tried to convince federal judges that their interpretation of history required the courts to recognize past injustices—namely, New York State's violations of the Trade and Intercourse (Nonintercourse) Acts that resulted in the dispossessed of millions of acres of Hodinöhsö:ni´ lands. I was one of the researchers in three separate cases—one Cayuga and two Seneca. My most extensive experience in federal court occurred in the summer of 2000 when I presented expert witness testimony based on research done for my book *Conspiracy of Interests: Iroquois Dispossession and the Rise of New York State*. I spent four days on the stand at the Hanley Federal Courthouse in Syracuse testifying about state failures to abide by the Nonintercourse Acts in negotiating the Treaty of Cayuga Ferry in 1795 that defrauded the Cayugas of approximately 64,000 acres. This experience in telling the truth resulted in retaliation by state officials, who attempted to fire me from my position as Distinguished Professor of History at the State University of New York at New Paltz.[2] In the two Seneca land claims cases, I collected copies of documents for the Senecas at various libraries and archives stretching from Albany to the Washington, DC, metropolitan area; wrote several reports for attorneys Arlinda Locklear, a Lumbee, and Jeanne Whiteing, a Blackfeet; and gave a deposition. During the legal efforts, I was amazed by how these two attorneys could quickly pick up 450 years of Seneca history that took me forty years to partially master![3]

Until the Supreme Court decision in the Oneida case in 1974, New York State officials' public reaction to these land claims suits was to minimize them as being far-fetched. Although these same officials admitted privately that much of central and western New York had clouded title based on its questionable land dealings from the end of the American Revolution through the Jacksonian era, they quickly dismissed Iroquois assertions.[4] After the state's 1974 loss in the Oneida case, the New York State Legislature began to allocate money for legal efforts to fight such suits because individual homeowners, local and county governments, and banks and title companies effectively lobbied in Albany. Opposition to Indian land claims also came from the New York Farm Bureau and state agencies such as the New York State Power Authority and New York State Thruway as well as from the New York State Department of Parks, Recreation, and Historic Sites.[5] New York officials also joined in with their counterparts in other states in seeking federal remedies. In 1982, Representative Gary Lee and Senator Alfonse D'Amato, both of New York, as well as Senator Strom Thurmond of South Carolina introduced the Ancient Indian Land Claims Settlement Bill into Congress. It called for a quick, "low-ball" monetary settlement, no land returned, and the extinguishment of all Indian land claims within six months after passage.[6] The bill sent shock waves through Iroquoia, with both elected and traditional tribal governments openly slamming the initiative. In his official capacity as Seneca Nation president, Barry Snyder Sr. sent a formal protest to Governor Hugh Carey. The bill eventually died in committee.[7]

In 1985, the Oneidas had brought a second test case before the Supreme Court involving more than 700 acres in their vast claim. The justices, in a five to four decision, held that New York State had violated the Federal Trade and Intercourse Act of 1790 and had negotiated a transfer of land title to the state without the required presence of a federal treaty commissioner, Senate ratification, or its official proclamation by the president.[8] In the same year, responding to this second Oneida success, the Seneca Nation of Indians filed a land claims suit against New York State for lands around Cuba Lake on the Oil Spring Reservation in Cattaraugus and Allegany Counties. Eight years later the Senecas filed a second land claim for Grand Island in the Niagara River in Erie County. Despite New York State officials' claims that the violations of the Trade and Intercourse Acts were merely procedural errors, Arlinda Locklear, who successfully argued the second Oneida case in 1985 and later was the attorney in the two Seneca land claims suits, has pointed out that this and other eastern land claims litigation were no "technical disputes hatched by clever lawyers," but rather "long-standing pleas for justice by the tribes, pleas that are based on established legal principles well known to New York State, and have been asserted by the tribes for generations in every form available to them."[9] Locklear's assessment is confirmed by a look at the Senecas' claims to Cuba Lake and Grand Island.

The Oneida Nation's use of the Federal Trade and Intercourse Act arguments in its 1974 and 1985 Supreme Court cases was actually first employed by the Seneca Nation of Indians in the 1880s and 1890s. Nearly 125 years earlier, two brothers from Buffalo—John C. and James C. Strong—then serving as attorneys for the Seneca Nation, used this legal argument for the first time in a case before the New York State Court of Appeals in 1891, which the Supreme Court dismissed on appeal in 1896.[10] The case centered on the Senecas seeking legal redress for the Ogden Land Company's fraudulent takes of lands at Cattaraugus in 1826 and the failure to protect Seneca interests as required by the federal Trade and Intercourse Acts. The litigation started as an ejectment suit against Harrison Christy, who fifty years earlier had secured 100 acres of Cattaraugus lands from the Ogden Land Company. The Seneca Nation brought the action first in state court under an 1845 New York law that gave the Indian nation the right to prosecute and maintain any action, suit, or proceeding in all courts of law and equity.[11]

The Senecas continued to pursue their land claims in the first three decades of the twentieth century even though their efforts to seek the

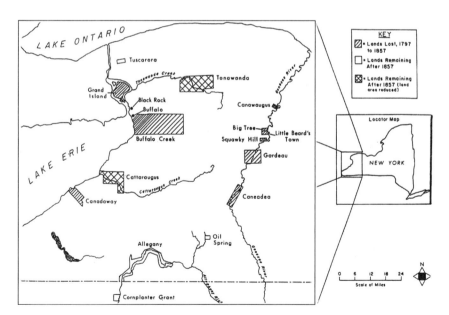

Map 6. Seneca Indian lands lost after the Treaty of Big Tree, 1797. Map by Ben Simpson. Author's collection.

return of their land had been denied in the *United States v. Christy* decision of 1896. In a ploy to get around this negative decision in which the court had in the end dismissed the Federal Trade and Intercourse Acts argument, the Seneca Nation, with the aid of its able Rochester attorney George Decker, attempted to seek compensation for the loss of riparian rights along the Niagara River. From 1912 to 1914, Decker and the Senecas unsuccessfully appealed directly to Congress for redress.[12] In the 1920s, a major Iroquois land claims movement emerged after the Everett report, an investigation by a committee of the New York State Legislature that threw light on how the Six Nations had been dispossessed of millions of acres of their lands after the American Revolution.[13] In 1927, however, the federal courts dismissed the Six Nations' claim to these lands.[14]

The Senecas also pursued claims under the Buffalo Creek Treaty of 1838, which had set aside more than 200,000 acres of Indian Territory in compensation for their and other Iroquois nations' removal. Federal officials had later sold off these lands, however, and the money had gone into the US Treasury. The Senecas had brought suit for these losses in the US Court of Claims. Eventually, after the Senecas pursued this claim through the lengthy legal process, the United States in 1898 awarded $1,998,744.46 to the "New York Indians."[15]

On August 13, 1946, Congress passed the Indian Claims Commission Act, which provided for the creation of a commission of three persons, later enlarged to five, with appropriate staff, to adjudicate claims against the United States on behalf of "any Indian tribe, band, or other identifiable group of Indians residing within the territorial limits of the United States or Alaska." Before the ICC's work ended in 1978, the act allowed tribes to file claims against the United States for Washington officials' failures in managing resources and enforcing treaties. Under the act, all claims had to be filed within five years; awards would be monetary, and no land or other property would be returned. Judges could deduct "offsets"—that is, deduct money spent by the US government for the benefit of the claimant. ICC decisions could be appealed to the Court of Claims.[16] To many Native Americans and their supporters inside and outside government, the Indian Claims Commission Act was originally seen as their opportunity to be heard, their day in court to seek redress. Yet the act was also part of the termination-era philosophy advanced by numerous members of Congress—a final accounting of Indian grievances, a payout, and the beginning of federal withdrawal from Indian affairs.[17]

In 1949, the Senecas hired attorney Paul G. Reilly of the firm of Earle and Reilly (later Reilly, Fleming, and Reilly) to bring several actions before the ICC. In 1951, the Seneca Nation filed its first petition seeking monetary damages from the United States for not carrying out its fiduciary responsibilities in protecting the Senecas' interests. This omnibus filing included the land loss of millions of acres from the Phelps-Gorham cession of 1788 through the Ogden Land Company cessions at the Buffalo Creek Treaties of 1826 and 1838; it also included the leasing agreements—Salamanca and the other congressional villages on the Allegany Indian Reservation. In 1958, the ICC directed the Seneca Nation to file separate petitions for these multiple claims of land loss. In 1963, the ICC rejected the Seneca Nation's claim, excluding the separate lease issue.[18] The treaty land-loss case was appealed to the Court of Claims. This court differentiated between Seneca claims of land loss prior to the Trade and Intercourse Act of 1790 and land loss after it. It held that the United States did have a trust responsibility after the passage of the 1790 act and that the Senecas had received "an unconscionably low consideration," only 43 cents per acre.[19] When the case was remanded back to the ICC, the Seneca Nation was eventually awarded $5,649,585.04 for its claims relating to its post-1790 cessions.[20] The debate over whether the Senecas should accept this award and how the moneys should be distributed led to bitter tribal infighting, especially at Cattaraugus.[21] The tribal dispute was finally settled by a referendum in which less than 30 percent of those eligible voted—659 for acceptance and 75 for rejection of the award (see the discussion on this controversy in chapter 8). Eventually 80 percent of the award was distributed per capita—approximately $800 for every enrolled Seneca—and an elders' fund was established.[22]

Previous to this award, Reilly had refiled a claim in November 1958 before the ICC seeking compensation from the US government because of its failure to supervise leasing arrangements on the Allegany Indian

Reservation. Nearly two decades later, in February 1977, the ICC awarded the Senecas a pittance, $600,000, because federal officials—namely, those in Washington's Office of Indian Affairs and Indian agents in the field—had failed "to properly protect the interest of the Seneca Nation within the boundaries of the Allegany Reservation, the major portion of which lands were and are within the present boundaries of the city of Salamanca, New York."[23]

Although the Senecas as early as the mid-1960s were apparently aware that the Oneidas were proceeding with their land claims case in federal courts and that the Cayugas, many of whom were intermarried with Senecas, had filed their litigation in 1977, they delayed pushing in a similar direction. However, the growing tensions with Albany policymakers over the construction of the Southern Tier Expressway and the state's insistence in applying the sales tax on Indian lands fueled the Senecas' commitment to file the Cuba Lake case in 1985. Although their Cuba Lake and Grand Island land claims produced very different outcomes, both cases were a reflection of the Senecas' greater assertiveness in taking on the State of New York. Attempting to redress past injustices, these cases united the Senecas internally and mitigated tensions that existed in their two very diverse communities. They balanced the interests and real concerns of the two Seneca communities at Allegany and Cattaraugus.

The Cuba Lake case, involving lands reserved for the Seneca prophet Sga:nyodai:yoh (Handsome Lake) in an 1801 codicil to the Treaty of Big Tree of 1797, also brought them into conflict with the Allegany State Park Commission, which administered the state park there. The commission was one of twelve governmental bodies established by Robert Moses in his master park plan for New York State during Al Smith's governorship. The Grand Island case brought the Senecas into conflict with the New York State Thruway, which administered Interstate 190 and the twin Grand Island bridges, built in 1935 and rebuilt from 1962 to 1965—projects also promoted by Moses and constructed by his assistant, William S. Chapin, the chief engineer.[24]

Despite the small size of the lands claimed in the Cuba Lake case compared to other larger takes by New York State, this suit was no minor one to the Senecas, especially to the elders of the nation and to the followers of the Longhouse religion. The loss of lands on their Oil Spring Reservation was of special importance to them. Oil Spring, a one-mile-square territory, had been personally given to Handsome Lake, the Seneca prophet, in 1801 by the Holland Land Company as an appendage to the 1797 federal Treaty of Big Tree. This land, which contains a petroleum spring used medicinally by the Indians from at least the seventeenth century on, is a sacred place to Senecas because it is associated with the prophet, his life, and his religious practices. It was protected by the venerated Allegany Seneca chief Governor Blacksnake, Handsome Lake's nephew, who in a legal action in the 1850s helped save this Seneca territory.[25]

At the heart of the later Seneca litigation known as the "Cuba Lake case" was the construction of the Genesee Valley Canal beginning in the late 1830s. The canal, 128 miles long, connected the Erie Canal near Rochester to the New York and Erie Railroad at Olean, New York, a major railway that had opened in 1851. This canal had only a twenty-year history of use, from 1858 to 1878. Yet for the Senecas it has had a major impact. From the 1850s onward, it led to court actions, federal hearings, and congressional legislation. The Genesee Valley Canal required the acquisition of land as a feeder for the canal. The Oil Spring Reservoir (Cuba Lake) was created in 1855 by construction of a dam on Oil Creek fifty-six feet in height. In 1863 and then again in 1868, the New York State Legislature authorized the raising of the water level of Oil Spring Reservoir. By the late 1860s, the New York State Canal Board, which funded, built, and managed the operations, took between 45 and 47 acres of the Oil Spring Indian Reservation. Another take followed in 1872. In that year, the water level of the Oil Creek Reservoir was again raised, this time probably five or six feet, and a further appropriation of 120 acres was made. This and other raisings (at least three other raisings after 1858) were necessary because it had been impossible to furnish enough water to permit traffic to go on in the canal during the dry summer months.[26] In 1866, the New York State comptroller paid the Senecas $1,396.04 for a portion of some of the lands taken. No other payments were made to the Senecas.[27] Thus, the Senecas' tribal lands were used as part of the bed of the man-made reservoir, renamed

Cuba Lake, for the spillway, and for a road constructed around the lake. The Genesee Valley Canal was abandoned by the late 1870s, but the artificial lake nevertheless remained state property even though the federal government had never acceded to the New York State purchase and expropriation of this Indian land.

By the first decade of the twentieth century, with the creation of its Conservation Department, New York State began requiring fishing licenses. The Town of Cuba encouraged tourism, and the lake became well stocked with fish. Officials who administered the Cuba Reservation (a 650-acre park) soon required anglers to have New York State fishing licenses. Indians were harassed and arrested for failing to have these licenses. Meanwhile, the Senecas insisted that outsiders be required to have Seneca Nation–issued licenses on their lands.[28]

Despite the controversy, non-Indians began building cottages around the lake without any federal or New York State legal authority and without knowledge and/or concerns for Indian claims to part of Cuba Lake and its shoreline. Just before World War I, state officials subdivided the lakefront property into building lots, built boat launches, and constructed a road around the lake, once again impinging on Seneca tribal lands. In 1913, the New York State Legislature gave the New York State Conservation Department the authority to lease these lots as vacation homes for boating, fishing, and other recreational activities. The white lessees as well as earlier squatters sold and resold their lots and the cottages they built on them, even though they had no legal right to do so. As early as 1914, state officials readily admitted that they had no accurate surveys indicting where state boundaries ended and Indian lands began.[29]

On January 5, 1927, Congress passed "[a]n Act to grant to the State of New York and the Seneca Nation of Indians jurisdiction over the taking of fish and game within the Allegany, Cattaraugus, and Oil Spring Reservations." Section 3 of the bill made reference to New York State's acquisition of Oil Spring "by condemnation proceedings" despite the fact that the federal government had never previously given its assent to the acquisition or carried out its responsibilities as set forth in the Trade and Intercourse Acts.[30]

In May 1928, Congress passed House Resolution 12446, "[a]n Act to approve a deed of conveyance of certain leases in the Seneca Oil Spring Reservation, New York." This second federal act granted "by quitclaim title a tract of land having a radius of seventy-five feet from the center of the oil spring located on the Oil Spring Reservation, New York, and a right of way three rods wide to such spring from the public highway now passing through the reservation." It retroactively confirmed a conveyance dated December 20, 1927, between the Seneca Nation of Indians and the Seneca Oil Spring Association, Inc. The Seneca Nation of Indians received $500, and the Seneca Oil Spring Association received the land for the specific purpose of preserving the spring as a historical monument. The act had a reversionary clause: "That the purpose for which the land is hereby conveyed shall be for the preserving of the spring as a historical monument only, and title to said land shall revert to the Seneca Nation of Indians if said land is ever placed to any other use."[31]

Most Senecas never accepted these congressional acts that on their surface retroactively confirmed New York State's position on lands at Cuba Lake. They later brought an action before the ICC. In a ruling in 1963, although admitting that New York State took Seneca lands—47.25 acres in 1858 or 1859 and 3.7 acres between 1863 and 1872—for the building of the Genesee Canal without any consent or approval by Congress or any federal government agency, the ICC decided that the United States had no fiduciary responsibility to protect Seneca lands at Cuba Lake because, it claimed, the Federal Trade and Intercourse Acts did not apply to Indian lands in New York as one of the original thirteen states.[32]

The issue lay dormant until the Oneida case of 1974, which allowed the Senecas access to federal courts to bring a land claims suit. In 1985, the Seneca Nation sued New York State in the Western District of New York for the return of the lands taken between 1858 and 1872. In 1993, individual lessees of the state cottages were added to the case as defendants.[33] As a result of Arlinda Locklear's legal groundwork, the US Department of Justice entered the case four years later as plaintiff-intervenor in support of the Senecas' position. On October 31, 1998, Locklear and attorney Jeanne Whiteing won a major decision. That day, the US District Court for the Western District of New York granted the Seneca Nation's motion for summary judgment against the state and the lessees, concluding that Oil Spring lands were illegally appropriated in violation of Seneca treaty rights and the federal Indian Nonintercourse Act.[34] The decision was affirmed on appeal in 1999.[35] The US Supreme Court denied the state's appeal for a hearing in 2000.[36] On January 22, 2002, Judge John T. Curtin, who had heard the original case before the Western District of New York in 1998, appointed Louis Coffey, a prominent attorney from Philadelphia associated with the American Arbitration Association, as the mediator to attempt to work out a land claims settlement. The mediation process was to take place for three years, during which there was a gubernatorial and presidential election, two elections of the Seneca Tribal Council, a restructuring of the Seneca's settlement committee, and the dismissal of both the Seneca Nation's attorney general and one of its two lead attorneys.[37]

Finally, in the early winter of 2005, Coffey worked out an agreement between the Seneca Nation Land Claims Committee—headed by Arlene Bova, a tribal councilor, and its attorney Jeanne Whiteing—and federal and state officials.[38] The accord was the *first* land claims settlement ever made by New York State with a federally recognized Indian nation! The *Seneca Nation of Indians' Official Newsletter* hailed the "returning of lands by the state" as "a historic moment in the nation's history." Later, President Barry Snyder Sr., praising the work of Councilor Bova and the Seneca Land Claims Committee, called it "a significant victory. This land has been kept from our nation since it was condemned in 1858 [by the state for canal use]. . . . [S]ince that time, we have tried to regain what has always been ours."[39]

The Cooperative Management Agreement Relating to Cuba Lake between the Seneca Nation of Indians and the State of New York, dated March 14, 2005, was signed by President Snyder; Daniel D. Hogan, commissioner of the New York State Office of General Services; and Michael D. Olson, acting principal US deputy assistant secretary of the interior for Indian affairs. It should be noted that state officials were willing to settle because the acreage involved was quite small—only 51.3 acres—in sharp contrast to other Iroquois land claims involving thousands and even hundreds of thousands of acres in more valuable parts of the state.

The agreement received state officials' support because the federal government agreed to facilitate the settlement by allocating $1.75 million to the overall pot of $3,882,000. In the end, the Senecas regained title and sovereignty over lands taken, "joint jurisdiction with the state over the public road, part of which is not on tribal land; and the regulation of use of the lake, part of which is not on tribal land." The federal government helped fund nineteen buyouts of lessees on Cuba Lake that impinged on Indian lands. Because the state retained joint control over the lake surface level and fishing and boating there, those occupants of lakefront lots not on tribal lands were largely unaffected by the accord.[40]

The Senecas' victory in the Cuba Lake case was not repeated in their second major land claims case, involving Grand Island, Erie County, New York. Grand Island, a massive land mass of 17,385 acres, divides the Niagara River into eastern and western branches. The island is the main access route between two of New York State's major cities: Buffalo and Niagara Falls. The New York State Thruway Authority maintains the major road and twin bridges that connect these two Niagara frontier cities. Today, the island contains seventeen thousand permanent residents, well-appointed suburban-style homes, a regional amusement park, two golf courses, two state parks, and sandy beach facilities.[41]

Grand Island has been associated with Seneca Indian history since the seventeenth century. Although centered from Canandaigua Lake westward to Genesee country prior to Euroamerican contact, the Senecas expanded their influence and territory well westward and southward in the middle decades of the seventeenth century. In 1651, they defeated the Neutrals, who occupied Grand Island and other islands in the Niagara River, and finally, after decades of conflict, the Eries in 1680, who had occupied lands south of the present city of Buffalo and lands along Lake Erie.[42] The history of Grand Island has been a convoluted one since the end of the French and Indian War, with different claims of jurisdiction and sovereignty by the Senecas, New York, the United States, and British Canada. The Senecas based their claim of ownership not only on the mid-seventeenth-century conquest of the Neutrals and the Eries, but also on the re-ceding of the Niagara River islands to them by the United States in the Treaty of Canandaigua in 1794, thirty years after the Senecas had turned over control of these lands to the British Crown in 1764.[43] They also maintained that the New York State–Seneca accord of September 12, 1815, that specifically ceded the islands was illegal because it violated the Federal Trade and Intercourse Acts in that no federal treaty commissioner was present and the US Senate never ratified the land transfer.[44]

Behind this 1815 treaty council was Peter B. Porter, the most influential white man in western New York dealing with the Iroquois in the first three decades of the nineteenth century. The state's leading entrepreneur in marketing salt, he was also chief agent of the Ogden Land Company, founded in 1810. He was elected to Congress before the War of 1812 and served as a general later in the conflict. In the 1820s, during the John Quincy Adams presidency, Porter served as secretary of war.[45] In 1815, he was the principal New York State treaty commissioner in efforts to buy Grand Island and the other islands in the Niagara River. He was joined in the effort by Governor Daniel Tompkins and seven other commissioners. In return for "all the islands in the Niagara River between Lake Erie and Lake Ontario, and within the jurisdiction of the United States," the treaty provided $1,000 payment to the Senecas and $500 to their chiefs, sachems, and warriors. The Senecas also reserved "equal right and privileges with the citizens of the United States in hunting, fishing, and fowling in and upon the water on the Niagara river," as well as the right to camp on the islands.[46] At the end of the War of 1812, with increasing talk about concentrating Indian populations to the Allegany Reservation or removing the Iroquois altogether from the state, the Seneca strategy appeared to be agreeing to piecemeal cessions of lands in order to delay and prevent larger disasters from happening. With the hovering shadow of the planned Erie Canal, which the Indians knew would bring rapid changes and white population growth, they had little choice but to cede over the islands, lands that were less central to their cultural existence when compared to Buffalo Creek or their other reservation communities.

In 1816, Porter, then serving as New York State's secretary of state, was appointed by President Madison as head of the Anglo-American Mixed Boundary Commission provided for under the Treaty of Ghent, which ended the War of 1812.[47] By June 1819, Porter and the other federal commissioners had focused their attention on the Niagara River boundary, and soon thereafter Grand Island was "awarded" to the United States, along with every island except Navy Island. On June 18, 1822, the Anglo-American Mixed Boundary Commission's final report was finalized at Utica, New York; five weeks later it was formally presented to Secretary of State John Quincy Adams.[48] In 1824, the state authorized a survey of Grand Island into farm lots. The next year this survey was completed, and these lots were immediately put up for sale at the state's land office in Albany. New York State sold these lots for a total of $76,230.[49]

In the twentieth century, the Senecas had previously brought their case before the ICC. On December 30, 1968, the ICC found for the Senecas, both the Seneca Nation and Tonawanda Senecas, on their claim that Washington officials had ignored their responsibilities to protect tribal interests in allowing the Niagara strip and islands in the Niagara River to be lost to New York State in 1802 and 1815: "The Commission finds that the Senecas were granted, by the Treaty of 1794, a compensable interest in the southern strip and island (but not the riverbed) described in the conveyances to New York of 1802 and 1815. The Trade and Intercourse Act of 1790 imposed an obligation to the United States to insure [sic] that the Seneca received a proper consideration for these cessions; any failure to meet this standard would amount to less than fair and honorable dealings under the Indian Claims Commission Act."[50] However, the ICC suit dealt with monetary damages from the United States for failure to protect Seneca interests but did not address New York State's actions in what the Indians perceived as a fraudulent taking of tribal lands. In 1993, the Seneca Nation initiated its land claims case for Grand Island and several small islands in the Niagara River, bringing suit against the New York State Thruway Authority and six individuals and businesses representing Grand Island property owners. The Senecas once again used the Federal Trade and Intercourse Acts argument against the defendants.

Unlike the religious motivation behind the Cuba Lake case, the Grand Island filing was prompted by other factors. In part, it was payback for events that had transpired almost forty years earlier. At the announcement of the filing, President Barry Snyder Sr., a Cattaraugus Seneca, once again brought up the bitter memories of the New York State Thruway crisis of 1954.[51] Snyder and certain tribal councilors clearly understood that if the Senecas could win the case and be awarded a land settlement in the vicinity of Buffalo, then they could have a chance to develop profitable gaming operations there. Although the tribal leadership still had to convince their own people about the merits of starting a casino operation, they understood that section 8c of the Seneca Nation Settlement Act of 1990 allowed the repurchase of former lands—namely, Erie and Niagara Counties—and the placement of those reacquired lands into trust. There were other reasons behind the suit as well. Congress's passage of the Seneca Nation Settlement Act, a victory for the tribe in November 1990, had emboldened its leadership to take more aggressive actions, especially when state officials tried to collect sales taxes. Increasing tensions with Albany officials over this issue had come to a head in 1992 with major Seneca disruptions of commercial traffic on the Southern Tier Expressway and the New York State Thruway.

The Grand Island case was to be litigated for the next thirteen years. In 1997, the Tonawanda Band of Senecas intervened in the case as plaintiffs because in 1815 the two Seneca governments in New York had been one entity. The two Seneca communities had united on this claim to the Niagara River islands as early as 1914 and had signed a formal agreement to that effect.[52] As a result of the appeal by Arlinda Locklear, the US Department of Justice, as it had in the Cuba Lake case, entered the litigation in 1998 as plaintiff-intervenor.

In 1993, when the Grand Island case was first filed, I was focused entirely on my academic career at SUNY New Paltz and writing on the Six Nations in the Civil War era. Except for providing historical background and testimony requested by Representative Amory Houghton and Senator Daniel Inouye on a 1990 congressional bill involving the numerous inequitable leases on the Allegany Territory, I was more focused on events that occurred at Antietam in September 1862. However, when my Civil War research was completed in 1994, I began focusing on the Seneca treaty period, 1784–1857, the precise time of these Native people's dispossession from the bulk of their lands. In mid-1996, the Seneca Nation and its attorney, Arlinda Locklear, asked me to do historical research and report on several possible land claims, including one for Oil Spring and the other for Grand Island. On February 28, 1997, I submitted these reports detailing how the state had acquired both of these Seneca territories and had accomplished these dispossessions without a federal commissioner's presence, without US Senate approval, and without a formal proclamation by the president of the United States.

Later, on a rainy morning, February 11, 2000, I journeyed from the old Edison Hotel on Manhattan's west side to a corporate law office across town. Seated with me were attorneys Locklear and Whiteing as well as June Lorenzo, an attorney from the Indian Law Research Center who was representing the Tonawanda Senecas. Across the table was Peter Sullivan, the assistant attorney general of New York State, who I thought would depose me on questions related to the reports I had filed. A second attorney, representing the private landowners on Grand Island, failed to make the deposition because his flight from Boston had been grounded owing to inclement weather. A stenographer transcribed what turned out to be a fiasco. Instead of asking me questions about the Indians' presence and use of the islands in the Niagara River, about how the state had acquired Grand Island, about when and how the United States–Canada boundary line was set, or for specifics about the state–Seneca treaty of 1815, Sullivan blew smoke, obfuscating the deposition, spending most of the time attempting to confuse me about the geography of the Niagara River and its two branches around Grand Island. The whole deposition wasted my time and the hard-earned money of New York State taxpayers as well as that of the Senecas.

In 2002, federal district judge Richard Arcara awarded summary judgment to New York State. The judge ignored the fact that besides the Seneca claim, British Canada had claimed jurisdiction over all the islands in the Niagara River until 1822. Arcara insisted that the Empire State had acquired fee title to the lands even before the 1815 state treaty. His decision held that the Senecas' aboriginal title had been extinguished much earlier, either in 1764 after Pontiac's War, when these Indians transferred the Niagara River islands to the British Crown, or in 1784 at the US treaty with the Six Nations at Fort Stanwix, an accord that had never mentioned these islands. Arcara rejected the Seneca attorneys' claim that the United States transferred these islands, including Grand Island, back to the Senecas under the Treaty of Canandaigua of 1794.[53] On September 9, 2004, the US Court of Appeals affirmed Arcara's decision, and in 2006 the US Supreme Court denied the Senecas' appeal, refusing to hear the case, thus terminating the action.[54]

With the failure of both the Oneidas and Cayugas over the past seven years to employ similar arguments and the federal courts' application of the equitable doctrine of laches, an era appears to have come to an end. No longer are the federal courts looking with favor on Iroquois land claims as they had in the two decades after the 1974 decision in the Oneida case. In 2005, the Supreme Court made this quite clear in *City of Sherrill v. Oneida Indian Nation*. In stating its reasons for denying the Oneidas' claim, the high court insisted that these Indians had not made a timely effort, even though the Indians had no way to seek to gain back lands until 1974:

> Given the longstanding, distinctly non-Indian character of the area and its inhabitants, the regulatory authority constantly exercised by New York State and its counties and towns, and the Oneidas' long delay in seeking judicial relief against parties other than the United States, we hold that the Tribe cannot unilaterally revive its ancient sovereignty, in whole or in part, over the parcels at issue. The Oneidas long ago relinquished the reins of government and cannot regain them through open-market purchases from current titleholders.[55]

Thus, the Senecas were defeated in their claim to Grand Island and restricted by the *Sherrill* decision in pursuing other land claims against New York State. Nevertheless, their assertions of sovereignty had produced a significant settlement in the Cuba Lake case, a cause they had been championing for a century and a half. Despite the small size of the claim, this was no small accomplishment. The return of the land at Cuba Lake, because of its connection to Sga:nyodai:yoh, had special meaning to most Senecas. Indeed, no other Iroquois community had ever been able to get state officials to concede on any previous land claim!

The pursuit of these two claims also illustrates the broker aspect of Seneca politics. The Cuba Lake claim, because of this territory's association with the Seneca prophet, had more religious appeal to Allegany Senecas and Longhouse followers at both Coldspring and Newtown. The Grand Island claim, which involved Senecas suing the New York State Thruway

Authority, was to some degree payback for this authority's take of Cattaraugus lands in 1954. The Grand Island litigation was also a way to put pressure on Albany officials to come to the table to negotiate on a gaming compact after a door was opened in a congressional act of November 1990. The latter litigation—the Seneca Nation Settlement Act—was to dramatically transform this American Indian nation over the next two decades.

10

The Salamanca Albatross

AT THE MAY 18, 1963, House Subcommittee on Indian Affairs hearing at Allegany Territory, Carl Zaprowski, a forty-seven-year-old non-Indian motel operator in Salamanca, testified that he favored the dam project since he believed that his business would be enhanced by flooding Seneca lands to create the lower Allegheny Reservoir. He saw the project as attracting more tourists who were interested in fishing and boating. Questioning the compensation package proposed in House Resolution 1794 and stretching the truth, the motel operator claimed that he had observed Senecas who were hunting in the take area, but he had never seen a member a tribal member fishing "down there" since his childhood. He dismissed financial help for the Senecas' loss of herbs and basket-weaving material because he claimed there was no more than one basket maker and one medicine man down on that reservation. While challenging the compensation package, he proudly indicated that the Seneca Nation was charging him only one dollar in rent a year, which he paid in taxes to the municipality of Salamanca![1]

Despite Zaprowski's incredibly insensitive and inaccurate testimony, the Seneca Nation of Indians' lease issue had to be delayed until its resolution by Congress in 1990. Housing for Senecas flooded out by Kinzua and other more pressing concerns had to be dealt with first. Importantly, Congressman James Haley, an expert at resolving leasing problems faced by Native communities, retired from office in 1977, and no other congressman was to take up the Senecas' longstanding concerns again until the mid-1980s.

I first became involved in the Seneca lease renegotiation process in 1985, the same year the Senecas filed their Cuba Lake case. That academic year I was to serve as senior fellow at the Rockefeller Public Policy Institute doing research on state–Iroquois issues. In March 1986, I was granted an interview with longtime state senator Jess Present, a distinguished-looking Republican from Jamestown, New York. In the Legislative Office Building in Albany, he politely answered my questions and indicated to me that the city of Salamanca was an "albatross around his neck" because he had failed to help resolve its major leasing controversy with the Senecas.[2] Every high school student of my generation growing up in the 1950s had been exposed to Samuel Taylor Coleridge's epic poem *The Rime of the Ancient Mariner*, which was required reading then. I understood Present's reference but could not empathize with the state senator's perception of burden. His analogy to the cursed mariner who shot the albatross did not make much sense to me. Indeed, in my own thinking, the Senecas, despite being innocent of a crime, were the ones who carried a weight around *their* necks, one even greater than an albatross; for well over a century, non-Indians holding leases in the City of Salamanca and its environs had frequently lobbied in both Albany and Washington to win title to lands on the Allegany Reservation.

Four months earlier I had accompanied several Senecas to a historic hearing held by the subcommittee of the US House of Representatives Committee on Interior and Insular Affairs—a hearing that was to positively affect the Senecas. On November 7, 1985, the committee, chaired by Congressman Morris Udall of Arizona, held its session on Capitol Hill to determine what federal efforts needed to be taken by Congress to resolve a century-old leasing dispute on Seneca lands on the Allegany Indian Reservation. Eighty-five percent of the city of Salamanca, New York, sits on the reservation. Thousands of non-Indian residents of Salamanca and five villages surrounding the city—Carrolton (Carrollton), Great Valley, Red House, Vandalia, and West Salamanca—had lived and done business there for generations based on leases confirmed by Congress in 1875 and 1880 and based on an 1890 lease act for ninety-nine years beginning in 1892. Approximately three thousand substantially undervalued leases were set to run out on February 19, 1991. Thus, with less than six years remaining on these leases, Congress first began to take up the fate of the city and the future of the Seneca Nation of Indians.[3]

Congressman Stanley Lundine, later lieutenant governor of New York State, had initiated the November 1985 hearing. Lundine, who had a reputation for evenhandedness, hoped to get the lease-renewal effort off the ground and resolve the issue for both Indian and non-Indian constituents in his southwestern New York congressional district. The hearing was convened, ironically enough, in the antechamber used by the Aerospace Subcommittee. The walls were filled with murals of man's achievements on the New Frontier, while the residual problems of the old frontier—namely, the tensions between the Indian and non-Indian worlds and the impact of the railroad on Indian lands and sovereignty—echoed in the chamber. Amid scenes of moonscapes on the walls, with images of Alan Shepard and John Glenn staring down, Chairman Udall called the hearing to order while I sat in the back of the room trying inconspicuously to take notes of the proceedings.

The hearing proved significant for my career and even more eventful for the Seneca Nation of Indians. Reporters scribbled notes, and an NBC television crew attempted to boil the two-hour hearing down to a one-minute segment for the evening news. Seated on separate sides were delegates of the Seneca Nation and their adversaries, the Salamanca city officials. House staffers, including Native Americans who wore their hair in braids and draped themselves in turquoise and silver, attempted to facilitate the meeting.[4]

Fearing that congressional interference would work against the Senecas as it had so often in the past, Calvin Lay Jr., president of the Seneca Nation, adjusted his wide shoulders and then testified before the crowded hearing. He specified his people's willingness to negotiate new leases, taking into account the declining economic situation and fair market value, suggesting that no federal intervention was necessary. In response, the city's attorney, David Franz, beseeching the legislators for help, indicated—incorrectly—that the intent of Congress in granting ninety-nine-year leases was to give "tantamount title" to the non-Indian citizens of Salamanca. He then urged Congress to "buy the city from the Seneca Nation of Indians." Congressman Udall and Connecticut congressman

Sam Gedjenson angrily condemned this logic. They insisted that the US government frequently awards ninety-nine-year grazing leases on its public lands, and yet this arrangement is *not* "tantamount" to awarding title to the lessee.[5]

The 1985 hearing was a turning point for the Senecas' claim because the leaseholders found Congress unwilling to side with their position and promote their interests as they had done so often in the past. Until that hearing, with the exception of three years during Franklin D. Roosevelt's presidency, and for the past 150 years, Congress, the US Department of the Interior, and the New York State Legislature had favored the leaseholders' position. The federal government had abandoned its trust responsibilities to protect Senecas, their lands, and their interests, allowing squatters onto the Allegany Indian Reservation, not supervising and later retroactively confirming these leases.

On June 28, 1850, the Seneca Nation of Indians' Tribal Council had leased a 145-acre right-of-way for $3,000 to the New York and Erie Railroad, later the Erie Railroad, for 11.66 miles of track through the Allegany Indian Reservation. Thirteen years later the Erie Railroad leased an additional 23.85 acres for $2,385 for the "construction, occupancy and maintenance" of its rail activities. These leasing arrangements had no required formal federal approval but rather were confirmed by actions of the New York State Legislature.[6] The result of this lease was an influx of whites onto the Allegany Indian Reservation; white farmers, persons in service occupations for the railroads, and others began to illegally occupy tracts of land on the reservation. By 1870, Salamanca alone had a population of 1,881 non-Indians.[7] Going against federal, state, and tribal laws, these non-Indians subsequently leased reservation lands at low rentals from individual Senecas. Five years later 420 leasing arrangements involving one-third of the lands on the reservation had been concluded, with a total investment by whites reaching well more than $1 million. By 1900, Salamanca's non-Indian population outnumbered the Senecas on Allegany by five to one.[8]

In 1865, the New York State Legislature passed private bills confirming the leasing arrangements. In 1871, aware that this action was illegal under federal laws and treaties, state legislators then approached Congress to confirm the leases.[9] The federal Indian agent at the time was also the attorney for the City of Salamanca and actually supported congressional confirmation of these illegal leases.[10] Senator Reuben E. Fenton, the US senator from nearby Jamestown, New York, who had been elected governor of the state, readily admitted the illegality of the leases but advocated that Congress take action to retroactively confirm them.[11] President William Nephew of the Seneca Nation and tribal councilors signed a petition challenging congressional action in support of the leaseholders, insisting that this action would violate treaties with the Senecas, the Federal Trade and Intercourse Acts, New York State laws, as well as "laws, customs, and usages of the Seneca tribe and Nation."[12]

In the winter of 1875, Congress confirmed the leases. On February 19, President Grant signed "[a]n Act to Authorize the Seneca Nation of New York Indians to Lease Lands Within the Cattaraugus and Allegany Reservations, and to Confirm Existing Leases." The act confirmed the existing railroad leases and created a commission of three members to "survey, locate, and establish proper boundaries and limits of the villages of Vandalia, Carrolton, Great Valley, Salamanca, West Salamanca and Red House with the said Allegany Reservation." These so-called congressional villages were subject to state legal jurisdiction. All existing individual leases were made valid and binding for a five-year period, after which they could be renewed for twelve years.[13] After seventeen years, Congress extended the leases, now totaling three thousand in number, for ninety-nine years, effective February 19, 1892.[14] All of these leases were substantially undervalued, ranging from $1 to $4 per year for residential property and $150 per year for prime commercial lots. And none of the leases had standard accelerator clauses attached to them to take inflation into account.

From 1892 to 1985, Salamancans believed that they could secure congressional approval for their efforts to secure title to these lands. By 1900, eight thousand non-Indians lived in the city. In 1902, Congressman Edward B. Vreeland, the president of the major bank in Salamanca, introduced a bill to force the allotment of the Seneca lands. If tribal lands that were collectively owned were divided up and distributed to individual Senecas in fee-simple title, Vreeland understood that this would facilitate sales to non-Indians. On the floor of Congress, he openly admitted: "I represent eight thousand people who live upon these [Seneca] reservations who hold ninety-nine-year leases from those Indians, and want to get a title to their lands."[15]

Although Vreeland's attempt failed, white Salamancans, as the 1985 congressional hearing later revealed, never completely lost their hope of securing title. After a while, many of these leaseholders stopped paying these minuscule rents to the Seneca Nation, and federal Indian agents failed to pursue delinquent lessees. Many Salamancans saw these lease payments as "inconsequential" obligations, in part because they were infinitesimal and in part because the white lessees assumed that the Indians were powerless to force them to pay.

After years of seeking redress on nonpayment or on the undervalued nature of the leases, the Seneca Nation finally found a favorable ear at the Public Lands Division of the US Department of Justice in the 1930s. By 1939, the Seneca Nation, with this department's aid, canceled eight hundred of the delinquent leases. At the centerpiece of Justice Department and Seneca concern was the "Forness case." Fred and Jessie Forness operated a large garage in the commercial center of the city. Under the Seneca Nation formula, the Fornesses' $4 per year rental of choice commercial property should have been raised to $230 per year. Their lease had been canceled because they had not paid their rent for eleven years. The Justice Department brought the test case on behalf of the Senecas to determine whether the Indians had the right to cancel the Fornesses' lease and other federally authorized leases because of nonpayment.[16]

In *United States v. Forness*, decided in the Federal Circuit of Appeals in January 1942, Justice Jerome Frank insisted that when the Salamanca leases were confirmed, Congress had a trust responsibility to protect the Indians from exploitation and that the case "represents the culmination of a long struggle by the Indians to enforce their economic rights." Finding against the Fornesses, the court restricted the application of state laws, insisting that the lessees were "customarily lax about paying their rent"; that all too frequently in the past they had been in default; and that the Senecas had attempted to cancel the delinquent leases in the past.[17]

As a result of the *Forness* decision, 627 leases were renegotiated upward. Partly in response to this decision, the New York State Legislature on March 8, 1943, created the Joint Legislative Committee on Indian Affairs. In February 1944, the committee issued a report that focused almost entirely on the Salamanca lease controversy and the Forness decision, which it characterized as a "reproach" both to the state and to the nation. Calling for the transfer of federal jurisdiction over the Indians to the state, the report recommended that the Salamanca lease issue be resolved by allowing the city to purchase Seneca lands.[18]

Adding insult to the indignities already suffered by the Seneca Nation, in 1950 Congress passed the Seneca Rental Act, which went into effect the next year. Because the BIA New York Agency was now closed, leaseholders under the provisions of the act paid their rental money directly to the City of Salamanca; the city would then forward the money to the Seneca Nation. Although this facilitated payment and replaced the role of collection undertaken by the Indian agent in the past, the legislation created the false impression that the city had paramount authority over "its residents" and that the Indians were simply ordinary landowners, not a federally recognized Indian nation.[19]

In the wake of Kinzua, the Senecas prepared to deal with the lease. In January 1967, the Seneca Tribal Council created its first lease-negotiating committee and named its membership: Floyd Bucktooth, Ralph Bowen, Calvin "Kelly" John, Leonard Redeye, Cornelius Seneca, and Martin Seneca Sr.[20] The council was undoubtedly inspired to push in this direction because the Senecas' advocate, Congressman Haley, was close to legislatively rectifying a similar long-term lease situation affecting the Agua Caliente Indians of Palm Springs, California. Haley was later hailed for his determined work in resolving Indian leasing problems. However, the Senecas apparently were sidetracked by the more immediate crisis over the Southern Tier Expressway.

In 1969, going against the wishes of the Seneca Nation and not consulting with tribal leaders, the New York State Legislature created the Salamanca Lease Authority, giving it official sanction to negotiate a settlement.[21] While city officials were attempting to strengthen their position by lobbying in Albany, Salamanca was in steady decline. Citing an article in the *Wall Street Journal*, the city's representatives blamed this economic downturn on the unsettled situation with the lease, implying that it was the Senecas' fault. On a radio program, President William Seneca, accompanied by Treasurer Calvin "Kelly" John, responded by insisting that the city's economy had long been stagnant and that city officials had done nothing to stem the downward spiral and bring new industry to the area. He reminded his listeners that the city's economy had been built on rail service, having three rail lines at one time, but now there were only abandoned yards.[22]

By the early 1980s, the lease controversy lingered despite the intense lobbying by representatives of the congressional villages. Mayor Ronald Yehl of Salamanca, Assemblyman Daniel Walsh, and state senator Jess Present lobbied for relief for the leaseholders and for state and federal intervention to aid the depressed region of southwestern New York, part of northern Appalachia. But the situation had substantially changed.[23] In 1988, the Seneca Nation Tribal Council established the Seneca Nation Salamanca Lease Negotiation Committee. It appointed Loretta Crane Seneca and Mae Chambers as co-chairpersons. Although changes in its membership occurred over time, the committee initially included George Abrams, Rovena Abrams, Iva Brant, Opal Frank, Art Hill, (Alice) Jean Jemison, Marlene Johnson, Max Lay, Rhoda Leaffe, Suzanne Smith, and Tessie Snow. For two years, the Lease Committee members met at the Senecas' Genevieve Plummer Tribal Building in Jimersontown to discuss strategies as well as with Cattaraugus County officials, including the mayor and city attorney of Salamanca. At every committee meeting, a BIA representative was in attendance to monitor and report back to Washington. Seneca attorney Loretta Crane and the tribe's Washington attorney Douglas Endreson also led the legislative lobbying effort.[24]

Crane, a Cattaraugus Seneca, was the daughter of former Seneca president Martin Seneca Sr., who had helped guide these Indians during the latter days of the Kinzua crisis. Her brother Martin, the first Seneca Harvard Law School graduate, had served from the early 1970s on in key posts in the US Department of the Interior, including being second in command at the BIA during Gerald Ford's presidency. Her uncle William, an expert on tribal housing needs, was president of the Seneca Nation in the early 1980s. Thus, Crane, who returned to Cattaraugus from Utah in the 1980s to work for the Seneca Nation, had the skills—legal and political—to understand both tribal and national politics, skills that aided her in her work from 1987 to 1991 helping to resolve the lease controversy. She and her family were well schooled in the deal-making politics of the Beltway and, at the same time, understood the highly charged political world of the Seneca Nation. Endreson, an attorney of Navajo ancestry, had previously worked for the Native American Rights Fund before becoming the Seneca attorney. Married to a Seneca, he had worked within the nation in Salamanca until he was hired by the major Washington, DC, law firm Sonofsky and Chambers. Marvin Sonofsky had long worked for various Indian communities and had participated in ICC cases, and his partner, Reid Chambers, had been the solicitor of the Interior Department during the Carter administration. Endreson was an outgoing person with a great knowledge of both Seneca history and politics. The two attorneys were to make a formidable team.[25]

While the Seneca Lease Negotiation Committee was holding its strategy sessions and preliminary meetings, the Seneca leadership was beginning to meet with Congressman Amory Houghton Jr. and his staff on ways to deal with the leasing controversy. Houghton was no run-of-the-mill congressman. His great-great-grandfather had founded Corning Glass Works in 1851. His grandfather had been a congressman and had served as US ambassador to Germany and later to Great Britain. His father had served as US ambassador to France. Hence, Amory Houghton Jr. was a member of one of upstate New York's most prominent and wealthiest families. Although a patrician, he had served in the US Marine Corps during World War II and was later educated at Harvard. From 1964 to 1983, he had been the chief operating officer of Corning Glass. He also served on several boards of trustees, including those for IBM, Citigroup, and Procter & Gamble.[26]

In 1986, Houghton was elected to Congress and was subsequently reelected easily eight more times until his retirement. In Congress, he founded the Republican Main Street Partnership, aimed to work across the aisle with Democrats on mutual interests.[27] He became an outspoken advocate on environmental protection, civil rights, and the promotion of the arts and historical preservation while generally being conservative fiscally on most other government funding issues.

Houghton's congressional office, as I observed it, was administered as if he were still CEO of Corning Glass. His disciplined staff was well prepared and businesslike on all matters, and so delays were not tolerated. Houghton's ability to "close the deal" carried over to his political career and made him a true force in Congress. Unlike most other members of New York State's congressional delegation, he, because of his sizable family wealth, was not beholden to others and was not in need of securing outside funding for his reelection campaign. His district was heavily Republican, and thus he had no challenges from local Democrats. His generous monetary contributions to his national political party and its candidates gave him great standing within Republican circles. Thus, at a time of Republican Party political ascendancy during the Reagan–Bush era, from 1980 to 1992, he was the right man in the right place at the right time to help the Senecas.[28]

While the non-Indian old guard in Salamanca continued to hold to their hard-line stance, three Seneca presidents from 1987 onward—Bob Hoag, Dennis Lay, and Calvin "Kelly" John—as well as members of the Senecas' Lease Committee presented themselves to Houghton as reasonable leaders willing to sit down with representatives of the congressional villages and negotiate as equals. To their credit, the Seneca leadership understood that Houghton was a key for them to achieve a satisfactory lease settlement. The Senecas furthered their cause by adopting Houghton into their nation, a method that they had used in the past in attempts to gain access to politicians. They also began working with Houghton's able staff on a bill to resolve the lease impasse. Houghton tried to break the lease deadlock by going in person to address the Cattaraugus County legislature, but he was soundly rebuffed. Although the representatives of the other congressional villages were willing to settle, those representing Salamanca refused to budge until May 1990.[29]

Realizing the city was close to bankruptcy, Salamanca's mayor Antonio Carbone had sought some quid pro quo in a settlement with the Seneca Nation. The *New York Times* accurately described the depressed conditions in Salamanca at that time: "Half the stores on Main Street are closed, giving the place a half-sleeping look, and many young people have already left to find jobs elsewhere."[30] Houghton's worked-out formula was thus appealing to the mayor and the city council. To sweeten the pot, the congressman would convince the Seneca Nation leadership to use a small portion of the future settlement money provided in the proposed bill for the city's future economic development. In July 1990, Carbone informed Houghton that he and the Common Council of the City of Salamanca had voted to accept the proposal worked out by the Seneca Nation and the Salamanca Lease Authority.[31]

Now Houghton needed to gain Albany Democrats' support for his bill. Because of a crisis at the Akwesasne Mohawk Indian Reservation involving differences over the establishment of a casino, Houghton was to get Democrat support and Governor Mario Cuomo's endorsement. In 1989 and 1990, an internal Mohawk tribal dispute led to civil strife on the reservation. Albany officials ignored the warning signs, and their statements and policies only aggravated the situation. These same officials had for years failed to deal seriously with legitimate concerns, including the Mohawks' major environmental crisis as well as land claims issues; they had also insisted on imposing the state sales tax on Mohawk sales of cigarettes and gasoline, a move that further exacerbated the situation. In addition, Governor Cuomo reacted slowly in his response to violence occurring there. Only after a killing and continue threats of retaliation did the governor send state police to end the conflict. The governor's credentials as a liberal and an advocate for human rights were called into question, so he needed to rebuild his image by fostering cooperation with another Hodinöhsö:ni´ nation. As a result, Houghton, a master of persuasion, facilitated Albany's acceptance of his efforts in the Seneca leasing issue. Governor Cuomo's representative, attorney Robert Batson, was later to testify in support of the settlement.[32]

Houghton's proposal, known as the "40/40 bill," called for a $35 million payment by the federal government and $25 million by New York State for past inequities and failure to protect the Indians' interests. The Senecas would agree to renew the leases for the congressional villages for forty years, with the option for another forty years, providing the leases were not in default. Of the $35 million from federal coffers, $30 million would go directly to the Seneca Nation as a cash payment for them to manage, invest, or use. Importantly for compromise with the leaseholders, $5 million would be used by the Seneca Nation for economic development, including within the City of Salamanca. Section 8(c) of the proposed bill contained a provision for the acquisition of land by the Indians "within or near proximity of former reservation land" that could be added to the Seneca Nation territory in accordance with procedures set forth by the secretary of the interior. This provision in the bill later proved especially important, allowing the Seneca Nation to build and manage gaming operations off the Allegany and Cattaraugus Reservations at Niagara Falls and Buffalo.[33] Houghton was soon to win support from the New York State congressional delegation, including from Republican senator Alfonse D'Amato and Democrat senator Daniel Patrick Moynihan, the powerful chairman of the Senate Finance Committee. Both were sponsors of the identical Houghton bill in the Senate.[34]

The Senecas then hired the eminent economist Joseph Stiglitz, then of Stanford University, to evaluate the impact of the undervalued leases on their nation. This scholar—who later won the Nobel Prize for Economics, headed President Clinton's Council of Economic Advisers and served as chief economist of the World Bank—developed a detailed report that the Senecas later submitted to both the House Committee on Interior and Insular Affairs and the Senate Select Committee on Indian Affairs. His report concluded that the Seneca Nation had lost $262,196,000 in potential revenues because of the leases in the City of Salamanca alone, not counting those in the other five congressional villages. Stiglitz's calculations were based on what would have been fair-rental-valued leases and investment of these moneys in safe government securities.[35]

Although not all Senecas favored Houghton's plan and wanted more payback for the past racist treatment they had endured, they agreed to the congressman's formula, realizing that the Senecas' economy was at that time tied to the city's survival. Some Senecas were married to non-Indian residents of the city, and so familial ties required compromise. On the other side, non-Indian Salamancans were divided as well. Although many non-Indian residents recognized that they were paying grossly minimal rental amounts, ranging from $1 a year for residential property up to $125 a year for prime commercial lots in Salamanca, and that the total payment by the city to the Seneca Nation was merely $17,000 a year, others refused to admit that the Indians had been taken advantage of in the past or that the inequities were continuing in 1990.[36] A local organization opposing congressional action, the Salamanca Coalition of United Taxpayers (SCOUT), arose and refused to accept the mayor's accord with the Seneca Nation. Call-in radio in Cattaraugus County spewed hate and condemned Carbone, Houghton, and the Senecas.

In early to mid-August 1990, I received several telephone calls from Sheila Seelye, a legislative assistant in Congressman Houghton's office; from Pete Taylor of the Senate Select Committee on Indian Affairs; and from Cheryl Ray, the treasurer of the Seneca Nation, about testifying before two committees of Congress based on my two decades of research and writings about the Seneca leases. Taylor had read one of my articles and had suggested to Senator Daniel Inouye, chair of the Senate Select Committee on Indian Affairs, that I should provide testimony. I later found out that the Seneca Lease Committee had shared my writings on the subject with Congressman Houghton and his staff. I received a formal invitation to testify in early September.[37]

In the second week of September 1990, I arrived at the Hotel Lombardy, about a three-mile walk from Capitol Hill. There I met a delegation of Senecas, members of the Seneca Lease Committee, including Marlene Johnson, Mae Chambers, and Rovena Abrams. The next day I accompanied these women, along with attorneys Crane and Endreson, to the Rayburn Building, where we met with Senate Committee on Interior and Insular Affairs member Ben Nighthorse Campbell, then a Colorado Democratic congressman—he later switched parties to run as a Republican for the Senate. Campbell was a member of the Northern Cheyenne Nation. On the walls of his congressional office, I saw the many honors that Campbell had received as a world-class judo champion and as a Native American artist. However, there was an uneasiness to the meeting. I could easily see the gulf that existed between the Washington Beltway and the reservation and between Plains Indians and eastern Native peoples. Although polite, Campbell appeared to be something out of a Hollywood movie, giving his support to his "blood brothers," but not really connecting with the Seneca delegation that was going to appear the next day before the House Committee on Interior and Insular Affairs.

On September 13, the House committee convened—with Congressman Campbell presiding in the absence of Morris Udall, who was suffering from the effects of Parkinson's disease—to hear testimony on Houghton's bill. I was guided to the witness table and seated next to Congressman Houghton. I listened to Houghton's testimony all the while beginning to find myself nervously thinking about my testimony that was scheduled to follow. Besides submitting written testimony, I was to summarize in less than ten minutes my twenty years of research on the history of the Salamanca leases. As a college professor so used to lecturing before undergraduates while moving around the classroom, I now had to testify seated before an august congressional committee, with the president of the Seneca Nation, his opponents, congressional staffers, and journalists seated behind me. Five days later I had to repeat the testimony about the history of the leases before Senator Daniel Inouye's Senate Select Committee on Indian Affairs, but this time there were glaring lights that blinded me so that I couldn't see the committee members in the front of the room and that made the room uncomfortably warm.[38]

Seneca representatives followed my testimony at the House hearing on September 13 and again on September 18 at the Senate hearing. President Dennis Lay recounted the long and difficult work done by the Seneca Nation Lease Negotiation Committee, to which the Tribal Council had given wide authority. He indicated that the Department of the Interior had been involved in the settlement process and that a BIA representative had attended the negotiating sessions. Lay insisted that "six generations of Seneca people have now lived with this controversy," confirming my earlier opinion that the Senecas were the ones with the albatross around their necks. Although feeling angry about how the Senecas "have been treated for one hundred years, and about how much we have lost," the Seneca president, a former police officer on the Cattaraugus Indian Reservation, carefully described how his nation's government had decided to push for a congressional settlement bill. Lay mentioned that before the Senecas signed any new leases, the inequities of the past had to be resolved first. The Seneca president went on: "We can never be fully compensated—we cannot regain one hundred years of lost control of our lands," and "no amount of money could compensate us for what we have lost." He then indicated how the money provided in the bill could aid his people, with $14 million earmarked for economic development and other amounts for land acquisition, aid to the elderly, education, environmental protection, youth programs, substance abuse counseling, and development of a tribal archives.[39]

Marlene Johnson, a tribal councilor and a nationally known educator who chaired the National Advisory Council on Indian Education, testified after the Seneca president. As a member of the Seneca Nation Salamanca Lease Negotiation Committee, her aim in providing testimony was to explain why congressional action was so necessary. She noted that the original confirmation of the leases by Congress in the late nineteenth century occurred during an ugly era of national policy, one that led to immense losses of Indian lands and the abandonment of federal trust responsibilities to Indian nations.[40] Next, attorney Loretta Crane pointed out other aspects of the negotiated settlement with the City of Salamanca, emphasizing that "during the first ten years of the new leasing arrangement, a portion of the interest generated by economic development funds" would be "used for community and economic development purposes within the city." She said that the Seneca Nation conceded about issuing two 40/40 leases but felt that extending leases well into the future would "promote economic security for city residents and the city itself" because it would "enable city residents and businesses to obtain mortgages, provide security for existing businesses, and encourage development of new businesses." Crane indicated that the total annual rent was to jump to $800,000 per year and escalate according to changes in property values in the city. Objective reappraisals of property would be made every three years for congressional villages and every four years for the City of Salamanca. She insisted: "Never again will the Nation accept the same inadequate rent, year after year, regardless of property values or economic conditions."[41]

At the two hearings, there was limited testimony opposing Houghton's bill. Patrick Cleveland, a spokesman for SCOUT, testified in opposition, claiming that the Salamanca Lease Authority had negotiated with the

Seneca Nation "without any benefit of preliminary studies and without a public hearing or referendum." He described the poor economic climate in Salamanca and stated that the city would face bankruptcy.[42] Cleveland was followed by Dennis Toboloski, the Cattaraugus County government attorney, who strongly objected to section 8(c) of the bill, which allowed the Seneca Nation to buy lands in surrounding areas that would then be put in trust by the Department of the Interior. With nontaxable lands in Allegany State Park and three nontaxable Indian reservations, and with the possibility of the Seneca Nation acquiring other lands and putting them into trust, Toboloski insisted that the county's towns and school districts would face an unbearable burden that would fall on the shoulders of the county's non-Indian citizens.[43]

Houghton and his staff carefully guided the bill through both houses, winning support by presenting the legislation as more than just providing new leases, but as rectifying an injustice done to the Senecas and promoting conflict resolution between Indians and non-Indians. Written into the bill were other stated purposes. Its aims were "to provide stability and security" to the city (Salamanca), the congressional villages, and their residents; "to promote the economic growth of the city and the congressional villages"; and "to promote cooperative economic development efforts on the part of the Seneca Nation and the city." Importantly, there was one more stated purpose, a not-so-veiled threat of future litigation. Passage of the bill was a way "to avoid the potential legal liability on the part of the United States that could be a direct consequence of not reaching a settlement."[44]

This Houghton bill, the exact same one in both houses of Congress, was favorably reported out of committee in early October. Houghton continued to speak out on behalf of the proposed legislation. On October 10, on the floor of the House of Representatives, he stated: "Mr. Speaker, the Seneca Nation has lost millions of dollars of revenue and land value over the last one hundred years solely because of the actions of the United States in authorizing and facilitating the lease of tribal lands at bargain basement prices. The bill recognized the moral responsibilities of the United States and the State of New York by requiring compensation to the tribe. . . . I urge the House to pass this bill which corrects an ancient wrong done to this tribe of Indians."[45]

The Seneca Nation Settlement Act passed the House and Senate by acclimation and was signed into law by President George H. W. Bush on November 3, 1990, as Public Law 101-53.[46] Three months later the Seneca Nation prepared to hold lease renewal sessions with the individual lease-holders to carry out the act.[47] Yet for a decade more after the "40/40 act" went into effect, the Senecas had to battle with a small group of white Salamancans, members of SCOUT, who refused to sign new leases. The Seneca Nation Tribal Council, nevertheless, in an attempt at reconciliation, delayed ejectment proceedings against these recalcitrants and repeatedly held public lease-signing days. Moreover, in the 1990 act there was also a provision for the creation of a panel to mediate and attempt to gain acceptance of the settlement. Three mediators were eventually chosen—Randy John, Patrick Callahan, and Michael Chiariello. Both John, a Seneca, and Chiariello, a non-Indian resident of Salamanca, were faculty members at St. Bonaventure University, and the Brooklyn-born Callahan was a social studies teacher in the Salamanca public schools. Although Callahan had been a member of the Salamanca Lease Authority, he had strong misgivings about SCOUT, its rhetoric and actions, and its unrealistic attempts to challenge the 40/40 lease.[48]

Despite the mediators' efforts, a few hard-liners in Salamanca led by Joseph Fluent continued to challenge the Settlement Act, refusing to sign lease renewals. To bolster his limited support, Fluent claimed to represent a group of 1,200 militant residents of Salamanca, infuriated by the congressional action and President Bush's signing of the Seneca Nation Settlement Act. He maintained that fifty families were ready to dynamite their homes if they were evicted by the Senecas. Fluent angrily asserted: "If I can't have it, nobody is going to have it."[49] These families hired the young and inexperienced Buffalo-based attorney Jennifer Coleman of Sleight, Lustig and Brown to fight the constitutionality of the act, even while most of their neighbors accepted the changed situation and signed their renewal leases with the Seneca Nation.

The Senecas waited until 1995 to initiate ejectment proceedings. By that time, fewer than twenty-two Salamancans had not signed their lease renewals.[50] After the Senecas began ejectment proceedings, twenty SCOUT holdouts, including Joseph and Alice Fluent, brought suit in the US

Court of Federal Claims in 1999, arguing that Congress had violated the leaseholders' constitutional rights in passing the Seneca Nation Settlement Act. The court quietly gave summary judgment to the United States and dismissed the case.[51] In 2001, the US Court of Appeals held that the ownership of the land as well as the improvements made on the land, including housing built by the leaseholders, reverted to the Seneca Nation at the expiration of the leases. The three appeals judges included Alan Gajarsa, who before his federal appointment to the bench had served as the lead attorney for the Cayugas in their land claims case. The judges affirmed the Court of Federal Claims decision that the ejected leaseholders had "no compensable property interest" and dismissed SCOUT's last-ditch effort. They insisted: "The Act of 1990 specifically disavows the role of the United States in approving the lease" and makes it clear that the Seneca Nation of Indians alone is solely responsible for negotiation of the leases . . . and approval of any such lease by the United States is not required."[52]

Racial tensions in Salamanca and environs have substantially subsided from the days prior to and immediately after the passing of the Seneca Nation Settlement Act of 1990. The Salamanca economy has been infused by the Seneca Nation's local investments, especially by the opening of the Allegany Casino in 2004 and businesses dependent on it. The casino alone has created employment for nearly two thousand Indians and non-Indians. In order to stem decline, the nation has also contributed to city improvements in its recreational facilities as well as in other areas. In this vein, the Seneca Tribal Council has recently modified the 40/40 lease into an eighty-year lease within the congressional villages. This move is intended to give individuals and businesses leasing in Allegany Territory long-term stability, allowing them to get easier lending terms from banks.[53]

11

Smoke Shops to Casinos

THROUGHOUT THE 1970S, the Senecas on both residential territories faced myriad serious economic problems—few employment opportunities, undervalued leases, limited entrepreneurial and educational skills, and growing dependence on federal and state grants and programs. Senecas were not helped by the rapid decline of manufacturing and the closing of steel mills in western New York. Their longtime employment in construction in western New York dried up, and unemployment skyrocketed. The tribal government had grown to 165 employees at this time, but almost all were hired on grants provided by the federal government programs created during the Johnson and Nixon presidencies. Moreover, despite a commitment to fund economic development made by the state in the Southern Tier Expressway Memorandum of Understanding in 1976, Albany officials soon reneged on their promises. As late as 1979, the Seneca Nation collected only $65,695.49 in tribal revenues, mostly from leasing and a limited bingo operation.[1]

Three decades later, however, the Seneca Nation of Indians had been transformed into a major economic juggernaut in western New York, with annual revenues of greater than $1 billion. It employed 5,200 people, non-Indians as well as Indians. Indeed, the Seneca Nation had become the largest employer in Cattaraugus and Niagara Counties. In 2012, at its major casino and hotel operations at Niagara Falls alone, 3,700 men and women were employed, and one-third of these workers lived in the city. They had a combined yearly salary of $100 million. Quite significantly, until federal legislation in 2010, Seneca entrepreneurs had become major distributors of cigarettes on the Internet and were the primary distributors for 275 smoke shops throughout Iroquoia. Nearly three thousand people in Iroquoia were employed in this burgeoning enterprise. In 2009 alone, privately owned Seneca smoke shops took in $329.9 million, and Seneca Nation–owned one stops (convenience stores) made $180 million largely in cigarette and gasoline sales.[2]

How and why did this transformation take place? Much, if not all, of the credit belongs to Native Americans themselves on reservations from Florida to Mississippi to California. These changes did not emanate from within the Washington Beltway. Native leaders were to lead the way in bringing economic improvements, developing diverse strategies, and expanding opportunities for themselves.

From the mid-1970s well into the 1980s, federal policies claiming to promote tribal self-determination and economic development had limited success at best. In 1977, the American Indian Policy Review Commission reported that 60 percent of the BIA budget was "committed to providing social welfare services," whereas only 9.5 percent was used to "protect the remaining natural resources of Indians and further development of Indian Country." The report pointed out that even casual observers' "have been startled by the stark contrast in economic conditions between reservation lands and adjoining non-reservation lands and communities. There has been an obvious lack of meaningful development of tribal lands, while one can observe prospering communities just beyond the reservation borders." It continued: "To develop, Indian people must move away from the dependency relationship. The consensus of Indian opinion is that self-sufficiency is the goal, self-reliance is the only possible means." It advocated continued federal funding, with the federal government serving as a facilitator "to provide a favorable climate for economic development." "Self-reliance means determining a truly Indian development process, using Indian labor, Indian resources, and Indian creativity." Despite its criticism of past policies that generated dependence, the commission refused to break totally with the past, insisting that future independence did not mean "scorning all federal assistance" but required "effective and wise use of that assistance"—"increased appropriations for capitalization of necessary community facilities, enterprise development projects, and other essential community support systems, and by alternate means for capital resources." The report recommended the establishment of "new Indian financing mechanisms (e.g., development banks) and investment procedures" and the fostering of basic skills and technologies.[3]

Native Americans had heard these arguments before and were to hear them again. They dismissed much of the American Indian Policy Review Commission's rhetoric, knowing that federal funding was always elusive and subject to congressional whims and changes in presidential administrations in Washington, DC. Such was the case in the 1980s, when federal policy shifted to a more conservative approach. The election of Ronald Reagan brought cuts to Indian programs funded by the federal government and a new conservative impetus to promote private enterprise on reservations.[4] At the time of Reagan's election, 41 percent of reservation Indians were living in households below the poverty line, and the unemployment rate for Indian males between ages twenty and sixty-four was 58 percent.[5]

On January 24, 1983, after Secretary of the Interior James Watt received harsh criticism from Native Americans as well as from environmental groups, the president issued an "American Indian policy statement." He acknowledged that since the passage of the Indian Self-Determination and Educational Assistance Act of 1975, there "has been more rhetoric than action." He added that federal policies "have by and large inhibited the political and economic development of the tribes. Excessive regulation and self-perpetuating bureaucracy have stifled local decision-making, thwarted Indian control of resources, and promoted dependency rather than self-sufficiency." Reagan promised to reverse this trend and remove obstacles to provide a favorable environment for the development of healthy reservation economies. The president then laid out his agenda, emphasizing the rejection of past termination policies, a firm commitment to carrying out the "highest standards" of the federal government's trust responsibilities; direct funding of block grants to Indian tribal governments; special assistance to build managerial capacities; seed money to promote economic development projects; better coordination of all federal Indian programs; efforts to reduce federal regulations; and the establishment of a presidential commission to improve reservation economies.[6]

Ten days earlier Reagan had created the President's Commission on Indian Reservation Economies by Executive Order Number 12401.[7] He appointed Ross Swimmer, the tribal chairman of the Cherokee Nation of Oklahoma, and Robert Robertson, a non-Indian who had served in Indian policy formulation during the Nixon presidency, as co-chairmen of the commission, which was composed of six Native Americans, all from the Trans-Mississippi West, and three non-Indians. The commissioners submitted their report a year later. Among its recommendations, the report called for modernizing tribal government to achieve effective separation of governmental powers and corporate business functions; the creation of an Indian trust services administration to "strengthen tribal autonomy, authority and accountability, and simultaneously protect Indian trust resources against termination"; the establishment of a national commission of Indian business development to promote the private sector and coordinate with the efforts of federal agencies; and the taking of steps to further capital formation and encourage private ownership of tribal enterprise.[8] This conservative alternative included more of the same, once again adding new levels to an already bureaucratic administration of Indian affairs.

The Reagan administration subsequently created the Task Force on Indian Economic Development. Its recommendations included the creation of reservation enterprise zones with tax incentives to private investors and regulatory relief to attract businesses; Indian preference in contracting in set-aside programs throughout the federal government; encouraging the BIA to undertake economic policy studies to improve the quality and quantity of its data; and the creation of the Office of Economic Development to consolidate existing BIA programs within its purview and to coordinate economic activities carried out by federal agencies outside of the Interior Department.[9] Yet by the end of the Reagan presidency, economic policies set forth in the American Indian Policy Review Commission final report of 1977 and the two conservative efforts in the 1980s were judged as failures.[10]

The congressional passage of the Indian Gaming Regulatory Act (IGRA) in 1988 and its incredible long-term impact were to blur the reality of federal failures to promote reservation economic development during the Carter and Reagan years. Much of what came out of the nation's capital was pure rhetoric, assertions of self-determination without much substance. Although too often Native American communities do not get enough credit, they largely on their own, with little assistance from the BIA or other agencies in Washington, reacted to these failures to develop ways to bring economic improvements to their people.

The economic turnaround for the Senecas started in the 1980s from within their own ranks. In the mid-1980s, they still had to face a hostile administration in Albany headed by Governor Mario Cuomo, intent on expanding the state's revenue stream. After New York State officials broke their promises to President Hoag to provide economic development moneys, the Senecas turned to other alternatives. As we saw with the establishment of health services on the reservations, contact with other Native American communities strongly influenced changes within the Seneca Nation. Tribal councilors and tribal personnel in their official capacities journeyed to numerous regional and national meetings, including to the National Congress of American Indians' annual convention. There they became more aware of what was happening in other parts of Indian Country. Delegates would discuss ways to improve reservation economies and lessen dependence on federal grant programs.

Two of the many ideas discussed at these meetings were that (1) Native communities needed to establish small business operations, including smoke shops, within their communities that would hire Native peoples and keep capital within the community for further economic development, and (2) tribal gaming operations could produce needed revenues. In the 1970s, visits to the Florida Seminoles, then under the dynamic leadership of Chairman Howard Tommie, and to the Mississippi Choctaws under the business acumen of Chairman Philip Martin, were obligatory for representatives of other Native communities seeking ways to overcome dependence on the federal government. These eastern leaders had tremendous influence on Native Americans nationally, including on the Seneca Nation of Indians.

In the mid-1970s, the Senecas at Allegany had established a small tribal bingo operation at Steamburg that was later shifted to Seneca Lanes, the tribal bowling alley complex in Salamanca. They also had established a bingo operation in the abandoned United States Pillow Corporation complex at Cattaraugus. Later, in its critical need to provide for the needs of its growing population and to increase employment, the Seneca Nation also converted its Newtown Arena, used by its people for lacrosse and ice hockey, into a bingo hall.

Four federal court decisions—*Seminole Tribe of Florida v. Butterworth* (1981), *California v. Cabazon Band of Mission Indians* (1987), *Oklahoma Tax Commission v. Citizen Band of Potawatomi Tribe* (1991), and *[New York State] Department of Finance v. Milhelm Attea & Bros.* (1994)—were to affect the Senecas.[11] In the 1970s, the Seminoles had opened a bingo hall in Hollywood, Florida, that proved to be an overnight bonanza. Their achievement reverberated throughout Indian Country.[12] However, the Seminole Nation immediately found itself faced with litigation over its high-stakes bingo operation in that the stakes set there far exceeded state limits. The sheriff of Broward County threatened to arrest Seminole tribal leaders. In response, the Seminoles sued Broward County, seeking a declaratory judgment and claiming tribal sovereignty. State officials argued that they had the policing power to shut down this gaming operation based on the potential for high-stakes bingo to be infiltrated by organized crime and on the state's jurisdiction in criminal matters with passage of Public Law 280 in 1953. In *Seminole Tribe of Florida v. Butterworth* in 1981, the federal Court of Appeals decided that Florida could not interfere with the Seminoles' high-stakes bingo operations because the state's approach to bingo was regulatory in nature and "not criminal or prohibitory." As a result, numerous Native American communities nationwide, including the Seneca Nation, expanded their limited bingo operations.

In the 1980s, two federally recognized Native communities in California—the Cabazon and Morongo Bands of Mission Indians—opened bingo halls on their reservation, which soon became extremely profitable. Yet, according to California law, no bingo operation was allowed in the state except for the purposes of raising money for charities. The law allowed only a maximum pot of $250. As a consequence, in the mid-1980s the state attempted to enforce this law, arguing that California had criminal jurisdiction under Public Law 280 and therefore had the legal right to apply its criminal laws to the two reservations. In response, the two Native communities brought suit, challenging California's right to regulate their gaming operations. In 1987, in *California v. Cabazon Band of Mission Indians*, the US Supreme Court held for the two Indian nations. Because California did not prohibit all gambling, but only some forms of it, and allowed other types of gambling such as horse racing and a state lottery, the court concluded that it had powers only to regulate Indian gaming, but not "criminal/prohibitory powers," and thus the state could not shut down these Mission Indians' gaming operations. The court decided that the state was not authorized by Public Law 280 or by any other federal law to enforce its criminal jurisdiction over bingo or other gaming operations on California's reservations. The door was thus opened for casino operations.

In response, California and other states lobbied Congress into enacting the IGRA, which was passed and signed into law in 1988. The IGRA's stated purposes were to promote "tribal economic development, self-sufficiency, and strong tribal government" and, at the same time, to protect Indian nations "from organized crime and other corrupting influences." The act divided Indian gaming into three classes: Class I, traditional gaming conducted during tribal ceremonies with minimal prizes; Class II, bingo, card games already under state law, lotto, and pull tabs, which were not prohibited by existing state law and subject to regulation by the National Indian Gaming Commission, a three-person board created by the IGRA in the Interior Department; and Class III, "all forms of gaming that are not Class I or Class II gaming," including slot machines, craps, roulette, blackjack, and baccarat. To establish Class III, the Indian gaming operation had to be located within a state that permitted such gaming.[13]

Before Indian casinos could be established, however, a federally recognized tribe had to negotiate a binding compact with the state. The IGRA gave the states a significant role in regulating aspects of Indian gaming. Indian nations had to negotiate gaming compacts dealing with monetary payments to the state before they could establish Class III gaming operations—that is, establish casinos. In order to finalize these compacts, the Indian nations also had to accede to state criminal jurisdiction in casino facilities. In each of these areas, Indian nations' inherent right to engage in gaming as set forth in the *Cabazon* case was sharply restricted and defined. Moreover, Indian nations faced penalties from the act's creation of the

National Indian Gaming Commission, an independent federal regulatory authority, if they violated regulations established by this new agency housed in the Department of the Interior. The act specified that Indian tribes had "the exclusive right to regulate gaming activity on Indian lands if the gaming activity is not specifically prohibited by federal law and is conducted within a state which does not, as a matter of criminal law and public policy, prohibit such gaming activity."[14] As a result of this legislative initiative, casino development rapidly expanded in Indian Country. By 2010, Indian casinos produced nearly $27 billion in revenues, and more than 250 establishments were operating from Connecticut to California.[15] Yet it was to take a decade and a half after the *Cabazon* decision for the Seneca Nation to open its first Class III gaming operation at Niagara Falls.

In the 1980s and 1990s, individual Seneca entrepreneurs opened numerous smoke shops on their two residential territories. Once again, this phenomenon was motivated by forces at work in other parts of Indian Country. At the forefront of this change was Maurice "Mo" John Sr., a magnetic personality who illustrates the new direction taken by the Seneca Nation in the early 1980s to deal with its economic problems and, at the same time, to ward off what was (and still is) perceived as the state's intrusion. John was the key figure in the push for the establishment of smoke shops that challenged state regulation, including Albany's attempt to collect sales taxes within the territories of the Seneca Nation. Willing to stand up to state authorities and even going to jail based on principles of Seneca sovereignty, this colorful figure created a new style of activist leadership in Seneca Country. For a quarter of a century, John clearly understood how to make use of the media to generate headlines by his bold, sometimes over-the-top statements and actions.[16]

John, an Allegany Seneca, was born at Onoville and grew up as the Kinzua Dam was being constructed. As a teenager, he would see the houses burned, his ancestors' bones dug up in cemetery relocation, and the land cleared to make way for the Allegheny Reservoir. He would sit on benches listening to the elders talk about Kinzua and remembered seeing his father, a tribal councilor at the time, cry when this was happening. As a result, he was full of anger. His grandparents would tell him: "Never let them take our land; land is everything." During the Vietnam era, he went off to enlist in the US Air Force, serving until 1972. He returned to Allegany and was soon elected as a tribal councilor for two terms. John was proud of certain accomplishments in his four years on the council: the establishment of IHS services, senior centers, and recreational facilities such as the Newtown Arena, Seneca Lanes Bowling Alley, and tennis courts. However, with the lack of employment opportunities—he could only find some work parking cars at the newly established bingo hall at Steamburg—his disgust for tribal politics grew exponentially. With no job prospects and a chip on his shoulder, John left Allegany and went west to work in construction in Colorado and California. There, in Denver and Los Angeles, he had life-changing experiences. In these urban settings, he met numerous activist Indians who had been relocated by federal government policies. He also met a Lakota, whom he married. During these important years of his life, he became drawn to Plains Indian theology and rituals, taking part in the Sun Dance. In 1982, he returned to Allegany as a changed man.

In the 1970s and early 1980s, reservation communities throughout Indian Country began an expansion of both tribally owned and privately operated smoke ships. In New York, these smoke shops first appeared at Akwesasne and Onondaga. Before John returned to Seneca Territory, the idea for smoke shop development there had first been brought up in the Tribal Council by then treasurer Calvin Lay Jr., later president of the Seneca Nation. However, there were regulations on the books that had stymied this move. Lay had been active in Seneca politics from 1970 onward. He served as a tribal councilor from Cattaraugus from 1970 to 1974 and again from 1980 to 1984; treasurer of the Seneca Nation from 1974 to 1976; and president from 1976 to 1978 and again from 1984 to 1986. Beginning in the early 1970s, he and other councilors and tribal personnel in their official capacity journeyed to numerous regional and national meetings, including to the National Congress of American Indians' annual convention, where they attended talks and had private meetings about economic development. Despite Lay's efforts, however, and the fact that smoke shops had already opened in other parts of Iroquoia, the Seneca Nation Tribal Council initially did not look favorably on John's proposal to establish his own smoke shop. However, with the help of his influential relative, longtime tribal councilor Wayne Printup, John was to open the door to the smoke shop era in Seneca Country and get permission to sell cigarettes.

In July 1983, John was to start selling cigarettes—merely thirteen cartons—out of the back of his van at an abandoned service station on the eastern end of Allegany Territory, just off the present Seneca Junction exit on the Southern Tier Expressway. Barry Snyder Sr., who had served as an economic development officer and councilor within the Seneca Nation in the early 1970s, was to follow suit the next year, establishing the Seneca Hawk smoke shop on the western end of the Cattaraugus Territory, just off the Irving exit at the New York State Thruway. Others were to follow their example. Snyder later expanded his operation to make it a major truck stop selling tax-free gasoline. Well-known Seneca families—Abrams, Heron, (Ross) John, Schindler, Seneca, Watt—were to follow John and Snyder's example.

Mo John "danced to the beat of his own drum." After he began selling cigarettes, he soon faced a challenge: state troopers confronted him about selling unstamped cigarettes. According to John, "I took out my 30-30 [hunting rifle], and they backed down. . . . The Creator gave me sovereignty, not the state of New York." Unfortunately for John and other Senecas who followed his example, Albany authorities never abandoned their attempt to apply the sales tax to cigarette sales to non-Indians on Indian lands. John's entrepreneurial efforts expanded, formally establishing a smoke shop enterprise; however, he and other smoke shop entrepreneurs faced a backlash from both the state and other Senecas. John and his family suffered greatly. To many Senecas, John became a hero, asserting treaty rights and sovereignty and resisting the dreaded enemy in Albany; other Senecas, however, saw him as simply a headline grabber, much like Wallace "Mad Bear" Anderson, whom John admired. His Seneca critics were also peeved by what John had set in motion by his smoke shop—namely, what they interpreted as individualistic and materialistic tendencies that they believed ran counter to the overall tribal culture. To be fair, not all of the smoke shop entrepreneurs were like John, a man who was committed to question authority and shake things up.[17]

These Seneca businessmen's significant economic success had political consequences. A bitter split developed between families who ran smoke shops, joined by their loyal employees, and other members of the Seneca Nation. The internal crisis raged throughout the 1990s at a time when Albany officials were attempting to apply the sales tax to the Hodinöhsö:ni´ territories throughout New York. At times, the internal battle turned mean-spirited and quite ugly, even violent. However, it should be noted that although the number of entrepreneurs and the extent of their wealth was new, class distinctions in Iroquois communities were not new in Iroquoia. They had existed well before the 1980s.

For more than two hundred years, observers had pointed out class distinctions in Hodinöhsö:ni´ communities. In an interview I conducted with the highly respected elder Ernest Benedict in the early 1980s, the Mohawk chief referred to Joseph Brant, George Smoke Johnson, and Henry Martin Johnson, founders of the Six Nations Reserve community at Ohsweken, Ontario, as "the aristocratic Mohawks." In the 1980s, archaeologists uncovering Brant's original Mohawk settlement there were to find fancy china, snuff boxes, and other items indicating wealth.[18] In the first years of the nineteenth century, observers including Governor De Witt Clinton noted the personal wealth of the aged Oneida chief Skenando, as evidenced by his impressive residence in central New York.[19] The official Iroquois census for New York State in 1845 clearly showed disparity in individual families' wealth—size of plots and acreage tilled—on most reservations in New York State.[20] At Tonawanda in the first half of the nineteenth century, the family of Ely S. Parker, the famous Seneca sachem, Civil War officer, and first Indian to be appointed commissioner of Indian affairs, lived in an impressive farmhouse, unlike many of their Seneca neighbors who lived in log cabins. In the twentieth century, prominent Tonawanda Senecas such as Chief Nick Bailey, a prominent musician, and other Carlisle-educated Indians along Meadville Road lived in more substantial housing than Tonawandas in the "Down Below District," the area where many Longhouse followers resided.[21]

In a recent, most insightful book, *Rich Indians: Native People and the Problem of Wealth in American History*, Alexandra Harmon has perceptively observed that Native American societies have too often been viewed as static, having an egalitarian, spiritual traditionalist underpinning and not having a "competitive, materialistic, activist, non-Indian ethos." She describes misconceptions held by both Native peoples and non-Indians about wealth, observing that to Native Americans "[white people's] improvement became proof of [their] greed and disdain for the life-sustaining ethic of reciprocity." Harmon concludes that many contemporary Native Americans "have taken satisfaction in the implication that their humble material circumstances reflected values at odds with the self-interested accumulation of Euro-Americans."[22] Some Euro-Americans, uneasy with the adverse effects of their society's greater materialism, agree; they interpret Indians' poverty as evidence of adherence to more admirable ideals, such as spirituality and generosity. Thus, in the 1980s and 1990s, to many Native and non-Native peoples, economic ambition, as expressed by owners of smoke shops, was seen, rightly or wrongly, as contrary to Indian mores. Even though these smoke shops provided much needed jobs for hundreds of Senecas, opponents of smoke shops pointed an accusatory finger at owners of these privately owned enterprises, who did not pay into the nation's coffers or follow certain tribal regulations.[23] From 1990 onward, the result of these differing views was bitter internal tribal struggles throughout Hodinöhsö:ni´ territories, including within the Seneca Nation.

Smoke shops brought great personal profits to individuals and led to internal debate about their role in Seneca society. New York State initiated efforts to apply its sales tax on reservation purchases of cigarettes and gasoline by non-Indians. State attempts to tax the Senecas were not new in the 1980s, but in fact dated back to the first half of the nineteenth century. In the aftermath of the Buffalo Creek Treaty of January 1838, the New York State Legislature attempted to extend its jurisdiction, including its taxing power, to Seneca Country. In May 1840, the New York State Legislature, without federal authorization, passed "[a]n Act in relation to the roads and bridges within the Allegany and Delaware Creek [sic] Reservations." The act gave the county boards of supervisors in Erie, Chautauqua, and Cattaraugus Counties the right to assess highway taxes on all lands within the Allegany and Cattaraugus Indian Reservations as they did neighboring non-Indian communities, which "they may deem reasonable and necessary, to put highways and bridges within said reservation in good repair."[24] The next year, the legislature, without federal authorization, passed "[a]n Act authorizing the construction and repair of roads and bridges on the Indian lands in the Counties of Erie and Cattaraugus." The act permitted the county boards of supervisors in the two counties to survey and construct roads across three of the Seneca communities: Buffalo Creek, Cattaraugus, and Allegany Indian Reservations. Significantly, the cost of these two-year road-building projects would be borne by the Indian residents of each reservation: $5,000 per year at Buffalo Creek and $4,000 per year at Cattaraugus and Allegany, a clear attempt to drive the Iroquois west out of their homeland. If these taxes were not paid, the state comptroller could "proceed to advertise and sell said lands in the manner now provided by law." The law gave the Indians an assurance of their continuing right of occupancy after tax foreclosure. "But no sale for the purpose of collecting said taxes shall in any manner affect the right of the Indians to occupy said land."[25] Nevertheless, to Senecas, taxation was clearly associated with dispossession, forcing them to abandon their tribal status and become US citizens if they could not pay the taxes. In 1866, the US Supreme Court held in *In Re New York Indians* that the New York State Legislature's acts of 1840 and 1841 were illegal. Justice Samuel Nelson said that a state law in 1857 had guaranteed that no tax could "be assessed on either of the two reservations (Allegany and Cattaraugus), or on any property of the Seneca Nation, and that all acts of the state conflicting with the provisions of this section are hereby repealed." Justice Nelson added that because the Indians were under federal treaties, they "were still in their ancient possessions and occupancy, and till removed by the United States, were entitled to undisturbed enjoyment of them."[26]

Events transpiring in other parts of Indian Country were to have repercussions in western New York. In 1987, the Oklahoma Tax Commission served a $2.7 million bill on the Citizen Band of Potawatomi Tribe of Oklahoma for its cigarette sales from 1982 to 1986. The US Supreme Court decided the case in 1991. Chief Justice William Rehnquist, who wrote the court's opinion, maintained that a state may tax cigarette sales to non-Indians on tribal territory; however, because of sovereign immunity, the state had no way to enforce its taxes on a federally recognized Indian community.[27] Even before this decision, New York State and the Internal

Revenue Service were already attempting to find a way to collect taxes from on-reservation cigarette sales to non-Indians.[28]

In response to criticisms I made in my Rockefeller Public Policy Institute report sent to the governor's office in July 1986 and abstracted in a popular article that appeared in *Capital Region* magazine, Dr. Henrik Dullea, the director of state operations and his staff, undertook to write the "Preliminary Report to the Governor on State–Indian Relations." The Dullea report, completed in 1988, pointed out what it considered one of the major problems souring state relations with the Six Nations—namely, the failure to collect sales taxes on non-Indian purchases of cigarettes, gasoline, and diesel fuel on Indian reservations. "Off-reservation vendors and their distributors have complained to legislators and others about what they regard as unfair competition." However, "the Indian representatives counter that they are not taking unfair advantage, but are seeking only to obtain economic self-sufficiency"; and they emphasize "that in giving up most of their land base, and as a result of racial prejudice, they have been prevented from developing to the same extent as the dominant society." The report, which was forwarded to Governor Mario Cuomo, concluded that "non-Indians were liable for taxes on purchases made on Indian reservations," but that there was no practical way for the state to obtain those taxes if the vendors continued to refuse collection.[29]

The same year the New York State Department of Taxation and Finance adopted regulations limiting the quantity of unstamped—meaning untaxed—cigarettes that wholesalers could sell and distribute to tribes and tribal vendors. The state based this quota on its own projections or through negotiations with tribal leaders and then issued a certain number of tax exemptions to the tribes or Native vendors or both. This state agency had imposed record-keeping requirements and had limited the number of untaxed cigarettes that could be delivered to and sold on reservations. Among the other requirements, a smoke shop owner had to hold a valid state tax-exempt certificate, make monthly reports, and collect taxes on nonexempt sales, meaning sales to all non-Indians purchasing cigarettes on reservations. The delivery amount would be determined by negotiations and on the average statewide consumption of cigarettes. The state sales tax on the cigarettes delivered to the reservation would be paid by the wholesaler, not by the smoke shop retailer. The state then attempted to enforce these same regulations.[30]

The state's relations with the Six Nations went from bad to worse. In May 1990, the governor gave an interview to the *New York Times* in which he demonstrated his lack of understanding of the Iroquois, their history, and their cultural sensitivities. Without realizing that his words would exacerbate tensions, Mario Cuomo bluntly insisted: "You have this first problem which is that they [the Six Nations], many of them, regard themselves as part of a nation. They're a conquered nation. And they will not accept that you obliterated their existence as a nation just because you're more powerful than them."[31]

In 1989, the New York State Department of Finance brought a suit in state court against Milhem Attea and Bros., Inc., a federally licensed non-Indian wholesale distributor of cigarettes to smoke shop retailers on the Allegany and Cattaraugus Territories. Attea then countersued the Department of Finance, refusing responsibility for the state's collection of taxes. The case eventually reached the US Supreme Court in 1994. In the court's decision, Justice John Paul Stevens wrote that the states may impose on reservation retailers "minimal burdens reasonably tailored to the collection of valid taxes from non-Indians." The Court held that "Indian traders are not wholly immune from state regulation that is reasonably necessary to the assessment or collection of lawful state taxes." Despite the state's victory in court, the decision did not resolve New York's enforcement problem.[32]

Well before the Attea decision was handed down, Barry Snyder Sr. was to seize upon the sales tax issue, which directly threatened his family's operations and profits at the Seneca Hawk as well as at the growing number of smoke shops. Snyder had grown up in poverty, living in a dilapidated house with a wood stove and no indoor plumbing in the Bucktown section of the Cattaraugus Indian Reservation. In 1957, he joined the US Army after graduating from Gowanda High School. In the early 1970s, Snyder worked in the Seneca Nation's Office of Economic Development in the role of the nation's purchasing director and served on the Tribal Council. In this decade, he also served as treasurer, an office he held again in the early 1980s. Although his political enemies accused him of corruption and intimidation, Snyder was to be elected president of the

Seneca Nation five times—in 1980, 1992, 2004, 2008, and 2012. Even when he was not an elected president, treasurer, or councilor, he was still the most powerful individual within the Seneca Nation for more than three decades. Although he and his allies on both the Allegany and Cattaraugus Reservations were on occasion voted out of power, their voices were never silenced in council because they were major employers of Senecas on both residential territories.[33]

Despite receiving constant criticism, legitimate or otherwise, Snyder did transform the Seneca Nation. Even numerous critics who viewed him with disdain would acknowledge his abilities. Indeed, in his first ventures into tribal government during the Hoag era, he had learned much about ways to "rule" in the often unruly world of Seneca politics as well as about how to handle his opponents. Snyder was also his own man, adding to Hoag's style of leadership. He skillfully co-opted his tribal opposition by wrapping himself around Seneca sovereignty and treaty rights. He presented himself as the great defender of the Seneca people against the aggressive actions of the State of New York. The issue that effectively mobilized his numerous Seneca supporters was that Albany could not force Native-owned businesses on sovereign, federally recognized treaty lands to collect sales taxes.[34]

In response, Snyder and his non-Indian attorney Joseph Crangle, the former head of the Democratic Party in New York State, also helped establish the Iroquois Businessmen's Association. This organization, with affiliates in several other Six Nations communities, such as Oneida and Akwesasne, became a major force, pushing the Senecas and other Hodinöhsö:ni´ to challenge the state's right to levy sales taxes on Indian enterprises in federally recognized Indian communities. They also promoted a movement, "Honor Our Treaties," with T-shirts and banners. Members lobbied state legislators, testified at Albany hearings, drew media attention, and staged demonstrations. In 1992 and 1997, they rallied Senecas of all political stripes and closed down the New York State Thruway and the Southern Tier Expressway by occupying these two major routes and burning tires.[35]

Much to the anger of many Senecas who viewed any individualistic trend as a threat to common tribal goals, smoke shop owners set out on their own, no longer willing to wait for solutions from Washington and Albany or permission from their tribal government to regulate them. Ever so protective of their right to establish these smoke shops that sold tax-free cigarettes and gasoline at their truck stops, they insisted that federal treaties allowed them to do so. To some Senecas, they were defenders of sovereignty against the hated enemy in Albany. To others, they were corrupting influences on Seneca values in their individualist pursuit of profits and their resistance to tribal regulation. With the hiring of numerous employees dependent on newly created jobs, however, they generated increasing political support.

While the *Attea* case was proceeding up through the judicial system, eventually landing before the US Supreme Court, I attended an eye-opening joint hearing of the New York State Senate Standing Committee on Corporations, Authorities, and Commissions and the Assembly Subcommittee on Corporate Law, which was considering legislation to further regulate cigarette and gasoline sales to non-Indian purchasers on reservations and to enforce collecting these revenues. I had been invited to hear the testimony, which was held on May 27, 1992, by President Calvin "Kelly" John and sat through the entire hearing by his side. As a witness to this hearing, chaired by state senator John Daly of Niagara Falls and later commissioner of transportation under Governor George Pataki, I observed how state officials dismissed the Senecas and their leadership. The hearing began promptly at 10:00 AM in a crowded amphitheater in the State Legislative Office Building in Albany with the brief testimony of the chiefs of the Iroquois Grand Council. They were followed by approximately sixteen Indian and non-Indian entrepreneurs and lobbyists. By the time President John was allowed to present testimony against the state's application of the sales tax, it was 4:00 PM, and the room had emptied. Spokespersons representing non-Indian convenience-store operators asked the legislators to impose the sales tax to provide a level playing field, arguing that untaxed cigarettes and gasoline sold on Indian reservations gave Native-owned smoke shops and convenience stores an unfair advantage.

Bypassing Native protocol, Snyder was one of the Seneca entrepreneurs who testified ahead of President John. He insisted that the state officials' reasoning behind the legislation was "political expediency." After citing federal treaties with the Senecas in 1784, 1789, 1794, and 1842 as a defense against state-imposed taxation, Snyder defiantly questioned the state legislators' motives: "Just look how quickly this bill has come before you for discussion. I am knowledgeable enough to know that some serious pressure has been applied to get a tax bill this far so fast. And why is that? Because it is equitable? Because it is just? No, the bill has been speeded up because you [New York State] need money and the Seneca entrepreneurs are making more money than you ever thought they could, and gentlemen, that's simply not a good enough reason to break a treaty." Snyder continued with a rhetorical question: "What did we get in return?" He answered: "Resolutions for enterprise initiatives? Praise for [our] energy? Praise for our perseverance? Accolades for doing things and achieving things the white man's way? No." Instead, he added, "we get called cheaters, tax evaders, and all the vile names you can think of because we have been successful." Snyder then concluded: "We're the ones who have been cheated. Forget about the broken treaties that set up our [present] land[holdings]. The rules make it harder for us to survive, let alone thrive. But we have taken a single competitive edge guaranteed by federal treaty and turned it into our advantage. We aren't playing by the rules? Well, gentlemen, it's simply not true. We are playing by the rules, your rules, remember, and just because we are succeeding doesn't mean you can change these rules to suit yourselves."[36]

Six hours after the hearing began, President John, a proud seventy-year-old Allegany Seneca who had battled the state since jurisdictional transfer in the late 1940s, was allowed to speak. He reiterated his people's arguments against state sales tax enforcement, indicating, in his characteristically mild-mannered way, that the state's planned actions were in violation of federal treaties.[37] John was followed by J. C. Seneca, a successful Seneca businessman and vice president of the Northeast Area of the National Congress of American Indians. Seneca condemned the legislators for how they had treated President John, calling the delaying of the president's testimony "disrespectful to an Indian leader." Seneca was even more combative than Snyder in his testimony. He indicated that the Senecas would not just consider levying fees on state workers crossing into Seneca territories, as suggested in earlier testimony, but would consider shutting down "the railroad or Thruway." He threatened: "I am one of the young Senecas . . . that are tired of being pushed around [by New York State] and seeing our people taken advantage of as I grew up. From this time, we will no longer put up with the encroachments on our rights as aboriginal people. No more!"[38]

Hearing J. C. Seneca's testimony, I knew full well that a storm was brewing. I wondered if the legislators took Seneca's words seriously. After the end of my semester teaching responsibilities at SUNY New Paltz, I began to prepare to teach Seneca history at Saint Bonaventure University, which is less than twenty miles from the tribal office at Jimersontown on the Allegany Territory. In July 1992, when I started the course there, I soon found myself a witness to what Seneca had outlined in his May testimony.

On July 17, a date that today is commemorated as Unity Day within the Seneca Nation, about two hundred tribal members established roadblocks on the New York State Thruway and on the Southern Tier Expressway. They also dropped burning tires off the thruway overpass on the Cattaraugus Indian Reservation to protest Albany's efforts. Thirteen protesters were arrested. Three state troopers and three protesters were injured during the melee. After two hundred additional state troopers were sent as backup, the Senecas dismantled the roadblocks and ended their demonstration.[39]

By visibly leading opposition to the sales tax and organizing his growing number of loyal followers in demonstrations, Snyder saw his political fortunes rise significantly within the Seneca Nation. That November he used the sales tax once again to capture the presidency of the Seneca Nation.[40] The issue dominated his campaign; nevertheless, casino development was also clearly on Senecas' minds. One opponent of casinos, the late Barry White, an academic at SUNY Buffalo and member of the Newtown Longhouse on the Cattaraugus Indian Reservation, observed: "We're in a transition very much like we were when we started fur trading with the Europeans. It's a whole new level of thinking, a whole new level of economics. And people are hungry for that. That's why I would rather have them think deeper about the implications of economic development."[41]

On November 4, 1992, Snyder was elected to the presidency of the Seneca Nation, receiving 816 to Emory Williams's 687 and J. C. Seneca's 355 votes. At his swearing-in ceremony as president before a crowd of six hundred Senecas, Mohawk chiefs, and local, state, and federal officials, Snyder's opponents, including Susan Abrams, head of the Senecas' United People's Party, demonstrated, calling the election rigged, accusing Snyder and his Seneca Party of vote buying, and thus delaying his inauguration.[42]

Although within the Seneca community a few individuals on both sides of this debate were out to take personal advantage of the casino issue for political and economic gain, most Senecas were caught in the crossfire, literally and figuratively, in this fight that too often became mean-spirited. Both sides of the debate drew inspiration and strength from traditional teachings. The Iroquoian Great Law of Peace advised: "Never consider your own interests but work to benefit the people and for the [seven] generations not yet born." It advised tribal leaders (chiefs) to stand tall and learn to bear severe criticism: "You will receive many scratches and the thickness of your skin shall be seven spans [also referred to as 'having skin seven thumbs thick']. You must be patient and henceforth work in unity." Yet neither side heeded a clear warning in the Great Law: "And when it shall come to pass that the chiefs cannot agree, when they continually throw ashes at one another, then the people's heads will roll."[43] This is precisely what happened in the decade-long casino fight.

Unknown to outside observers, the struggle was not simply a local factional fight over casinos but had long-standing roots in Iroquoia and reflected historical Seneca political behavior. Since 1848, when the Seneca Nation had replaced its chieftainship with an elected republic, its populace had struggled to maintain its fragile, confederated political governmental structure. From Willie Hoag to Bob Hoag to Barry Snyder Sr., the Seneca polity was characterized by an intense, often chaotic style, politics that resulted in frequent charges of corruption—real or imaginary—character assassination, and, unfortunately, occasional intimidation and violence. Both the advocates of casinos and their opponents understood that in order to win the electorate to their position, they had to use traditional metaphors, evoke treaties that they claimed recognized tribal sovereignty, and challenge the Senecas' enemies in Albany to deflect criticism and overcome divisions.

As early as 1992, I had become aware that Indian Country was undergoing seismic changes. I was an invited guest to the grand opening of

Foxwoods, the Mashantucket Pequot Tribal Nation's casino in Ledyard, Connecticut. In the mid-1980s, I had previously worked as a consultant to the Pequots, helping them to organize and hold a major historical conference, publish its proceedings, and collect documents for their planned museum.[44] On President Lincoln's birthday in 1992, I journeyed with my late friend Roy Black, a Native American artist, and his wife, Gloria, to the casino opening. John Peters, the Mashpee Wampanoag medicine man, gave the invocation, and Pequot tribal officials cut the blue ribbon and officially opened the casino. By the end of that day, approximately three thousand patrons poured into the casino, heading for the slot machines, craps and blackjack tables, and roulette wheels. Both my friend Roy and I realized that we had been witnesses to history that day. We understood full well that other eastern federally recognized Native communities would follow the Pequots' lead and take advantage of the IGRA to establish Class III gaming, even though in 1992 the majority of Senecas were opposed to this new direction. Our conclusion was to be reinforced when the Oneida Nation in central New York opened the highly profitable Turning Stone Casino the following year.[45]

In the 1990s, the Seneca Nation was torn apart by whether to pursue or reject casino development. Where issues such as land claims and taxation generated consensus, casinos did just the opposite—nearly tearing the Senecas apart in internecine conflict that even led to violence and three deaths. Many traditionally minded Senecas, fearful of outside influences and control, had real concerns about the IGRA, especially the requirement of signing a compact with their historic enemy in Albany. After all, in 1976, after the Senecas signed their most recent "compact" with the state, the Memorandum of Understanding concerning the Southern Tier Expressway, Albany officials had never carried out the promises made to the Senecas. Even after the opening of Indian-run casinos, the Iroquois Grand Council of Chiefs at Onondaga repeatedly condemned the move. The chiefs repeatedly maintained: "Casino culture destroys the social, cultural and spiritual fabric of our people, and will lead to more serious disruption of the overall health and welfare of our people."[46] Even though the Seneca Nation was a separate entity outside the framework of the Iroquois Grand Council's purview, some Senecas looked for direction from the sachems at Onondaga. Senecas were well aware of events that had transpired at Akwesasne in 1990, when a debate over casino development resulted in a civil war, a murder, a major schism in the Longhouse, and the rise of the Warriors Movement intent on bringing down elected tribal governments and challenging the actions of the Iroquois Grand Council.[47]

Seneca advocates of casino development presented themselves as the true forward-thinking alternative to overcoming the historic, debilitating effects of poverty and dependence on state and federal governments. They characterized their opponents as naive and living in the past. In contrast, anticasino advocates presented themselves as the true upholders of Seneca and Hodinöhsö:ni´ values—unlike their opponents, whom they viewed as sacrificing tribal sovereignty to the dreaded enemy in Albany for personal gain.

Pro-casino Senecas clearly had the advantage. Smoke shop proprietors who favored the expansion of gaming had the wealth and power to shape the agenda, hiring significant numbers of employees, who made up a sizable proportion of the tribal electorate. Senecas were well aware that Indian Country was now rapidly accepting the idea of casinos to boost tribal economies with needed capital. The Senecas desperately needed an infusion of capital to overcome dependence and to plan for the future, referred to in Iroquoian terms as "looking ahead seven generations." Although the Seneca economy had made major gains in the 1980s, in 1992 the Indian nation's unemployment rate was still 27 percent, triple that of Cattaraugus County, one of the poorest counties in New York State.[48] Tribal bingo, one stops, and the Seneca Nation Settlement Act payments were not enough to build a viable economy for the future, and casinos seemed to be both a quick and right fix for these economic problems.

The casino/anticasino debate intensified in 1993, when the New York State Assembly's Subcommittee on Indian Affairs, chaired by Edward Griffith of Buffalo, held hearings in Buffalo and Albany in May to discuss state–Indian relations.[49] At the downtown Buffalo and Erie County Public Library on May 13, seven Senecas testified, six of whom were from Cattaraugus. Midge Dean Stock, a well-respected Allegany Seneca, then head of this Indian nation's Education Department, brought up Seneca educational needs.[50] However, two issues received the most attention: the

sales tax and casinos. Ross John and Larry Ballagh, two Seneca councilors and members of the Iroquois Businessmen's Association, testified that the sales tax was a violation of Seneca sovereignty and treaty
rights.[51] Yet the hearing was dominated by Seneca opponents of casinos.
At the hearing, the most detailed testimony in opposition to casinos was
presented by John Mohawk, the well-known Seneca journalist, philoso-
pher, and historian who taught at SUNY Buffalo. To differentiate himself
from Ballagh and John, he indicated that he was representing the Iroquois Confederacy's Grand Council at the hearing and was not an official
representative of the Seneca Nation Tribal Council. Mohawk then argued
against casino gaming; he believed that it was highly susceptible to the
"invasion of organized crime or other sources of criminal behavior" and
that there was "no enforceable process to prevent and/or punish political corruption." He asked the state legislators to carry out its obligations
to its citizens and to the Indian communities by avoiding the creation
of environments that would "deteriorate the quality of life." Ironically,
this spokesman of Hodinöhsö:ni´ sovereignty was beseeching the New
York State Legislature, often seen as the enemy of his people, not to aid
pro-casino Senecas in their efforts to win support for a gaming compact
with Albany.

In responding to a query by the subcommittee's chairman, Edward
Griffith, about the potential economic benefits of casinos to reservations,
Mohawk maintained that casino development required the Senecas to
obtain significant infusion of capital for "fantasy palaces" and hotels, but
that in the end it would lead to "vicious competition." "In the long run
it's a bell curve, and in the long run, probably twenty years from now,
the Indians wouldn't profit from the gambling casino or at last not in any
great measure." Mohawk added that most of the casino workers would
"make relatively low wages" and that most of the jobs would go to non-
Indians. He suggested that the pro-casino elements within the Iroquois
communities were few in number and found mostly in communities with
elected governments. Yet, to him, a positive decision to make a compact
with a Six Nations community would "affect everybody's lives inside the
Indian Country, and I say that it will distort and change things in New
York State."

Bud Mahoney, the subcommittee's counsel, asked Mohawk about Native religious prohibitions against gaming. Mohawk, a member of the Newtown Longhouse, responded:

> Okay, the culture, the Iroquois culture has an admonition and the admonition is essentially something along the lines of a sin for people to gamble away all of their money which they needed in order to support their families, and in a sense in our modern context we will call that the gambling compulsion, but at any rate people interpret that in many, many degrees. Some people say that that means you can't have any gambling of any kind whatsoever. Other people say you can have some kind if it's just for fun. Others say you can if you don't lose too much money, so all the ways up and down the line I think there's no question about it that gambling was not seen in the Seneca Handsome Lake's point of view.[52]

Calvin Lay Jr., former president of the Seneca Nation, followed. He adamantly opposed casinos. Lay made six points in his argument: (1) that the Seneca Nation had survived many years without gambling and could continue to do so in the future without it; (2) that the efforts by the Seneca Council in considering a gaming compact with the state were threats to tribal sovereignty and that negotiating away "these sovereign rights" for the almighty dollar was unconscionable; (3) that gaming would undermine the Senecas' culture; (4) that Senecas were not suited to be casino workers and that, in the long run, the casino would hire mostly non-Senecas; (5) that the costs of building and operating a facility had not been determined and that it was very possible it would become a "white elephant" and increase the Senecas' debt burden; and (6) that the locations of the Seneca Nation reservations were away from high-population areas, thereby requiring the Senecas "to spend megabucks" to attract customers.[53]

Susan Abrams, who had led the demonstration at President Snyder's inaugural six months earlier, focused on sovereignty issues and the alleged actions of the Seneca president, attorney, and Tribal Council in pushing for casinos. Abrams claimed that she and her anticasino allies' lives were being threatened. She insisted that her anticasino group numbered between 150 and 250 members and that they were allied with the chiefs on other reservations, who opposed casino compacts with the state because they perceived them as a threat to tribal sovereignty. Abrams questioned Barry Snyder's honesty as well as that of Tribal Council members. She maintained that Snyder stifled discussions and debates in the Tribal Council, and she accused him and attorney Joseph Crangle of negotiating with state officials "underhandedly." She challenged the alleged claims made to state officials that the majority of Senecas favored a gaming compact.[54]

In July 1993, one day after the Oneida Nation opened Turning Stone, the first legalized Indian casino in New York, the Seneca Nation Tribal Council gave President Snyder the authorization to look into the possibility of operating its own tribal casino.[55] The next month the Seneca Nation Tribal Council suspended tribal employees for joining in an anticasino protest at the Seneca Nation's One Stop at Cattaraugus. In reaction to the suspensions, confrontations between gaming and antigaming Senecas turned more violent, and a gas bomb was tossed in the direction of President Snyder's tribal office at Cattaraugus.[56] To calm the situation, the Tribal Council announced that it was rescinding the authorization for Snyder to pursue gaming opportunities. It also authorized a nonbinding referendum on the issue and set the vote to take place on May 10, 1994. The referendum resulted in a vote of 714 opposed and 444 in favor of Class III gaming.[57]

Two other events in 1994 were to lead to a political upheaval within the Seneca Nation. The first was the US Supreme Court decision in the *Attea* case described previously. The second event was the election of Dennis Bowen to the presidency of the Seneca Nation in November 1994. Bowen was elected president by a mere three-vote margin. He immediately tried to remove Ross John and Art John from their seats on the Tribal Council because they had been appointed as replacement tribal councilors by President Snyder and had not been elected by popular vote. In reaction to Bowen's move, his opponents attempted to have him removed from the presidency and replaced by Karen Bucktooth. Attempts to resolve this tribal dispute went before the Seneca Peacemaker's Court as well as before state and federal courts, the latter finally remanding the issue back to the Seneca Nation Tribal Council.[58]

In late February 1995, supporters of Bucktooth, still steaming after the close election and Bowen's efforts to remove the two councilors, seized and occupied one of the Senecas' governmental buildings at Cattaraugus. Shots rang out on February 27. Community members began to fear that the Senecas were about to repeat the Akwesasne experience, and they were not so far off. On March 25, tragedy ensued: three supporters of Bucktooth—Myron Kettle, Samuel Powless, and Charles Thompson—lay dead. A fourth—David Rice, a supporter of Bowen—was wounded in a barrage of bullets in a clash between armed gaming and antigaming Senecas. Six days later BIA officials intervened and recognized Bowen as the legitimate president of the Seneca Nation.[59]

Early in 1995, after George Pataki's election as governor, the New York State Division of Military and Naval Affairs drew up a secret contingency plan against so-called warrior nations "in the event of civil disturbances at Akwesasne, Cattaraugus, and Onondaga." A New York National Guard unit was organized—as both an "air mobile force and a mechanized infantry force"—to assist the New York State Police "anywhere within the Indian reservations clearing built-up areas or in a direct assault against an armed force." The purpose of this directive was clear:

a. Department of State Police (DSP) will assist Dept of Taxation and Finance SNY [State of New York] establish collection activity for due/past due NYS Taxes from the sale of gasoline, alcohol, tobacco and gaming revenues on Indian Reservations bordered within the State of New York. DSP is expected to be met with resistance from the pro-gambling warrior society dissidents who have demonstrated violent/militant resistance to occupation or intervention by the DSP in the past.

b. DSP may require Military Forces to move against the Indians armed with automatic weapons.

c. The Governor will order the National Guard to State Active Duty.

d. The New York Army National Guard may be required to conduct combat operations.

e. Civil Disturbances may occur on/off the Indian Reservations.[60]

Although this plan never went into effect, its mere existence vividly illustrates the heightened level of tensions between state officials and the Six Nations.

In the same month, Assemblyman David R. Townsend Jr. submitted a legislative report, *Claims Casino: A Report on State–Indian Relations in New York State*, to Governor Pataki.[61] Townsend, a Republican from Sylvan Beach, represented the 115th Assembly District, which was in the heart of the traditional Oneida Nation territory. Non-Indian residents and business owners in this area had been directly affected by the sizable Oneida Indian land claim, the establishment of the Oneidas' Turning Stone Casino and Resort complex, and the tribe's acquisition of land and businesses with the profits from gaming. Until his defeat in 2010, Assembly Townsend was the most ardent supporter of the New York State Convenience Store Association, which lobbied for the state imposition of sales taxes on Indian reservations because their own non-Indian businesses had been undercut by cheaper tax-free cigarettes and fuel dispensed by Indian-owned stores.

Although Townsend's report was directed largely at Ray Halbritter, the Oneidas' tribal chairman, his lengthy analysis also dealt with other Native communities in New York State. Its conclusions were clearly spelled out in his transmittal letter to the governor: New York State should go ahead and collect its sales taxes and demand more concessions from Indian nations seeking gaming compacts. Townsend condemned federal officials for allowing Indian land claims to proceed without taking into consideration offsets for the state's alleged generosity in providing state services over two centuries. The assemblyman insisted that the result was "ever-increasing free local and state services to increasingly wealthy Indians, and ever-increasing taxes from non-Indians to support these services." He added:

> The federal government has forced Indian casinos down our throats. Federal courts implicitly have ordered what could be a financially suffocating settlement of an Oneida land claim. Federal law makes it almost impossible to collect state or local taxes from Indians on reservations or engaged in commerce. . . . As our report shows, federal and state governments have been paying for these services for years, and are continuing to do so. Things will not get much better until Washington recognizes that federal Indian policy is causing major problems for local and state governments. However, I do not believe that we can wait until Washington awakens

to the harm that it is causing. New York must abandon its timid non-role of acquiescing to each Indian request and demand as if it came from Mother Teresa. Our Indian friends are making huge sums of money and our response has been to drive them to the bank. On the simple grounds that each of us should pay his or her share of state and local services, New York should establish an Indian policy that mandates the financial protection that our taxpayers have every reason to expect.[62]

The Townsend report also noted the state's services toward the Senecas, especially in the areas of education, health, housing, state police, social services, and transportation. It indicated that the Seneca Nation received $166,448 for library funding; that the state had allocated $1,066,315 toward construction of 105 housing units; and that the Erie County Sheriff's Department was paying hundreds of thousands of dollars for deputies, and the New York State Police had assigned four troopers on both day and night shifts to keep the peace at Cattaraugus after the three murders four months earlier. The report indicated that the state was providing $208,000 and the federal government $4,208,000 for Seneca health care, although it never explained the reasons for the disparity or described the historic failures of Albany to meet the health and social services needs of its reservation populations.[63]

The Townsend report noted that the Senecas had filed land claims to Grand Island and Cuba Lake but indicated that the majority of Senecas, unlike the Oneidas, were not disposed toward pursuing casino gambling. It quickly treated past acquisition of Seneca Indian lands as if Albany and Washington had been respectful of Native communities and generous with payments. The report also mentioned that the state's contribution to settle the Salamanca lease was $25 million. Without going into great detail, it—incredibly—added: "The Senecas also received substantial sums for easements taken for the Southern Tier Expressway and for land flooded by the Kinzua Dam project in Pennsylvania by the Army Corps of Engineers." Later in the report, Townsend, in an effort to justify the Southern Tier Expressway land take, indicated that the state had paid $2,264 an acre, $494,386, to the Seneca Nation for the easement and $1.3 million in compensation to individual Senecas. Much to Townsend's chagrin, the state had had to agree to exchange 795 acres (750 acres of Allegany State Park and 45 privately owned acres) with the Seneca Nation for this easement, requiring state officials later to purchase other lands for the Allegany State Park.[64] Unlike state senator Frank Padavan of Queens, a major opponent of the expansion of gaming based on his moral objections and law enforcement concerns, Townsend, until his defeat in 2010, was more focused on economic competition and land claims issues.[65]

Despite Albany officials' hardened stance in the summer of 1995, their position was to shift by the following year. A split had developed within the Pataki administration. Some were pushing for casino development, but New York's constitution prohibited Albany from establishing its own type of state-run gaming enterprise. Establishing compacts with tribes besides the Oneidas would allow the establishment of Indian-run casinos according to the provisions of the IGRA. It would provide revenues to the state and create jobs, especially in economically hard hit upstate New York. Michael Urbach, the New York State commissioner of taxation and finance, claimed that the state was losing $125 million in revenues because non-Indians were trekking to the reservations to fill up their gas tanks and buy cigarettes.[66] He saw the real economic possibilities of allowing the expansion of gaming. As a key member of the New York State Task Force on Casino Gambling established by Governor Pataki's Executive Order Number 36.1, Urbach and Taxation and Finance Commission members pointed out that since the passing of the IGRA in 1988, a total of 180,000 direct gaming jobs and 250,000 indirect jobs had been created nationally.[67]

Late in 1996, the Pataki administration began to draft sales tax compacts with several Hodinöhsö:ni´ communities. When these efforts were revealed, a backlash followed in Iroquoia, and leaders who dared negotiate with the enemy—namely, state politicos in Albany—were condemned. Even some of the most eloquent voices of sovereignty on the Grand Council at Onondaga were now viewed as traitors. The reaction spilled over into Seneca politics.[68] Despite the growing crisis in Iroquoia, Governor Pataki's position once again hardened after the Seneca Tribal Council and other Iroquois communities refused to accept a tax compact worked out with certain tribal leaders. He gave the Senecas and other Hodinöhsö:ni´ a deadline of April 1, 1997, after which the state would impose taxes of $.43 to $.47 a gallon on gasoline and $5.30 per carton of cigarettes to non-Indian customers of Indian-owned convenience stories. Seneca president Michael Schindler, a mild-mannered man and member of the Newtown Longhouse at Cattaraugus, tried to meet with the governor to work out an agreement over the sales tax in an attempt to prevent a violent confrontation from occurring.[69]

On April 20, 1997, approximately a thousand Senecas and their supporters once again blocked the New York State Thruway to protest the state's intention to levy sales taxes on Indian lands. Fifty-five state troopers in riot gear responded. A brief scuffle ensued. The Senecas claimed that they were peaceful protesters, a fact later questioned by the state police. A number of protesters scuffled with the police, and some state troopers and some Senecas were injured in the fray. The incident resulted in the closing of several thruway exits from Hamburg to Fredonia.[70] Frustrated and faced with internal criticism, President Schindler responded to the riot, trying to explain its origins to the press. He insisted that the Senecas as a whole believed that the state was "trying to destroy" their nation. "Our people say, 'Don't make any agreements with the state because they don't live up to their agreements.'"[71] One month later Governor Pataki, fearful of bad press, backed away from trying to collect sales taxes on transactions on Indian lands and dumped the question into the hands of the state legislature. Despite the lobbying efforts by the New York State Association of Convenience Stores to have the state collect those sales taxes, the Legislature failed to act.[72]

When Governor Pataki backed down in enforcing sales tax collection, Seneca attention once more shifted to the casino issue. In February 1998, three hundred casino opponents prevented a tribal vote allowing for a referendum on the issue after the Niagara Falls Development Corporation had revealed its plans to work with the Senecas in establishing a $140 million Indian casino in Niagara Falls. After the confrontation the year before, many Senecas questioned the state police's jurisdiction in a future casino; they were also vehemently opposed to sharing profits with the state.[73] Yet in early May 1998, by a vote of 710 to 547, the Senecas approved a resolution permitting talks with New York State officials about building a casino outside of the Senecas' reservations. After being threatened by anticasino proponents, President Schindler nullified the vote but the next day reversed himself, claiming that he had overturned the vote while under duress.[74]

It is important to note that beginning with the election of Barry Snyder Sr. in November 1992, gaming advocates had held private conversations with Albany officials about casinos. They were well aware that section 8c of the Seneca Nation Settlement Act of 1990 had permitted the Senecas to acquire land "within or near proximity to former reservation land."[75] Under this provision, the Senecas had the legal right to establish gaming operations throughout any of its historic territory recognized under federal treaties from the time of the federal Treaty of Big Tree of September 15, 1797, which first recognized the existence of eleven Seneca reservations, totaling hundreds of thousands of acres in western New York, including the entire present city of Buffalo.[76] Indian lands in Niagara County were historically Seneca, some of which were sold to the Tuscaroras in 1803, when this Iroquoian nation was resettled there on a reservation in the Lewiston–Sanborn area.[77]

From the Seneca protest in 1997 to the preliminary accord on casinos in 2001, Governor Pataki and his administration played down the sales tax issue and did not threaten to enforce it on the reservations. Although Assemblyman Townsend continued to lead the legislative opposition to the state's nonpolicy on the sales tax, the executive office of the governor was more conciliatory. One top official of the state's Department of Law calmed fears by maintaining that "[t]he state has no ability to take action on reservations. We don't have police power with respect to the laws."[78]

Because the economy of western New York was in severe decline, with Buffalo alone losing 40 percent of its population since 1950, the governor presented his support for Indian casinos as a way to breathe new life and jobs into the city and region.[79] But there were other factors as well. Niagara Falls, New York, an equally economically depressed community, was now faced with severe competition from Niagara Falls, Ontario, its sister city across the border, which had invested $2 billion and opened a successful casino that earned $597 million in 2000. Officials in Niagara Falls, New York, sought ways to infuse new economic life into the fading city to compete for tourist dollars, and a casino, they thought, would do just that. The Niagara Falls Development Corporation was to sweeten the pot by offering to the Senecas its outdated and failing convention center complex, which had been designed by Philip Johnson and opened in 1974, as a possible casino site.[80]

The governor and his staff saw the rapid growth of Indian casinos nationwide as an economic stimulus for western New York, one that would result in employment gains and additions to the state coffers. He was well aware that the New York constitution did not allow the state to establish a full-scale casino operation with highly profitable slot machines. Pataki also understood that any lobbying campaign to amend the state's constitution would be time-consuming and politically risky because he had some powerful opponents, especially Townsend and Padavan, within his own party. As a consequence, Pataki saw the establishment of Indian casinos as the state's fast track to economic development. He also had another reason to support Indian casinos: he hoped to use this issue to help him negotiate favorable Indian land claims settlements for the state.[81]

In 1993, during Barry Snyder's presidency, the Seneca Nation had filed suit for Grand Island. Although the Senecas had a long-standing claim to this territory that connected two of New York State's major cities, this action was clearly one to press the state to sign a compact for an Indian casino or two in Erie and Niagara Counties. It was also aimed at retaliating for the New York State Thruway's take of lands at Cattaraugus, Snyder's home territory, in 1954. The New York State Thruway, one of the defendants in the filed land claims case, administered the Grand Island Twin Bridges and the main roadway from Buffalo to Niagara Falls. Snyder understood that attacking two agencies of the New York State government—the Department of Taxation and Finance and the New York State Thruway—was good politics within the Seneca Nation and furthered his image as a defender of tribal sovereignty. Instead of filing a claim for the Senecas' historic homeland in the Genesee Valley, as one of the Senecas' attorneys had suggested, Snyder and the Seneca Tribal Council sued for Grand Island, hoping to exert pressure for a favorable settlement with the state over an Indian casino compact because he was already aware that Albany officials in the Cuomo administration had earlier floated the idea of a trade. It should be noted that Snyder's chief adviser in this matter was attorney Joseph Crangle, a major figure in western New York politics and a former head of the Democratic Party in the state.

In 2001, less concerned about the social costs of gaming and faced with declining revenues from state race tracks, Governor Pataki gave his full support for Indian casinos to be established in the state. With five Indian nations—the Cayuga, Mohawk, Oneida, Stockbridge-Munsee, and Seneca—pursuing land claims litigation against New York State, Pataki also envisioned making accords with some or all of these Native American nations whereby the state would sign gaming compacts in trades for settling these cases. Although initially the Pataki administration insisted that the Senecas' Grand Island claim had to be settled before state officials would agree to a gaming compact, the governor later backed away from this position. In order to quiet opposition from Assemblyman Townsend as well as from Assemblyman Sam Hoyt of Buffalo, the voice of Grand Island residents in the New York State Legislature, Pataki indicated that the state would indemnify property owners if the Grand Island case were lost in federal court.[82]

The governor, although receiving criticism from powerful Buffalo Democrats such as Deputy Assembly Speaker Arthur Eve, head of the Black Caucus of the New York State Legislature, as well as from Townsend and Padavan for his determined push for Indian casino development, did have significant Republican support for it.[83] Former western New York Republican congressman William Paxon served as a consultant to the law firm Akin, Gump, which led the Seneca Nation lobbying effort for a gaming compact. Local legislators—Republican state senators George Maziarz and Dale Volkers as well as Assemblyman William T. Stachowski—pushed for approval as well.[84] Stachowski insisted: "We need to keep our dollars in Niagara Falls."[85] Pataki's supporters were reinforced by articles in business-oriented publications such as the *Wall Street Journal* and *Business Week*, which increasingly devoted more and more attention to Native American entrepreneurial efforts and viewed this trend as a positive economic change. The doubling of casino revenues from 1997 to 2001—from $6 billion to $12.8 billion—and the hiring of hundreds of thousands of workers nationwide were also factors that turned the tide to approval of a state–Seneca gaming accord.[86]

With the election of Duane Ray to the Seneca Nation presidency in November 1998, the nation's representatives had already begun formal negotiations with John O'Mara, an attorney representing the New York State governor. They had also met with Niagara Falls officials; a Malaysian investor, K. T. Lin, son of one of the wealthiest men in the world, who had financed the Mashantucket Pequots' Foxwoods Resort and Casino in Connecticut; and six separate developers, including G. Michael "Mickey" Brown, who was the former president of Foxwoods and head of the New Jersey Division of Gaming Enforcement.[87] On June 21, 2001, Seneca and Albany officials signed a preliminary casino agreement that called for the establishment of three casinos: the first in the Niagara Falls Convention and Civic Center to be opened by April 2002; the second in downtown Buffalo, to open at the end of 2002; and the third at or adjacent to the Cattaraugus Indian Reservation sometime after that. This executed new Memorandum of Understanding outlined the basic tenets of the agreement but required a Seneca referendum before a formal compact would go into effect.[88]

Some Senecas believed that if the nation approved this preliminary gaming compact, it would threaten what they saw as its inherent sovereignty. The Seneca Nation had to agree to share 25 percent of the slot machine profits with New York State and its local communities (the same model that the Mashantucket Pequots had agreed to with Connecticut in 1992). Although the Senecas received the Niagara Falls Convention and Civic Center for one dollar, they had to promise to hire some union workers on the project, assume the center's substantial debt, and later deal with asbestos contamination at the site. New York State troopers were allowed jurisdiction on casino grounds and were permitted state law enforcement criminal checks on casino employees, which would restrict those convicted of DWI, DUI, and felonies from being hired. Because there was a requirement that the Seneca Nation would conduct a referendum accepting or rejecting the compact, the issue was still unsettled after the preliminary accord was reached.[89] On May 14, 2002, the Seneca voted, addressing the question whether tribal members favored entering into an agreement with New York State for Class III gaming off their existing territories. By a vote of 1,077 to 976 (52.5 percent to 47.5 percent), the Seneca Nation accepted the creation of two Indian casinos—in Niagara Falls and Buffalo—away from their residential populations on the Allegany and Cattaraugus Indian Territories.[90]

On August 18, 2002, Cyrus Schindler Sr. and George Pataki signed the final version of the New York State–Seneca Gaming Compact allowing for the creation of three casinos. The Senecas were to receive the exclusive right to operate casinos with slot machines in the fourteen counties of western New York, a provision that was later violated by Albany officials' establishment of racinos. At the ceremony, President Schindler insisted that the compact was a major step toward making the Seneca Nation "more self-sufficient. Today is important and historic because it will lead to better housing, better health care, and more educational opportunities for our people." After calling the accord a model compact for other Native communities, he evoked the *Guswentha*, the two-row wampum that contains two parallel purple rows of shell interspersed by three rows of white shell. To the Six Nations, the two purple strands represent two vessels—an Iroquois canoe and a Euro-American ship—symbolic of two distinct peoples traveling down the river of life. The canoe represents the Iroquois world; the ship represents the Euro-Americans and their laws, mores, and values. In order to successfully navigate the river, the vessels must not interfere with each other, meaning that the Indians and non-Indians have to respect each other's way of life. Schindler was teaching a lesson to the Albany officials in attendance—namely, that they needed to recognize the separate and distinct status of the Seneca Nation of Indians. At the ceremony, even though the state was given certain new authority and jurisdiction in the compact, Governor Pataki acknowledged that the "Seneca Nation is a sovereign nation" and claimed that the compact recognized that fact and did nothing to subvert it.[91]

Two and a half weeks earlier, the Seneca Nation Tribal Council had created the Seneca Niagara Gaming Corporation, a separate entity required by the National Indian Gaming Commission, to establish, manage, and run casino operations. This new tribal entity then hired Klewin Building Corporation to refurbish the fifty-five-acre Niagara Falls Convention and Civic Center site as a temporary casino. Major investors included the Lin family, who provided the $100 million loan for the casino.

Mickey Brown was soon hired to establish and manage casino operations. He had worked with the Lins previously in their Foxwood Casino operation in Connecticut and thus was skilled in securing investors. All of these early initiatives were gambles because they preceded the turning over of the Niagara Falls site to the Senecas and were initiated several months in advance of the New York State Assembly approval and before the required approval by the secretary of the interior.[92]

The casino issue still remained the major divisive one within the Seneca Nation until the last months of 2002. In an election in November of that year, Rickey L. Armstrong Sr. of the pro-gaming Seneca Party defeated Arnold Cooper, the incumbent Seneca Nation treasurer and candidate of the Keepers of the Western Door Party, which had opposed signing gaming compacts. In a record turnout of voters, Armstrong easily defeated Cooper 1,306 to 865, insisting that he and gaming advocates had won a mandate "to open the [Niagara Falls] casino on schedule" and urging all Senecas to finally "get over their divisiveness and come together as one."[93] The Seneca Nation Tribal Council soon pushed forward in promoting the establishment of two other casinos—one off reservation in Buffalo and the other on the Allegany Indian Reservation in West Salamanca. Although Buffalo's mayor and civic and religious groups challenged the Senecas' legal and moral right to build a casino on the city's waterfront, the Seneca Tribal Council voted to hold another referendum, this time on whether to build a casino on Seneca Territory. In September 2003, the Senecas voted to develop the casino within their residential territory on the Allegany Territory adjacent to the Southern Tier Expressway. At the same time, they pursued in federal court the option of the casino in downtown Buffalo.

On May 1, 2004, the Seneca Allegany Casino opened. Cars were backed for several miles through the streets of Salamanca. I was accompanied by two Seneca women with "connections," so I was allowed to skirt the line and get to the casino's opening ceremony, amazed by the draw of this gaming operation in this largely rural and poor northern Appalachian region of New York. The same year, the Seneca Nation opened a four-star hotel at the Seneca Niagara Falls Casino and renamed the complex the "Seneca Niagara Falls Casino and Resort" and started construction of an eleven-story, 220-room hotel at the Seneca Allegany Casino.[94] In 2007, after much resistance by Erie County politicians and civic and religious groups, the Senecas opened a third, much scaled-down casino in downtown Buffalo.[95]

In November 2004, Barry Snyder once again emerged from his behind-the-scenes leadership of the Seneca Party and was elected president for the third time, taking the reins of tribal government after successfully pushing through Seneca acceptance of three casinos. Frequently charged with corruption and intimidation, he nevertheless had achieved an economic transformation of the Seneca Nation. Whether supporting him or not, Senecas would acknowledge that Snyder was the "puppet master" who could get things done. Thirteen months after his election, Snyder fittingly presided over the groundbreaking ceremony at the third Seneca casino in downtown Buffalo, the Seneca Buffalo Creek Casino, proudly pointing out that the two previously opened casinos had already created four thousand new jobs, added $72 million in payroll to the local economy, hired 1,200 union construction workers, and provided $100 million in revenues to New York State and $21 million to the cities of Niagara Falls and Salamanca. Then Snyder struck a chord that Senecas could clearly understand. With a sense of history, he referred to the importance of the site chosen for the casino. Snyder, whose own ancestors had been dispossessed and removed from the Buffalo Creek Reservation after the fraudulent federal treaty of 1838, stated: "And so it is with tremendous pride, as we stand here today on land that our ancestors lived, hunted, and raised their families that I announce that the Seneca Nation has returned to Buffalo Creek after 167 years." He concluded his speech by signaling a warning that there was a "a looming threat" to the Senecas' treaties, lands, and population. "Last year in violation of the Canandaigua [1794] and Buffalo Creek [1842] treaties, the State Legislature directed all goods and services sold to non-Indians in our territory be subject to state sales taxation."[96]

Snyder's warnings proved prescient. Later New York State governors–Elliot Spitzer, David Patterson, and Andrew Cuomo—continued to push policies judged by most Senecas as threats to their sovereignty and their efforts at promoting economic betterment. Both Spitzer in his short-lived governorship and his successor Patterson supported efforts by the state Legislature to require sales tax enforcement. Proponents of these

Growth in Gaming Revenues in Past 10 Years
($ in Billions)

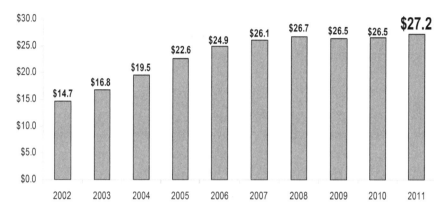

Chart 1. Growth of Indian gaming revenues nationwide, 2002–11. *Source*: US Department of the Interior, National Indian Gaming Commission.

measures included diverse lobbyist groups ranging from non-Indian-run convenience stores that totaled three thousand in the state and employed sixty-eight thousand people to antismoking health advocates such as the American Cancer Society.[97] Their lobbying efforts intensified with the incredible growth of Seneca cigarette distribution on the Internet. By 2009, Seneca cigarette sales, largely attributed to the explosion of Internet marketing, totaled hundreds of millions of dollars a year.[98] Even before Senecas had started rolling their own cheaper cigarettes and distributing their own brands throughout the state, thereby bypassing wholesalers as well as the New York State Department of Taxation and Finance, major tobacco giants such as Philip Morris, pressured by state and federal officials, convenience store operators, and wholesalers, had turned against the Indians.[99]

The result was the push for new federal legislation. On March 31, 2010, President Barack Obama signed a bill introduced by two Democrat congressman—Representative Andrew Weiner of New York and Senator Herbert Kohl of Wisconsin. The bill's stated aims were to fight criminal activities and to stop terrorist organizations from profiting from trafficking in illicit cigarettes; to prevent billions of dollars in revenues from being lost to federal, state, and local governments by ensuring the collection of taxes on cigarettes and smokeless tobacco sold on the Internet or in mail-order sales; and to make tobacco products less accessible to America's children. Antitobacco advocates, in and out of Congress, also viewed the bill as a major effort to enhance public health by helping to prevent and reduce the use of tobacco. The bill—the Prevent All Cigarette Trafficking (PACT) Act—required all individuals and businesses that sold cigarettes and smokeless tobacco on the Internet or other mail-order sales to pay all applicable federal, state, local, or tribal tobacco taxes and to affix tax stamps before delivering these products to customers in a state; to comply with various state and local laws that were required of non-Internet sellers; to register with and make periodic reports to state tax-collection officials; and to check the age and identification of customers to ensure that no children under the age of eighteen would purchase cigarettes and smokeless tobacco on the Internet. Importantly, PACT also made tobacco products unmailable, thus stopping Internet sellers from using the US mail to evade compliance. Violators of the act would be faced with strong penalties and would be subject to prosecution under federal law as well as by states and localities and by Indian tribes. Despite not being specifically mentioned in PACT, private mail delivery companies, including Fed-Ex and UPS, have voluntarily complied with the act and have refused mailings and deliveries of cigarettes and smokeless tobacco products. Although it was insisted that the act was not aimed at limiting tribal sovereignty, it clearly had a devastating economic impact throughout Indian Country, including in New York. Seneca cigarette and smokeless tobacco sales dropped by more than 80 percent in the year after PACT went into effect.[100]

Besides the never-ending sales tax controversy that still sours Seneca relations with Albany, the two parties have clashed over gaming operations. Soon after the opening of the Senecas third casino in Buffalo in 2007, Albany clearly broke the 2002 agreement that had been federally approved by the US Department of the Interior. The compact agreement gave the Seneca Nation the exclusive right to have casinos with slot machines in a fourteen-county area, the Senecas' traditional homeland in today's western New York State. In return, the Seneca Nation was to provide 25 percent of its profits from slot machine operations to the state. Nevertheless, Albany officials allowed non-Indian operated racinos at Batavia, Farmington, and Hamburg to install video lottery terminals, similar to slot machines, in a clear attempt to get around the restriction set forth in the gaming compact.[101]

Until the summer of 2013, the Seneca Nation held back its required payments to Albany under the exclusivity provision on slot machines set forth in the compact. These moneys were supposed to be forwarded to the state government in Albany to share with the cities of Niagara Falls, Salamanca, and Buffalo, where the three Seneca casinos are located.[102] Late in 2011, Governor Andrew Cuomo announced and quickly received legislative approval for a referendum on a new amendment to the New York State constitution that would allow the state to license seven full-scale gaming operations, not racinos, throughout New York. A statewide referendum on this amendment is scheduled to take place in November 2013, with the possibility that construction would follow the next year.[103] Seneca leadership was faced with this impending competition and the economic fallout from PACT. To meet these challenges, President Robert Odawi Porter's administration, among other things, attempted to network with legislators to try to win support for Seneca concerns; testified at state legislative and congressional hearings; used the print and television media to explain Seneca positions on issues; agreed to mediation over the state's violations of the gaming compact; and began to pursue the FERC hydropower license at the Kinzua Dam.[104]

On November 4, 2012, Barry E. Snyder Sr. was elected president of the Seneca Nation of Indians for the fifth time. He immediately named Mo John as his special assistant. Snyder made it clear that he was determined to continue to withhold slot machine revenues to the Empire State until Albany officials honored the Seneca Nation of Indians' exclusivity agreement. In his inaugural address of November 13, he definitely insisted: "We also pledge that no casino revenue will be paid to New York State without the continued assurance that our exclusivity rights are honored as the compact intended, and proliferation of the state's licensed casinos stops at our [fourteen-county] exclusive territory."[105]

By May 2013, the war of words between New York State and Seneca officials became more acrimonious. At a time when mediators were hoping to resolve the dispute peacefully, Governor Andrew Cuomo floated the idea of locating a new non-Indian casino in Niagara Falls to compete with the Seneca Niagara Falls Casino. Non-Indian racino/racetracks in Batavia, Hamburg, and Farmington New York continued to present themselves in newspaper advertisements and on road signs as full functioning casinos. In response, the Senecas continued to withhold 25 percent of their slot machine revenues at their casinos from state coffers, as required by the 2002 gaming compact, moneys that Albany officials were supposed to share with the City of Buffalo, Niagara Falls, and Salamanca. There was even talk that the state would not renew the gaming compact in 2016, a compact that many Senecas believed was automatically built into the 2002 agreement.[106] On May 17, 2013, at a treaty commemoration ceremony at West Seneca, New York, President Barry Snyder Sr. blasted the governor, accusing him of employing "playground bully tactics" in squeezing his Seneca people.[107]

In late May and early June, both the Oneida Nation of New York and the Akwesasne Mohawks worked out accords with the state to ensure that non-Indian casinos would not compete within their regions in central and northern New York. On June 12, 2013, despite the threats and counterthreats, the Seneca Nation and the governor's office were to come to an accord. The Senecas agreed to resume payments, a total of $630 million to the state for the benefit of the three cities. In return, the state formally extended its approval of the gaming compact with the Senecas to 2023. State officials recognized the Seneca Nation's' exclusivity zone and agreed not to approve a full-scale non-Indian casino in the fourteen counties of western New York. Although racinos were allowed to continue operations at Batavia, Hamburg, and Farmington, they could no longer advertise as casinos. Both Seneca and New York State officials have hailed this accord as a new day in their relations; however, based on their rocky relationship in the past, one cannot be overly optimistic.[108]

PART IV **||||** *Conclusion*

12

Looking Ahead Seven Generations

IN 2013, the Senecas live in the shadow of land losses that occurred in the postwar era. It is important to point out that the generation that grew up from childhood in the two decades after World War II are still in major political offices of the nation. For them, the past is a present reality, clearly affecting current Seneca reactions to state and federal policies. Today, interest in finding how and why the Kinzua project came about continues to be the subject of talks and panel discussions at Remember the Removal Day, an annual event on the last Saturday in September. Various presentations and exhibits sponsored by the Seneca-Iroquois National Museum keep memories of this painful era alive. To a large degree, this interest led to the creation of the Kinzua Dam Relicensing Commission (KDRC). The KDRC, headed by Wendy Huff from 2010 to 2012, is seeking the federal license to operate and manage the hydropower production at the Kinzua Dam.

The Kinzua Dam project shaped nearly every aspect of Seneca life—culturally, economically, educationally, and politically—over the past half-century. Besides the loss of approximately 10,000 acres of Seneca territory, the dam project sped up New York State's acquisition of Indian lands for highway development that had begun with thruway planning in the postwar years. Although the dam had its original roots in flood control, its hydropower potential was part of the conversation at least since the late 1930s; by the late 1950s, hydropower became an important factor in the push for the project. The Kinzua Dam was not simply the result of lobbying by Pennsylvania interests, the Army Corps of Engineers, or congressmen seeking pork-barrel funding for their districts. It was the result of the interplay of federal termination and energy policies in Cold War America; New York State's historic dismissal of the rights—civil and treaty—of its Native American populations as well as its insatiable desire to expand or protect its interests and land base for highways in its efforts to promote tourism and other forms of economic development; and Pennsylvania officials' and corporate interests' desire to foster industry in the western part of the state by preventing floods, *but also by developing more hydropower* to overcome the state's overdependence on coal, which had resulted in massive pollution problems. It was the interplay of these forces that empowered the Army Corps of Engineers to design Kinzua and condemn Seneca lands, ultimately allowing Penelec to transform the dam into a hydroelectric-generating station.

The Seneca Nation did survive Kinzua in spite of federal termination policies and Pennsylvania's and New York State's aggressive actions to acquire Indian lands. The Kinzua take resulted in the loss of approximately one-fifth of the Seneca Nation's entire tribal landholdings and delayed tribal efforts to resolve the century-old Salamanca lease controversy and its initiatives to file land claims suits. Yet the Haley bill, House Resolution 1794, enacted by Congress as the Seneca Nation Compensation Act in 1964, resulted in certain beneficial changes within the Seneca Nation. The nation constructed new homes, a museum, two libraries, two community centers, two IHS facilities, as well as a modern tribal governmental structure, albeit a large and bureaucratic one. Under immense pressures, Cornelius Seneca, George Heron, Basil Williams, and Martin Seneca Sr., the four presidents during the Kinzua Dam era (1956–66), along with the Seneca Nation Tribal Council, volunteers on the Kinzua Planning Committee, and, later, members of the Health Action Group, planted the seeds of the contemporary Seneca Nation, no small achievement. Numerous Senecas were now able to seek higher education for the first time because of funds provided in the 1964 act. Looking back today, I am amazed that the Senecas achieved what they did when *everything* was stacked against them.

One of the failures of the generation of leaders who fought the Kinzua Dam was in economic planning for the nation. Because these leaders had neither the formal education nor the managerial experience to handle the people's disparate economic needs, their efforts went nowhere until new leaders, however controversial their methods, emerged in the 1980s. After New York State officials broke their promises to President Hoag made in 1976 about providing economic development moneys, the Senecas turned to other alternatives. Debate over the direction of tribal economic development—the responsibility of smoke shop owners to the Seneca Nation and the decision to establish casinos—exacerbated the tensions and further polarized the Senecas. However, when new outside threats—state land acquisition for the Southern Tier Expressway and especially Albany's insistence on imposing state sales taxes—Allegany and Cattaraugus Senecas began to coalesce.

Whether it was in economic development, in the improvement of health care delivery, or in the pursuit of tribal land claims, the Senecas were strongly influenced by their contact with other Native American communities. Councilors and tribal personnel in their official capacity journeyed to numerous regional and national meetings. There, they became more aware of what was happening throughout Iroquoia as well as in other parts of Indian Country. Importantly, the results were the establishment of IHS facilities and dramatically improved medical services. This greater contact with tribal leaders around the United States also led to the push for privately owned smoke shops and gas stations as well as tribally run One Stop convenience stores; it also eventually led to gaming—tribal bingo operations and the establishment of three Seneca casinos.

By the mid-1980s, smoke shop owners at both Allegany and Cattaraugus began to prosper. The sale of tax-free cigarettes and gasoline became attractive to both Indian and non-Indian customers drawn to the Seneca reservations by their proximity and easy access off major roads— the Southern Tier Expressway and the New York State Thruway. Smoke shop owners set out on their own, no longer willing to wait for solutions from Washington and Albany. They sought to take care of their extended families rather than wait for their own nation to act. Despite questions raised by Native peoples and non-Indians alike about the operations of some of these emerging entrepreneurs and their commitment to the Seneca Nation as a whole, such operations stoked the fires that were to heat the tribal economy, eventually leading to three casinos.

At the present time, the leadership of the Seneca Nation faces immense pressure to find ways to expand the Seneca economy to support its more than eight thousand tribal members, approximately 50 percent of whom live on its two residential territories. Over the past decade, Seneca efforts have been focused largely on expanding gaming operations, building the three casinos and two major hotel complexes. In related moves, the Seneca Nation has acquired land for casino office facilities, parking, and recreational activities in the cities of Buffalo and Niagara Falls. Yet to diversify and plan for the Senecas' future residential needs, it has also purchased 54 acres in Cuba, New York, adjacent to its Oil Spring Territory—the idle Acme Electronics Plant—and 50 acres in the Town of Collins, bordering the Cattaraugus Territory.[1] In a greater attempt to serve all its tribal members, the Seneca Nation has developed new initiatives to provide health and services to the 50 percent of its population that live off its territory, the majority in Buffalo and its environs.[2]

Today, the Seneca Gaming Corporation, a wholly owned, tribally chartered corporation of the Seneca Nation of Indians, has three subsidiaries—the Seneca Niagara Falls Gaming Corporation, the Seneca Territory Gaming Corporation, and the Seneca Erie Gaming Corporation, which operates three casinos. In 2012, the tribal economy is driven largely by gaming, which has pumped $1.1 billion dollars and more than five thousand jobs into the western New York State economy. Although individual enterprises on the Seneca territories have emerged, including the highly successful Seneca Tobacco Company at Allegany, which rolls tobacco into cigarettes and cigars under tax licensing agreements with individual states, most of the Senecas today are employed by the tribal government and its subsidiaries.[3]

With the establishment of Seneca Holdings, Inc., and the appointment of David Kimelberg, a grandnephew of Cornelius Seneca, as its chief operating officer, the Senecas have attempted to diversify its existing gaming economy. Kimelberg, who previously worked on Wall Street at Goldman Sachs, has no easy task because his role requires getting his nation to make heavy financial commitments and take significant risks. Although not political, he has to contend with Senecas' ever-present distrust of their leadership. Seneca Holdings, a private equity investment arm of the Seneca Nation, has several subsidiaries, including Seneca Telecommunications, SCMC LLC Executive Protection Systems, Nexus Technologies, Seneca Broadcasting, and Seneca Construction Management Corporation. It has invested and acquired a telecommunications company; formed a green-energy subsidiary to focus on wind, hydro, and solar power production; and focused on seeking federal government contracting work. The Seneca Construction Management Corporation recently won a major contract to build a counterterrorism Army Reserve Center in Schenectady.[4]

The Senecas face many challenges from the outside. Over the past quarter-century, litigation to fight state policies, especially the state's imposition of sales tax, has run into the hundreds of millions of dollars and has sapped both the tribal leadership's energy and the nation's financial resources. It has also diverted much attention away from other needs. At the federal level, the growing conservative tide in Congress that produced the PACT Act has stymied economic growth and reduced employment. Unfavorable decisions made in the US Supreme Court have brought Seneca land claims litigation to a halt. Moreover, funding for IHS services has been steadily reduced.

The Seneca Nation also has to contend internally with numerous challenges as well. Although health care has substantially improved since the Kinzua crisis, Senecas also face crises in their major health care delivery system. Diabetes is an epidemic, and determined Seneca programs to combat this disease and to fight drug and alcohol abuse have had limited success. Although many Senecas now go on to college, the nation's high school dropout rate has led to tribal discussions about creating a charter school. Although there have been several distinct tribal efforts to encourage language retention since the late 1960s, only a few Senecas, less than 1 percent of the population, are fluent native speakers today.[5]

On February 25, 2012, in his State of the Nation address to the Seneca Nation, President Robert Odawi Porter spoke of the changes that had occurred since Kinzua. He pointed out the "unbelievable progress" that his nation "has made to recover from the devastation [of] 175 years of poverty up until the Kinzua era. Forty years ago, the Seneca Nation had virtually no money, no employees, and provided no services." He added: "No one living forty years ago would have guessed that the Seneca Nation government would have achieved such great things by the present day." Porter, who initiated the push to seek the federal license for hydropower production at the Kinzua Dam, maintained that threats continue to grow and that decisions have to be made to ensure the future of the Seneca Nation. In his address, he pointed out that Seneca Holdings had established five operating companies, the largest being Seneca Construction Management Corporation, in order to diversify "the Nation's revenue stream"; however, he urged support for further economic investment to provide more jobs and a more stable economy for future generations. Porter emphasized that the Senecas need to create development zones on parts of their two residential territories and work with school districts to better educate the nation's children to counter the drug epidemic. In his conclusion, his emphasis was on education. Porter observed that the Seneca Tribal Council had committed itself to fund the training of one hundred Seneca language teachers over the next five years "in an effort to help inculcate a stronger connection to [the nation's] traditional culture, faith, and way of life." However, Porter warned that his nation "remains at a crossroads."[6]

Porter later commented to me that the Senecas have to contend not just with officials attempting to assert state jurisdiction, apply the sales tax, and seek rights of way and lands through Allegany and Cattaraugus territories, but with internal factors as well. Because of the growth of numerous tribal services and employment opportunities within the Seneca Nation, its population has ever-increasing expectations. Instead of a nation concerned with its immediate survival and depending solely on volunteers, with no full-time employees, as was the case before and during the first years of the Kinzua crisis, the Seneca Nation of Indians' governmental structure is large and bureaucratic today, providing services to its members in numerous areas unheard of in the period 1956–66. In overcoming dependence on the federal and state governments, the Senecas are heavily dependent on programs established by their own tribal government.[7]

Thus, there are immense pressures to find ways to expand its economy to support its current membership and plan for future generations.

The Kinzua generation of leaders understood the need to hold onto Seneca nationhood by rebuilding their communities, and in that regard they succeeded. Despite having to deal with outside forces that nearly overwhelmed them as well as with internal tensions caused by the Senecas' own great diversity, they recognized the need for change; nevertheless, they at the same time retained their federated political structure established in 1848. Just as in the past Senecas recovered from the Denonville Expedition in 1687, the Sullivan–Clinton scorched-earth campaign in the American Revolution, and Jacksonian removal policies that split their nation, the Senecas were to recover from the disaster of Kinzua.

The Senecas' elasticity, a feature long recognized in the anthropological literature, has been clearly evident to me in my many visits to Seneca Country over the past four decades. I would usually stop in the two community centers funded under the Seneca Nation Compensation Act—the Saylor Building on Cattaraugus Territory and the Haley Building on Allegany Territory, the latter recently replaced by a much larger, all-inclusive community center in Jimersontown. There, I would attend events, be fed Seneca-style corn soup, sit with Seneca and Cayuga elders, listen to them talk about the days before the dam, and watch the young girls and boys there social dancing or playing games in and around these buildings. In many ways, this was my postgraduate education, my introduction to the world of the contemporary Seneca Nation. It was also my first understanding of the impact of the Kinzua Dam on these Native peoples. Although the Haley Building (renamed the Jo Jo Redeye Building a decade ago) was razed in 2013, the existence of these two important centers and their invaluable service to the Seneca peoples for more than four decades provided me with real insights about Seneca resilience.

Although the postwar Seneca leadership did not succeed in stopping the building of the dam or in all their efforts to rebuild their nation, they did their part in transforming the Seneca Nation. They were largely unaware of some of the powerful forces promoting the Kinzua project, had virtually no economic or political power to sustain a successful campaign, and had limited educational and managerial training to carry out all that was needed for their nation after the dam opened in 1966. However, when their time in office was over, they left behind a sense of Seneca nationhood. They had done their best under unbelievable pressures, and they should be credited with allowing the post-Kinzua generation—those many children I saw dancing and playing, now adults today—the opportunity to build on their efforts. *Nyawëh* to them!

Notes \\\\\\ *Bibliography* \\\\\\ *Index*

Notes

ABBREVIATIONS

APS	American Philosophical Society
ATU	*Albany Times Union*
BIA	US Bureau of Indian Affairs
BN	*Buffalo News*
DDEL	Dwight David Eisenhower Presidential Library
FERC	Federal Energy Regulatory Commission
FPC	Federal Power Commission
FSC	Florida Southern College
KPN	*Kinzua Planning Newsletter*
JPJ	*Jamestown Post Journal*
KDRC	Kinzua Dam Relicensing Commission
MR	microfilm reel
MSS	manuscript collection
NA	National Archives, Washington, DC
NA II	National Archives, College Park, MD
NYSA	New York State Archives, Albany
NYSDH	New York State Department of Health
NYSDOT	New York State Department of Transportation
NYSDPW	New York State Department of Public Works
NYSL	New York State Library
NYT	*New York Times*
OSI	Office of the Secretary of the Interior
PSA	Pennsylvania State Archives, Harrisburg
RG	Record Group
SNI	Seneca Nation of Indians
SRP	*Salamanca Press (Salamanca Republican Press)*
SU	Syracuse University, Bird Library

SUNY   State University of New York
WHS   Wisconsin Historical Society, Madison

PREFACE

1. Laurence M. Hauptman, *The Iroquois Struggle for Survival: World War II to Red Power* (Syracuse, NY: Syracuse Univ. Press, 1986), 85–122; and Laurence M. Hauptman, "General John S. Bragdon, the Office of Public Works Planning, and the Decision to Build Pennsylvania's Kinzua Dam," *Pennsylvania History* 53 (July 1986): 181–200.

2. Hauptman, *The Iroquois Struggle for Survival* and "General John S. Bragdon." For more on the dam's impact, see Joy Bilharz, *The Allegany Senecas and Kinzua Dam: Forced Relocation through Two Generations* (Lincoln: Univ. of Nebraska Press, 1998). For the impact on tribal elders, see Randy A. John, *The Social Integration of an Elderly Native American Population* (New York: Garland, 1995), 27–93. William N. Hoover's *Kinzua: From Cornplanter to the Corps* (New York: Universe, 2004) contains valuable maps and a timeline on the project's development and impact as well as photographs of dam construction.

3. Transcript of hearings at Salamanca High School, Allegany Indian Reservation, Feb. 24, 2011, in Federal Energy Regulatory Commission (FERC), *In the Matter of Scoping Document for Kinzua Pumped Storage Project (P-13880-000)* (Washington, DC: FERC, 2011), 21–28, available at the FERC website, http://www.ferc.gov/.

4. Shane Titus testimony in ibid., 41–45.

5. Rebecca Bowen testimony in ibid., 34–35.

6. George Heron, interviewed by the author, Sept. 28, 1984, Allegany Indian Reservation.

7. Hauptman, *The Iroquois Struggle for Survival*, 85–122.

8. William N. Fenton, ed., *Symposium on Local Diversity in Iroquois Culture*, Bureau of Ethnology Bulletin no. 149 (Washington, DC: US Government Printing Office, 1951).

9. For the Tonawanda schism, see Laurence M. Hauptman, *The Tonawanda Senecas' Heroic Battle against Removal: Conservative Activist Indians* (Albany: State Univ. of New York [SUNY] Press, 2011).

10. Robert Odawi Porter, personal communication to the author, Sept. 29, 2006. Porter was later elected president of the Seneca Nation of Indians in November 2010. He said: "What appears to the outside as chaos is what makes us who we are." The *Buffalo News* (*BN*) frequently reports on the Seneca Nation and often focuses on its internal political divisions. For a recent sample, see Dan Herbeck, "Resentments Abound in Seneca Power Struggle," *BN*, Nov. 14, 2011. For Seneca criticisms of the way newspapers handle news reporting on the Seneca Nation, see Robert Odawi Porter, "Senecas Are the Target of Ugly Media Stereotypes in Handling of Seneca Stories," *BN*, Feb. 20, 2012.

11. Thomas S. Abler uses the term *factionalism* in his excellent dissertation but clearly states that Seneca politics is no carbon copy of non-Indian politics off the reservation. Thomas Abler, "Factional Dispute and Party Conflict in the Political System of the Seneca Nation (1845–1895)," PhD diss., Univ. of Toronto, 1969, 27.

12. Bernard Cohn, "History and Anthropology: The State of Play, " *Comparative Studies in Society and History* 22 (Apr. 1980), 221.

13. I have described my methodological approach in "Beyond Forensic History: Observations Based on a Forty-Year Journey through Iroquois Country," *Journal of the West* 49 (Fall 2010): 10–19.

14. Edmund Wilson, *Apologies to the Iroquois* (1960; paperback reprint, Syracuse, NY: Syracuse Univ. Press, 1991), 172.

15. Anthony F. C. Wallace, *The Death and Rebirth of the Seneca* (New York: Random House, 1970).

16. William N. Fenton to Walter Taylor, Jan. 28, 1965, Walter Taylor MSS, Microfilm Reel (MR) 14, Wisconsin Historical Society (WHS), Madison.

17. For my review of Bilharz's work, see *Journal of the Royal Anthropological Institute* 5 (Sept. 1999): 495.

18. For the expansion of the Seneca economy and its great impact on western New York State, see Jonathan B. Taylor, *The Seneca Nation Economy: Its Foundations, Size, and Impact on New York State and the Western New York Region* (Sarasota, FL: Taylor Policy Group, 2010); "Seneca Nation Ad Focuses on $1 Billion Investment," Seneca Nation of Indians (SNI) press release, Jan. 12, 2012, SNI Archives, Salamanca, Allegany Indian Reservation; "Seneca Nation Economic Impact Crucial to WNY," SNI press release, Feb. 28, 2012, SNI Archives.

19. Pauline Seneca, interviewed by the author, June 4, 1978, Cattaraugus Indian Reservation. The late Mrs. Seneca, a Cayuga schoolteacher, was the wife of Cornelius Seneca, president of the Seneca Nation in the 1940s and 1950s.

20. Carole Moses, interviewed by the author, Sept. 28, 1984, Allegany Indian Reservation.

1. THE SENECA NATION OF INDIANS: DIVERSITY AND ADAPTATION

1. Myrtle Peterson, interviewed by the author, Apr. 7, 1978, Cherokee, NC; "Myrtle Peterson Dies at 88," *Randolph Register*, June 28, 2000.

2. Treaty of Buffalo Creek, 7 Stat. 550 (Jan. 15, 1838). For analysis, see Henry S. Manley, "Buying Buffalo from the Indians," *New York History* 28 (July 1947): 313–29; Laurence M. Hauptman, *Conspiracy of Interests: Iroquois Dispossession and the Rise of New York State* (Syracuse, NY: Syracuse Univ. Press, 1999), 175–90.

3. Treaty with the Seneca at Buffalo Creek, 7 Stat. 586 (May 20, 1842). For analysis, see Laurence M. Hauptman, "State's Men, Salvation Seekers, and the Senecas: The Supplemental Treaty of Buffalo Creek, 1842," *New York History* 78 (Jan. 1997): 51–82; and Hauptman, *The Tonawanda Senecas' Heroic Battle against Removal*.

4. Thomas Abler, "Friends, Factions, and the Seneca Nation Revolution of 1848," *Niagara Frontier* 21 (Winter 1974): 74–79; George H. J. Abrams, *The Seneca People* (Phoenix: Indian Tribal Series, 1976), 61–70.

5. The documents related to the establishment of the Seneca Nation of Indians in 1848 can be found in David Wilkins, ed., *Documents of Native American Political Development: 1500s to 1933* (New York: Oxford Univ. Press, 2009), 72–81, 101–4.

6. Interviews by the author: Rovena Abrams, Feb. 23, 2011, Allegany Indian Reservation; Calvin "Kelly" John, May 4, 1997, Allegany Indian Reservation; Carole Moses, Sept. 28, 1984, Allegany Indian Reservation; Genevieve Plummer, July 28, 1977, Allegany Indian Reservation; and Wini Kettle, July 28, 1977, Cattaraugus Indian Reservation.

7. Both Thomas Abler and Robert Berkhofer have described Seneca politics as factionalized before the Seneca Revolution of 1848. Abler, "Friends, Factions, and the Seneca Nation Revolution of 1848," 74–79, and "Factional Dispute and Party Conflict"; Robert F. Berkhofer Jr., "Faith and Factionalism among the Senecas: Theory and Ethnohistory," *Ethnohistory* 12 (1965): 99–112.

8. *Webster's Twentieth Century Dictionary Unabridged.*

9. Chad S. Rector, *Federations: The Political Dynamics of Cooperation* (Ithaca, NY: Cornell Univ. Press, 2009), 4, 179, 1–10.

10. Staff listing, *O He Yoh Noh*, Apr. 29, 1970; "Appeal for Support of *O He Yoh Noh*," *O He Yoh Noh*, July 23, 1975; Rick Jemison, interviewed by the author, Mar. 21, 2012, Cattaraugus Indian Reservation; Rovena Abrams interview, Feb. 23, 2011. I surveyed every available issue of both *O He Yoh Noh* and *Si Wong Geh* published from 1970 to 1976, available on microfiche at Princeton University Library. *O He Yoh Noh* clearly expressed harsher opinions of the national Red Power movement as well as of the increasing activism at Cattaraugus. See its articles "Concerning Red Power," Apr. 1, 1970; "Alcatraz," June 17, 1971; and "Trail of Broken Treaties," Dec. 13, 1972. For *O He Yoh Noh*'s focus on culture and language, see, for example, "The Way to Any Culture Is Language," Jan. 6, 1972; "Indian Names," Apr. 29, May 6, 1970; "Halliday Jackson's Journal," June 22, 1972.

11. William Engelbrecht, *Iroquoia: The Development of a Native World* (Syracuse, NY: Syracuse Univ. Press, 2003), 114–19.

12. José António Brandão, *"Your Fyre Shall Burn No More": Iroquois Policy toward New France and Its Native Allies to 1701* (Lincoln: Univ. of Nebraska Press, 1997), 31–116; Daniel Richter, *The Ordeal of the Longhouse: The Peoples of the Iroquois League in the Era of European Colonization* (Chapel Hill: Univ. of North Carolina Press, 1992), 30–74.

13. For Seneca adaptability in the eighteenth century, see Kurt A. Jordan, *The Seneca Restoration, 1715–1754: An Iroquois Local Political Economy* (Gainesville: Univ. Press of Florida, 2008).

14. Arthur C. Parker, "The White Man Takes Possession, 1783–1842," in *History of the Genesee Country*, 4 vols., edited by Lockwood R. Doty (Chicago: S. J. Clarke, 1925), 1:278.

15. Treaty with the Six Nations at Canandaigua, 7 Stat. 44 (Nov. 11, 1794). Seneca elders refer to this accord as the "Pickering Treaty."

16. Treaty of Big Tree, 7 Stat. 601 (Sept. 15, 1797). For Oil Spring, see Hauptman, *Conspiracy of Interests*, 162–74.

17. See Hauptman, *The Tonawanda Senecas' Heroic Battle against Removal*.

18. Timothy Pickering, "Indian Census of 1792," in Jasper Parrish MSS, Vassar College, Poughkeepsie; New York State Legislature, *Report Relative to Indian Affairs. Mar. 4, 1819*, Assembly Doc. no. 90 (Albany: New York State, 1819).

19. Barbara Graymont, *The Iroquois in the American Revolution* (Syracuse, NY: Syracuse Univ. Press, 1972), 259–96. For life at Buffalo Creek and its great cultural diversity, see Hauptman, *Conspiracy of Interests*, 107–16, and Alyssa Mt. Pleasant, "After the Whirlwind: Maintaining a Haudenosaunee Place at Buffalo Creek, 1780–1825," PhD diss., Cornell Univ., 2007.

20. Fred Kennedy and Jean Loret, interviewed by the author, Sept. 25, 2011, Dunkirk, NY.

21. Treaty with the Seneca, 7 Stat. 70 (June 30, 1802). For the 1826 treaty, see New York State Legislature, Assembly, *Report of the Special Committee to Investigate the Indian Problem of the State of New York Appointed by the Assembly of 1888*, Assembly Doc. No. 51 (Albany: Troy Press, 1889), 144–50 (better known as the *Whipple Report*). See also Laurence M. Hauptman, "*Seneca Nation v. Christy*: A Background Study," *Buffalo Law Review* 46 (Fall 1998): 947–77.

22. Thomas Donaldson, comp., *The Six Nations of New York*, Extra Census Bulletin of the 11th Census of the United States for the Year 1890 (Washington, DC: US Census Printing Office, 1892), 30–31.

23. Asher Wright, the Presbyterian missionary at Buffalo Creek, relocated his church to Cattaraugus. His religious education and linguistic efforts have been well chronicled: William N. Fenton, "Toward the Gradual Civilization of the Indian Natives: The Missionary and Linguistic Work of Asher Wright (1803–1875) among the Senecas of Western New York," *Proceedings of the American Philosophical Society* 100 (1956): 567–81; William N. Fenton, ed., "Seneca Indians by Asher Wright (1859)," *Ethnohistory* 4 (1957): 302–21; Thomas S. Abler, "Protestant Missionaries and Native Cultures: Parallel Careers of Asher Wright and Silas T. Rand," *American Indian Quarterly* 26 (Winter 1992): 25–27. For the extensive missionary presence at Buffalo Creek, see Frank Severance, ed., *Buffalo Historical Publications*, vol. 6, 2 parts (Buffalo: Buffalo Historical Society, 1906), and the full analysis in Mt. Pleasant, "After the Whirlwind." For the opposition to this missionary presence, see Granville Ganter's excellent edited volume *The Collected Speeches of Sagoyewatha or Red Jacket* (Syracuse, NY: Syracuse Univ. Press, 2006), xxiv–xxix, 243–49, 266–67.

24. Francis Kettle, interviewed by the author, July 27, 1977, Cattaraugus Indian Reservation.

25. For the Tuscarora protest, see the following articles in the *New York Times* (*NYT*): "Indians Protest a Niagara Power Project," Sept. 27, 1957; "Tuscarora Braves Repel Surveyors," Apr. 17, 1957; "Tuscaroras Stop Surveyors Again," Apr. 18, 1957; "Tuscaroras in Protest," July 2, 1958. For more on this protest, see Chief Clinton Rickard, *Fighting Tuscarora: The Autobiography of Chief Clinton Rickard*, edited by Barbara Graymont (Syracuse, NY: Syracuse Univ. Press, 1973), 138–52.

26. Wallace, *The Death and Rebirth of the Seneca*, 239–337.

27. William N. Fenton, "Pennsylvania's Remaining Indian Settlement," *Pennsylvania Park News* 44 (1945), 1–2.

28. Keith H. Basso, *Wisdom Sits in Places: Landscape and Language among the Western Apache* (Albuquerque: Univ. of New Mexico Press, 1996), 34. Besides Basso's exceptional book, I have benefited by rereading N. Scott Momaday, *The Names: A Memoir* (Tucson: Univ. of Arizona Press, 1976). For the importance of place—namely, the upper Allegheny River valley to the Senecas—see several articles by William N. Fenton: "Fishing Drives among the Cornplanter Senecas," *Pennsylvania Archaeologist* 12 (1942): 48–52; "Place-Names and Related Activities of the Cornplanter Seneca," *Pennsylvania Archaeologist* 15, no. 1 (1945): 25–29, no. 2 (1945): 42–50, no. 3 (1945): 88–96, no. 4 (1945): 108–18, and 16, no. 2 (1946): 42–57; "A Day on the Allegheny Ox-Bow," *Living Wilderness* 10 (1945): 1–8.

29. Donaldson, *The Six Nations of New York*, 27–28.

30. Treaty with the Six Nations at Canandaigua, 7 Stat. 44 (Nov. 11, 1794); Treaty of Big Tree, 7 Stat. 601 (Sept. 15, 1797).

31. Merle H. Deardorff, "The Cornplanter Grant in Warren County," *Western Pennsylvania Historical Magazine* 24 (Mar. 1941): 1–22; Donaldson, *The Six Nations of New York*, 29–30.

32. For a brief summary of the lease history, see Laurence M. Hauptman, "Compensatory Justice: The Seneca Nation Settlement Act of 1990," *National Forum* 71 (Spring 1991): 31–33.

33. The Senecas were excluded from the provisions of the General Allotment Act of 1887 (the Dawes Act) because of the existence of the Ogden Land Company's preemption to these Indian lands. See Laurence M. Hauptman, "Senecas and Subdividers: Resistance to Allotment of Indian Lands in New York, 1875–1906," *Prologue: The Journal of the National Archives* (Summer 1977): 105–17. In November 1985, I attended a US House of Representatives hearing at which Salamanca non-Indian city officials asked Congress to purchase the city from the Seneca Nation!

34. I have previously documented these efforts in *Formulating American Indian Policy in New York State, 1970–1986* (Albany: SUNY Press, 1988).

35. For Willie Hoag, see Charles E. Congdon, *Allegany Oxbow: A History of Allegany State Park and the Allegany Reserve of the Seneca Nation* (Little Valley, NY: Straight, 1967), 163; Donaldson, *The Six Nations of New York*, 27–28.

36. Martin Seneca Jr., interviewed by the author, June 11, 2011, Allegany Indian Reservation.

37. See the following articles in the *Seneca Nation of Indians' [SNI] Official Newsletter*: "WW II Veterans Were the Focus at the Allegany Casino Veterans Powwow," July 29, 2005; "Iroquois Post to Continue Honoring WW II Vets," Nov. 25, 2005; "Veteran's Day, Program," Dec. 25, 2009.

38. For interviews of Seneca World War II veterans, see Alberta Austin, comp., *Ne´ Ho Niyo´ Dë: Nö´—That's The Way It Was*, 2 vols. (Lackawanna, NY: Rebco Enterprises for

the Seneca Nation Education Department, Curriculum Development Project, 1986 and 1989), 1:13–14 (Edgar Cornfield), 1:48 (George Heron), 1:70 (Johnson Jimerson), 2:76 (Lambert Griffen), 2:195–196 (Lawrence Pierce), 2:208 (Clifford Redeye Sr.).

39. Congdon, *Allegany Oxbow*, 136–37.

40. Ibid., 137–38.

41. Ibid., 138.

42. "All-Indian Post of Legion Formed," *Buffalo Courier-Express*, Oct. 26, 1946; "Legion Has All-Indian Post," *NYT*, Oct. 26, 1946. In addition, the Seneca Nation has impressive monuments dedicated to its veterans at Allegany Reservation and Niagara Falls and holds a veterans' powwow every year to honor those who served.

2. FEDERAL POLICIES: TERMINATION

1. Calvin "Kelly" John, interviewed by the author, May 4, 1997, Allegany Indian Reservation, and May 2, 1987, Annual Peter Doctor Memorial Indian Scholarship Foundation Dinner, Allegany Indian Reservation. For John's obituary, see *Jamestown Post Journal* (*JPJ*), Oct. 9, 2004.

2. The Peter Doctor Indian Education Memorial Foundation was founded in 1941 by Reverend Peter Doctor (Tonawanda Seneca) and newspaperman Melvin Patterson (Tuscarora). Its roots go back to the Iroquois Temperance League founded in 1831 by Reverend Asher Wright. Until her death in 2010, Ramona Charles, a Tonawanda Seneca, was its longtime president.

3. President Calvin "Kelly" John influenced my Seneca research in a number of areas: he gave me the title of chapter 3, "Backlash," in my book *Iroquois Struggle for Survival*, 31–43. Our many discussions about Joseph Ellicott and Governor Blacksnake directly influenced my writings about them in *Conspiracy of Interests*, chapters 7 and 10, as well as in "Governor Blacksnake and the Seneca Indian Struggle to Save the Oil Spring Reservation," *Mid-America* 81 (Winter 1999): 51–73.

4. *United States v. Forness, et al.* (Salamanca Trust Co., et al., defendant-intervenor), 125 Fed. Rep., 2d Series, 928 (1942). For an homage to President Seneca, see his obituary in the Allegany Seneca newsletter: "Cornelius Vanderbilt Seneca," *O He Yoh Noh*, July 30, 1969. See also "Cornelius Seneca, Leader of Indian Nation, Is Dead," *NYT*, July 29, 1969.

5. New York State Legislature, Joint Legislative Committee on Indian Affairs, *Annual Report, 1943*, New York State Legislative Doc. no. 52 (Albany: New York State, 1943).

6. Ibid., 32. President Seneca was correct in his assessment. See the following articles in the *SRP*: "Sued by U.S. Government He Is Helping to Defend," Nov. 17, 1942; "Move to Stop Aid to Indians," Nov. 20, 1942; "Forness Case Decision Termed Reproach to State and Nation," Aug. 5, 1944.

7. New York State Legislature, Joint Legislative Committee on Indian Affairs, *Annual Report, 1945*, New York State Legislative Doc. No. 51 (Albany: New York State, 1945).

8. US Congress, Senate, Committee on Indian Affairs, *Survey of Conditions of Indian Affairs in the United States,* Partial Report No. 310, 78-1, Serial 10756 (Washington, DC: US Government Printing Office, 1943).

9. US Congress, House of Representatives, *Hearings on H.R. 166: Investigate Indian Affairs, Feb. 2, 1944,* 78th Cong., 2d sess., part 2 (Washington, DC: US Government Printing Office, 1944), 51–52.

10. William A. Brophy to Kenneth B. Disher, Sept. 20, 1940, William A. Brophy MSS, Box 2, Chronological File, Harry S. Truman Presidential Library, Independence, MO.

11. US Congress, Senate, Committee on the Post Office and Civil Service, *Hearings on S. Res. 41: Officers and Employees of the Federal Government,* 80th Cong., 1st sess. (Washington, DC: US Government Printing Office, 1947), pt. 3, 547.

12. R. Warren Metcalf, *Termination's Legacy: The Discarded Indians of Utah* (Lincoln: Univ. of Nebraska Press, 2002), 234–39; Donald L. Fixico, *Termination and Relocation: Federal Indian Policy, 1945–1960* (Albuquerque: Univ. of New Mexico Press, 1986), 21–44; Kenneth Philp, *Termination Revisited: American Indians on the Trail to Self-Determination, 1933–1953* (Lincoln: Univ. of Nebraska Press, 1999). For a recent new look at this era, see Brian Hosmer, ed., *Native Americans and the Legacy of Harry S. Truman* (Kirksville, MO: Truman State Univ. Press, 2010).

13. American Indian Policy Review Commission, *Final Report Submitted to Congress, May 17, 1977,* 2 vols. (Washington, DC: US Government Printing Office, 1977), 1:450–53; Francis Paul Prucha, *The Great Father: The United States Government and the American Indians,* 2 vols. (Lincoln: Univ. of Nebraska Press, 1984), 2:1013–59.

14. Fixico, *Termination and Relocation,* 21–44.

15. For Watkins's views, see Arthur V. Watkins, "Termination of Federal Supervision: The Removal of Restrictions over Indian Property and Person," *Annals of the Academy of Political and Social Science* 311 (May 1957): 47–55. The best work on Watkins is in Metcalf, *Termination's Legacy,* esp. 21–48.

16. Bess Furman, "Campaign to 'Free' the Indians," *NYT,* July 22, 1947; Hugh Butler, "It Is Time to Give Serious Consideration to Setting Indians Free," speech reprinted from *Congressional Record,* July 21, 1947, in Hugh Butler MSS, Box 211, Nebraska State Historical Society, Lincoln. For more on Butler and Daniel Reed, see Hauptman, *The Iroquois Struggle for Survival,* 41–56.

17. US Congress, Senate, Committee on Interior and Insular Affairs, Subcommittee on Indian Affairs, *Hearings on S. 1683, S. 1686, S. 1687: New York Indians, March 9–11, 1948* (Washington, DC: US Government Printing Office, 1948).

18. Ibid., 47 (John, Heron, Printup). For more on the late George Heron, see chapter 5 in this book; see also Alberta Austin's interview of George Heron, undated, in Austin, *Ne´ Ho Niyo´ Dë: Nö´,* 1:44–48.

19. For the "New York officials" claims, see, for example, the testimony of Leighton Wade, counsel for the New York State Joint Legislative Committee on Indian Affairs, in

US Congress, Senate, Committee on Interior and Insular Affairs, Subcommittee on Indian Affairs, *Hearings on S. 1683 . . . New York Indians*, 79–84, 213–23.

20. Ibid., 48.

21. Ibid., 51, 53–54, 56.

22. Ibid., 51, 53–54.

23. Ibid., 57.

24. Ibid., 194–202.

25. Ibid., 202.

26. I have written extensively about Alice Lee Jemison based on fieldwork at Cattaraugus, archival research, and use of the Freedom of Information Act to acquire Jemison's FBI file. I must acknowledge the helpful suggestions made to me by anthropologists Morris Opler and William N. Fenton, demographer Henry Dobyns, and historian Donald Berthrong to point me in the right direction. They encouraged my fieldwork, which allowed me to look beyond government-generated propaganda used by too many historians to interpret (and even slander) this Seneca activist. Jemison's family were and are well-respected officials within the Seneca Nation of Indians. For a summary of her life, see Laurence M. Hauptman, "Jemison, Alice Mae Lee," in *Notable American Women, the Modern Period: A Biographical Dictionary*, 4 vols., edited by Barbara Sicherman, Carol Hurd Green, Ilene Kantrov, and Harriette Walker, 4:379–80 (Cambridge, MA: Belknap Press of Harvard Univ. Press, 1980). Jemison was a zealot who was relentless in her criticism of the Bureau of Indian Affairs (BIA) and willing to brand her enemies, such as John Collier, as "Communists" and to work with extremist groups in her single-minded efforts to abolish this agency. See Laurence M. Hauptman, *The Iroquois and the New Deal* (Syracuse, NY: Syracuse Univ. Press, 1981), 34–69; "The American Indian Federation and the Indian New Deal: A Reinterpretation," *Pacific Historical Review* 52 (Nov. 1983): 378–402; and "Alice Lee Jemison: A Modern 'Mother of the Nation,'" in *Sifters: Native American Women's Lives*, edited by Theda Perdue, 175–86 (New York: Oxford Univ. Press, 2001).

27. Senate, Committee on Interior and Insular Affairs, Subcommittee on Indian Affairs, *Hearings on S. 1683 . . . New York Indians*, 21–27.

28. Ibid., 22, 25.

29. Ibid., 23–25, 26.

30. Ibid., 207–9.

31. Ibid., 162–65.

32. Ibid., 122–28.

33. Ibid., 94–95, 96–97. John Snyder, a Cattaraugus Seneca attorney, was not a practicing lawyer off the reservation because he had not passed the bar examination. In the late 1920s and early 1930s, he was accused of being involved in some questionable real estate dealings along Lake Erie. Jeanne Marie Jemison, interviewed by the author, Aug. 23, 1978, Tyson's Corners, VA. He was also controversial for, among other things, his support for Commissioner John Collier's Indian New Deal program and the Indian Reorganization

Act, which the Seneca Nation overwhelmingly rejected. See Hauptman, *The Iroquois and the New Deal*, 58.

34. 25 U.S.C. 232 (1948); 25 U.S.C. 233 (1950). For the ill-informed debate in the House of Representatives and its passing of the second act by a margin of 295 to 4 on September 13, 1950, see US Congress, House, *Congressional Record*, 81st Cong., 2d sess., Aug. 14, 1950, 12453–63. The lack of congressional interest in Indian affairs was manifested by the absence of 131 members.

35. Commission on Organization of the Executive Branch of the Government (Hoover Commission), "Report of the Committee on Indian Affairs," Philleo Nash MSS, Box 44, Truman Library.

36. Oscar Chapman to Harry Truman, Mar. 18, 1950, Harry Truman, White House Official File 6-C, Truman Library.

37. H.R. 108, 67 Stat., B132 (1954).

38. Herbert Lehman to Mrs. Edgar Anderson, Mar. 24, 1954, and Herbert Lehman to Mrs. Paul P. Burke, Mar. 28, 1955, Herbert Lehman MSS, Box 12, Ser. Leg. Dr. 12, Indians C-67-31, Butler Library, Columbia Univ. For Lehman's work as New Deal governor and his favorable interaction with the Senecas, see Hauptman, *The Iroquois and the New Deal*, 129, 157.

39. Orme Lewis (assistant secretary of the interior) to President Dwight David Eisenhower, Jan. 4, 1954, Irving Ives MSS, Box 45, #1913, Cornell Univ.

40. Ibid.

41. Ibid.

42. "20 Senators Attend Hugh Butler Rites," *NYT*, July 4, 1954. See also "Daniel Reed, 83, Dies in Capital: Served in House Forty Years," *NYT*, Feb. 20, 1959. Reed was succeeded by Charles Goodell, much more sympathetic and respectful to the Senecas. For Watkins, see "Seaton Appoints Watkins as Aide; Watkins Served in Senate," *NYT*, Apr. 11, 1959; "Watkins to Direct Indian Claims Unit," *NYT*, May 2, 1960; "Arthur V. Watkins Dies at 86," *NYT*, Sept. 2, 1973.

43. Thomas Clarkin, *Federal Indian Policy in the Kennedy and Johnson Administrations, 1961–1969* (Albuquerque: Univ. of New Mexico Press, 2001), 160–70. For Senator Anderson, see his book *Outsider in the Senate: Senator Clinton P. Anderson's Memoir* (New York: World, 1970).

44. Seneca Nation Compensation Act of 1964, 78 Stat. 738 (Aug. 31, 1964).

45. "Bill to End U.S. Control of Senecas Is Introduced [by Senator Henry 'Scoop' Jackson of Washington]," *NYT*, Sept. 6, 1967.

46. Richard M. Nixon, *Public Papers of President Richard Nixon, 1970* (Washington, DC: US Government Printing Office, 1970), 564–76. See also George Pierre Castile, *To Show Heart: Native American Self-Determination and Federal Indian Policy, 1960–1975* (Tucson: Univ. of Arizona Press, 1998). For some positive legacies of the Nixon administration in overhauling federal Indian policies, see Laurence M. Hauptman, "Finally Acknowledging Native Peoples: American Indian Policies since the Nixon Administration," in *"They Made Us Many*

Promises": The American Indian Experience, 1524 to the Present, edited by Philip Weeks, 210–28 (Wheeling, IL: Harlan Davidson, 2002).

47. The fear that the federal government would return to its terminationist agenda cast a pall over the Seneca Nation in the early 1970s. See "Senate Opposes Termination," *Si Wong Geh*, Feb. 9, 1972; "Indian Claims," *Si Wong Geh*, Mar. 13, 20, 1974. Calvin "Kelly" John wrote a series of articles explaining the rise and fall of termination policies: see "House Concurrent Resolution 108," *O He Yoh Noh*, Feb. 24, 1972, and "Termination History," *O He Yoh Noh*, Mar. 2, 1972. Seneca Keepers of the Faith (Jesse Armstrong, John Cook, Lorenza Dowdy, Worthington and Louise Green, Albert Jacobs, Johnson Jimerson, Calvin "Kelly" John, Geneva Jones, Lavina Logan, and Harry Watt) later attempted to calm fears by explaining the Seneca's past opposition to termination policies. *Si Wong Geh*, Sept. 26, 1973.

3. EMPIRE STATE POLICIES: THE THRUWAY

1. Francis Kettle, interviewed by the author, July 27, 1977, June 4, 1978, Cattaraugus Indian Reservation.

2. William N. Fenton, *The Great Law and the Longhouse: A Political History of the Iroquois Confederacy* (Norman: Univ. of Oklahoma Press, 1998), 694–95.

3. For a detailed treatment of the Erie Canal and its impact on the Senecas, see Hauptman, *Conspiracy of Interests*, 101–90.

4. J. N. P. Memorandum to Paul Lockwood, Feb. 19, 1946, Thomas E. Dewey MSS, Rush Rhees Library, Univ. of Rochester; New York State Governor's Office, news releases, Nov. 13, Nov. 20, 1952, Governors' Records: Thomas E. Dewey, Box 178, Folder 31: "Indian Services," MR 27, New York State Archives (NYSA), Albany; Elmer Thompson (Seneca Nation clerk) to Thomas E. Dewey, Jan. 25, 1954, Governors' Records: Thomas E. Dewey, 3rd term, Box 117, Folder 34, MR 59, NYSA.

5. For Wade's longtime role, see Hauptman, *The Iroquois Struggle for Survival*, 31–41, 62, 191–92.

6. "Dewey to Speak at Thruway Banquet Tonight," *JPJ*, Aug. 26, 1954; "Buffalo-Utica Thruway Stretch Open to Traffic: Dewey Opens 57-Mile WNY Link . . . ," *JPJ*, Aug. 27, 1954; "Ceremonies Mark Thruway Opening: Western N.Y. Segment Added to Dream Road," *SRP*, Aug. 26, 1954.

7. Rickard, *Fighting Tuscarora*, 142–49.

8. "Message of Governor Thomas E. Dewey to the Legislature, Jan. 3, 1945," Robert Moses MSS, Box 24, Manuscript Division, New York Public Library.

9. For the Moses–Sloan correspondence/debate over postwar planning, see Moses to Sloan, Jan. 29, Feb. 7, 13, 1945, and Sloan to Moses, Feb. 2, 10, 1945, Moses MSS, Box 26, File: Alfred P. Sloan Jr., 1945, Manuscript Division, New York Public Library. Moses insisted that the building of highways would be delayed but would resume at the end of the war once "priorities are lifted" (Jan. 23). The pushy Sloan advocated an even greater federal and state commitment for highways expansion at the end of the war.

10. C. R. Waters to President Cornelius Seneca, Jan. 15, 1946, BIA, New York Agency Records, 1938–49, Box 7, Folder: "Rights of Way; Roads," Record Group (RG) 75, National Archives (NA), Federal Record Center, New York City.

11. C. R. Waters to United States Indian Agency—attention Mrs. Anderson, Apr. 16, 1946, and J. Frank O'Marah to Charles H. Berry (superintendent of the New York Agency), May 7, 1946, BIA New York Agency Records, Box 4, Folder: "Surveys and Encroachments (Lands)," NA, RG 75, NA, Federal Record Center, New York City.

12. Oscar L. Chapman to J. Frank O'Marah, June 10, 1946, BIA, New York Agency Records, Box 7, Folder: "Rights of Way; Roads," NA, Federal Record Center, New York City.

13. "Bertram D. Tallamy, 87, Official for U.S. and New York Highways" (obituary), *NYT*, Sept. 25, 1989. For the Moses–Tallamy connection, see Robert Caro, *The Power Broker: Robert Moses and the Fall of New York* (New York: Random House, 1974), 272, 830.

14. Rickard, *Fighting Tuscarora*, 138–52; Hauptman, *The Iroquois Struggle for Survival*, 139–45, 151–78.

15. Neither the highly critical older assessment of Moses by Robert Caro nor the recent favorable assessments of him treat the master builder's views of or policies toward the Iroquois: see Caro, *The Power Broker*; Joel Schwartz, *The New York Approach: Robert Moses, Urban Liberals, and Redevelopment of the Inner City* (Columbus: Ohio State Univ. Press, 1993); Hilary Ballon and Kenneth T. Jackson, eds., *Robert Moses and the Modern City: The Transformation of New York* (New York: Norton, 2007); Peter Eisenstadt, *Rochdale Village: Robert Moses, 6000 Families, and New York City's Great Experiment in Integrated Housing* (Ithaca, NY: Cornell Univ. Press, 2010).

16. Robert Moses, *Tuscarora Fiction and Fact: A Reply to the Author of "Memoirs of Hecate County" and His Reviewers* (New York: privately printed, 1960), 7; Robert Moses, *Working for the People: Promise and Performance in Public Service* (New York: Harper, 1956), 3–4.

17. Robert Moses, "Tomorrow's Cars and Roads," 3, reprint of article in *Liberty Magazine*, in Robert Moses MSS, Box 1, Package #1, Reports: 1942–43, Bird Library, Syracuse Univ.

18. Governor's Memoranda on Legislative Bills Approved, Apr. 7, 1954, Issuance of Notes and Bonds of the New York State Thruway Authority, in New York State Governor's Office, *Public Papers of Thomas E. Dewey*, 12 vols. (Albany: New York State, 1944–57), 12:289–91.

19. George M. Shapiro (counsel to Governor Dewey) to R. Burdell Bixby (secretary to Governor Dewey), Nov. 11, 1953. The governor's executive assistant responded favorably to this lobbying effort for the thruway extension south from Buffalo to the Pennsylvania line: Holden A. Evans Jr. to Harold E. Smith (Park and Pollard Company: Dairy and Poultry Feeds), Dec. 31, 1953; Evans to Fred I. Inglehardt (Buffalo's Delaware Avenue Association), Dec. 24, 1953; Evans to Buffalo's West Side Business Men's Association, Dec. 23, 1953; Evans to Bernard Bodanza (Niagara Frontier Industrial Traffic League), Dec. 17, 1953; Evans to Mrs. Jessie Woodard (Chautauqua County Pomona Grange), Dec. 7, 1953; Evans to Rita E. O'Brien (United Florists of Western New York), Dec. 7, 1953; Evans to P. S. McLean (Central

Greyhound Bus Lines of New York), Dec. 4, 1953. All found in Governor's Records: Thomas E. Dewey, 3rd term, Series 6, Box 220, Folder 9: "Thruway-Niagara-Erie Section," MR 65, NYSA.

20. Harlow Curtice to Robert Moses, Jan. 14, 1954, and Moses to Curtice, Apr. 26, 1954, Moses MSS, Box 42, File: General Motors, 1954, Manuscript Division, New York Public Library. Moses's lobbying continued unabated. See his statement on behalf of the United States Conference of Mayors submitted to the President's Advisory Committee on a National Highway Program, Oct. 7, 1954, Moses MSS, Box 4, Vol. II, Bird Library, Syracuse Univ.

21. Mark Rose, *Interstate: Express Highway Politics, 1941–1956* (Lawrence: Regent Press of Kansas, 1979), 58–75. For Bragdon, see Hauptman, *The Iroquois Struggle for Survival*, 107–22.

22. Michael R. Fein, *Paving the Way: New York Road Building and the American State, 1880–1956* (Lawrence: Univ. Press of Kansas, 2008), 230; Rose, *Interstate*, 58–75.

23. New York State Thruway Authority, *Annual Report, 1954* (Albany: New York State, 1954); New York State Thruway Chronology, New York State Electronic Document, #THR500-4, THRCH95-11136, Manuscript Division, New York State Library (NYSL).

24. "Dewey to Speak at Thruway Banquet Tonight"; "Buffalo–Utica Thruway Stretch Open to Traffic"; "Ceremonies Mark Thruway Opening."

25. P. G. Baldwin's filed report to Bertram D. Tallamy, Sept. 10, 1954, of a meeting with the SNI Tribal Council, Aug. 28, 1954, New York State Department of Public Works (NYSDPW) Records, Deputy Superintendent's Files, #B0 251-84, Box 9 (1954), Folder: Indian Affairs, NYSA (hereafter "Baldwin report").

26. O'Neill had worked for the Justice Department between 1936 and 1942 and again between 1944 and 1954, just before his employment by the Seneca Nation. Walter Taylor claimed that O'Neill was forced out of the Justice Department after being criticized for providing legal advice to the Senecas. Walter Taylor to Arthur E. Morgan, Apr. 9, 1966, Taylor MSS, MR 7, WHS; Edward O'Neill, interviewed by the author, Jan. 10, 1984, Washington, DC; O'Neill's résumé in Folder 2: "O'Neill, Edward," 1959–60, William N. Fenton MSS, American Philosophical Society (APS), Philadelphia. The 1957 change in New York State Law rescinding the payment of the Seneca Nation attorney is noted in New York State Interdepartmental Committee on Indian Affairs, *Annual Report for 1957* (Albany: New York State, 1957), 4.

27. SNI Tribal Council, minutes of special session, Aug. 28, 1954, SNI Department of Justice Records, SNI Archives.

28. The Senecas' assertion and Baldwin's response are given in the Baldwin report (cited fully in note 25).

29. Ibid.

30. SNI Tribal Council, special session minutes, Aug. 28, 1954, SNI Department of Justice Records, SNI Archives.

31. Edward O'Neill to Ali David Good, Aug. 29, 1954, and P. G. Baldwin to Edward O'Neill, Aug. 31, 1954, NYSDPW Records, Deputy Superintendents' Records, Box 9(1954), NYSA.

32. SNI Tribal Council, minutes of special session, Sept. 18, 1954, SNI Department of Justice Records, SNI Archives.

33. P. G. Baldwin to Bertram D. Tallamy, Memorandum: "Settlement with the Seneca Nation of Indians," Sept. 20, 1954, NYSDPW, Deputy Superintendent's Records, #BO 251-84, Box 9 (1954), Folder: "Indian Affairs," NYSA.

34. For newspaper coverage of this accord and claims of $100,000 compensation to so-called Seneca landowners, see "Seneca Indians, State, Agree on Thruway Land [$100,000 earmarked for Owners, $75,000 for Nation]," *JPJ*, Sept. 18, 1954; "Senecas Expect $175,000 for Thruway Site," *SRP*, Sept. 20, 1954.

35. The Seneca Nation of Indians to the People of the State of New York, acting by and through the New York State Thruway Authority, "Conveyance of Permanent Ease-ment" (Memorandum of Closing of Title) and "Indenture," with attached minutes of the SNI Tribal Council meeting of Sept. 18, 1954, at the Allegany Indian Reservation Court-house, filed at the Erie County Clerk's Office, Oct. 5, 1954; Laurence M. Hauptman, FOIL Request #F08-0011 to New York State Thruway Authority, released to the author Feb. 12, 2008.

36. See note 35.

37. Arthur Lazarus Jr. (Seneca Nation attorney) to Ali D. Good, Sept. 21, 1971; Louis J. Lefkowitz (attorney general of New York State) and Edward R. Amend (assistant attorney general) to Lazarus, Oct. 1, 1971; Lazarus to Amend and Good, Nov. 23, 1971; Lefkowitz and Amend to Lazarus, Nov. 30, 1971; Lazarus to Merwin Pierce, Jan. 21, 1972; Irving Solomon (chief land claims examiner) to Arthur Levitt (New York State comptroller), Jan. 19, 1972, all in SNI Department of Justice Records, SNI Archives.

38. For the governor's planned visit to Dunkirk, New York, on Oct. 13, 1954, see "Dewey to Mark Start of County Thruway Work," *JPJ*, Oct. 6, 1954; New York State Governor's Office, *Public Papers of Thomas E. Dewey*, 1954, 811.

39. Michael James, "Thruway Section Reaches Border," *NYT*, Aug. 22, 1957.

40. "Tuscaroras Stop Surveyors Again," *NYT*, Apr. 18, 1958; "Indian Women Protest Niagara Power Survey," *Rochester Democrat and Chronicle*, July 2, 1958; "Tuscaroras in Pro-test," *NYT*, July 2, 1958.

41. For the Onondaga road protest, see Harvey Flad, "The City and the Longhouse: A Social Geography of American Indians in Syracuse, New York," PhD diss., Syracuse Univ., 1973, 162–73; "Onondagas, State Reach Accord on Route 81 Controversy," *Syracuse Herald-American*, Oct. 31, 1971.

42. Carolyn Thompson, "Seneca Nation Targets New York Thruway in Tax Dispute," *Indian Country Today*, July 15, 2011.

43. I was teaching at St. Bonaventure University, fifteen miles from the Allegany Indian Reservation, and was witness to the Seneca protest in 1992 along the New York State Thruway as well as in the city of Salamanca. "Senecas Clash with Police over Tax Ruling," *NYT*, July, 17, 1992. One of my former students was directly involved in the protest: Carole

Moses, interviewed by the author, July 18, 2001, Allegany Indian Reservation. For the 1997 protest, see Bilharz, *The Allegany Senecas and Kinzua Dam*, 135–36.

44. Rick Jemison, interviewed by the author, Mar. 21, 2012, Cattaraugus Indian Reservation. Mr. Jemison was a Seneca Nation tribal councilor in the 1990s and was the Seneca representative who helped negotiate the New York State–Seneca Gaming Pact.

45. See the following articles in the *SNI Official Newsletter*: "Seneca Nation Delivers Bill to New York for Thruway Use; Nation Starts Assessing Thruway Authority for Vehicular Use of Tribal Land," June 15, 2007; "Senecas Erect Sign on Nation Land Beside New York State Thruway; Messages to State and Motorists Indicate the Roadway No Longer Has Right of Way," Sept. 14, 2007. The toll booth idea was first put forth by Standing Arrow (Francis Johnson), a Mohawk Indian, protesting state policies and asserting Indian land claims in the 1950s. See Wilson, *Apologies to the Iroquois*, 39–57.

46. "New York Senecas Vote to Rescind Thruway Pact," *NYT*, Apr. 20, 2007.

4. KEYSTONE STATE POLICIES: POWER TRIP

1. Paul C. Rosier, "Dam Building and Treaty Breaking: The Kinzua Dam Controversy, 1936–1958," *Pennsylvania Magazine of History and Biography* 119 (Oct. 1995), 347.

2. Ibid., 345–68. Rosier does mention energy/utilities companies but never explores their major role in pushing the project forward. In another study focusing on the politics of flood control, Roy E. Brant suggests that hydropower at Kinzua was initially considered merely "an incidental byproduct of flood control." He adds, but only in one passing sentence, that interest "continued to run high, leading to its eventual inclusion." Unfortunately, he never follows up this point. Roy E. Brant, "A Flood Control Dam for the Upper Allegheny River; Forty Years of Controversy," PhD diss., Univ. of Pittsburgh, 1970, 41.

3. US Congress, House of Representatives, Committee on Appropriations, Subcommittee on Public Works, *Hearings on H.R. 8090: Public Works Appropriations for 1958, March 28–May 10, 1957*, 2 vols., 85th Cong., 1st sess. (Washington, DC: US Government Printing Office, 1957), 2:1047; James Haley to President John Fitzgerald Kennedy, June 20, 1961, James A. Haley MSS, Haley Seneca Indian File, Florida Southern College (FSC), Lakeland; US Congress, House of Representatives, Committee on Interior and Insular Affairs, Subcommittee on Indian Affairs, *Hearings on H.R. 1794, H.R. 3343, and H.R. 7354: Kinzua Dam (Seneca Indian Relocation), May 18–December 10, 1963*, 88th Cong., 1st sess., May 18, Dec. 10, 1963 (Washington, DC: US Government Printing Office, 1964), 143–44 (fourteen separate days of hearings); Wilson, *Apologies to the Iroquois*, 195–96.

4. Jerry Zremski, "Senecas Seek Kinzua Dam Hydropower," *BN*, Nov. 30, 2010; President Robert Odawi, statement at news conference, Nov. 30, 2010, Allegany Indian Reservation, handout in author's possession.

5. US Army Corps of Engineers, Pittsburgh District, *Kinzua Dam and Allegheny Reservoir*, pamphlet (May 2009), for distribution at Kinzua Dam Visitor Center; FirstEnergy publicity video, *Kinzua Dam*, Dec. 28, 2005, Kinzua Dam Visitor Center.

6. Statistics found at the FirstEnergy Corporation website, https://www.firstenergy corp.com/. Other statistics about payments by FirstEnergy to the federal government and the profitability of the dam were provided by David Kimmelberg, director of the Seneca Nation of Indians Holding Company, Sept. 26, 2011, Allegany Indian Reservation.

7. Rosier, "Dam Building and Treaty Breaking," 348. For more on disastrous floods along the Allegheny–Monongahela–Ohio and their impact on politics, see Roland Smith, "The Politics of Pittsburgh Flood Control, 1908–1936," *Pennsylvania History* 42 (Jan. 1975): 5–24; Roland Smith, "The Politics of Pittsburgh Flood Control, 1936–1960," *Pennsylvania History* 44 (Jan. 1977): 3–24; Allen Lee, "The Kinzua Dam Project: A Case Study in the Politics of Flooding," PhD diss., Univ. of Pittsburgh, 1959; and Brant, "A Flood Control Dam for the Upper Allegheny River."

8. 49 Stat. 1570 (June 22, 1936); 52 Stat. 1215 (June 28, 1938); 55 Stat. 638 (Aug. 18, 1941).

9. Merrill Bowen, interviewed by the author, Aug. 26, 1983, and Sept. 28, 1984, Allegany Indian Reservation. Bowen, the Cornplanter Seneca spokesman during the Kinzua crisis and editor of the *Kinzua Planning Newsletter*, went with several Seneca delegates to Harrisburg to protest in 1936. For the Interior Department's initial opposition to the Kinzua Dam during the New Deal, see John D. Reeves and A. D. Wathen to Commissioner of Indian Affairs, Dec. 30, 1936, and Oscar L. Chapman (assistant secretary of the interior) to Louis Johnson (assistant secretary of war), June 6, 1940, BIA Central Classified Files, 1907–39, #2691-29-052 (N.Y.), RG 75, NA. See also Chapman to Secretary of War, Aug. 28, Nov. 23, Dec. 31, 1940, and E. K. Burlew (acting secretary of the interior) to Secretary of War, May 2, 1940, New York Agency Records, Box 4, Folder: "Cornplanter Dam," NA, Federal Record Center, New York City; "Threat to Seneca Land Averted," *Indians at Work* (BIA), Apr. 15, 1937.

10. The Covell report is reprinted in US Congress, House of Representatives, *House Document 300: Hearings: Allegheny River, N.Y. and Pennsylvania, Allegheny Reservoir,* 76th Cong., 1st sess. (Washington, DC: US Government Printing Office, 1939), 22–87. I previously traced the Army Corp's involvement in the project, making use of the records of the Office of the Chief of Engineers, Civil Works, 1923–42, River and Harbors Files, Allegheny River, RG 77, NA, National Records Center, Washington, DC, formerly at Suitland, MD. See Hauptman, *Iroquois Struggle for Survival,* 91–93, 261 nn. 12–14. These records are now in a "black hole" in the National Archives system, possibly in storage at Atlanta.

11. Covell report (see note 10), 85, 38–45.

12. Charles E. Congdon, interviewed by William N. Fenton, Dec. 4, 1964, Fenton MSS, Folder: "Kinzua Dam, III," APS. For the history of the Allegany State Park, see Congdon, *Allegany Oxbow.*

13. Elmer Thompson (Seneca Nation clerk) to Charles H. Berry (New York State Indian superintendent), June 8, 1945; Thompson to President Harry Truman, with Seneca Nation resolution opposing Kinzua Dam, June 23, 1945; Seneca Nation resolution of Dec. 8, 1945 (filed Mar. 4, 1946); Thompson to Nora Anderson (assistant to Superintendent Berry), Apr. 27, May 6, July 29, 1946; Thompson to Senator James Mead, Aug. 28, 1945. All in BIA, New

York Agency Records, 1938–49, Box 4, Folder: "Cornplanter Dam," RG 75, NA, Federal Record Center, New York City.

14. "State Council of Parks Backs Federal Plan to Buy Reservation and Remove Indians: Linked with Kinzua Dam; Would Develop Allegany Valley for Recreation," *SRP*, Jan. 21, 1946. Other state park officials objected to trading Allegany State Park lands; see Kenneth B. Disher (Allegany State Park Commission) to Charles Berry (BIA New York superintendent), July 11, 1945, BIA, New York Agency Records, 1938–49, Federal Records Center, New York City. The Senecas also initially rejected this idea: Elmer Thompson to Senator James Mead, Aug. 28, 1945, BIA, New York Agency Records, 1938–49, Federal Records Center, New York City; "Don't Like Park Land, Say Indians: Seneca Clerk [Thompson] Attacks Plan to Trade Land," *SRP*, Aug. 13, 1946.

15. Lafayette Kennedy testimony in New York State Joint Legislative Committee on Indian Affairs, Hearings at the Tonawanda Indian Community House, Nov. 17, 1961, Akron, NY, transcript in NYSL.

16. For Goddard, see Reed M. Smith, *State Government in Transition: Reforms of the Leader Administration, 1955–1959* (Philadelphia: Univ. of Pennsylvania Press, 1961), 97 nn. 204–5. For George Leader's reform administration, see M. Nelson McGeary, *Pennsylvania Government in Action: Governor Leader's Administration* (Philadelphia: Univ. of Pennsylvania Press, 1982). For David L. Lawrence, see Roy Lubove, *Twentieth Century Pittsburgh: Government, Business, and Environmental Change* (New York: New Viewpoints, 1969), 106–41; Bruce M. Stave, *The New Deal and the Last Hurrah: Pittsburgh Machine Politics* (Pittsburgh: Pittsburgh Univ. Press, 1970); and especially Michael P. Weber, *Don't Call Me Boss: David L. Lawrence* (Pittsburgh: Univ. of Pittsburgh Press, 1988).

17. Maurice K. Goddard to Congressman Clarence Cannon (chairman, House Appropriations Committee), May 6, 1957, Governors' Records: David Lawrence, Box 40, Pennsylvania State Archives (PSA), Harrisburg.

18. Senator Joseph S. Clark news release of statement to be presented to the House Public Works Subcommittee of the Committee on Appropriations, May 15, 1957, John S. Bragdon MSS, Box 51, Dwight D. Eisenhower Presidential Library (DDEL), Abilene, KS; Senator Joseph S. Clark news release, May 20, 1958, July 21, 1959, Apr. 13, 1960, and summary of public works meeting, Feb. 26, 1959, Joseph S. Clark MSS, Box 202, Folder: "Public Works," Historical Society of Pennsylvania, Philadelphia.

19. Rickard, *Fighting Tuscarora*, 138–54.

20. For the extensive effects by Pennsylvania officials to obtain Niagara power, see "Fact Sheet" (undated) related to congressional Niagara power bills and their implications for Pennsylvania; William R. Devlin (Pennsylvania Department of Commerce) to Robert Moses, Aug. 5, 1957; Devlin to Thomas D. McBride (Pennsylvania attorney general), Aug. 5, 1957; Devlin to David W. Randall (secretary to Governor Leader), Oct. 22, 1956; Devlin to William C. Wenner (Allegheny Electric Cooperative), Aug. 5, 1957; George Leader to Devlin, June 28, 1957; Wenner to Leader, Oct. 9, 15, 1956, Sept. 18, 1957; Leader to Wenner, Oct. 26,

1956; Leader to Governor Averill Harriman (New York), Oct. 26, 1956; Leader to Senator Robert Kerr (chairman, US Senate Public Works Committee), July 14, 1955, Apr. 12, 1957; Wenner to Henry Leader, June 21, Aug. 7, 1956; Senator Joseph Clark telegram to Governor Leader, July 24, 1956; Thomas Buchanan to Herbert V. Cohen (Pennsylvania attorney general), July 9, 1955; Thomas Kerrigan (acting counsel, Pennsylvania Public Utility Commission) to Henry Rubin (Pennsylvania attorney general), July 9, 1955; Thomas Kerrigan (acting counsel, Pennsylvania Public Utility Commission) to Henry Rubin (Pennsylvania Public Utility Commission), July 5, 1956; Joseph M. Barr (Pennsylvania Democrat Party chairman) telegram to Governor Leader, Feb. 7, 1956, with attached letter by Robert Kemp (attorney/lobbyist for Allegheny Electric Cooperative), Feb. 1, 1956. All in Governors' Records: George M. Leader, RG 207, #9-0190, Box 39, Folder: "Niagara Power," PSA.

21. Wenner to Governor George Leader, Oct. 15, 1956.

22. Maurice Goddard for Governor George Leader to Colonel H. E. Sprague, Jan. 31, Feb. 4, 1958, Governors' Records: George W. Leader, #9-0199, Subject Files: Water Conservation, Stream Purification, and Flood Control, Box 51, Folder: "Army, U.S.," PSA. Goddard met with congressional representatives as well as with representatives from the Army Corps, the Department of Agriculture (National Forests), the Department of the Interior, and both private and cooperative power companies. Summary of public-works meeting, Feb. 26, 1959, Clark MSS, Box 202, Folder: "Public Works," Historical Society of Pennsylvania; Status of Recreation Areas, June 10, 1962, Clark MSS, Box 201, Historical Society of Pennsylvania.

23. Colonel H. E. Sprague to Governor George Leader, Jan. 13, 1958, with attached report of activities of the US Army Corps of Engineers, Pittsburgh District, in western Pennsylvania for 1957–58, Governors' Records: George W. Leader, RG 207, #9-0199, Subject Files: Water Conservation, Stream Purification, and Flood Control, Box 51, Folder 1: "Army, U.S.," PSA.

24. Maurice Goddard to William Wenner, May 20, 1959, Governors' Records: David Lawrence, #9-0373, Water Conservation, Box 40, Folder 17: "Kinzua," PSA, emphasis mine. Wenner had brought up the hydropower possibilities at the proposed Kinzua Dam pushed by ten electricity distribution cooperatives and justified it as an effective plan because electricity was too costly in Pennsylvania. From his first days as governor, Governor Lawrence pushed the Kinzua Dam project. Governor David Lawrence, telegram to Pennsylvania congressional delegation et al., Jan. 22, 1959, Governors' Records: David Lawrence, #9-0373, Subject Files: Water Conservation, Box 40, Folder 17: "Kinzua," PSA.

25. Clark news release, May 15, 1957, Clark MSS, Box 202, Folder: "Public Works," Historical Society of Pennsylvania.

26. Brant claims that Javits and Keating opposed the dam, that New York's congressional delegation was unanimously opposed to the dam, and that the Pennsylvania delegation was split on the issue. Brant, "A Flood Control Dam for the Upper Allegheny River," 73–74. Yet neither Javits nor Keating formally testified against the dam, and their collections of

correspondence reveal only token opposition to the project. In Pennsylvania, Congressman John Saylor fought against the dam's construction from the beginning. Congressman Haley, who was born in Alabama, later voted against the historic Civil Rights Act of 1964. During the Kinzua crisis, he wrote to his Florida constituents, "One of the most surprising things that has occurred was that the two alleged champions of civil rights in minority groups, Senators Javits and Keating of New York, never made any effort to my knowledge to appear before my Subcommittee during the hearings or act to protect the rights of the Seneca Indians (some of whose lands are located in the State of New York) in this serious problem." James A. Haley to Lilian and Emily Dixon, June 15, 1961, Haley MSS, Haley Seneca Indian File, FSC.

27. Arthur E. Morgan, *Dams and Other Disasters: A Century of the Army Corps of Engineers in Civil Works* (Boston: Sargent, 1971), 310–66.

28. Arthur E. Morgan, *The Community of the Future and the Future of the Community* (Yellow Springs, Ohio: Community Service, 1957), 156–59. Morgan wrote sixteen books, including two on Edward Bellamy.

29. For Morgan and the TVA, see Arthur E. Morgan, *The Making of the TVA* (Buffalo: Prometheus Books, 1974); Thomas McCraw, *Morgan v. Lilienthal: A Feud within TVA* (Chicago: Loyola Univ. Press, 1970); and Thomas McCraw, *TVA and the Power Fight, 1933–1939* (Philadelphia: Lippincott, 1971). For the displacement of rural populations and the resettlement of the dispossessed, see the excellent treatment by Michael J. McDonald and John Muldowny, *TVA and the Dispossessed: The Resettlement of Population in the Norris Dam Area* (Knoxville: Univ. of Tennessee Press, 1982). For a contrast with Morgan, see David E. Lilienthal, *TVA: Democracy on the March* (New York: Harper and Row, 1953).

30. Arthur E. Morgan, "Intelligent Reasonableness and the Utilities: Democratic Decency or Chronic Bitterness," *Vital Speeches* 3 (Feb. 1, 1937), 232–33.

31. Morgan, *Dams and Other Disasters*, 310–66.

32. US Congress, House of Representatives, Committee on Appropriations, Subcommittee on Public Works Appropriations, *Hearings on H.R. 7509: Public Works Appropriations for 1958*, 86th Cong., 1st sess. (Washington, DC: US Government Printing Office, 1957), 676–89.

33. US Congress, Senate, Committee on Appropriations, Subcommittee on Public Works Appropriations, *Hearings on Public Works Appropriations for 1958*, 85th Cong., 1st sess. (Washington, DC: US Government Printing Office, 1957), 425–53.

34. Cornelius Seneca to President Dwight D. Eisenhower, Mar. 26, 1957, Eisenhower Records, Alpha Series, Box 1699, File: Kinzua Dam (3), DDEL. Seneca continued to appeal directly to Eisenhower, hoping to get an audience with him. That never happened. Seneca to Eisenhower, June 26, 1957, Eisenhower Records, Official File 155-E (1957[2]), DDEL.

35. Minutes of a [White House] Meeting [John S. Bragdon, assistant secretary of the army and chief of the Army Corps of Engineers] to discuss Allegheny Dam and Reservoir, PA, Sept. 6, 1957, Bragdon MSS, Box 51, DDEL; E. L. Tippetts, *Abbett, McCarthy, Stratton,*

Report Plans 1, 2, 3: Allegheny Reservoir; a Review of Authorized Plan and Alternative for the U.S. Army Corps of Engineers Division, Ohio River, Apr. 1958, in Arthur E. Morgan MSS, Antioch College, Yellow Springs, OH; "General James S. Stratton, Flood-Control Specialist," *NYT,* Mar. 21, 1984.

36. For more on Morgan's efforts, see Hauptman, *The Iroquois Struggle for Survival,* 108–15, 118–21.

37. Philadelphia Yearly Meeting of Friends, *The Kinzua Dam Controversy: A Practical Solution—without Shame* (Philadelphia: Philadelphia Yearly Meeting of Friends, 1961). The Quakers sent Walter Taylor of the American Friends Service to help the Senecas, subsidized his work for five years, and underwrote the *Kinzua Planning Newsletter* to help the Senecas "recover" (see chapter 5). Wilson, *Apologies to the Iroquois.* Brooks Atkinson wrote sympathetic columns in the *New York Times* describing the plight of the Senecas. See, for example, his article "Critic at Large: Proposed Dam That Would Violate Treaty with the Senecas Poses Moral Questions," *NYT,* Apr. 12, 1961. See also Brook Atkinson, *Tuesdays and Fridays* (New York: Viking, 1963).

38. *Seneca Nation of Indians v. Wilbur M. Brucker, et al.,* 462 F. Supp. 580, 262 F. 2d 27, 360 U.S. 909 (1959); Edward O'Neill, interviewed by the author, Jan. 10, 1984, Washington, DC.

39. Brant, "A Flood Control Dam for the Upper Allegheny River," 75–76.

40. Ibid.; John Bragdon memorandum for the president, Aug. 24, 1959, Ann Whitman Files, Eisenhower Diary Series, Box 43, Staff Notes, Aug. 1959 (1), DDEL; Bragdon to Mrs. [Ann] Whitman (president's secretary), Oct. 17, 1959 Bragdon MSS, Box 51, DDEL; Phillip S. Hughes (Bureau of the Budget) to the Secretary of the Interior, June 22, 1959, Eisenhower Records, White House Central Files, Official File 155-E 1957 (2), Box 837, DDEL.

41. Del Laverdure (deputy assistant US commissioner of Indian affairs), presentation at Seneca Remember the Removal commemoration, Sept. 25, 2011; Marjane Ambler, *Breaking the Bonds: Indian Control of Energy Development* (Lawrence: Univ. Press of Kansas, 1990), 204–13, 311 n. 4.

42. US Department of the Interior, Bureau of Reclamation, *The Reclamation Program, 1953–1959* (Washington, DC: US Government Printing Office, 1959), v–vi; US Department of the Interior, Bureau of Reclamation, *Reclamation Project Data—Supplement* (Washington, DC: US Government Printing Office, 1966), iii.

43. US Department of the Interior, Bureau of Reclamation, *Project Data* (Washington, DC: US Government Printing Office, 1961), v–vi.

44. Michael L. Lawson, *Dammed Indians: The Pick-Sloan Plan and the Missouri River Sioux, 1944–1980* (Norman: Univ. of Oklahoma Press, 1982), 59–62; see also Michael L. Lawson, *Dammed Indians Revisited: The Continuing History of the Pick-Sloan Plan and the Missouri River Sioux* (Pierre: South Dakota State Historical Society, 2010). For a sampling of the impact of dams on other Native American communities in the United States and Canada, see George W. Aguilar Sr., *When the River Ran Wild: Indian Traditions on the Mid-Columbia and the Warm Springs Reservation* (Seattle: Univ. of Washington Press, 2005); Katrine Barber, *Death of Celilo*

Falls (Seattle: Univ. of Washington Press, 2005); Benedict J. Colombi, "Indigenous Peoples, Large Dams, and Capital-Intensive Energy Development: A View from the Lower Colorado River," in *Indians and Energy Exploitation and Opportunity in the American Southwest*, edited by Sherry Smith and Brian Frehner, 89–109 (Santa Fe: School for Advanced Research Press, 2010); Andrew H. Fisher, *Shadow Tribe: The Making of Columbia River Indian Identity* (Seattle: Univ. of Washington Press, 2010); Sean McCutcheon, *Electric Rivers: The Story of the James Bay Project* (Montreal: Black Rose Books, 1991).

45. Douglas McKay's address before the Pennsylvania Electric Association, Sept. 22, 1953, and Jerome K. Kuykendall's address before the Association of Edison Illuminating Companies, Oct. 7, 1954, Office Files of Theodore Stevens (assistant to the secretary of the interior, legislative legal counsel), 1956–60, Box 8, Folder: "Power Policy—General & Misc.," Office of the Secretary of the Interior (OSI) Records, RG 48, NA II, College Park, MD. For the Interior Department's "accomplishments" in this area during the Eisenhower presidency, see Commissioner of Reclamation to Legislative Counsel, Office of the Solicitor, stamped May 13, 1959, with attached report: "Accomplishments of the Interior Department and Construction of Water and Power Resource Projects, 1953–1962," Office Files of Theodore Stevens, Box 8, Folder: "Power Clippings," OSI Records, RG 48, NA II.

46. Bragdon memorandum for the record, July 23, 1957, Bragdon MSS, Box 51, DDEL. The Senecas had rejected swapping tribal lands since 1946. See "Senecas Don't Want to Swap Reservation Lands for Park Lands," *SRP*, Aug. 14, 1946.

47. O. Hatfield Chilson to President Eisenhower, Apr. 11, 1957, Fred Seaton MSS, Subject Series, Box 17, Kinzua Dam (Seneca Indians), DDEL, emphasis mine.

48. This conclusion is based on my examination of the Interior Department's briefing books at the Eisenhower Library. Moreover, until 1974 the commissioner of Indian affairs was not on the same policy level as other divisions in the department. In 1974, the commissioner's status was raised to assistant secretary for Indian affairs.

49. D. Ivan Fritts, "GOP Power Policies Cause Great Damage," *Oregon Democrat*, Nov. 10, 1957; William E. Leuchtenberg, "The Issue of Public Power," *Current History* (Jan. 1955): 48–52, found in Office Files of Theodore Stevens, OSI Records, Box 8, Folder: "Power Clippings," RG 48, NA II.

50. Haley to Kennedy, June 20, 1961; US Congress, House, Committee on Interior and Insular Affairs, Subcommittee on Indian Affairs, *Hearings on H.R. 1794 . . . Kinzua Dam (Seneca Indian Relocation)*, 143–44. For Haley's views on private power development, see Haley to Arthur Davidson, Aug. 25, 1961; Ray Littrell, Oct. 19, 1961; Harold Bray, Dec. 14, 1961; and Edward J. Kemper, Sept. 19, 1962. See also Congressman Haley's news release, May 12, 1961. All in Haley MSS, Folder: "Electric Power; Public and Private," 1961–63, FSC. As a persistent critic of Interior Department, Haley also opposed the Knowles Dam in Montana, a far greater hydroproject than Kinzua, which would also have condemned Indian lands. This dam was never built. For Haley's criticisms of the Knowles Dam project in Montana, see

US Congress, House, *Congressional Record*, 88th Cong., 1st sess., Aug. 19, 1963, 23638; Dec. 17, 1963, 14530–33.

51. "News Release: Remarks of Governor David Lawrence at Groundbreaking, Allegheny River Reservoir, Kinzua, Pennsylvania," Oct. 22, 1960, Governors' Records: David L. Lawrence, Box 40, PSA.

52. "Secretary of the Interior Enunciates Broad Power Policy for Department," US Department of the Interior news release, Feb. 14, 1961, Office and Subject Files of Kenneth Holum (assistant secretary of the interior for water and power), Box 11: Power Projects, Folder: "Power Policy Statements," OSI Records, RG 48, NA II. For the pressures on Udall, see Robert Dean, "'Dam Building Still Had Some Magic Then': Stewart Udall, the Central Arizona Project, and the Evolution of the Pacific Southwest Water Plan, 1963–1968," *Pacific Historical Review* 66, no. 9 (1997): 81–98.

53. Stewart Udall, "Memorandum on Power Policy to All Staffs of the Department of the Interior," Feb. 13, 1961, Clark MSS, Box 172, Folder: "FPC [Federal Power Commission]," Historical Society of Pennsylvania.

54. Knowland J. Plucknett to Assistant Secretary—Water and Power Development, through Assistant and Chief Engineering Research Adviser, Mar. 2, 1962, and Holum to Secretary of the Interior, July 19, 1961, with attached report on meeting with the Department of the Interior, the Army Corps of Engineers, and Pennsylvania Power Company representatives, re: Kinzua project—Pennsylvania, July 18, 1961, Office Files of Kenneth Holum, Box 5, Folder: "Kinzua Project," OSI Records, RG 48, NA II.

55. "Electrical Generating Plant at Kinzua Reservoir Studied," *Warren Times-Mirror*, Mar. 3, 1960; "Generation of Electricity as Phase of Multiple Use of Kinzua Dam Is Feasible," *Warren Times-Mirror*, Apr. 27, 1960.

56. "Penelec–Warren Cooperative Propose Kinzua Dam Reservoir 'Storage Battery' Power Plan," *Warren Times-Mirror*, Sept. 28, 1960.

57. Pennsylvania Electric Company (Penelec), *Annual Report for 1964*, Pennsylvania Public Utilities Commission, Harrisburg. According to its *Annual Report for 1965* (Pennsylvania Public Utilities Commission, Harrisburg), Penelec put up 20 percent and Cleveland Electric Illuminating 80 percent of the $30 million cost of constructing the "Seneca Pumped Storage Hydroelectric Station" (p. 2).

58. Pennsylvania Electric Company Notice of Application for a Preliminary Permit from the Federal Power Commission, Project No. 2280, Oct. 31, 1960, FPC Records, FERC, Washington, DC.

59. Pennsylvania Electric Company, Project No. 2280, 25 F.P.C. 909 (May 3, 1961), FPC Records, FERC.

60. Ibid.

61. Pennsylvania Electric Company Preliminary Report to Federal Power Commission, Oct. 3, 1961, Kinzua Dam Regulatory Commission (KDRC) Records, SNI Archives.

62. Arthur Lazarus Jr. to Seneca Nation Tribal Council, Feb. 26, 1962, SNI, KDRC Records, SNI Archives.

63. US Congress, House, Committee on Interior and Insular Affairs, Subcommittee on Indian Affairs, *Hearings on H.R. 1794 . . . Kinzua Dam (Seneca Indian Relocation)*, 99, emphasis mine.

64. US Congress, Senate, Committee on Interior and Indian Affairs, Subcommittee on Indian Affairs, *Hearings on S. 1836 and H.R. 1794: Kinzua Dam (Seneca Indian Relocation), March 2, 1964*, 88th Cong, 2d sess. (Washington, DC: US Government Printing Office, 1964), 182.

65. See Congressman Haley's statements comparing Montana's proposed Knowles Dam, which the congressman also opposed, and the Kinzua Dam: US Congress, House of Representatives, *Congressional Record*, 88th Cong., 1st sess., Aug. 19, 1963, 14530–33.

66. Memoranda of Understanding between Pennsylvania Electric Company and U.S. Department of Agriculture, Apr. 10, 1963, and June 18, 1965, FPC Records, FERC.

67. *Warren County Observer* article reprinted as "As Others See It: Power of Kinzua," *SRP*, Apr. 12, 1965.

68. Pennsylvania Electric Company and Cleveland Electric Illuminating Company, Project 2280 (May 26, 1965), KDRC Records, SNI Archives; Penelec, *Annual Report for 1965*.

69. Penelec, *Annual Report for 1965*.

70. "Kinzua Dam Is Hailed at Dedication," *Pittsburgh Post Gazette*, Sept. 17, 1966.

71. Scranton quoted in "Scranton Hails the Kinzua Dam as a Boon to Entire Region," *NYT*, Sept. 17, 1966.

72. Taylor, *The Seneca Nation Economy*; David Kimelberg interview.

73. Clarkin, *Federal Indian Policy in the Kennedy and Johnson Administrations*, 1–60, 111–39; for Kinzua, see 49–57.

74. *Report to the Secretary of the Interior by the Task Force on Indian Affairs*, July 10, 1961, Haley MSS, File: Task Force on Indian Affairs, FSC.

75. George Heron, interviewed by the author, Sept. 28, 1984, Allegany Indian Reservation. For the American Indian Chicago Conference and its meaning to eastern tribes, see Laurence M. Hauptman and Jack Campisi, "The Voice of Eastern Indians: The American Indian Chicago Conference, 1961, and the Movement for Federal Recognition," *Proceedings of the American Philosophical Society* 132 (Dec. 1988): 316–29.

76. Michael Harrington, *The Other America: Poverty in the United States* (New York: Macmillan, 1962).

77. Robert L. Bennett oral history, Lyndon Baines Johnson Presidential Library, Austin. For Udall's awakening on Indian issues, see Clarkin, *Federal Indian Policy in the Kennedy and Johnson Administrations*, 196–226.

78. Stewart Udall to Franklin Delano Roosevelt Jr., Apr. 9, 1964, and "Udall Lauds Electric Utility Expansion Plans to Aid Appalachia," US Department of the Interior news release, Mar. 27, 1964, Office and Subject Files of Kenneth Holum, OSI Records, Box 11:

Power Projects, Folder: "Power Policy Statements," RG 48, NA II. Although New York State's southern tier counties such as Cattaraugus and counties in northwestern Pennsylvania are included in the Appalachian Regional Commission's northern focus, the Senecas, unlike the Eastern Band of Cherokees in North Carolina, have largely been ignored in the literature on Appalachia. Ninety-nine percent of the literature on Appalachia focuses on West Virginia and states south of it. Finally, in 2006, an article on the Senecas in connection with Appalachia was published: Midge Dean Stock, "The Seneca-Iroquois National Museum," in *Encyclopedia of Appalachia*, edited by Rudy Abramson and Jean Haskell, 1507–8 (Knoxville: Univ. of Tennessee Press, 2006). Although Karl B. Raitz, Richard Ulack, and Thomas Leinbach's book *Appalachia: A Regional Geography: Land, People, and Development* (Boulder, CO: Westview Press, 1984) is filled with valuable information, it is typical in ignoring the Seneca presence in Appalachia.

79. Howard Morgan to President John Kennedy, Jan. 23, 1963, Clark MSS, Box 172, Folder: "FPC," Historical Society of Pennsylvania.

5. GEORGE HERON, THE KINZUA PLANNING COMMITTEE, AND THE HALEY ACT

1. SNI press release, May 27, 2011, SNI Archives. For more on George Heron, see "From the President's Desk," *SNI Official Newsletter*, Feb. 27, 2009; "George D. Heron," *JPJ*, May 27, 2011; "George D. Heron, 92, Served Two Terms as President of the Seneca Nation of Indians," *BN*, May 27, 2011.

2. "Transcript of the President's News Conference on Domestic and World Affairs," *NYT*, Mar. 9, 1961.

3. Lee White to William N. Fenton, Aug. 25, 1961, Fenton MSS, Folder: "Kinzua Dam," APS.

4. John Fitzgerald Kennedy to Basil Williams, Aug. 9, 1961, reprinted in US Congress, House, Committee on Interior and Insular Affairs, Subcommittee on Indian Affairs, *Hearings on H.R. 1794 . . . Kinzua Dam (Seneca Indian Relocation)*, 145.

5. US Department of the Interior, Bureau of Indian Affairs, *Seneca Indians Who Will Be Affected by the Kinzua Dam Reservoir* (Billings, MT: Missouri River Basin Investigations Project, 1963).

6. Philleo Nash to Seneca Nation Tribal Council, Sept. 19, 1964, quoted in Philleo Nash to James A. Haley, Jan. 21, 1966, Haley MSS, Folder: "Indian Affairs Comm.: Seneca Indians," FSC. Even when the BIA was including Senecas in post-Kinzua program planning, it was still committed to federal withdrawal. Ibid. See also James E. Officer (interim commissioner of Indian affairs) to James A. Haley, Mar. 7, 1966, Haley MSS, Folder: "Haley Seneca Indian File," FSC.

7. Clarkin, *Federal Indian Policy in the Kennedy and Johnson Administrations*, 80–83, 165–66.

8. *Kinzua Planning Newsletter* (*KPN*), Mar. 25, 1964. Bowen was forced to apologize in fear that the subcommittee would not approve the compensation bill. Merrill Bowen to Senator Peter Dominick, May 27, 1964, Haley MSS, Haley Seneca Indian File, FSC.

9. US Congress, House, Subcommittee on Indian Affairs, *Hearings on H.R. 1794 . . . Kinzua Dam (Seneca Indian Relocation)*, 50–51, 297; Rosier, "Dam Building and Treaty Breaking," 346 n. 2.

10. US Congress, House, Committee on Interior and Insular Affairs, Subcommittee on Indian Affairs, *Hearings H.R. 1794 . . . Kinzua Dam (Seneca Indian Relocation)*, 53–59.

11. US Department of the Interior, *Seneca Indians Who Will Be Affected by the Kinzua Dam Reservoir*, 11–20.

12. Testimony of Maribel Printup in US Congress, House, Committee on Interior and Insular Affairs, Subcommittee on Indian Affairs, *Hearings on H.R. 1794 . . . Kinzua Dam (Seneca Indian Relocation)*, May 18, 1963, 71–72.

13. Testimony of Basil Williams, May 18, 1963, in ibid., 51.

14. Nearly every issue of the Seneca *KPN* from 1961 to its demise in 1965 is filled with news about the subcommittees created in response to the Kinzua crisis. For membership on the subcommittee, see *KPN*, Apr. 24, Apr. 30, Oct. 8, Nov. 30, 1962; Jan. 10, Mar. 23, Apr. 17, 1963; Jan. 29, 1964.

15. Jack Preston to Theodore Hetzel, Nov. 16, 1961, Taylor MSS, MR 6, WHS. The late Jack Preston was my colleague at SUNY New Paltz, where he taught ethnomusicology in the Anthropology Department for a decade. William N. Fenton to Preston, Aug. 31, Oct. 28, 1961, and Preston to Fenton, Sept. 8, Oct. 15, 1961, Fenton MSS, Folder: "Kinzua Dam," APS; *KPN*, Oct. 11, 1961. Dr. Hazel Dean John was the first Seneca to receive a doctorate in linguistics in North America. She later became the director of the Native American Indian Education Unit in the New York State Department of Education in Albany.

16. For example, Cornelius Seneca and the Tribal Council in 1956–57 were accused of making natural gas leases at ridiculously low rates. After hearing criticism about these leases, I asked Seneca's widow about his role. She informed me that her husband and the Tribal Council were in dire economic straits at the time and, as a result, made some of these bad agreements to secure desperately needed moneys to fight the Kinzua Dam. Pauline Lay Seneca, interviewed by the author, July 17, 1982, Cattaraugus Indian Reservation. Interviews collected by William N. Fenton in his fieldwork at Allegany clearly reflect these criticisms. Fenton MSS, Folder: "Kinzua Dam," APS. Several Cornplanters were especially critical. Heron acknowledged what he faced. George Heron, interviewed by the author, Sept. 29, 1984, Allegany Indian Reservation.

17. One cannot minimize the role of the remarkable Walter Taylor. Taylor was quoted as saying: "I am convinced that the Indian is not against progress and I am amazed at his generosity with regard to many projects but he objects to being 'forced' to conform with the white man's laws, many of which he agrees are good and needed." Quoted in Jack Berger, "Indians Oppose Conformity Not Progress," *SRP*, Apr. 8, 1966. For an appreciation of Taylor's work, see Flora Heron, "Senecas Are Grateful to Mr. and Mrs. Taylor" (letter to the editor), *SRP*, Apr. 12, 1966. For a summary of Taylor's work, see Taylor to George Heron, May 1, 1964, Apr. 9, 1966, Taylor MSS, MR 7, WHS. See also Taylor to Lee White, June 13, 1961; Taylor

to Chuck Horner (NBC television), Jan. 3, 1962; Taylor to Governor Nelson Rockefeller, May 28, 1963; Taylor to President Lyndon Johnson, Feb. 23, 1964; Taylor to Congressman Wayne Aspinall, all in Theodore Hetzel MSS, Coll. #1168, Friends Kinzua Dam Project Summary, 1956–64, Magill Library, Haverford College. Taylor to Congressman James A. Haley, May 29, 1961; Taylor to Commissioner Philleo Nash, Jan. 15, 1964; Taylor to Senator Peter Dominick, June 5, 1964, all in Taylor MSS, MR 5, WHS.

18. Lazarus was especially effective in monitoring the progress of the Seneca Nation compensation bill in Congress. Arthur Lazarus Jr. to Lee White, May 2, 1962, and Lazarus to Philleo Nash, May 3, 1962, Taylor MSS, MR 6, WHS; minutes of the House Subcommittee on Indian Affairs, Nov. 1, Dec. 9, 13, 1963, Haley MSS, FSC; Arthur Lazarus Jr. to James A. Haley, Jan. 23, 1963, Haley Seneca Indian File: Kinzua Dam Official, May 1960–Dec. 1963, and Lazarus to Haley, Jan. 28, Mar. 23, 31, 1964, Haley MSS, Seneca Indian File: Kinzua Dam Official, Jan.–Mar. 1964, FSC; Lazarus to Haley, Apr. 22, 1964, Haley MSS, Haley Seneca Indian File: Kinzua Dam Official, Apr. 1–Oct. 31, 1964, FSC; Lazarus to Haley, May 7, May 15, June 11, 1964, Haley MSS, Haley Seneca Indian File: Kinzua Dam Correspondence, FSC.

19. Hauptman and Campisi, "The Voice of Eastern Indians"; American Indian Chicago Conference, *The Declaration of Indian Purpose: The Voice of the American Indian* (Chicago: American Indian Chicago Conference, 1961).

20. Philadelphia Yearly Meeting of Friends, *The Kinzua Conference*.

21. American Indian Chicago Conference, *Declaration of Indian Purpose*, 37.

22. US Congress, Senate, Committee on Interior and Insular Affairs, Subcommittee on Indian Affairs, *Hearings on H.R. 1794 . . . Kinzua Dam (Seneca Relocation)*, 109–11.

23. See Heron's revealing testimony before the New York State Joint Legislative Committee, a body that had earlier pushed for the transfer of criminal and civil jurisdiction from the federal to the state government. The Senecas and most other Iroquois detested its counsel, Leighton Wade of Olean, who had frequently opposed their interests. Heron nevertheless appeared before this hostile committee seeking state funds for housing and education during the Kinzua crisis. New York State Legislature, Joint Legislative Committee on Indian Affairs, minutes of hearing at the Tonawanda Indian Community House, Nov. 9, 1963, 28–38, 79–100, transcript in NYSL.

24. The push for women's suffrage included Reva Cooper Barse, Genevieve Plummer, and Martha Bucktooth. Barse was perhaps the most outspoken voice pushing for women's suffrage. She was also a frequent critic of Seneca leadership.

25. Basil Williams to Nelson Rockefeller, May 9, Aug. 29, 1962, Taylor MSS, MR 14, WHS; "Governor Rockefeller Adopted into the Hawk Clan of the Seneca Nation," *KPN*, May 16, 1962. Anthropologist William N. Fenton, who himself had been adopted into the Hawk Clan earlier, had tried unsuccessfully to help the Senecas get an audience with Rockefeller in Albany. Fenton was Rockefeller's classmate at Dartmouth College. Fenton to Nelson Rockefeller, May 2, 1960, Fenton Notes, Feb. 24, 1960, Fenton MSS, Kinzua Dam Folder II, APS.

26. Walter Taylor to William N. Fenton, May 29, 1963; Taylor to Nelson Rockefeller, Aug. 7, 1963, Oct. 26, 1963, Nov. 13, 1964; Rockefeller to George Heron, Aug. 7, 1963, all in Taylor MSS, MR 14, WHS.

27. DeForrest Billy to Congressman Wayne N. Aspinall, Mar. 13, 1963, Haley MSS, Haley Seneca Indian Files: Kinzua Dam Official, Jan. 1963–Oct. 1964, FSC.

28. Ibid.

29. Heron testimony in New York State Legislature, Joint Legislative Committee on Indian Affairs, minutes of hearing at the Tonawanda Indian Community House, Nov. 9, 1963, 28–38, transcript in NYSL. Attorney Lazarus presented the Senecas' case at federal hearings and in the courts. US Congress, House, Committee on Interior and Insular Affairs, Subcommittee on Indian Affairs, *Hearing on H.R. 1794 . . . Kinzua Dam (Seneca Indian Relocation)*, 356–60.

30. William N. Fenton, "From Longhouse to Ranch-Type House: The Second Housing Revolution of the Seneca Nation," in *Iroquois Culture, History, and Prehistory: Proceedings of the 1965 Conference on Iroquois Research*, edited by Elisabeth Tooker, 3–22 (Albany: New York State Museum, 1967). See also Bilharz, *The Allegany Senecas and the Kinzua Dam*, 62–71.

31. Ingrid Jewell, "Engineers Warned on Kinzua: Demand New Homes, Roads before Dam Is Closed," *Pittsburgh Post Gazette*, Aug. 13, 1963.

32. Fenton, "From Longhouse to Ranch-Type House," 7.

33. Ibid., 7, 17.

34. Cornelius Seneca to John Saylor, Mar. 8, June 27, 1957; Saylor to President Eisenhower, Jan. 16, 1959; Heron to Saylor, Jan. 12, 1959, all in John Saylor MSS, Box 39, Indiana Univ. of Pennsylvania, Indiana, PA; "Statement of Honorable John Saylor on H.R. 1794," Haley MSS, Haley Seneca Indian Files: Kinzua Dam Official, FSC; Thomas G. Smith, *Green Republican: John Saylor and the Preservation of America's Wilderness* (Pittsburgh: Univ. of Pittsburgh Press, 2006), 133–40, 225–27; "Rep. Saylor Accuses Army Engineers of Ignoring Plight of Seneca Indians," *Washington Post*, July 16, 1963.

35. Harry A. Kersey Jr., *An Assumption of Sovereignty: Social and Political Transformation among the Florida Seminoles, 1953–1979* (Lincoln: Univ. of Nebraska Press, 2007), 25–26; Stewart O'Nan, *The Circus Fire* (New York: Anchor Books/Random House, 2000), 196, 210–11, 292–95, 300–305, 314–15, 330–31; "James A. Haley Dies; Former Congressman," *NYT*, Aug. 8, 1981. Haley called the 1964 Civil Rights bill "monstrous," a bill that could not have passed without the "vulture in the galleries." Quoted in Joseph L. Rauh Jr., "The Role of the Leadership Conference on Civil Rights in the Civil Rights Struggle of 1963–1964," in *The Civil Rights Act of 1964: The Passage of the Law That Ended Racial Segregation*, edited by Robert D. Loevy (Albany: SUNY Press, 1997), 65.

Saylor acknowledged Haley's lead on the floor of Congress: "Mr. Speaker, first I would like to commend our colleague, the gentleman from Florida [Mr. Haley]. Mr. Haley took up the problems of the Seneca Indians as a personal crusade, realizing that their treaty had been broken and that it was incumbent upon the people of the United States to do something to take care of this great tribe. As a result of his efforts alone, we are here today with a conference report which gives the Seneca Indians the necessary money which will enable them to rehabilitate themselves. This is a tremendous credit to the gentleman from Florida; it is a tribute to him." US Congress, House, *Congressional Record*, 88th Cong., 1st sess., Aug. 18, 1963, 19525. Frank Church, chairman of the Senate Subcommittee on Indian Affairs in 1964 and an advocate of termination, credited Haley as well. Church to Haley, Aug. 21, 1964, Haley MSS, Haley Seneca Indian File, FSC.

36. Vine Deloria Jr. and Clifford M. Lytle, *The Nations Within: The Past and Future of American Indian Sovereignty* (New York: Pantheon Books, 1984), 196–97. Haley's congressional colleagues honored him for his work on behalf of Native Americans. US Congress, House of Representatives, Committee on Interior and Insular Affairs, *Proceedings, July 27, 1976: Unveiling of a Portrait of the Honorable James A. Haley* (Washington, DC: US Government Printing Office, 1976). They passed a resolution: "he has been unswerving in his efforts to enact legislation that will improve the lot of the American Indians and has championed their causes when it was politically unpopular to do so, thereby earning the gratitude of the entire Indian community and the respect of his colleagues."

37. James A. Haley to Theodore Edison, Apr. 20, 1964, Haley MSS, Haley Seneca Indian File: Kinzua Dam Correspondence, FSC; "Rehabilitation Expenses for Missouri River Indian Tribes" (expenses contrasted with costs expenses proposed for Seneca [Kinzua Dam] rehabilitation), Haley MSS, Haley Seneca Indian File: Kinzua Dam Official (1963–64), FSC.

38. "Rep. Haley Irked: Criticism Voiced on Kinzua Issue," *Buffalo Courier-Express*, Aug. 16, 1961.

39. Haley quoted in Jerry Blizin, "Rep. 'Deh-Gawh-Weh-Goh,' Him Friend of the Indians," *St. Petersburg Times*, Mar. 2, 1964.

40. "Senecas Adopt Rep. Haley at Hearing," *SRP*, May 20, 1963; James A. Haley to Dorothy Jimerson (Seneca Heron clan mother), June 14, 1963, Haley MSS, Indian Affairs Committee: Seneca Indians, FSC.

41. James A. Haley to Hugh Downs, Jan. 22, 1963, Haley MSS, Haley Seneca Indian File: Kinzua Dam Correspondence, FSC. See also George Heron to James Haley, Dec. 17, 1962, Feb. 1, Oct. 31, 1964, Haley MSS, Haley Seneca Indian File: Kinzua Dam Correspondence, FSC.

42. Kersey, *Assumption of Sovereignty*, 25–26, 45–47. For Haley's statements favoring federal withdrawal in the long run, see "Government Should Be out of the Indian Business in 25 Years," *Grand Junction Daily Sentinel* (Colorado), Aug. 24, 1958; "Haley Seeks New Policy in Indian Affairs Field," *Sarasota Herald Tribune*, Oct. 16, 1960. Yet Haley continued to take up the Senecas' cause: "Block Is Thrown at Kinzua Project," *JPJ*, May 13, 1960; "Rep. Haley Says Indians [Senecas] Wronged by Kinzua Dam," *BN*, May 18, 1963.

43. James A. Haley to Lilian Dixon, June 15, 1961, Haley MSS, Indian Affairs Comm.: Seneca Indians, FSC; Jacob Javits to Haley, Feb. 11, 1964, Haley MSS, Haley Seneca Indian File: Kinzua Dam Correspondence, FSC. Javits to Frank Church (chair of Senate Subcommittee on

Indian Affairs), Mar. 14, 1964, reprinted in US Congress, Senate, Committee on Interior and Insular Affairs, Subcommittee on Indian Affairs, *Hearings on S. 1836 . . . Kinzua Dam (Seneca Relocation),* 197–99. Senator Joseph Clark of Pennsylvania, a major proponent of the Civil Rights Acts of 1964 and 1965 and leading congressional voice in favor of building the Kinzua Dam, also later supported Haley's bill to "compensate" the Senecas. Clark's wife was the sister of Nelson Rockefeller's first wife. According to Walter Taylor, once Kinzua was being built, Senator Clark was "politically free to criticize the [Army] Corps in a manner impossible for him before." Walter Taylor to Arthur Morgan, Apr. 9, 1966, Taylor MSS, MR 7, WHS.

44. For news coverage of the historic hearing at Salamanca High School, the first of its kind in Seneca Country, see "Congressmen Hold Public Meeting on Seneca Settlement," *Warren County Observer* (Pennsylvania), May 20, 1963; "Hope Expressed after Hearing for Agreement on Seneca Legislation," *SRP,* May 20, 1963; "Rep. Haley Says Indians 'Wronged' by Kinzua Dam," *BN,* May 18, 1963.

45. Heron's and Haley's testimony in US Congress, House, Committee on Interior and Insular Affairs, Subcommittee on Indian Affairs, *Hearings on H.R. 1794 . . . Kinzua Dam (Seneca Relocation),* 49–50.

46. Williams's testimony in ibid., 59.

47. See "Congressmen Question Lack of Indians on County Planning Board," *SRP,* May 18, 1963.

48. Stouffer's testimony in US Congress, House, Committee on Interior and Insular Affairs, Subcommittee on Indian Affairs, *Hearings on H.R. 1794 . . . Kinzua Dam (Seneca Relocation),* 64.

49. Ibid., 65–67.

50. George Heron to Walter Taylor, May 1, 1964, Taylor MSS, MR 7, WHS.

51. Philleo Nash to James A. Haley, Jan. 21, 1966, Haley MSS, Indian Affairs Committee: Seneca Indians, FSC.

52. Printup's testimony in US Congress, House, Committee on Interior and Insular Affairs, Subcommittee on Indian Affairs, *Hearings on H.R. 1794 . . . Kinzua Dam (Seneca Relocation),* 72–75. Bilharz claims that only two students were enrolled in postsecondary programs from 1961 to 1965. Yet table 1 (p. 74) in the federal hearing of May 18, 1963, indicates that twelve Senecas would be enrolled in their second year of postsecondary education in 1964. Bilharz, *The Allegany Senecas and Kinzua Dam,* 90.

53. Bilharz, *The Allegany Senecas and Kinzua Dam,* 89–90.

54. Merle Watt Sr., interviewed by the author, Feb. 1, 2012, Allegany Indian Reservation.

55. Randy John, personal communication to the author, June 21, 2012. Dr. John served as assistant to President Robert Odawi Porter in 2011. Both men's higher education—John at Yale and doctoral training at Syracuse, Porter at Syracuse and Harvard Law School— were supported by the Seneca Educational Foundation. The same was true of Wendy Huff, executive director of the KDRC, and Becky Bowen, acting director of the Seneca Nation Archives. Lori Quigley, the former head of the Seneca Nation Education Department and

now graduate dean of Education at Russell Sage College, also benefited by this foundation's support.

56. Bilharz, *The Allegany Seneca and the Kinzua Dam*, 60–61; Hoover, *Kinzua*, 48–49. For the "salvage archaeology," see George H. J. Abrams, "The Cornplanter Cemetery," *Pennsylvania Archaeology* 35 (Aug. 1965): 59–73; "Indian Graves Moved; Roads to be Built," *SRP*, July 2, 1965.

57. Petition by Cornplanter Heirs to Army Corps of Engineers, Sept. 8, 1963; Lee White transmittal letter, Dec. 4, 1963, with memorandum relative to the Army Corps of Engineers; Colonel Bert de Melker to Merrill Bowen, Feb. 11, 1964; Merle H. Deardorff to de Melker, Feb. 11, 1964; de Melker to Deardorff, Feb. 18, 1964; Walter Taylor reports on Cornplanter Cemetery relocation to Indian Committee of the Philadelphia Yearly Meeting of Friends, Mar. 30, 1964, Apr. 21, 1965, all in Hetzel MSS, Folder: "Hetzel, Theodore, Friends Kinzua Dam Project Summary," 1962–64, Magill Library, Haverford College. Merle H. Deardorff to Merrill Bowen, Jan. 5, Feb. 12, Feb. 19, 1964; Bowen to Deardorff, Jan. 25, Feb. 26, 1964; Bowen to Colonel James E. Hammer, Apr. 21, 1965; Weber–Cornplanter Agreement Related to Cornplanter Cemetery, all in Merle H. Deardorff MSS, MG 220, PSA.

58. Bilharz, *The Allegany Seneca and the Kinzua Dam*, 60–61

59. 78 Stat. 738 (Aug. 31, 1964).

60. George Heron to James A. Haley, Oct. 31, 1964, Haley MSS, Haley Seneca Indian File: Kinzua Dam Correspondence, FSC.

61. Martin Seneca Sr. to James A. Haley, Mar. 15, 1966, and Arthur Lazarus Jr. to Haley, Feb. 28, May 23, June 23, 1966, Haley MSS, Indian Affairs Committee: Seneca Indians, FSC; James A. Haley, "A Reminder of Our Obligations," speech at dedication of Seneca Nation of Indians' Haley Building, May 21, 1966, Haley MSS, FSC.

62. Harry Watt to James A. Haley, Nov. 19, 1966, Haley MSS, Indian Affairs Committee: Seneca Indians, FSC.

63. Calvin "Kelly" John to James A. Haley, Mar. 8, 1967, Haley MSS, Indian Affairs Committee: Seneca Indians, FSC.

64. Martin Seneca Sr., "The State of the Seneca Nation of Indians," speech reprinted in *Seneca Nation Newsletter*, Jan. 1966, emphasis added. This newsletter, which succeeded the *Kinzua Planning Newsletter*, was edited by Merrill Bowen and Maribel Printup and whose staff included Shirley Crowe and Nora Crouse; it is different from the *SNI Official Newsletter* and was defunct by 1967.

65. James A. Haley to Chief [*sic*] George Heron, Mar. 10, 1964, Haley MSS, Haley Seneca Indian File, FSC; "Work to Start Soon on First Factory on Lands of Senecas," *SRP*, Dec. 3, 1966.

66. Seneca, "The State of the Seneca Nation of Indians" (Jan. 1966); Bilharz, *The Allegany Senecas and the Kinzua Dam*, 93–95, 133; David George-Shongo Jr., *Onö´dowa´ga:´ Gano´kyëdoh Nogeh´oweh (Seneca Nation of Indians): The 160 Years of Republican Government* (Allegany Indian Reservation: Seneca Nation of Indians, Archives Department, 2009), 36, 46.

67. George-Shongo, *Onö´dowa´ga:´ Gano´kyëdoh Nogeh´oweh*, 36.

68. Bilharz, *The Allegany Senecas and the Kinzua Dam*, 133.

69. George-Shongo, *Onö´dowa´ga:´ Gano´kyëdoh Nogeh´oweh*, 46.

70. Clarkin, *Federal Indian Policy in the Kennedy and Johnson Administrations*, 123–33; Castile, *To Show Heart*, chaps. 2 and 3; and George P. Castile, *Taking Charge: Native American Self-Determination and Federal Policy, 1975–1993* (Tucson: Univ. of Arizona Press, 2006), 12–16.

71. On May 23, 1964, in a very light voter turnout, Seneca women were granted the right to vote by a margin of 169 to 99. In April 1966, in a vote 146 to 140, Seneca women were given the right to seek and hold Seneca tribal offices. Interestingly, in this second referendum, the vote at the Allegany Reservation was 68 to 51 against women holding office. "Seneca Women Given Right to Hold Office," *SRP*, Apr. 7, 1966.

72. "Seneca President Is Working on Full-Time Executive Basis," *SRP*, Dec. 15, 1966.

6. THE IROQUOIA PROJECT AND ITS LEGACIES: FAILURE?

1. Rovena Abrams, interviewed by the author, Feb. 23, 2011, Allegany Indian Reservation; Rovena Abrams, "Remember the Removal: My Story," *SNI Official Newsletter*, Oct. 12, 2012. Rovena Abrams and Maribel Printup are the daughters of the late Nettie Watt, one of the most accomplished Seneca artists of her generation. "Nettie Watt, Authority on Indian Basketry" (obituary), *BN*, Aug. 19, 1987. Their uncle, Harry Watt, was a prominent traditional leader of the Coldspring Longhouse.

2. See Bilharz, *The Allegany Senecas and Kinzua Dam*, 96–106.

3. George Heron, interviewed by the author, Sept. 29, 1984, Allegany Indian Reservation.

4. The Iroquoia project history is summarized in the following sources: in Neilan Engineers and Development Counselors International, *Iroquoia: A Practical Action Program for the Recreation–Tourist Development of the Allegany Reservation* (Washington, DC: US Department of Commerce, 1969), 3–145; Childs and Waters, Inc., "Preliminary Report Iroquoia Planning Committee," Oct. 1965, fourth draft, in Taylor MSS, MR 15, WHS; and US Department of Interior, Bureau of Indian Affairs, *BIA Analysis on the Brill Engineering Corporation Proposed Recreation and Industrial Development Plan, Allegany Indian Reservation*, Seneca-Iroquois National Museum Records, Allegany Indian Reservation. See also Johnson, Horrigan and Yeaple to Calvin "Kelly" John (president of the Seneca Nation of Indians), Aug. 1967, enclosing "Summary Report; Seneca Nation of Indians and Recreation Program, 1966," Recreation/Tourism Development—"Iroquoia," Seneca-Iroquois National Museum Records.

5. *O He Yoh Noh*, Mar. 5, 1971; "Council Notes," *Si Wong Geh*, Aug. 14, 1974.

6. US Congress, House, Committee on Interior and Insular Affairs, Subcommittee on Indian Affairs, *Hearings on H.R. 1794 . . . Kinzua Dam (Seneca Indian Relocation)*, 224–50.

7. George Heron to Philleo Nash, attention to Paul Hand, Oct. 2, 1962, with two attached resolutions of the Seneca Nation of Indians Tribal Council, Sept. 29, 1962, Taylor MSS, MR 14, WHS.

8. Sadie Kennedy et al. of Cattaraugus to the Senate Subcommittee on Indian Affairs, Feb. 12, 1964, reprinted in US Congress, House, Committee on Interior and Insular Affairs, Subcommittee on Indian Affairs, *Hearings on H.R. 1794 . . . Kinzua Dam (Seneca Indian Relocation)*, 190.

9. Brill reports in ibid., 226.

10. US Department of Interior, Bureau of Indian Affairs, *BIA Analysis.* For a brief summary of previous projects, see Neilan Engineers, *Iroquoia,* 8–11; *KPN,* June 25, 1963.

11. US Congress, House, Committee on Interior and Insular Affairs, Subcommittee on Indian Affairs, *Hearings on H.R. 1794 . . . Kinzua Dam (Seneca Relocation)*, 226.

12. Ibid., 226–27.

13. Ibid., 227.

14. Ibid., 228–33, 243.

15. Ibid., 236, 240–41, 250.

16. Ibid., 234–35, 248.

17. Ibid., 232–39.

18. Ibid., 232, 250. For more on "Iroquoia," see also ibid., 375–78.

19. Seneca Nation Tribal councilors quoted about the Brill report in Neilan Engineers, *Iroquoia,* 10.

20. Childs and Waters, "Preliminary Report," fourth draft; Neilan Engineers, *Iroquoia,* 8–11.

21. Bilharz assumes that William Fenton directed the project for a much longer period and was unresponsive to Seneca views. Bilharz, *The Allegany Senecas and Kinzua Dam,* 96–102. Both points are incorrect. Fenton was appointed in January 1965 and announced his resignation as chair in the Provisional Committee's report in November 1965, recommending that a Seneca be appointed in his place. He recommended Wayne Printup. "Report of the Provisional Committee for Iroquoia: A Cultural and Recreational Development on the Allegany Reservation to Seneca Nation Council," Nov. 1, 1965; William N. Fenton to Walter Taylor, Oct. 19, 1965; Wayne Printup to William N. Fenton, Oct. 4, 14, 1965, all in Taylor MSS, MR 15, WHS.

22. Members of the committee are listed in "Recreational Development: Iroquoia," *KPN,* June 1965.

23. President Martin Seneca Sr., "The State of the Seneca Nation of Indians," Jan. 11, 1965, *KPN,* Mar. 1965. For more on the committee's membership, see "Seneca President [Martin Seneca Sr.] Appoints New Iroquois Committee," *SRP,* Dec. 2, 1965. Martin Seneca Sr. followed Fenton's advice in appointing Printup as chair.

24. William N. Fenton to O'Neill, Feb. 21, 1958, New York State Museum Records, Box 10, Folder 19, NYSA; Fenton to O'Neill, June 17, 1957, July 19, 29, 1958, New York State Museum Records, Box 11, Folder 31, NYSA; O'Neill to Fenton, Sept. 16, 1958, Fenton MSS, Series II.a, Fenton Notes for O'Neill (for US Army Corps of Engineers' public hearing, Apr. 1, 1957), undated, Folder: "Kinzua Dam," APS.

25. US Congress, Senate, Committee on Interior and Insular Affairs, Subcommittee on Indian Affairs, *Hearings on S. 1836 . . . Kinzua Dam (Seneca Indian Relocation)*, 109–11; "Senecas Oppose Kinzua Project with New Lawyer," *Warren Times-Mirror*, Oct. 20, 1959; William N. Fenton, interviewed by the author, May 18, 1983, Albany. For more on Fenton's role, see my article "On and Off State Time: William N. Fenton and the Seneca Nation in Crisis, 1954–1968," *New York History* 93 (Spring 2012): 182–232.

26. Fenton to Taylor, Oct. 19, 22, 1965; Printup to Fenton, Oct. 4, 14, 1965.

27. "Report of the Provisional Committee for Iroquoia," Nov. 1, 1965.

28. William N. Fenton to Walter Taylor, Jan. 28, June 16, 1965; Taylor to Fenton, Sept. 24, 1965; Taylor Memorandum to Harry Watt, Richard JohnnyJohn, Coleman John, and Chief Freeman Johnson, June 28, 1965; Taylor to Fenton, Dec. 23, 1965, all in Taylor MSS, MR 14 and 15, WHS.

29. Fenton to Taylor, Jan. 28, 1965. See also note 28.

30. Printup to Fenton, Oct. 4, 14, 1965.

31. William N. Fenton to Walter Taylor, Oct. 11, 1965, and Taylor to Arthur Lazarus Jr., Oct. 23, 1965, Taylor MSS, MR 15, WHS.

32. Walter Taylor to Robert Haines and Theodore Hetzel, Sept. 12, 1965; Taylor to Hetzel, Sept. 22, 1965; Taylor to William N. Fenton, Sept. 19, 1965; Taylor to Fenton, Sept. 19, 1965; Taylor to Fenton, Oct. 20, 1965; Fenton to Taylor, Oct. 25, 1965, all in Taylor MSS, MR 14 and 15, WHS.

33. William N. Fenton, "Iroquoia's Theme," with note "Elisabeth [Tooker] replace commentary," Fenton MSS, Folder: "United States Department of the Interior. Re: Iroquoia Project," 1965, APS.

34. William N. Fenton to Elisabeth Tooker, Mar. 10, 1965, and Tooker to Fenton, Mar. 12, 1965, Taylor MSS, MR 15, WHS.

35. Fenton, "Iroquoia's Theme."

36. Neilan Engineers, *Iroquoia*, 8–11.

37. "Report of the Provisional Committee for Iroquoia." Prior to the Childs and Waters report in October, Fenton was optimistic about the Iroquoia project—as was George Heron. At the 1965 Iroquois Research Conference, Fenton lauded the idea of Iroquoia. See Fenton, "From Longhouse to Ranch-Type House," 21–22.

38. Martin Seneca Sr., "The State of the Seneca Nation of Indians" (Jan. 1966).

39. Rovena Abrams interview, Feb. 23, 2011.

40. For the state's historic failure to provide quality education and library services, see Hauptman, *Formulating American Indian Policy in New York State*, 75–88; New York State Interdepartmental Committee on Indian Affairs, *Annual Report, 1973–1974* (Albany: New York State, 1974), 23; Charles Townley to Dorothy Smith, Philip Tarbell, and Lincoln White, June 5, 1974, Native American Indian Education Unit Correspondence, 1954–85, Box 2, Folder: "Legislation," New York State Department of Education Records, NYSA; John McAvin Field Reports, Jan. 14–15 and Mar. 24–25, 1971, Mar. 9–10 and Mar. 15, 1972, and

Townley to Jean Connor, May 15, 1971, Office of Library Development Records, Folder: "Indian Library Advisory Board," NYSL.

41. The annual reports of these Iroquois Conferences—not to be confused with the Iroquois Research Conference at Rensselaerville, New York, the annual convocation of scholars—can be found in the Office of Library Development, NYSL. One of these sessions was formally published: Roy H. Sandstrom, ed., *Educating the Educators: A Report of the Institute on "The American Indian Student in Higher Education"* (Canton, NY: St. Lawrence Univ. and Xerox Corporation, 1971). Also, Marlene Johnson, interviewed by the author, Aug. 15, 2001, Cattaraugus Indian Reservation.

42. Interviews by the author: Marlene Johnson and Ethel Bray, Aug. 15, 2001, Cattaraugus Indian Reservation; Lana Redeye, Aug. 23, 2001, Allegany Indian Reservation.

43. Bernard Finney, telephone interview by the author, June 5, 2001; SNI Tribal Council Minutes, Nov. 12, 1977–July 14, 1979, SNI Archives.

44. Bonnie Biggs, "Bright Child of Oklahoma: Lotsee Patterson and the Development of America's Tribal Libraries," *American Indian Culture and Research Journal* 24 (2000): 55–67.

45. Dadie Perlov to Governor Hugh Carey, July 13, 1977, Legislative Bill Jacket, New York State Statutes, chap. 476 (1977), NYSA.

46. Regents of the University of the State of New York, *Position Paper No. 22: Native American Education* (Albany: New York State Education Department, 1975).

47. James Donovan, interviewed by the author, Apr. 17, 1986, Albany; McKinney's 1977 Session Laws, chap. 476, Aug. 1, 1977, 681–85; Legislative Bill Jacket, New York State Statutes, chap. 476 (1977), NYSA; Laura Chodos, interviewed by the author, Feb. 24, 1986, Albany. The New York State Indian Library Act of 1977 has been hailed as a "landmark statute." See US National Commission on Libraries and Information Science, *Pathways to Excellence: A Report on Improving Library and Information Services for Native American Peoples* (Washington, DC: US National Commission on Libraries and Information Science, 1992); Elisabeth Rockefeller-MacArthur, *American Indian Library Services in Perspective* (Jefferson, NC: McFarland, 1998), 79–82.

48. Interviews by the author: Ethel Bray, Aug. 15, 2001, and Marilyn Douglas (director, Office of Library Development, New York State Library), Aug. 1, 2001, Albany; for Bray's own views, see Ethel Bray, "The Seneca Nation Library," *The Bookmark* (Summer 1988): 246–47. Joseph Schubert, "Native American Libraries and Their Library Systems in New York State," statement to US National Commission on Libraries and Information Science, Hartford, Conn., Oct. 24, 1990, Office of Library Development Records, Folder: "Indian Libraries," NYSL; Joseph Shubert to Midge Dean Stock, Sept. 28, 1994, Office of Library Development Records, Folder: "Indian Library Correspondence," NYSL.

49. Lana Redeye interview, Aug. 23, 2001; George Abrams, personal communication to the author, July 31, 2001.

50. Tooker to Fenton, Mar. 12, 1965.

51. George Abrams, *Tribal Museums in America* (Nashville: Association of State and Local History, 2002); "Seneca Nation Will Build New Museum in Salamanca," *SRP*, June 8, 1976.

52. Stock, "Seneca-Iroquois National Museum," 1507–8.

53. Rovena Abrams interview, Feb. 23, 2011.

54. I have made presentations four times over the past thirty-five years at the Seneca-Iroquois National Museum, including at its twenty-fifth anniversary celebration in August 2002 and most recently on May 15, 2011. I have known and worked with the museum's four directors since the early 1980s.

55. Abrams, "[A Report on] Tribal Museums in America"; "Seneca Nation Will Build New Museum in Salamanca."

56. Seneca Nation of Indians, *Annual Report for 2008* (Allegany Reservation: SNI, 2008).

7. THE HEALTH ACTION GROUP: LIONEL JOHN AND THE POWER OF WOMEN

1. William Millar, interviewed by the author, Oct. 24, 1987, Mashantucket Pequot Indian Reservation, Ledyard, CT.

2. For Willie Hoag, see Hauptman, "Senecas and Subdividers." Although earlier administrations initiated some of these projects, Bob Hoag's administration often took credit: "Seneca Lanes Opens," *O He Yoh Noh*, Sept. 10, 1975; "$850,000 Hockey–Lacrosse Center to Be Constructed by the Seneca," *Si Wong Geh*, Apr. 23, 1975; "Groundbreaking Ceremonies," *Si Wong Geh*, May 21, 1975; "Work Completed on First Cabins at Seneca Camp Site," *Si Wong Geh*, Apr. 30, 1975; "Highbanks Campgrounds," *Si Wong Geh*, May 28, 1975; "Portrait of Bob Hoag," *Oh He Yoh Noh*, Jan. 23, 1976; Donna Snyder, "Hoag: A Man Eyeing the Future," *BN*, Aug. 19, 1987; "Robert Hoag, 53, Ex-head of Seneca Tribe," *NYT*, July 15, 1989.

3. New York State, "Profile Summary of Allegany and Cattaraugus Reservations," New York State Legislature, Assembly, Standing Committee on Governmental Operations, Subcommittee on Indian Affairs, Subject and Hearing Files, 1968–72, Box 3, NYSA.

4. "History of T. I. S. Clinic," *Si Wong Geh*, May 28, 1975.

5. Ibid.

6. For the Senecas' attempt to convert the Thomas Indian School, see New York State Governor's Committee on the Utilization of the Thomas Indian School, meeting minutes, Oct. 29, 1956, and Jan. 31, 1957, Fenton MSS, New York State Museum Records, Box 19, Folder 18, NYSA; William N. Fenton report, Dec. 12, 1957, NYSM, Box 10, Folder 19, NYSA.

7. For the horrors of life at the Thomas Indian School, see Ron Douglas's documentary *Unseen Tears: The Impact of Native American Schooling in Western New York*, Channels—Stories from the Niagara Frontier by Squeaky Wheels Media Resources (Buffalo: Community Foundation for Greater Buffalo in Cooperation with Native American Community Services of Erie and Niagara Counties, 2009). Over the years, I have greatly benefited by discussions with Marlene Johnson, a former residential student at the Thomas Indian School, and

her daughter Lori Quigley, dean of education at Russell Sage College, about the long-term negative effects of this schooling on Seneca children. Both Johnson and Quigley served as chair of the National Advisory Commission on Indian Education. For more favorable Seneca views on the school, see two interviews in Austin, *Ne′ Ho Niyo′ Dë: Nö′* (Virginia Snow, 1:192–98, and Arthur Nephew, 2:155–56). Calvin Kettle noted that he and other Senecas believed that the ruins of the school were haunted by ghosts! Interview in Austin, *Ne′ Ho Niyo′ Dë: Nö′*, 1:88–90.

8. Quoted in Karen Kalaijian and Anthony Golda, "Indian Health Services in Western New York State: Past, Present, and Future," report to the New York State commissioner of health, July 1975, New York State Department of Health (NYSDH) Records, Subject Files of the Executive Deputy Commissioner, Box 16, Folder: "Indian Health Services," NYSA.

9. New York State Legislature, Assembly, Standing Committee on Governmental Operations, Subcommittee on Indian Affairs, *Report* (Albany: New York State, 1971), 41.

10. *KNP*, Oct. 23, 1962, 9.

11. New York State Interdepartmental Committee on Indian Affairs, *Annual Report, 1968–1969* (Albany: New York State, 1969), 6–8, 16.

12. New York State Interdepartmental Committee on Indian Affairs, *Annual Report, 1970–1971* (Albany: New York State, 1971), 6.

13. Kalaijian and Golda, "Indian Health Services in Western New York."

14. Alice Lee Jemison to President Franklin D. Roosevelt, June 20, 1935, Roosevelt Records, Official File 296, Franklin D. Roosevelt Library, Hyde Park, NY; Nora M. Anderson (acting superintendent, BIA New York Agency) to Commissioner of Indian Affairs, May 13, 1946, New York Agency Records, 1938–49, BIA, RG 75, NA, Federal Record Center, New York City; Joseph Reilly (chair, Assembly Subcommittee on Indian Affairs) to Henry Diamond (commissioner of Department of Environmental Conservation), Apr. 10, 1970, and Diamond to Reilly, Aug. 14, Sept. 3, 1970, New York State Legislature, Assembly, Standing Committee on Governmental Operations, Subcommittee on Indian Affairs, Subject and Hearing Files, 1968–72, Box 2, Folder 9, NYSA; "Pollution," *Si Wong Geh*, Oct. 6, 1971.

15. New York State Department of Environmental Conservation, "Report Finds Scant Progress 21 Years after West Valley Cleanup Pact," *Environment DEC* (June 2008), available at the New York State Environmental Conservation website, http://www.dec.ny.gov/pubs/379.html; Union of Concerned Scientists, "A Brief History of Reprocessing and Cleanup in West Valley, N.Y." (fact sheet), Mar. 2008, available at the Union of Concerned Scientists' website, http://www.ucsua.org/nuclear-power/nuclear-power-risk/nuclear-profile/.

16. A new $333 million clean-up effort began in 2011. "B&W Announces $333 million West Valley Demonstration Project Cleanup Contract Award," Reuters, July 26, 2011. Seneca Nation officials continue to protest the failures to clean up West Valley. President Robert Odawi Porter, address opposing West Valley Nuclear Storage Site, Public Hearing of President's Commission on America's Nuclear Future, Harvard Univ., Oct. 12, 2011, SNI press release, SNI Archives; "President's Desk," *SNI Official Newsletter*, Oct. 28, 2011.

17. "Senecas' Problems Aired for Assembly Group," *JPJ*, Aug. 28, 1970.

18. John Hudacs, interviewed by the author, Mar. 10, 1986, Albany; and Fred DiMaggio, interviewed by the author, Apr. 17, 1986, Albany.

19. New York State Legislature, Assembly, Standing Committee on Governmental Operations, Subcommittee on Indian Affairs, *Report*, 41–42.

20. Ibid., 42–43.

21. I have written previously about Seneca women and their roles. See Laurence M. Hauptman, *Seven Generations of Iroquois Leadership: The Six Nations since 1800* (Syracuse, NY: Syracuse Univ. Press, 2008), 65–79, 191–202.

22. For a fuller treatment of Iroquois activism in the late 1960s and early 1970s, see Hauptman, *The Iroquois Struggle for Survival*, 215–29.

23. Marilyn Jemison Anderson, interviewed by the author, Sept. 26, 2011, Cattaraugus Indian Reservation.

24. "Health Services," *Si Wong Geh*, July 4, 1973.

25. Ibid.

26. See, for example, the following articles in *Si Wong Geh*: "Clinic News," Nov. 21, 1973; "Health Action Group News," Feb. 13, 1974; "Health Action Group Meeting," Feb. 20, 1974; "Health Action Group Meeting," Feb. 27, 1974; "Communicable Diseases," May 22, 1974; "Health Action Group News," May 29, 1974; "Happy Anniversary Health Action Group," June 17, 1974; "Health Action Group," Oct. 3, 1974; "Seneca Nation Will Take New Health Clinic Project," May 12, 1976.

27. For example, see the following articles in *Si Wong Geh*: "What Is Epilepsy?" Sept. 25, 1974; "Questions and Answers on Mumps," Oct. 23, 1974; "Questions and Answers on Rubella," Oct. 30, 1974; "Questions and Answers on Poliomyelitis," Nov. 6, 1974; "Pap Tests," Nov. 13, 1974; "High Blood Pressure (Hypertension)," June 25, 1975; "Why Risk Heart Attack? Six Ways to Guard Your Health," Oct. 22, 1975; "New Venereal Disease Type Spreading in the County," Nov. 26, 1975.

28. "Happy Anniversary Health Action Group," *Si Wong Geh*, June 17, 1974.

29. For the New York State law on Indian health care at the time, see New York State Public Health Law, amendment to chap. 22, sec. 201 (Mar., 1962).

30. "Happy Anniversary Health Action Group."

31. "Health Action," *SNI Health Action Newsletter*, Feb. 1976; "WIC," *O He Yoh Noh*, Dec. 8, 1976.

32. "Health Action"; "WIC"; Marilyn Jemison Anderson interview, Sept. 26, 2011.

33. Anita Lillian Taylor and Norma Kennedy, interviewed by the author, June 14, 2011, Allegany Indian Reservation; Rovena Abrams, interviewed by the author, Feb. 23, 2011, Allegany Indian Reservation.

34. Seneca Nation of Indians, *Seneca Nation of Indians Health Department, 1976–2009* (Allegany Indian Reservation: SNI, 2009), 7; George-Shongo, *Onö´dowa´ga:´ Gano´kyëdoh Nogeh´oweh*, 52.

35. Kalaijian and Golda, "Indian Health Services in Western New York"; Ralph Dwork to Dean Williams (president of the Seneca Nation of Indians), Jan. 30, 1974, and Williams to Hollis Ingraham (New York State commissioner of health), June 6, 1974, NYSDH Records, Commissioner's Subject Files, Box 36, Folder: "Indians, 1963–1976," NYSA; NYSDH news release (about Indian Health Aide Program), Mar. 8, 1972, NYSDH Records, Commissioner's Subject Files, Box 36, Folder: "Indians, 1963–1976," NYSA; "Council Reports of Regular Session," *O He Yoh Noh*, Jan. 20, 1972.

36. In 1977, I was the coordinator of a conference on Native American health concerns in New York State at SUNY New Paltz. There, Senecas—Marilyn Anderson, Wini Kettle, and Norma Kennedy—complained about previous medical studies, one undertaken without tribal approval, that had not been shared with or benefited their nation. Both Staub and Hoekelman had tribal approval and shared their results with the Senecas. Interviews by the author: Marilyn Jemison Anderson, Sept. 26, 2011; Wini Kettle, July 28, 1977, Cattaraugus Indian Reservation; Marilyn Jemison Anderson, Norma Kennedy, Wini Kettle, and Dr. Henry Staub, May 4, 1977, New Paltz, NY.

37. Henry Staub and Robert Hoekelman, "Health Supervision of Infants on the Cattaraugus Indian Reservation in New York: The Record Is No Better Than in Big City Slum Areas," *Clinical Pediatrics* 15 (Jan. 1976): 44–52. For the follow-up article, see Henry Staub, "American Indians: New Opportunity for Health Care," *New York State Journal of Medicine* 78 (June 1978): 1137–41.

38. "Report of Health Planning Commission—Indian Health Services—in Governor's Office in New York City," Aug. 15, 1975, and Dr. Robert Baker (Community Health Services), "Report of a Meeting with the Seneca Nation Representatives in Buffalo, May 27, 1976," NYSDH Records, Executive Deputy Commissioner's Files, Box 16, Folder: "Indian Health Services," NYSA.

39. Robert Whalen (New York State commissioner of health) to Everett Rhoades (American Indian Policy Review Commission), Jan. 5, 1976, and Gilda Ventresca (NYSDH liaison in Washington, DC), Aug. 25, 1975, NYSDH Records, Commissioner's Subject Files, Box 36, Folder: "Indians, 1963–1976," NYSA; David A. Solomon (NYSDH) to Donald J. Solomon (USET), Mar. 5, 1976, NYSDH Records, Deputy Executive Commissioner' Files, Box 16, Folder: "Indian Health Services," NYSA.

40. Robert Whelan to Louis Lefkowitz (New York State attorney general), Mar. 21, 1976, and Lefkowitz to Whalen, Oct. 18, 1976, NYSDH Records, Commissioner's Subject Files, Box 36, Folder: "Indians, 1963–1976," NYSA.

41. Kalaijian and Golda, "Indian Health Services in Western New York"; Karen Kalaijian, interviewed by the author, May 7, 1986, Albany.

42. 68 Stat., 674 (Aug. 5, 1954).

43. US Congress, Senate, Committee on Government Operations, *Hearings before the Permanent Subcommittee on Investigations: Indian Health Care, Sept. 16, 1974*, 93rd Cong., 2d sess. (Washington, DC: US Government Printing Office, 1974), 154–62. See also American

Indian Policy Review Commission, *Final Report*, 1:372; American Indian Policy Review Commission, Task Force Six, *Report on Indian Health*, 2 vols. (Washington, DC: US Government Printing Office, 1977); Prucha, *The Great Father*, 2:1149–53.

44. Jane Lawrence, "The Indian Health Service and the Sterilization of Native American Women," *American Indian Quarterly* 24 (Summer 2000): 400–419.

45. US Congress, Senate, Committee on Government Operations, *Hearings . . . Indian Health Care*, 154–57.

46. "Welcome USET," *O He Yoh Noh*, June 22, 1972; "Council Minutes: Executive Reports," *Si Wong Geh*, June 10, 1972.

47. George-Shongo, *Onö´dowa´ga:´ Gano´kyëdoh Nogeh´oweh*, 52–54.

48. William Millar interview, Oct. 24, 1987.

49. Indian Self-Determination and Education Act, 88 Stat. 2203–14 (Jan. 4, 1975); Indian Health Care Improvement Act, 90 Stat., 1400–1412 (Sept. 30, 1976).

50. Patricia Sullivan, "Emery A. Johnson, 78: Headed Indian Health Service," *Washington Post*, July 6, 2005.

51. George-Shongo, *Onö´dowa´ga:´ Gano´kyëdoh Nogeh´oweh*, 49, 55–56.

52. "Health Services, " *Si Wong Geh*, Jan. 15, 1975.

53. "Seneca Nation of Indians: IHS Proposal (Abstract)," *Health Action Newsletter* 1, no. 2 (1975), reprinted in *Si Wong Geh*, June 25, 1975; "SNI Indian Health Services Proposal Prepared with the Assistance of David W. Kaplan, M.D., Harvard School of Public Health, Boston, Massachusetts," Mar. 1, 1975, SNI Archives. See also George-Shongo, *Onö´dowa´ga:´ Gano´kyëdoh Nogeh´oweh*, 55; SNI, *Seneca Nation of Indians Health Department, 1976–2009*, 7. The rate of diabetes among the Senecas, the major health problem today, appears to have been even higher than what was found in this Seneca survey in 1975: 33.3 percent or higher between 1969 and 1978. See L. A. Frohman, T. D. Doeblin, and F. G. Emorlin, "Diabetes in the Seneca Indians," *Diabetes* 18 (1969): 38; Russell Judkins, "Diabetes and Perception of Diabetes among Seneca Indians," *New York Journal of Medicine* 78 (July 1978): 1320–23.

54. George-Shongo, *Onö´dowa´ga:´ Gano´kyëdoh Nogeh´oweh*, 56.

55. SNI, *Seneca Nation of Indians Health Department, 1976–2009*, 7.

56. Whelan to Rhoades, Jan. 5, 1976.

57. 88 Stat., 2203–14.

58. 90 Stat., 1400–412.

59. Ibid.

60. Ibid.

61. SNI, *Seneca Nation of Indians Health Department, 1976–2009*, 11–19; Rick Jemison, interviewed by the author, Mar. 22, 2012, Cattaraugus Indian Reservation.

62. George-Shongo, *Onö´dowa´ga:´ Gano´kyëdoh Nogeh´oweh*, 49.

63. SNI, *Seneca Nation of Indians Health Department, 1976–2009*, 7–19.

64. "From the President's Desk," *SNI Official Newsletter*, Apr. 15, 2011.

65. SNI, *Annual Report for 2008*; SNI Health Department website at http://www.sni .org/departments/healthsystem/, accessed July 5, 2011.

66. Quoted in SNI, *Seneca Nation of Indians Health Department, 1976–2009*, 22.

67. US Department of Health and Human Services, Public Health Service, Indian Health Service, "Indian Health Service Fact Sheets: Diabetes," available at http://www.ihs .gov/PublicAffairs/IHSBrochure/Diabetes.asp, accessed July 5, 2011.

68. "Seneca Nation Announces Health Care Incentive Program," *SNI Official Newsletter*, Jan. 25, 2008.

69. US Department of Health and Human Services, "Substance Use and Substance Use Disorders among American Indians and Alaska Natives," in *NSDUH Report: National Survey on Drug Use and Health* (pamphlet) (Washington, DC: US Department of Health and Human Services, Office of Applied Studies, Substance Abuse and Mental Health Services Administration, 2007).

70. "From the President's Desk," *SNI Official Newsletter*, Sept. 23, 2011.

71. Ibid.

8. SHOWDOWN ON THE FORBIDDEN PATH

1. Paul A. W. Wallace, *Indian Paths of Pennsylvania* (Harrisburg: Pennsylvania Historical and Museum Commission, 1965), 46–48. Despite its title, this book also describes trails through much of New York Colony. See also Robert S. Grumet, ed., *Journey on the Forbidden Path: Chronicles of a Diplomatic Mission to the Allegheny Country, March–September, 1760* (Philadelphia: American Philosophical Society, 1999). I was told of the Munsee–Seneca cooperation on the Forbidden Path. Calvin "Kelly" John, interviewed by the author, May 2, 1987, Allegany Indian Reservation.

2. Gwyn Thomas to E. B. Hughes (superintendent of Public Works), Jan. 9, 1961, NYS-DPW Records, Deputy Superintendent Files, Box 2, Folder: "Highways—Legislation," NYSA.

3. E. B. Hughes to Gwyn Thomas, Feb. 7, 1961, NYSDPW Records, Deputy Superintendent Files, Box 2, Folder: "Highways—Legislation," NYSA.

4. J. Burch McMorran (NYSDPW superintendent) to Senator Kenneth Keating, Mar. 2, 1961, NYSDPW Records, Superintendent's Correspondence and Subject Files, Box 21, Folder: "Docks and Dams," 1961, NYSA.

5. New York State Department of Public Works, *Annual Report, 1962* (Albany: New York State, 1962), 5.

6. Ibid.

7. New York State Governor's Office, press release, Feb. 2, 1962, with attached letter to US secretary of commerce, Jan. 29, 1962, NYSDPW Records, Superintendent's Correspondence and Subject Files, Box 59, Folder: "Southern Tier Expressway," 1962–63, NYSA.

8. *Laws of New York*, chap., 878 (Apr. 29, 1962), 3019–22.

9. An act of Congress in 1930 (46 Stat. 163) granted New York State authorization to construct, operate, and maintain a highway across the Allegheny River within the Allegany Reservation. Section 53 of the New York State highway law authorizes the New York State Department of Transportation (NYSDOT) to construct, maintain, and improve highways and bridges constructed by the state on Indian reservations, and section 31 authorizes the DOT to enter into agreement for land exchanges between the state and Seneca Nation that the Seneca Tribal Council deems just and reasonable. In 2007, the DOT and the Seneca Nation Tribal Council signed an agreement for the DOT to replace and rehabilitate the Red House Bridge on old Route 17. Despite this agreement, the DOT failed to carry out the agreement, and a Seneca woman was killed and her companion injured when they fell through holes in the bridge. "Woman Dies, Man Survives 20-foot Fall from Bridge; State Fault State for Failed Repairs," *BN*, Mar. 31, 2012; New York State Department of Transportation Agreement with the Seneca Nation of Indians, Re: Maintenance of Red House Bridge, Dec. 14, 2007, SNI Archives.

10. Saul C. Corwin to Warren Ashmead (counsel for New York State Legislature, Ways and Means Committee) Mar. 6, 1962, NYSDPW Records, Deputy Superintendent Files, Box 4, Folder: "Legislation, 1962–1963," NYSA.

11. J. Burch McMorran, memorandum to the governor, Apr. 9, 1962, re: Assembly Bill 4338, New York State Legislative Bill Jacket, chap. 878 (Apr. 29, 1962), Governor's Records: Nelson Rockefeller, NYSA.

12. Alfred W. Haight (first deputy comptroller, New York State), memorandum to the governor, Apr. 9, 1962; T. Norman Hurd, memorandum to the governor, Apr. 10, 1962; Louis J. Lefkowitz, memorandum to the governor, Apr. 16, 1962, Re: Assembly Bill 4338, New York State Legislative Bill Jacket, chap. 878 (Apr. 29, 1962), Governor's Records: Nelson Rockefeller, NYSA.

13. Memorandum to John Van Laak, Gerald Dunn, and J. Norman Hurd, Apr. 17, 1962, re: Assembly Bill 4338, New York State Legislative Bill Jacket, chap. 878 (Apr. 29, 1962), Governor's Records: Nelson Rockefeller, NYSA.

14. Telegrams sent by J. Leland Rickard (Route 17 Association) to Governor Nelson Rockefeller, Apr. 27, 1962; Robert Miller (Chautauqua County) to Rockefeller, Apr. 27, 1962; Carl Maier (Cattaraugus County) to Rockefeller, Apr. 27, 1962; Amory Houghton (Corning Glass) to Rockefeller, Apr. 29, 1962; all in NYS Legislative Bill Jacket, chap. 878 (Apr. 29, 1962), Governor's Records: Nelson Rockefeller, NYSA.

15. New York State Department of Public Works, *Annual Report, 1960* (Albany: New York State, 1960), 20–21.

16. McMorran to Senator Keating, Mar. 2, 1961.

17. "Highlights of Meeting with Corps of Engineers, June 21, 1962," *KPN*, July 9, 1962.

18. Brooks Atkinson, "Triumph over Morality," *NYT*, July 17, 1962, reprinted in Atkinson, *Tuesdays and Fridays*, 262–64.

19. "Highway Meeting—New York State Department of Public Works," *KPN*, Nov. 30, 1962.

20. Arthur Lazarus Jr. testimony in US Congress, House, Committee on Interior and Insular Affairs, Subcommittee on Indian Affairs, *Hearings on H.R. 1794 . . . Kinzua Dam (Seneca Indian Relocation)*, 358–59.

21. Ibid., 359, my emphasis. For the 1875 lease legislation, see *U.S. Statutes at Large*, 43rd Cong. 2d sess., chap. 90 (Feb. 19, 1875), 330–31.

22. District court opinion in Arthur Lazarus Jr. MSS, Series II, Box 4, Legal Briefs, Beinecke Library, Yale Univ. For an analysis of this case, referred to as *Seneca II*, see Charles F. W. Wilkinson and John M. Volkman, "Judicial Review of Indian Treaty Abrogation: 'As Long as Water Flows or Grass Grows upon the Earth,' How Long Is That?" *California Law Review* 63 (May 1975), 642–44.

23. *Seneca Nation v. William M. Brucker, et al.*, 338 F2d 55 (2d Circ. 1964); "Senecas Lose Bid to Bar Highway: Court Upholds U.S. Seizure of Reservation Lands," *NYT*, Oct. 30, 1964.

24. *Seneca Nation v. Brucker, cert. denied*, 380 U.S. 952 (1965).

25. See the following articles in *SRP*: "Senecas Must Be Consulted," Dec. 8, 1965; "Map Shows Proposed Expressway and Alternate Route in City," Jan. 5, 1966; "Construction of Southern Tier Expressway ahead of Schedule on New Route West of City Open for Traffic in October," Aug. 9, 1967; "The United States Takes Steps to Condemn Lands Senecas Refused to Sell," Mar. 3, 1968.

26. I have previously written about the Interstate 81 protest. See Hauptman, *The Iroquois Struggle for Survival*, 217–22.

27. Ibid., 231–44.

28. New York State Legislature, Assembly, Standing Committee on Governmental Operations, Subcommittee on Indian Affairs, *Report*, 44.

29. Hauptman, *The Iroquois Struggle for Survival*, 217–22.

30. [President James George], "Fact Sheet: The Seneca Nation and Fisher-Price," *Si Wong Geh*, June 15, 1972.

31. New York State highway law, in *Laws of New York*, chap. 962 (June 8, 1973), emphasis mine.

32. Louis J. Lefkowitz, memorandum to the governor, June 1963, Re: Assembly Bill 4020, Senate Bill 20,005-a, Legislative Bill Jacket, chap. 962 (1973), NYSA.

33. Ibid.

34. For the tribal leadership's justification for the toy factory project, see *Si Wong Geh*, Mar. 8, 1972; [George], "Fact Sheet," June 15, 1972. President James George blasted the project's critics and even accused them of working with Communists. Note in *Si Wong Geh*, July 12, 1972. For the opponents of the toy factory and their appeals, see Charles Williams and John Mohawk (Seneca Constitutional Rights Convention) to Henry Coords (president of Fisher-Price), with copies to Chief Leon Shenandoah and *Akwesasne Notes*, Aug. 25, 1972, reprinted in *O He Yoh Noh*, Sept. 27, 1972.

35. For the controversy, see the following articles in *O He Yoh Noh*: "Fisher-Price," Jan. 20, 1972, and "Federal Funds for Toy Factory," Aug. 30, 1972; and in *Si Wong Geh*: "Seneca Nation Sued over Land for Toy Factory," Apr. 12, 1972; "Judge Weighing Senecas' Plans for Toy Factory," Apr. 26, 1972; "Reservation Plant Seen as a Bonanza for Fisher-Price," Oct. 18, 1972; "Senecas Lose Court Battles," Aug. 9. 1972; "Court Denies Seneca Bid," Oct. 18, 1972. See also "Seneca Contract Is Upheld," *BN*, May 26, 1972.

36. Fred Kennedy and Jean Loret, interviewed by the author, Sept. 25, 2011, Dunkirk, NY. The Van Aernam family was involved in earlier Seneca protests over highway improvements of Route 17. In 1940, a photograph of Mrs. Ethia Van Aernam, protesting the road, appeared in several newspapers. "Squaw Holding Last Frontier against White Men," International News Photo, July 20, 1940.

37. John Mohawk, interviewed by the author, Mar. 20–21, Buffalo. For more on the Iroquois Unity Movement and the founding of *Akwesasne Notes*, see Hauptman, *The Iroquois Struggle for Survival*, 214–29. See also [John Mohawk], *Basic Call for Consciousness* (Rooseveltown, NY: Akwesasne Notes, 1978). The late John Mohawk helped promote and draft the United Nations Declaration of Indigenous Rights. For the Newtown Longhouse at Cattaraugus and criticisms of Seneca leadership, see "Disputes over Claims Money," *Si Wong Geh*, Sept. 19, 1973; "Cattaraugus Indians Uptight," *JPJ*, Oct. 6, 1973, reprinted in *Si Wong Geh*, Oct. 10, 1973.

38. According to *Si Wong Geh*, the Constitutional Rights Committee included the following members: Charles Williams (president), Anita Thompson (vice president), Abbie Brooks (treasurer), Rhoda I. Leaffe (secretary), John Mohawk, Ruth John, Edna Van Aernam, James Bennett, Sr., Aileen Williams, Beatrice Renand, Eileen Williams, Shirley Schindler, Bette Metros, Edward Schindler, Ernest Mohawk, Elsie Mohawk, Janet Parker, Jean Kennedy Loret, Judith Kennedy Williams, Sonja Kennedy, Edward Kennedy, Jr., David Kennedy, Fred Kennedy, Henry Kennedy, Lillian Kennedy, Mary Kennedy, Barry White, Doris Harris, Karen Keyes, Audrey Williams, Suzanne Williams Pearce, Joseph Gorenfle, Lucille White, John D. Leaffe, and Marilyn Schindler. See "Seneca Nation Sued over Land for Toy Factory."

39. Quoted in "Seneca Leader Mulls Decision of Fisher-Price," *Si Wong Geh*, Nov. 22, 1972.

40. "Seneca President Owes Upset Win to Factory Issue," *Si Wong Geh*, Nov. 29, 1972.

41. "Fisher-Price Drops Plans to Build on Reservation," *Si Wong Geh*, Nov. 29, 1972.

42. "Indian Plan Here Called Dangerous," *Si Wong Geh*, June 6, 1973.

43. "Claims Meeting," *Si Wong Geh*, Sept. 12, 1973.

44. "Dispute over Claims Money," *Si Wong Geh*, Sept. 19, 1973.

45. Ibid.; Calvin "Kelly" John, Harry Watt, et al. to Stewart L. Udall (former secretary of the interior), Aug. 11, 1967, reprinted in *Si Wong Geh*, Sept. 26, 1973. The letter clearly showed that the Seneca leadership firmly rejected termination.

46. "Cattaraugus Indians Uptight," *Si Wong Geh*, Oct. 10, 1973.

47. "Senecas Vote to Divide $4 Million," *Si Wong Geh*, Apr. 3, 1974.

48. *Si Wong Geh*, Aug. 28, 1973.

49. "Sovereignty Question," *Si Wong Geh*, Sept. 19, 1973. Quinn was later arrested allegedly for extortion of $217,000 from the Santa Fe Railroad and for failing to appear for sentencing in Oklahoma. He and Marlene Kennedy were subsequently charged with reckless endangerment and menacing and for firing a rifle at the New York State Police. "Quinn Arrested," *Si Wong Geh*, Apr. 28, 1976. Marlene Kennedy had also previously challenged the right of Niagara Mohawk Power and New York Telephone linesmen to charge monthly fees and to enter Cattaraugus and carry out the two utility companies' operations. "Threats Curtail Utilities Work on Indian Reserve," *Si Wong Geh*, Sept. 18, 1974.

50. "Dissidents May Be Expelled from Senecas' Reservation," *Si Wong Geh*, Jan. 29, 1975.

51. "$850,000 Hockey–Lacrosse Center to Be Constructed by the Senecas," *Si Wong Geh*, Apr. 23, 1975; "New Lacrosse, Hockey Arena Opens in June," *Si Wong Geh*, Apr. 28, 1976; "High Banks Campgrounds," *Si Wong Geh*, May 28, 1975; "Robert Hoag, 53, Ex-head of Seneca Tribe," *NYT*, July 15, 1989.

52. "Seneca Tie Land Deal on Southern Tier Expressway to Selection of Route 219," *Si Wong Geh*, Apr. 23, 1975; "Senecas Demand a Rt. 219 Corridor in X-way Talks," *SRP*, Apr. 17, 1975.

53. Harold Faber, "Senecas and State of New York Strike Historic Pact as Equals," *NYT*, July 11, 1976; *Seneca Nation of Indians v. State of New York*, cv-1971-528 (July 24, 1975).

54. Governor Hugh Carey, press release, Jan. 31, 1975; Carey to the Traditional Seneka [*sic*] Peoples Government, Feb. 4, 1975; Raymond Harding (Governor Carey's secretary) to James Tully (commissioner of taxation and finance), Apr. 23, 1975; Harding to Peter C. Goldmark Jr. (director, Division of the Budget), Apr. 23, 1975; Harding to Vito Castellano (first deputy commissioner of commerce), Apr. 23, 1975; Harding to President Robert C. Hoag (Seneca Nation of Indians), Aug. 22, 1975; Carey to Hoag, Sept. 4, 1975; Raymond Schuler (commissioner of transportation) to Carey, July 7, 1976; Carey to Hoag, July 28, 1976; Harding to Carey, Jan. 22, 1975; Carey to Elliot Tallchief (Traditional Seneka Peoples Government), Aug. 5, 1975; Traditional Seneka Peoples Government to Carey, May 30, 1975. All in Governor's Records: Hugh Carey, Subject Files, MR 104, NYSA. Also, Cornelius Abrams Jr., interviewed by the author, Sept. 29, 1984, and Mar. 21, 1986, Allegany Indian Reservation.

55. SNI Tribal Council special session, minutes, June 28, 1976, SNI Archives; Agreement between the Seneca Nation of Indians and the People of the State of New York for the Southern Tier Expressway, Cattaraugus County, July 28, 1976 (Robert C. Hoag and Raymond T. Schuler, signatories), and Memorandum of Understanding between New York State Department of Transportation and Seneca Nation of Indians, July 28, 1976, SNI Archives. State officials hyped this agreement, labeling it a "historic" treaty. Harold Faber, "Senecas and State of New York Strike Historic Pact as Equals," *NYT*, July 11, 1976; Raymond Schuler, interviewed by the author, June 3, 1986, Albany; William C. Hennessy, interviewed by the author, July 9, 1986, Albany.

56. Agreement between the Seneca Nation and the People of the State of New York for Southern Tier Expressway, Cattaraugus County, July 28, 1976, SNI Archives.

57. Ibid.

58. Memorandum of Understanding, July 28, 1976, emphasis mine; Schuler interview, June 3, 1986.

59. For the hype, see New York State Department of Transportation, *Annual Report, 1976* (Albany: New York State, 1976), 5.

60. Faber, "Senecas and State of New York Strike Historic Pact as Equals."

61. Lou Grumet to Secretary of State Mario Cuomo, July 19, 1977, New York State Department of State Records, Moss Lake Indian Negotiations, NYSA.

62. George Abrams, interviewed by the author, Aug. 26, 1983, Allegany Indian Reservation. For thirteen years, Abrams, a Cornplanter Heir, was the director of the Seneca-Iroquois National Museum. John Mladinov (NYSDOT executive deputy commissioner), interviewed by the author, Feb. 26, 1986, Albany.

63. The Senecas were well aware of the precedent-setting Oneida case. "Landmark Oneida Case," *Si Wong Geh*, Apr. 24, 1974; Norma Kennedy, interviewed by the author, May 15, 2011, Allegany Indian Reservation.

64. Barry Snyder (president of the Seneca Nation of Indians) to Governor Hugh Carey, Mar. 8, 1982, Governor's Records: Hugh Carey, Subject Files, MR 65, NYSA. See also US Congress, Senate, Select Committee on Indian Affairs, *Hearings on S. 2084: Ancient Indian Land Claims*, 97th Cong., 2d sess. (Washington, DC: US Government Printing Office, 1982); H.R. 5494, 97th Cong., 1st sess., Feb. 9, 1982.

65. Bilharz, *Allegany Senecas and Kinzua Dam*, 120–22. I was a participant in the first Remember the Removal commemoration in 1984 and in subsequent years as well. Carole Moses was later Peacemaker judge at Allegany. She was my student at SUNY New Paltz. Carole Moses, interviewed by the author, Sept. 28, 1984, Allegany Indian Reservation.

66. "Dissident Senecas Hold March," *Olean Times Herald*, Feb. 25, 1985; "Protesting Senecas March on Highway," *BN*, Feb. 24, 1985; Erie Paddock, "Senecas Bar Construction on Expressway," *Bradford Era* (Pennsylvania), Feb. 21, 1985; Erie Paddock, "Standoff: DOT Hopes Seneca Nation Can Intercede," *Bradford Era*, Feb. 23, 1985; Rosemary Daley, "Hennessy Seeks Facts from Senecas," *Olean Times Herald*, May 31, 1985; list of demands (handout), Feb. 23, 1985, copy in author's possession.

67. Quoted in "Indian Group Blocks Work on Highways," *NYT*, Aug. 4, 1985.

68. Bilharz, *Allegany Senecas and Kinzua Dam*, 123–25.

69. See the articles on the controversy listed in notes 66–67.

70. Bilharz, *Allegany Senecas and Kinzua Dam*, 125–26.

71. Ibid.

72. Ibid., 123–24; "Indian Group Blocks Work on Highway," *NYT*, Aug. 4, 1985; "Police Charge Dissident Blocked Highway Work," *Schenectady Gazette*, Aug. 14, 1985.

9. ONE WIN, ONE LOSS: SENECA LAND CLAIMS

1. *Cherokee Nation v. Georgia*, 30 U.S. 1 (1831); *Oneida Indian Nation of New York v. County of Oneida, et al.*, 414 U.S. 661 (1974). The attorney for the Oneidas wrote a memoir of his involvement in the case: George Shattuck, *The Oneida Land Claims: A Legal History* (Syracuse, NY: Syracuse Univ. Press, 1991).

2. *Cayuga Nation of New York and Seneca-Cayuga Tribe of Oklahoma and United States of America as Plaintiff-Intervenor*, 165 F. Supp. 266 (N.D.N.Y., 2001). For the political fallout from my testimony and threats to academic freedom, see Laurence M. Hauptman, "'Going off the Reservation': A Memoir," *Public Historian* 25 (Fall 2003): 81–102.

3. Cornelius Abrams Jr., interviewed by the author, Mar. 21, 1986, Allegany Indian Reservation; Duwayne "Duce" Bowen, interviewed by the author, Mar. 21, 1976, Allegany Indian Reservation. I have known attorney Arlinda Locklear for nearly thirty years and have worked with Jeanne Whiteing for a decade.

4. Louis Lefkowitz (New York State attorney general) and Jeremiah Jochnowitz (New York State assistant attorney general) to Gajarsa, Liss, and Sterenbech, Esq., Sept. 27, 1976, Governor's Records: Hugh Carey, Subject Files, MR 104, NYSA; New York State Power Authority attorney Thomas F. Moore Jr. and former New York assistant attorney general Henry Manley quoted in Exhibit III: Memorandum of Law and Fact, contained in petition of Feb. 9, 1968, attached to a letter of Joseph Califano to Jacob Thompson, Feb. 28, 1968, White House Central Files, Box 3, IN/AZ, Johnson Library. I have treated this case previously at greater length. See Hauptman, *Formulating Indian Policy in New York State*, 21–25, 104–7.

5. For a sampling of the early opposition to Indian land claims cases, see Gary Lee to Governor Hugh Carey, Feb. 21, 1979; Madison County [NY] Legislature resolution re: extinguishment of the aboriginal titles to the land claimed by Native Americans, Sept. 8, 1981; Peter Borzilleri (New York State Winegrowers) to Hugh Carey, Sept. 18, 1978; Richard McGuire (New York Farm Bureau) to Hugh Carey, May 27, 1980; Frederick B. Clark (chair, New York State Power Authority) to Robert J. Morgado, Mar. 6, 1978, all in Governor's Records: Hugh Carey, Subject File, MR 65, NYSA.

6. US Congress, House of Representatives, Committee on Interior and Insular Affairs, *Hearings on H.R. 6631: Settlement of the Cayuga Indian Land Claims in the State of New York, Mar. 3, 1980*, 96th Cong., 2d sess. (Washington, DC: US Government Printing Office, 1980). For an excellent treatment of this bill and the Reagan administration's response to it, see Dean J. Kotlowski, "From Backlash to Bingo: Ronald Reagan and Federal Indian Policy," *Pacific Historical Review* 77 (Nov. 2008), 630–33.

7. Barry Snyder Sr. to Governor Hugh Carey, Mar. 8, 1982, and Grand Council of the Haudenosaunee Six Nations Council to President Ronald Reagan, Feb. 14, 1982, Governor's Records: Hugh Carey, Subject Files, MR 65, NYSA.

8. *County of Oneida, et al. v. Oneida Indian Nation of New York*, 414 U.S. 226 (1985). For the Federal Trade and Intercourse Act of 1790, see 1 Stat., 137–38.

9. Arlinda Locklear, "Tribal Land Claims: Before and after Cayuga," *New York State Bar Association Government, Law, and Policy Journal* 8 (Spring 2006), 40.

10. *Seneca Nation v. Christy*, 2 N.Y.S. 546 (Sup. Ct. 1888), affirmed 27 N.E. 275 (N.Y. 1891), appeal dismissed, 162 U.S. 208 (1896). I must acknowledge the help of attorney George Shattuck, former attorney of the Oneida Nation and the lawyer who successfully argued the 1974 US Supreme Court case. Shattuck first taught me about the *Christy* case and how it shaped all later Iroquois land claims efforts. George Shattuck, interviewed by the author, Aug. 25, 1983, Syracuse, NY.

11. *Seneca Nation v. Christy*. For more on this case, see Hauptman, *"Seneca Nation of Indians v. Christy:* A Background Study."

12. "G. P. Decker, 74, Lawyer, Friend of Indian," *Rochester Democrat and Chronicle*, Feb. 25, 1936; see also Hauptman, *Seven Generations of Iroquois Leadership*, 127–42. For Decker's appeal on behalf of the Senecas' riparian rights along the Niagara River, see "Trace of Title of Seneca Indians," in US Congress, House of Representatives, Committee on Foreign Affairs, *Hearings on H.R. 2498, 11756, 16542, 16547, and 16587: Diversion of Water from the Niagara River, July 15, 1914*, 63rd Cong., 2d sess. (Washington, DC: US Government Printing Office, 1914), 26–27.

13. New York State Legislature, Assembly, "Report of the Indian Commission to Investigate the Status of the American Indians Residing in the State of New York . . . , Mar. 17, 1922," unpublished, referred to as the "Everett report," transcript in NYSL.

14. *Deere, et al. v. St. Lawrence River Power Co., et al.*, 22 F.2d 851 (1927).

15. *New York Indians v. United States*, 40 Ct. Cl. 448 (1905); Thomas Abler, "The Kansas Connection: The Seneca Nation and the Iroquois Confederacy Council," in *Extending the Rafters: Interdisciplinary Approaches to Iroquoian Studies*, edited by Michael Foster, Jack Campisi, and Marianne Mithun, 81–93 (Albany: SUNY Press, 1984). For the fraudulent Buffalo Creek Treaty of 1838 and its aftermath, see Hauptman, *Conspiracy of Interests*, 175–220.

16. 60 Stat., 1049–56.

17. Fixico, *Termination and Relocation*, 21–44.

18. The ruling came down in *Seneca Nation of Indians v. United States*, 39 Ind. Cl. Comm. 355 (1977).

19. *Six Nations v. United States*, 173 Ct. Cl. 917 (1965).

20. Ibid., 922–26.

21. "Senecas Vote to Divide $4 Million Approved," *Si Wong Geh*, Apr. 3, 1974.

22. "Seneca Nation of Indians Notice of Public Hearing Regarding Proposed Settlement of Claims against the U.S.A.," *Si Wong Geh*, July 14, 1976.

23. *Seneca Nation of Indians v. United States* (1977).

24. For Moses's dominance along the "Niagara Frontier," see Caro, *Powerbroker*, esp. 254. For the longtime relationship between Moses and Chapin, see ibid., 271, 484, 867–68.

25. Arlene Bova, interviewed by the author, Feb. 1, 2012, Allegany Indian Reservation. Bova was the head of the Seneca Nation of Indians' Land Claims Committee, which

negotiated the return of lands at Oil Spring in 2005. For the history of this special parcel of Seneca territory before the Civil War, see Hauptman, "Governor Blacksnake and the Seneca Indian Struggle to Save the Oil Spring Reservation." For a fuller discussion of this Seneca territory prior to the Genesee Valley Canal, see Hauptman, *Conspiracy of Interests*, 162–69; Congdon, *Allegany Oxbow*, 194–207.

26. Noble E. Whitford, *History of the Canal System of the State of New York*, 2 vols. (Albany: Brandon Printing for the New York State Engineer and Surveyor Office, 1906), 1:708–727, 1010–15; New York State Legislature, Assembly, *Document No. 168, Feb. 8, 1836* (Albany: New York State, 1836), 1–4.

27. The New York State Canal Fund paid "D. Sherman Atty. $1396.04" in 1865. Sherman was the attorney for the Senecas as well as the federal Indian agent! New York State Treasurer's Records, May 12, 1866, vol. 176 (Oct. 1864–Sept. 1865), 312, NYSA. See also Congdon, *Allegany Oxbow*, 205, and New York State Board of Land Commissioners, *Proceedings of the Commissioners for 1924* (Albany: J. B. Lyon, 1924), 109–12. The New York State Legislature considered further compensation but never acted on it. New York State Legislature, *Senate Journal* (1869), 288–91, 442–43, 562–65, 604–5; New York State Legislature, *Assembly Journal* (1869), 562–63, 634–35, 1180–81, 1114–15. They also failed to act on damages (trespass, timber stripping) done to Seneca lands at their three territories, including Oil Spring. New York State Legislature, Senate, *Document No. 72* (Apr. 3, 1868).

28. George P. Decker, "The New York Iroquois and State Game Laws," typescript, NYSL; Hauptman, *The Iroquois and the New Deal*, 6, 45–46, 186–87 n. 14.

29. F. A. Gaylord, "Report on State Land in the Vicinity of Cuba Lake" (1913); F. A. Gaylord to A. B. Strough, July 13, 1914; Albert E. Hoyt to Delbert Snyder, all in SNI Department of Justice Records, SNI Archives.

30. *U.S. Statutes at Large* 64, Part 2 (Jan. 5, 1927), 932–33. See U.S. Congress, *House Report 1322*, 69th Cong., 1st sess. (May 27, 1926), Serial Set No. 8534; U.S. Congress, *Senate Report 980*, 69th Cong., 1st sess. (June 2, 1926), Serial Set No. 8526. Not surprisingly, this bill was pushed by Congressman Daniel Reed of Dunkirk, New York. On the push for and against the bill, see New York State Attorney General to Senator James W. Wadsworth Jr., Apr. 6, 1926; Harry Nevins (attorney for the Seneca Nation) to Commissioner of Indian Affairs (Charles H. Burke), June 3, 1926; Burke to Daniel Reed, June 3, 1926, all in Office of Indian Affairs Records, BIA Central Classified Files, 1907–39, #16229-1926 (New York)—115, RG 75, NA. For the growing Iroquois land claims movement in the 1920s and other evident of state officials' concerns, see New York State Board of Land Commissioners, *Proceedings of the Commissioners for 1924*, 109–12, as well as the Everett report.

31. *U.S. Statutes at Large* 6v, part 2 (May 22, 1928), 1857. See US Congress, *Senate Report 1112*, 70th Cong., 1st sess. (May 3, 1928), Serial Set No. 8833; US Congress, *House Report 12446*, 70th Cong., 1st sess. (Apr. 12,1928), Serial Set No. 8842. For a copy of the conveyance, see BIA Central Classified Files, 1907–39, #54575-1926 (New York)—322, RG 75, NA.

32. *Seneca Nation of Indians v. United States*, 12 Ind. Cl. Comm. 552 (1963).

33. "Settlement of Cuba Lake Claim," *SNI Official Newsletter,* Feb. 11, 2005.

34. *Seneca Nation of Indians v. New York,* 26 F.Supp. 2d 555 (W.D.N.Y., 1998).

35. *Seneca Nation of Indians and United States of America v. New York,* 178 F.3d 959 (2d Circ., 1999).

36. *New York v. Seneca Nation of Indians,* 528 U.S. 1073 (2000).

37. Louis Coffey, "Mediated Settlement of a Native American Land Claim," *CPA Journal* (June 2006): 1–6. Coffey was the mediator appointed by Judge Curtin.

38. Arlene Bova and Jeanne Whiteing, interviewed by the author, Feb. 1, 2012, Allegany Indian Reservation.

39. Snyder quoted in "Settlement of Cuba Lake Claim," *SNI Official Newsletter,* Feb. 11, 2005. See also "U.S. Court Approval Clears Way for Restoration of Seneca Nation Sovereign Land" and "New York State Senator Cathy Young Visits Seneca Nation," *SNI Official Newsletter,* July 29, 2005.

40. Cooperative Management Agreement Relating to Cuba Lake between the Seneca Nation of Indians and the State of New York, Mar. 17, 2005, SNI Archives; US Department of the Interior, Office of the Assistant Secretary for Indian Affairs, "BIA Fiscal Year 2005 Budget Request Supports Trust, Indian Education and Law Enforcement Programs," news release, Feb. 2, 2004.

41. Robert W. Bingham, ed., *Niagara Frontier Miscellany,* Buffalo Historical Society Publications no. 34 (Buffalo: Buffalo Historical Society, 1947), 59–78. I have written previously about Grand Island and this Seneca claim. See Laurence M. Hauptman, "Who Owns Grand Island (Erie County, New York)?" *Oklahoma City University Law Review* 23 (Spring–Summer 1998): 151–74.

42. Bingham, *Niagara Frontier Miscellany*; Hauptman, "Who Owns Grand Island?"

43. The Senecas had inflicted a major defeat along the Niagara escarpment during Pontiac's War in 1763. This "Devil's Hole Massacre," as it came to be known, eventually led the Senecas to attempt to repair their relations with the British Crown the next year in an effort to restore the "Covenant Chain." For the Seneca transfer of the islands to the British Crown in 1764, see Edmund B. O'Callaghan and Berthold Fernow, eds., *Documents Relative to the Colonial History of the State of New York,* 14 vols. (Albany: Weed, Parsons, 1853–57), 7:621–23, 8:652–653. For the Treaty of Canandaigua, see 7 Stat. 44 (Nov. 11, 1794). For President Washington's commissioner to the Six Nations (Timothy Pickering) and his views in 1794, see Timothy Pickering to Henry Knox (secretary of war), Nov. 12, 1794, and Pickering to Knox, Timothy Pickering MSS, MR 60 and 62, Massachusetts Historical Society, Boston. See also *Seneca Nation of Indians v. United States, Tonawanda Seneca Indians v. United States,* 20 Ind. Cl. Comm. 177 (1968), at 181.

44. New York State Legislature, Assembly, *Report of the Special Committee to Investigate the Indian Problem of the State of New York* (*Whipple Report*), 211–13.

45. For more on Peter Porter, see Hauptman, *Conspiracy of Interests,* 121–44.

46. New York State Legislature, Assembly, *Whipple Report.*

47. Treaty of Ghent, 8 Stat., 218 (Dec. 24, 1814). For memoirs of two individuals involved in the work of the boundary commission, see Joseph Delafield, *The Unfortified Boundary*, edited by Robert MacElroy and Thomas Riggs (New York: privately printed, 1943), and William A. Bird, "Reminiscences of the Boundary Survey between the United States and the British Provinces," in *Buffalo Historical Society Publications*, no. 4, 1–14 (Buffalo: Buffalo Historical Society, 1896).

48. 8 Stat., 274–77 (June 18, 1822); Delafield, *Unfortified Boundary*, 61 n. 87.

49. Bingham, *Niagara Frontier Miscellany*, 65–69.

50. *Seneca Nation of Indians v. United States, Tonawanda Seneca Indians v. United States.*

51. Agnes Palazzetti, "Seneca Nation Filing Law Suit Laying Claim to Grand Island; Leader Says Land Was Illegally Sold," *BN*, Aug. 25, 1993; "Seneca Nation Files Suit to Reclaim Grand Island," *NYT*, Aug. 26, 1993. In May 1992, at the invitation of President Calvin "Kelly" John, I attended a revealing state legislative hearing on the sales tax chaired by state senator Daley. Chairman Daley clearly insulted the Seneca president by putting him at the end of the six-hour hearing when there were few people left in attendance. Nearly every non-Indian critic and lobbyist—about eighteen witnesses—testified before President John was allowed his turn. Laurence M. Hauptman field notes, May 1992, and see the description of this hearing and the insult to John in chapter 11.

52. "Agreement between the Seneca Nation of Indians and Tonawanda Band of Senecas, July 1914," George Decker MSS, Lavery Library, St. John Fisher College, East Rochester, NY.

53. *Seneca Nation of Indians and Tonawanda Band of Senecas (and the United States plaintiff-intervenor) v. State of New York, New York State Thruway, et al.*, 206 F.Supp. 2d 448 (W.D.N.Y., 2002).

54. 382 F.3d 245, U.S. Court of Appeals (2d Circ., 2004), 126 S. Ct. 2351; "Supreme Court Declines to Review Seneca Land Claim Case," *NYT*, June 6, 2006.

55. See *City of Sherrill v. Oneida Indian Nation*, 125 S.Ct. 1478 (2005); *Cayuga Indian Nation v. Pataki*, 413 F.3d 266 (2d. Circ. 2005). This Federal Court of Appeals decision reversed the federal district's decision based on the *Sherrill* decision. I was the expert witness on a finding of fact for the Cayugas in the federal district court that had previously awarded these Indians $247 million. On July 20, 2011, the US Supreme Court refused to overturn the decision in the *Sherrill* case. See *USA v. New York*, No. 10-1404, 10-1420.

10. THE SALAMANCA ALBATROSS

1. Testimony of Carl Zaprowski, in US Congress, House, Committee on Interior and Insular Affairs, Subcommittee on Indian Affairs, *Hearing on H.R. 1794 . . . Kinzua Dam (Seneca Indian Relocation)*, 42–45.

2. State senator Jess Present, interviewed by the author, Mar. 12, 1986, Albany.

3. Author's notes on hearings on Salamanca lease, US Congress, House of Representatives, Committee on Interior and Insular Affairs, Nov. 7, 1985.

4. In September 1990, I provided oral and written testimony before the House of Representatives Committee on Interior and Insular Affairs and the Senate Committee on Indian Affairs on the history of these leases and its impact on the Senecas. See US Congress, House of Representatives, Committee on Interior and Insular Affairs, *Hearings on H.R. 5367: To Provide for the Renegotiation of Certain Leases of the Seneca Nation, September 13, 1990*, 101st Cong., 2d sess. (Washington, DC: US Government Printing Office, 1991); US Congress, Senate, Select Committee on Indian Affairs, *Hearings on S. 2895: To Provide for the Renegotiation of Certain Leases of the Seneca Nation, September 18, 1990*, 101st Cong., 2d sess. (Washington, DC: US Government Printing Office, 1990). Although this chapter is different from my past treatments of the lease controversy, I have written about the issue on several occasions over the years. See *Iroquois Struggle for Survival*, 15–43; *The Iroquois in the Civil War: From Battlefield to Reservation* (Syracuse, NY: Syracuse Univ. Press, 1993), 117–27; *The Historical Background to the Present Day Seneca Nation–Salamanca Lease Controversy: The First Hundred Years*, Rockefeller Institute Working Paper no. 20 (Albany: Rockefeller Institute of Government, 1985), reprinted in *Iroquois Land Claims*, edited by Christopher Vecsey and William A. Starna, 101–22 (Syracuse, NY: Syracuse Univ. Press, 1988); and "Compensatory Justice."

5. Hauptman, notes on hearings on Salamanca lease, Nov. 7, 1985.

6. Abrams, *The Seneca People*, 70; Thomas E. Hogan, "City in a Quandary: Salamanca and the Allegany Leases," *New York History* 55 (Jan. 1974), 84.

7. US Bureau of the Census, *Ninth Census of the United States, 1870* (Washington, DC: US Census Printing Office, 1872), 207.

8. Abler, "Factional Dispute and Party Conflict," viii, 169–73; Thomas E. Hogan, "A History of the Allegany Reservation, 1850–1900," MA thesis, SUNY Fredonia, 1974, 8. See also Hauptman, "Senecas and Subdividers," 106.

9. *Laws of New York*, 88th sess., chap. 133 (Mar. 16, 1865) and chap. 211 (Mar. 25, 1865); John Hoffman (governor of New York State), Letter of Transmittal of Joint Legislative Resolution of New York State Legislature, Jan. 18, 1871, Office of Indian Affairs, New York Agency Records, M234, MR 75, NA.

10. US Congress, Senate, *Congressional Record*, 43d Cong., 2d sess., pt. 2, Feb. 2, 1875, 913–14.

11. Ibid., 909–10, 913–14, 919.

12. US Congress, Senate, *Misc. Doc. No. 122: Protest of the President, Councilors, and People of the Seneca Nation of Indians Made in Their National Council against the Passage of the Bill (H.R. No. 3080) to Authorize the Seneca Nation to Lease Their Lands within the Cattaraugus and Allegany Reservations, and to Confirm Existing Leases*, June 3, 1874, 43d Cong., 1st sess., reprinted in US Congress, Senate, Select Committee on Indian Affairs, *Report No. 101-511: Providing for the Renegotiation of Certain Leases of the Seneca Nation and for Other Purposes to Accompany S. 2895, October 8, 1990*, 101st Cong., 2d sess. (Washington, DC: US Government Printing Office, 1990), 5.

13. 18 Stat., 330 (Feb. 19, 1875).

14. 26 Stat., 588 (Sept. 30, 1890).

15. US Congress, House, *Congressional Record*, 57th Cong., 2d sess., pt. 1 (1902), 337. For Vreeland's attempts to allot Seneca lands, see Hauptman, "Senecas and Subdividers," 105–17.

16. I previously discussed what led up to this case at greater length in *Iroquois Struggle for Survival*, 15–43.

17. *United States v. Forness, et al.* (Salamanca Trust Co., et al., defendant-intervenors), 37 F. Supp. 337 (Feb. 14, 1941). For Justice Frank's opinion on appeal in favor of the Senecas, see 125 Fed. Rep., 2d Ser., 928 (Jan. 20, 1942). See also "Our Indian Landlords Finally Get a Break," *NYT*, Jan. 21, 1942.

18. New York State Legislature, Joint Legislative Committee on Indian Affairs, *Annual Report, 1944* (Albany: New York State, 1944); "Forness Case Decision Termed Reproach to State and Nation," *SRP*, Aug. 5, 1944.

19. For the Seneca Rental Act, see "A Pact with Americans; House Passes Bill for Rent Collection from Senecas," *NYT*, Aug. 1, 1950.

20. "Senecas Name Lease Negotiation Committee," *SRP*, Jan. 18, 1967.

21. Cornelius Abrams Jr., interviewed by the author, Sept. 29, 1984, and Mar. 21, 1986, Allegany Indian Reservation. I worked directly with the late Mr. Abrams in my research on the Seneca leases. An able researcher and a knowledgeable Seneca historian, Abrams, the director of the Seneca Nation of Indians Maps and Boundaries Department, then reported to President Hoag and the Seneca Nation Tribal Council about the documents I was uncovering.

22. "SNI President and Treasurer on Radio Show," *O He Yoh Noh*, Sept. 3, 1970. The Salamanca city officials were reacting to a story by James S. Kaplan published in the *Wall Street Journal* on August 17, 1970, summarized in "*Wall Street Journal* Surveys Salamanca Lease," *O He Yoh Noh*, Aug. 20, 1970.

23. Mayor Ron Yehl to Governor Hugh Carey, Oct. 13, 1981, Governor's Records: Hugh Carey, Subject Files, MR 65, NYSA; see Yehl's comments in "Seek to Raise Lease Fees for Salamanca," *NYT*, Jan. 28, 1980; Daniel Walsh, interviewed by the author, Mar. 13, 1986, Albany. Walsh, the head of the Business Council of New York from Olean, was the former Democrat majority leader of the New York State Assembly and a strong supporter of the Salamanca leaseholders.

24. For background on the diligent workings of the Seneca Nation Salamanca Lease Negotiation Committee, see the testimony of Seneca president Dennis Lay, US Congress, Senate, Select Committee on Indian Affairs, *Hearings on S. 2895*, 32–34 (oral testimony), 83–84 (written testimony); US Congress, House, Committee on Interior and Insular Affairs, *Hearings on H.R. 5367*, 73–74 (written testimony); "The Seneca Nation Salamanca Lease Negotiating Committee," *SNI Official Newsletter*, Oct. 28, 2005. Please note that in the photograph illustrating this article, not all committee members were included.

25. The opinions expressed on Loretta Crane and Douglas Endreson are based on my daily observations of and conversations with them throughout the lease efforts on Capitol

Hill in September 1990. Martin Seneca Jr., interviewed by the author, June 11, 2011, Allegany Indian Reservation; "Martin Seneca, Jr., Seneca Indian, Named Director, Trust Responsibilities, Bureau of Indian Affairs," *O He Yoh Noh*, May 8, 1974.

26. "Amory Houghton, Jr.," in *Biographical Directory of United States Congress, 1774–Present*, available at http://bioguide.congress.gov/biosearch/biosearch.asp. For tributes to the tactful congressman, a master of compromise across party and regional lines, see "From Amo's Civility to Cantor's Walkout," *BN*, July 28, 2011, and U.S. Congress, House, *Congressional Record*, 108th Cong., 2d sess., part 18, Nov. 19, 2004, 24344–45. For Houghton's critical views on Albany politics and what was needed to correct the situation, see Amory Houghton Jr. and Sherwood Boehlert, "Restore Ethics to Albany through Voter Owned Election," *BN*, Apr. 10, 2010.

27. For the Republican Main Street Partnership, see http://www.republicanmain street.org/index.pho/BoardMembers.

28. My comments here are based on my August–September 1990 notes and contact with Congressman Houghton and his staffers, especially Sheila Seelye.

29. Calvin "Kelly" John, interviewed by the author, May 4, 1997, Allegany Indian Reservation; author's conversation in 2001 with Randy John and Michael Chiariello, two St. Bonaventure University professors who attempted to mediate the dispute after the passage of the Seneca Nation Settlement Act.

30. "A New York Town Finds Debt to Indians," *NYT*, June 11, 1990. See also Elizabeth Kolbert, "City on Seneca Indian Reservation Reaches New Lease with Tribe," *NYT*, May 22, 1990. According to Seneca president Dennis Lay, "When they [the Salamanca city officials] negotiated the original leases, they thought we [Senecas] weren't going to be here at the end. We fooled them." Quoted in "Revenge of the Senecas, " *Time*, July 2, 1990.

31. Antonio N. Carbone to Congressman Amory Houghton, July 12, 1990, reprinted in US Congress, House, Committee on Interior and Insular Affairs, *Hearings on H.R. 5367*, 56.

32. Without regard to cultural sensibilities, Cuomo stoked the fires of Native activism. The governor was quoted as saying that many Indians "regard themselves as part of a nation. They are a nation, a conquered nation. And they, some of them, will not accept that you obliterated their existence as a nation just because you're more powerful than them." Quoted in Sam Howe Verhoek, "Whose Law Applies When Lawlessness Rules on Indian Land?" *NYT*, May 6, 1990, and discussed more fully in chapter 11. For the state's failures to help mitigate the environmental crisis at Akwesasne, see Laurence M. Hauptman, "Circle the Wagons: New York State v. the Indians," *Capital Region* (Feb. 1987): 29–31, 52–53. See also Hauptman, *Formulating American Indian Policy in New York State*, 60–64, 91–92, 103–4. For the civil strife at Akwesasne, see the following articles in the *New York Times*: Elizabeth Kolbert, "Armed Standoff on Mohawk Reservation Dispute Embroils Indian Reservation," July 27, 1989; Sam Howe Verhoek, "Mohawk Reserve Quiet as Officials Meet," May 4, 1990; "Mohawk Editor Held in Killing," May 15, 1990. At the exact same time, the Canadian government was in an armed standoff with Mohawks at Kahnawake and Oka.

33. US Congress, House, Committee on Interior and Insular Affairs, *Hearings on H.R. 5367*, 47–49.

34. Ibid., 47–49, 115–16. The Senate bill was number 2895 (1990).

35. For Stiglitz's report submitted to Congress, see "Exhibit A: Estimates of Lease Payment Deficiencies: Salamanca Leases," in US Congress, House, Committee on Interior and Insular Affairs, *Hearings on H.R. 5367*, 89–118.

36. Nancy O'Brien, a Salamanca businesswoman who owned a dry-cleaning store, had a $24 a year lease, or $2 a month. She objected to her rental lease being raised by Houghton's bill to $2,000 a year, or approximately $167 per month! Elizabeth Kolbert, "A New York Town Finds Debt to Indians May Finally Be Due," *NYT*, June 11, 1990.

37. Senator Daniel Inouye to Laurence M. Hauptman, Sept. 7, 1990, in author's possession. Later, Pete Taylor, the Senate Select Indian Affairs Committee's chief counsel, wrote to me after Houghton's bill was passed: "Your contribution toward this legislation did not begin with the testimony you provided the House and Senate. It began with your research into the musty records and laws of the State of New York and the United States. When I began my research, I called the Library of Congress, Congressional Research Service, and asked if they had any background material on the lease controversy between the Seneca Nation and the City of Salamanca. They sent me your chapter from the recently published book, *Iroquois Land Claims*. It was this work that guided me in my research of the past Federal laws, hearings and Congressional debates, and enabled me to quickly understand the meaning and scope of what I was reading. It is not often a historian can directly trace a legislative solution to the product of his labors, but you certainly can in this case. P. L. 101-503 is a direct consequence of your work, and the very fine testimony you provided." Pete Taylor to Laurence M. Hauptman, Dec. 10, 1990, in author's files.

38. For my testimony, see US Congress, House, Committee on Interior and Insular Affairs, *Hearings on H.R. 5367*, 32–34 (oral testimony) and appendix (written testimony); US Congress, Senate, Select Committee on Indian Affairs, *Hearings on S. 2895*, 19–21 (oral testimony) and 57–64 (written testimony).

39. For Dennis Lay's testimony, see US Congress, House, Committee on Interior and Insular Affairs, *Hearings on H.R. 5367*, 66 (oral testimony), 162 (written testimony); US Congress, Senate, Select Committee on Indian Affairs, *Hearings on S. 2895*, 76–82 (written testimony).

40. For Marlene Johnson's testimony, see US Congress, House, Committee on Interior and Insular Affairs, *Hearings on H.R. 5367*, 73–74 (written testimony); US Congress, Senate, Select Committee on Indian Affairs, *Hearings on S. 2895*, 32–34 (oral testimony) and 83–84 (written testimony).

41. For Loretta Seneca Crane's testimony, see US Congress, House, Committee on Interior and Insular Affairs, *Hearings on H.R. 5367*, 76–78 (written testimony); US Congress, Senate, Select Committee on Indian Affairs, *Hearings on S. 2895*, 33–35 (oral testimony) and 85–87 (written testimony).

42. Patrick Cleveland's testimony is in US Congress, House, Committee on Interior and Insular Affairs, *Hearings on H.R. 5367*, 119–22 (oral testimony).

43. Dennis Toboloski's testimony is in ibid., 123–124 (oral testimony), and US Congress, Senate, Select Committee on Indian Affairs, *Hearing on S. 2895*, 42–43.

44. H.R. 5367 became 104 Stat., 1292 (Nov. 3, 1990).

45. Amory Houghton speech on the Seneca Nation Settlement Act of 1990 is in US Congress, House, *Congressional Record*, 101st Cong., 2d sess., Oct. 10, 1990, 9285–9291. Citing my research, the Senate report favorably reported on the bill; see US Congress, Senate, Select Committee on Indian Affairs, *Report No. 101-51*.

46. Seneca Nation Settlement Act, 104 Stat., 1292 (Nov. 3, 1990).

47. "SNI Tribal Council Authorizes Signing of Salamanca Leases, *SNI Official Newsletter*, Feb. 5, 1991.

48. I briefly taught at St. Bonaventure as the Reginald Lenna Fellow. Both Randy John and Michael Chiariello introduced me to Pat Callahan. John was at the time chairman of the Department of Sociology, and Chiariello was a professor of philosophy there. For Callahan's testimony, see US Congress, Senate, Select Committee on Indian Affairs, *Hearings on S. 2895*, 39–40 (oral testimony) and 122–23 (written testimony). I thank Randy John, who until recently was the assistant to the president of the Seneca Nation, for his many insights about these critical years in Seneca history.

49. Quoted in Lindsey Gruson, "Town Learns Indians Are Taking Most of It Back: New Lease Raises Revenue for Seneca Tribe, but Residents Fear Losing Their Homes," *NYT*, Dec. 2, 1991.

50. Donna Snyder, "Senecas Reaffirm Position on Leases; Salamanca Residents Who Did Not Sign May Be Closer to Eviction," *BN*, Oct. 13, 1993; Agnes Palazzetti, "Some Residents to Remain Defiant as the Seneca's Lease Renewal Deadline Nears," *BN*, Sept. 10, 1994; Agnes Palazzetti, "Eviction Process May Begin Soon in Salamanca; Justice Department Mulling Suits against 16 Who Didn't Sign Senecas' Lease," *BN*, Nov. 1, 1994; Agnes Palazzetti, "Senecas Plan to Evict 21 in Salamanca; Failure to Sign Leases Brings Action to Oust," *BN*, May 12, 1995.

51. *Gregory T. Banner, et al. and the Salamanca Coalition of United Taxpayers v. United States*, 44 Fed. Cl. 568 (1999).

52. Ibid., 238 F.3d 1348 (US Ct. App., Fed. Circ., Jan. 29, 2001).

53. "Seneca Nation Extends Salamanca Lease Terms," SNI press release, Mar. 14, 2012, SNI Archives.

11. SMOKE SHOPS TO CASINOS

1. George-Shongo, *Onö´dowa´ga:´ Gano´kyëdoh Hogeh´oweh*, 37.

2. Taylor, *The Seneca Nation Economy*; "Seneca Nation Economic Impact Crucial to WNY," SNI press release, Feb. 28, 2012, SNI Archives; Rick Jemison, interview by the author, Mar. 22, 2012, Cattauragus Indian Reservation; Charles Specht, "Falls' Gamble on Casino

Hasn't Paid Off," *BN*, Dec. 29, 2012. Specht's title contradicts the positive facts brought out in his article about the impact of Seneca Niagara Hotel and Casino on Niagara Falls and Niagara County.

3. American Indian Policy Review Commission, *Final Report*, 1:305, 306, 307–8.

4. See Castile, *Taking Charge*, 62–66, 73–76, 98–99.

5. Donald D. Stull, "Reservation Economic Development in the Era of Self-Determination," *American Anthropologist* 92 (Mar. 1990), 207.

6. Ronald Reagan, "Statement on Indian Policy," Jan. 24, 1983, in Ronald Regan, *Public Papers of the Presidents: Ronald Reagan* (Washington DC: US Government Printing Office, 1983), 96–98.

7. Executive Order No. 12401: President's Commission on Indian Reservation Economics, Sept. 21, 1983, in Reagan, *Public Papers of the Presidents*, 56.

8. President's Commission on Indian Reservation Economies, *Report and Recommendations to the President of the United States* (Washington, DC: US Government Printing Office, 1984), 25–48.

9. US Department of the Interior, Task Force on Indian Economic Development, *Report of the Task Force on Indian Economic Development* (Washington, DC: US Government Printing Office, 1986), 21–25.

10. Stull, "Reservation Economic Development in the Era of Self-Determination," 209–10.

11. *Seminole Tribe of Florida v. Butterworth*, 658 F.2d 310 (5th Circ. Ct. App., 1981); *California v. Cabazon Band of Mission Indians*, 480 U.S. 202 (1987); *Oklahoma Tax Commission v. Citizen Band of Potawatomi Indian Tribe*, 498 U.S. 505 (1991); *[New York State] Department of Taxation and Finance, et al. v. Milhelm Attea and Bros., Inc., et al.*, 512 U.S. 61 (1994).

12. Kersey, *Assumption of Sovereignty*; Harry A. Kersey Jr. and Julian M. Pleasants, eds., *Seminole Voices: Reflections on Their Changing Society, 1970–2000* (Lincoln: Univ. of Nebraska Press, 2010). See also Jessica R. Cattelino, *High Stakes: Florida Seminole Gaming and Sovereignty* (Durham, NC: Duke Univ. Press, 2008).

13. Indian Gaming Regulatory Act, 102 Stat., 2467–76 (Oct. 17, 1988).

14. Ibid.

15. See the National Indian Gaming Commission website at http://www.nigc.gov/.

16. Maurice "Mo" John, telephone interview by the author, May 30, 2012. The details about John's life come from this interview.

17. For more on John, see Dan Herbeck, "U.S., Seneca Indian Clashing over Taxes; IRS Lien Is Filed on Gas Station—to Press Demand for $3. 5 Million," *BN*, Apr. 4, 1990; Michael Beebe and Elmer Ploetz, "Senecas Bill State for Motorists' Use of Thruway Section," *BN*, June 13, 2007; Dan Herbeck, "Judge [Maurice M. John Sr.] for Tribe Fights IRS on Taxes," *BN*, Nov. 9, 2003; Lou Michael and Tom Precious, "Senecas Demand New Deal on Thruway—Call Issue Separate from Dispute over Tobacco, Gasoline," *BN*, Apr. 20, 2007.

18. Chief Ernest Benedict, interviewed by the author, Sept. 10–11, 1982; July 30, 1983; Aug. 1, 2006, Akwesasne Indian Reservation. Sir William Johnson's Indian descendants, including Chief John Smoke Johnson, were major figures at Grand River, and his son, Chief George Henry Martin Johnson, was the father of the great poet E. Pauline Johnson.

19. William W. Campbell, ed., *The Life and Writings of DeWitt Clinton* (New York: Baker and Scribner, 1949), 187–88; Jeremy Belknap, *Journal of a Tour from Boston to Oneida, June 1796*, edited by George Dexter (Cambridge, MA: John Wilson, 1882), 21–22; Julian Ursyn Niemcewicz, "Journey to Niagara, 1805," edited by J. E. Budka Metchie, *New-York Historical Society Quarterly* 74 (Jan. 1960), 95.

20. New York State [Henry Roe Schoolcraft, comp.], *Indian Census of 1845*, NYSA.

21. (Norma) Ramona Charles, interviewed by the author, July 21, 1982, and May 14, 1986, Tonawanda Indian Reservation. See the photograph of this farmhouse in Arthur C. Parker, *The Life of General Ely S. Parker, Last Sachem of the Iroquois and General Grant's Military Secretary*, Buffalo Historical Society Publications no. 23 (Buffalo: Buffalo Historical Society, 1919). For the Tonawanda log cabin typical of the pre–Civil War era, see Dorcas R. Brown, "The Reservation Log Houses," MA thesis, SUNY, Oneonta, and New York State Historical Association, 2000.

22. Alexander Harmon, *Rich Indians: Native People and the Problem of Wealth in American History* (Chapel Hill: Univ. of North Carolina Press, 2010), 9.

23. Ibid., 277.

24. *Laws of New York*, 63d sess., chap. 254 (May 9, 1840), 26–27.

25. Ibid., 64th sess., chap. 166 (May 4, 1841), 134–36.

26. *In Re New York Indians*, 72 U.S. 761 (1866).

27. *Oklahoma Tax Commission v. Citizen Band of Potawatomi Indian Tribe.*

28. Both the New York State Department of Taxation and Finance and the US Internal Revenue Service went after Maurice "Mo" John. He was prosecuted, sent to jail, and fined $9 million. Maurice "Mo" John Sr., telephone interview, May 30, 2012.

29. Henrik Dullea to All Agency and Department Heads, Mar. 10, 1988; Pete Schiff, transmittal letter to Lew Millenbach, June 10, 1988, attaching "Preliminary Report to the Governor on State–Indian Relations," May 1988, in Seneca Land Claims Records (of Peter Sullivan, assistant attorney general), 1994–2005, Series III; and Grand Island, Discovery and Background Research, Subseries C: Miscellaneous Background Research, all in Box 12, Folder 8, Charles B. Sears Law Library, SUNY Buffalo. My public-policy report was published as *Formulating American Indian Policy in New York State*. The popular article was "Circle the Wagons."

30. For an excellent survey of the literature on the Seneca–state controversy over sales tax enforcement, see Amanda M. Murphy, "A Tale of Three Sovereigns: The Nebulous Boundaries of the Federal Government, New York State, and the Seneca Nation of Indian Concerning Taxation of Indian Reservation Cigarette Sales to Non-Indians," *Fordham Law Review* 79 (Apr. 2011): 2301–46.

31. Quoted in Sam Howe Verhoek, "Whose Law Applies When Lawlessness Rule on Indian Land," *NYT*, May 6, 1990.

32. *[New York State] Department of Taxation and Finance v. Milhelm Attea and Bros., Inc., et al.*

33. "Biography: Barry E. Snyder, Sr.," *SNI Official Newsletter*, Nov. 30, 2012; Dan Herbeck, "In Dollars and Votes, the Senecas' Paragon of Power," *BN*, May 17, 2004.

34. Author's field notes, 1980–2010.

35. George Borelli, "Crangle Discovers There Is Life after Politics," *BN*, Dec. 3, 1989. I was witness to some of the demonstrations in 1992. President Snyder invited me to speak at the anniversary of the Seneca Treaty of 1842 at West Seneca, New York, on May 20, 2010, part of an event promoted by Honor Our Treaties.

36. Snyder testimony in New York State Legislature, Senate, Standing Committee on Corporations, Authorities, and Commissions, *In the Matter of a Public Hearing to Consider the Taxation of Motor Fuels and Cigarettes Sold to Non–Native Americans on Indian Reservations*, May 27, 1992 (Albany: New York State, 1992), transcript on file in NYSL, 238–43.

37. John's testimony in ibid., 297–303.

38. J. C. Seneca's testimony in ibid., 304–11.

39. Author's field notes, July 1992. See the following articles in the *New York Times*: "Senecas Clash with Police over Tax Ruling," July 17, 1992; Lindsey Gruson, "New Betrayal, Senecas Say and New Rage," July 18, 1992; and Lindsey Gruson, "Senecas Dismantle the Roadblocks after Claiming Victory on Tax," July 19, 1992.

40. "Smokeshop Owner to Head Seneca Nation," *NYT*, Nov. 5, 1992.

41. Quoted in "Seneca Journal: Sovereignty and Casino Beckon to a Tribe," *NYT*, Oct. 29, 1992.

42. Agnes Palazzetti, "Snyder Installed as Seneca Leader; Last-Minute Effort to Prevent Swearing-In Fails," *BN*, Nov. 11, 1992. Snyder's term was marked by demonstrations outside the Seneca Hawk and disruptions of his cigarette and gasoline sales and deliveries, leading to court cases. Lori Lytel (manager of the Seneca Hawk), court affadavit, Aug. 10, 1993, in *Barry Snyder v. Susan P. Abrams, et al.* (Seneca Peacemaker's Court, 1994), Howard Berman Collection, Box 16, Sears Law Library, SUNY Buffalo.

43. All quotations are from Seth Newhouse's version of the Great Law, in "The Constitution of the Five Nations," in Arthur C. Parker, *Parker on the Iroquois*, edited by William N. Fenton, (Syracuse, NY: Syracuse Univ. Press, 1968), 29.

44. This work resulted in Laurence M. Hauptman and James Wherry, eds., *The Pequots: The Fall and Rise of an American Indian Nation* (Norman: Univ. of Oklahoma Press, 1990). See also "Indians [Mashantucket Pequot] Dedicate Casino," *NYT*, Feb. 13, 1992.

45. See the following articles by James Dao in the *New York Times*: "Accord Signed for Casino in New York State," Mar. 11, 1993; "Cuomo Signs Pact with Indians [Oneidas] in Upstate New York," Apr. 17, 1993; "Once Destitute Oneida Tribe Braces for Flood of Gaming Profits," July 18, 1993.

46. Iroquois Confederacy Grand Council Statement, 2005, copy in the author's possession. Even after three nations—Oneidas, Senecas, and Mohawks—had opened casinos, the Grand Council objected to them.

47. Chris Wood, "Gunfire and Gambling," *MacLean's*, May 7, 1990. See also Douglas M. George-Kanentiio, *The Iroquois on Fire* (Lincoln: Univ. of Nebraska Press, 2008).

48. "Seneca Journal: Sovereignty and Casino Beckon to a Tribe," *NYT*, Oct. 29, 1992.

49. New York State Legislature, Assembly, Subcommittee on Indian Affairs, *Public Hearings In Re: State–Indian Relations. Buffalo, May 13, 1993, and Albany, May 25, 1993*, 2 vols. (Albany: New York State, 1993), transcript on file in NYSL.

50. Midge Dean Stock's testimony in ibid., May 13, 1992.

51. Larry Ballagh's testimony in ibid., 63–73; testimony by Ross John (who also testified on educational matters) in ibid., 73–96.

52. John Mohawk's testimony in ibid., 40–63.

53. Calvin Lay Jr.'s testimony in ibid., 96–98.

54. Susan Abrams's testimony in ibid., 99–124.

55. "Senecas Look at Casino Gambling," *Albany Times Union (ATU)*, July 23, 1993.

56. "Seneca Gambling Leads to Squabble," *ATU*, July 31, 1993.

57. "Seneca Nation Panel Say No to Casino Plans," *ATU*, Aug. 2, 1993.

58. For more on the political battle that raged in the Seneca Nation of Indians between anti- and pro-casino proponents and filed legal motions and court decisions about the possible removal of President Dennis J. Bowen Sr., see "Protest of June 8, 1994"; Dennis J. Bowen Sr. to George Pataki, Mar. 25, 1995; motions and decision in *Ross L. John, et al. v. Dennis Bowen, Sr.*, *Dennis J. Bowen, Sr. v. Vincent E. Doyle, et al*, and *Susan P. Abrams v. Barry Snyder, President and Tribal Council* (Seneca Peacemaker's Court, 1994), all in Berman Collection, Box 16, "Seneca Nations of Indians, 1994–1995: Crisis," Sears Law Library, SUNY Buffalo.

59. "Man Wounded after Ruling in Seneca Feud," *NYT*, Feb. 28, 1995; "Feuding Factions of Senecas Give Up Control of Finances," *NYT*, Mar. 1, 1995; Robert D. McFadden, "Seneca Feud Boils Over; 3 Are Slain," *NYT*, Mar. 26, 1995. I was on the Allegany Indian Reservation attending a funeral at the time of these shootings. For President Bowen's handling of this tragedy, see Dennis J. Bowen to George Pataki, with attached Seneca Executive Order, to George Pataki, Mar. 25, 1995, and Bowen to Franklin Keel (BIA), Mar. 8, 1995, Berman Collection, Box 16, "Seneca Nation of Indians, 1994–1995: Crisis," Sears Law Library, SUNY Buffalo.

60. HQ STARC-NY/ARQ-MS11, "Subj: WARNING ORDER—[NYS]—Division of Military and Naval Affairs—AID TO CIVILIAN AUTHORITIES," July 1995, Kinzua Dam Research Files, Seneca-Iroquois National Museum, copy in SNI Archives, copy sent to author by a journalist.

61. David R. Townsend Jr. (with the assistance of Ed Byrnes), *Claims Casino: A Report on State–Indian Relations in New York State, August, 1995* (Albany: New York State Legislature, Assembly, 1995).

62. David R. Townsend Jr., transmittal letter to Governor Pataki, July 31, 1995, attached to ibid.

63. Ibid., 17, 24, 32.

64. Ibid.

65. Alaina Potrikas, "Oneida Nation Launches Political Mailing Campaign against David Townsend," *Syracuse Post-Standard*, Nov. 1, 2010; Frank Padavan, *Rolling the Dice: Why Casino Gambling Is a Bad Bet for New York State*, Parts I and II (Albany: New York State Legislature, Senate, 1994); Frank Padavan, *The Dice Are Rolling: Gambling with New York State's Future, January 6, 1997* (Albany: New York State Legislature, Senate, 1997).

66. "Tribes Organize Strategy to Bargain over Taxing of Cigarettes, Gasoline," *ATU*, Feb. 24, 1996.

67. Governor George Pataki's Executive Order Number 36.1 created the New York State Task Force on Casino Gambling, which issued its findings on August 30, 1996. Headed by Robert Sise, it recognized the economic stimulus resulting from creating Indian casinos. Urbach was a member of this task force. See New York State Task Force on Casino Gambling, *Report to the Governor, August 30, 1996* (Albany: New York State, 1996), 147.

68. Author's field notes, 1997. I witnessed these events and saw signs on three reservations naming certain chiefs (whom I will not name) as sellouts.

69. "Compromise on Indian Taxes," *ATU*, Feb. 23, 1997; Michael Schindler, interviewed by the author, June 11, 2011, Allegany Indian Reservation.

70. "Indian Tax Protest Blocks Thruway," *ATU*, Apr. 21, 1977.

71. Quoted in Mark McGuire, "State Police, Senecas Agree to Renew Talks," *ATU*, Apr. 23, 1997.

72. Carolyn Thompson, "Pataki Asks Indian Tax Exemption," *ATU*, May 23, 1997; John Caher, "Indian Tax Exemptions Challenged," *ATU*, June 18, 1997.

73. "Crowd Halts Plan to Vote on Casino," *NYT*, Feb. 16, 1998; "Opponents Block Vote on Legalizing Seneca Casino," *ATU*, Feb. 16, 1998.

74. Carolyn Thompson, "Seneca Leader Voids Casino Vote," *ATU*, May 3, 1998; "Casino Plan in Chaos after Leader Flip Flops," *ATU*, May 4, 1998.

75. Seneca Nation Settlement Act, 104 Stat., 1292 (Nov. 3, 1990); Jerry Zremski, "Tribe Seeks Shortcut for Federal Approval for Casinos in Upstate New York," *BN*, July 19, 2001.

76. Treaty of Big Tree, 7 Stat., 601 (Sept. 15, 1797).

77. Anthony F. C. Wallace, *Tuscarora: A History* (Albany: SUNY Press, 2012).

78. Quoted in James M. Odato, "Pataki Eyes Reservation Tax Issues," *ATU*, June 9, 2000.

79. US Bureau of the Census, *Seventeenth Census of the United States* (Washington, DC: US Census Printing Office, 1950); US Bureau of the Census, *Twenty-third Census of the United States* (Washington, DC: US Census Printing Office, 2010).

80. "New York Governor Announces Approval of Three New Casinos in Buffalo Area," *BN*, June 21, 2001; Somini Sengupta, "Niagara Falls and Buffalo Proposed as Casino

Sites," *NYT*, June 21, 2001; "Niagara Falls Casino Likely, Seneca Spokesman Says," *ATU*, Oct. 31, 2001.

81. "Seneca Casino Bid Linked to Land Claim Settlement," *ATU*, Aug. 20, 1999.

82. Sengupta, "Niagara Falls and Buffalo Proposed as Casino Sites"; "Pataki Criticized over Seneca Indians Casino Deal," *ATU*, June 29, 2001.

83. For Assemblyman Arthur O. Eve's opposition, see "New York Governor Announces Approval of Three Casinos in Buffalo Area."

84. James M. Odato, "Senecas Talk with State, Developers on Casinos," *ATU*, May 18, 2001; James M. Odato, "Casino Bill OK'ed by Senate," *ATU*, June 22, 2001; James C. McKinley Jr., "Democrats Contend a Pataki Lobbyist Has a Conflict," *NYT*, Nov. 12, 2001.

85. Quoted in Somini Sengupta, "Lawmakers Are Ambivalent on Pataki's Casino Proposal," *NYT*, June 22, 2001.

86. See note 15.

87. Odato, "Senecas Talk with State, Developers on Casinos."

88. Sarah Kershaw, "Senecas Sign Pact for Casinos in Niagara Falls and Buffalo," *NYT*, Aug. 19, 2002. The Memorandum of Understanding became the basis of the final gaming compact. Nation–State Gaming Compact between the Seneca Nation and the State of New York, Aug. 18, 2002, SNI Archives; Cyrus M. Schindler Sr., telephone interview by the author, May 31, 2012.

89. See the following articles by James M. Odato in the *Albany Times Union*: "Senecas Balk at Gaming Plans," Nov. 10, 2001; "New York Governor Lets Tribe to Open Casinos Without Written Commitment to Unions," Apr. 16, 2002; "Pataki to Sign Casino Compact," Aug. 17, 2002; "Seneca Poised to Take Over Building for Casino," Sept. 17, 2002.

90. Shaila K. Dewan, "Senecas Vote to Approve Plan for 2 Casinos," *NYT*, May 15, 2002.

91. Cyrus Schindler, telephone interview, May 31, 2012; "SNI President Cyrus M. Schindler and New York State Governor George E. Pataki Sign Casino Compact on August 18, 2002," *SNI Official Newsletter*, Aug. 23, 2002.

92. Ibid.; "From the President's [Cyrus M. Schindler Sr.] Desk," *SNI Official Newsletter*, Aug. 9, 2002; Odato, "Seneca Poised to Take over Building for Casino"; "From the President's [Rickey Armstrong Sr.] Desk," *SNI Official Newsletter*, May 14, 2004 (on the history of gaming compact with the state, Akin Group, and approval by US Department of the Interior on October 25, 2002).

93. Quoted in "Seneca Party Sweeps 2002 Election: Voters Choose Pro-Casino Gaming Party Candidates in a Decisive Victory on Election Day," *SNI Official Newsletter*, Nov. 15, 2002.

94. See "From the President's [Rickey Armstrong Sr.] Desk," May 14, 2004. Much of this same issue of the *Seneca Nation of Indians' Official Newsletter* is devoted to the opening of the Seneca Allegany Casino. Author's field notes, May 1, 2004.

95. David Staba, "Temporary Seneca Casino Opens in Downtown Buffalo," *NYT*, July 4, 2007.

96. "Remarks by Barry E. Snyder, Sr. at the Buffalo Casino Groundbreaking Held on December 8, 2005," *SNI Official Newsletter*, Dec. 23, 2005.

97. Dan Herbeck and Lou Michel, "Senecas Blast Spitzer on Plan for Taxes on Cigarette Sales," *BN*, Mar. 14, 2007; Valerie Bauman, "New York Senate Passes Indian Reservation Tax," *News from Indian Country*, Aug. 8, 2008.

98. Taylor, *The Seneca Economy*.

99. Rick Jemison interview, Mar. 22, 2012; Randy John, interviewed by the author, Jan. 31, 2012, Allegany Indian Reservation.

100. Prevent All Cigarette Trafficking (PACT) Act, Pub. L. 111-154, 124 Stat., 1087 (Mar. 31, 2010); Jerry Zremski, "Obama Signs Bill Restricting Mail-Order Cigarette Sales," *BN*, Apr. 1, 2010.

101. Non-Indian gaming operations with video lottery terminals in the Senecas' historic territory are at the Hamburg Casino and Racetrack, Finger Lakes Casino and Racetrack in Canandaigua, and Batavia Downs Casino and Racetrack. See Tom Precious, "Revenue Sharing Dispute," *BN*, Dec. 13. 2011.

102. A three-person binding arbitration panel, chaired by Judith S. Kaye, former chief judge of the New York State Court of Appeals, and including an attorney chosen by the Seneca Nation and one by the state, was established in September 2012 to determine if New York had violated the exclusivity rights given to the Senecas under the 2002 gaming compact. Steve Bell, "Casino Arbitration Panel Set, Chaired by Judge Kaye," *SNI Official Newsletter*, Sept. 28, 2012.

103. Charles Specht, "State Deal Would Allow Non-Indian Casinos," *BN*, Dec. 6, 2011; "Seneca Nation Officials React to [Andrew] Cuomo Speech; President, Councilor Attend State of the State, Emphasize Nation's Zone [of Exclusivity]," SNI news release, Jan. 4, 2012, SNI Archives; "Seneca Nation President on Cuomo Casino Idea; President Interviewed on Fred Dicker Radio Show," SNI news release, Jan. 19, 2012, SNI Archives; "Seneca President Comments on Gaming Amendment," *SNI Official Newsletter*, Mar. 15, 2012.

104. "Porter Administrative Accomplishments List, 2010–2012," *SNI Official Newsletter*, Oct. 26, 2012.

105. "A Letter from the President [Barry E. Snyder Sr.]," *SNI Official Newsletter*, Nov. 7, 2012; Dan Herbeck, "Snyder Begins Fifth Term as Seneca President, Lashes Out at State," *BN*, Nov. 13, 2012.

106. Tom Precious, "Cuomo Plans Non-Indian Casino in the Falls," *BN*, Feb. 3, 2013, and "Cuomo Gives Ultimatum on Casino Funds," *BN*, May 9, 2013.

107. Jill Terreri, "Snyder: Cuomo Employing 'Playground Bully Tactics,'" *BN*, May 17, 2013.

108. "Governor Cuomo and Seneca Nation of Indians Announce Landmark Agreement," New York State Governor's Office news release, June 13, 2013, at http://www.gover nor.ny.gov; "Game Compact Arbitration Settlement," *SNI Official Newsletter*, June 28, 2013; Charles V. Bagli, "Seneca Tribe Reaches Deal with Cuomo on Gambling," *NYT*, June 13,

2013. The 1976 "Lieu Lands" agreement between Albany and the Senecas over the Southern Tier Expressway was also lauded as the beginning of a better day, one that actually set off conflict and litigation well into the future.

12. LOOKING AHEAD SEVEN GENERATIONS

1. "Ex-Acme Electronics Plant in Cuba Acquired by Seneca Nation," *BN*, Aug. 23, 208; Robert Mele, interviewed by the author, Aug. 11, Sept. 27, 2012, Cattaraugus Indian Reservation. Mele heads the Seneca Gaming Corporation. His mother, Betty Mele, was one of the most outspoken Senecas opposing the Kinzua Dam project. Betty Mele, interviewed by the author, Sept. 25, 2012, Allegany Indian Reservation.

2. "A Letter from the President [Robert Odawi Porter]," *SNI Official Newsletter*, Apr. 27, 2012; Lana Redeye, "President Meets with Buffalo Area Senecas," *SNI Official Newsletter*, May 11, 2012; and Lana Redeye, "Interim Buffalo Creek Community Committee Formed," *SNI Official Newsletter*, June 15, 2012.

3. Robert Odawi Porter, "City and State: Seneca Nation" (editorial), *SNI Official Newsletter*, Sept. 28, 2012; Tyler Heron, interviewed by the author, Aug. 10, 2012, Allegany Indian Reservation. Tyler Heron, the son of the late George Heron, heads the Seneca Tobacco Company and graciously gave me a tour of his facility. He was also the former executive director of the KDRC.

4. David Kimelberg, "Achieving Economic Diversification in Indian Country," *Indian Country Today*, Dec. 16, 2011; "Seneca Nation Forms Green Energy Company; Seneca Holdings Subsidiary Will Focus on Wind, Hydro, Solar Power," SNI press release, Feb. 14, 2011, SNI Archives; Steve Bell and Eric Mower, "Seneca Firm Wins $18.5 Million Army Contract," *SNI Official Newsletter*, May 11, 2012; David Kimelberg, interviewed by the author, Feb. 1, 2012, Allegany Indian Reservation.

5. Robert Odawi Porter, "Seneca Language Death," available at the Seneca Faithkeepers' website, http://www.sites.google.com/site/haudenosauneenw/faithkeepers-school, accessed Feb. 25, 2011. For recent attempts to preserve the language, see Melissa Borgia, "An Overview of Language Preservation at Ohi:yo´, the Seneca Allegany Territory," PhD diss., Indiana Univ. of Pennsylvania, 2010. Today, there are no more than fifty fluent speakers of the Seneca language.

6. Robert Odawi Porter, "State of the Nation Address, Feb. 25, 2012," *SNI Official Newsletter*, Mar. 16, 2012.

7. Robert Odawi Porter, personal communication to the author, May 14, 2012.

Bibliography

ARCHIVAL RECORDS AND MANUSCRIPT COLLECTIONS

American Philosophical Society, Philadelphia
  Fenton, William N., MSS
  Speck, Frank, MSS
  Tooker, Elisabeth, MSS
  Wallace, Anthony F. C., MSS
Antioch College, Yellow Springs, OH
  Morgan, Arthur E., MSS
Columbia University, Butler Library
  Lehman, Herbert, MSS
  Poletti, Charles MSS
Cornell University
  Ives, Irving, MSS
  Reed, Daniel, MSS
Dwight D. Eisenhower Presidential Library, Abilene, KS
  Bragdon, John S., MSS
  Eisenhower Records, White House Central Files, 1953–61
    Harlow, Bryce, MSS
    Seaton, Fred, MSS
    Whitman, Ann, Files
    Oral histories: Elmer Bennett; Herbert Brownell; N. R. Danielson; O.
      Hatfield Chilson; Wesley D'Ewart; Jacob Javits; Kenneth Keating;
      David Lawrence; Orme Lewis; Arthur Watkins
Federal Energy Regulatory Commission, Washington, DC
  Federal Power Commission Records

Transcript of testimony at hearings (related to renewal of hydropower license), Salamanca, NY, Allegany Indian Reservation, Feb. 24, 2011

Federal Records Center, National Archives, New York City
    New York Agency Records, 1938–49, Record Group 75

Florida Southern College, Lakeland
    Haley, James A., MSS

Franklin Delano Roosevelt Library, Hyde Park, NY
    Eleanor Roosevelt MSS
    President Franklin D. Roosevelt, Official Files

Harry S. Truman Presidential Library, Independence, MO
    Brophy, William A., MSS
    Chapman, Oscar A., MSS
    Myer, Dillon S., MSS
    Nash, Philleo, MSS
    Truman Records, White House Official Files, 1945–53
    Oral histories: Dillon Myer; Earl Warren

Haverford College, Magill Library
    Hetzel, Theodore, MSS
    Society of Friends, Indian Committee of the Society of Friends, Records of the Philadelphia Yearly Meeting

Historical Society of Pennsylvania, Philadelphia
    Clark, Joseph S., MSS
    Indian Rights Association MSS

Humanities Research Center, University of Texas, Austin
    LaFarge, Oliver, MSS

Indiana University of Pennsylvania, Indiana, PA
    Saylor, John, MSS

Jimmy Carter Presidential Library, Atlanta
    Exit interviews: Lloyd Cutler; Stuart Eizenstat

John F. Kennedy Presidential Library, Boston
    White House Central Files, 1961–63
    Robert Kennedy Files as Attorney General
    Lee White Files as White House Counsel
    Oral histories: Clinton P. Anderson; John Carver Jr.; Philleo Nash; Stewart Udall

Library of Congress
    Anderson, Clinton P., MSS
    Kemp, Jack, MSS

Krug, J. A., MSS

Lyndon Baines Johnson Presidential Library, Austin

    White House Central Files, 1963–68

    Oral histories: Clinton P. Anderson; Robert L. Bennett; Philleo Nash; Stewart Udall

Massachusetts Historical Society, Boston

    Pickering, Timothy, MSS

National Archives, Washington, DC

    Bureau of Indian Affairs Central Classified Files, 1907–36

    Bureau of Indian Affairs Records, Record Group 75

    Bureau of Indian Affairs Reservation Planning Studies

    Office Files of the Commissioner of Indians Affairs/Assistant Secretary of the Interior for Indian Affairs

        Bennett, Robert L.

        Bruce, Louis R., Jr.

        Emmons, Glen

        Thompson, Morris

National Archives II, College Park, MD

    Cartographic Records—Archives II

    Office of the Secretary of the Interior Records, Record Group 48

        Holum, Kenneth, Assistant Secretary for Water and Power, 1961–65

        Stevens, Theodore, Assistant Secretary of the Interior—Legislative Legal Council, 1956–60

    Records of the Indian Claims Commission, Record Group 279

National Records Center, National Archives, Suitland, MD

    US Army Corps of Engineers Records, Office of the Chief Engineer, Record Group 77

Nebraska State Historical Society, Lincoln

    Butler, Hugh, MSS

Newberry Library, Chicago

    Jennings, Francis, et al., eds., *Iroquois Indians: A Documentary History of the Six Nations and Their League.* 50 microfilm reels.

New York Public Library, Manuscript Division

    Moses, Robert, MSS

New York State Archives, Albany, NY

    New York State Board of Charities [Department of Social Welfare / Department of Social Services]

Thomas Indian School

New York State Department of Education, Native American Indian Education Unit

New York State Department of Health Records

New York State Department of Law, Litigation Bureau
Landmark Case Files

New York State Department of Public Works (Department of Transportation) Records
Superintendent of Public Works Files
Deputy Superintendent of Public Works Files
Transportation Legislation Planning Files
Internal Memoranda on Proposed Legislation

New York State Department of State, Moss Lake Indian Negotiations

New York State Governor's Office
Governor's Records: Thomas E. Dewey; Averill Harriman; Nelson Rockefeller; Malcolm Wilson; Hugh Carey; Mario Cuomo; George Pataki; Elliott Spitzer; David Patterson
Governor's Legislative Bill and Veto Jacket Files

New York State Legislature, Assembly, Standing Committee on Governmental Operations, Subcommittee on Indian Affairs, Subject and Hearings Files, 1968–72

New York State Museum Records, 1954–68

New York State Treasurer's Records, May 12, 1866

New York State Library, Manuscript Division
New York State Thruway Chronology, New York State Electronic Document, #THR500-4, THRCH95-11136
Parker, Arthur C., MSS
Stillman, Lulu, MSS

New York State Library, Office of Library Development
American Indian library files

New York State Thruway
Re: New York State Thruway easement across the Seneca Nation's Cattaraugus Indian Reservation, 1954, Freedom of Information and Privacy Act #F08-0011, released Feb. 12, 2008

Pennsylvania State Archives, Harrisburg
Deardorff, Merle H., MSS

Governor's Records: David Lawrence; George William Leader; William Scranton

Pennsylvania Public Utilities Commission, Harrisburg

Pennsylvania Electric Company (Penelec) annual reports

Princeton University, Princeton, NJ

American Civil Liberties Collection

American Indian Periodicals Collection

Association on American Indian Affairs Collection

Richard M. Nixon Presidential Library, Yorba Linda, CA, and College Park, MD

National Council on Indian Opportunity

Exit Interview: Bradley Patterson Jr.

Presidential Daily Diary

White House Central Files

White House Tapes

Ronald Reagan Presidential Library, Simi Valley, CA

White House Office of Records Management, White House Central Files

Seneca-Iroquois National Museum, Salamanca, Allegany Territory

Haiwadogēsta´ Collection

Kinzua Dam and Seneca Relocation Project documents and photographs

Materials on "Iroquoia" project

Pamphlet series on Seneca Culture

Photographic Collection

Seneca Nation of Indians Archives, Salamanca, Allegany Territory

Agreement between Seneca Nation of Indians and the People of the State of New York for the Southern Tier Expressway, Cattaraugus County, July 28, 1976

Cooperative Management Agreement Relating to Cuba Lake between the Seneca Nation of Indians and the State of New York, Mar. 17, 2005

Department of Justice Records

Cuba Lake Land Claims Case File

New York State Thruway File

HQ STARC-NY/ARQ-MS11, "Subj: WARNING ORDER—[NYS]—Division of Military and Naval Affairs—AID TO CIVILIAN AUTHORITIES," July 1995

Kinzua Dam Relicensing Commission Records

Seneca Pumped Storage Project documents

Initial Study Report
  Cultural Resources Study
  Fisheries Study
  Impingement and Entrainment Study
  Invasive Botanical Study
  Mussel Study
  Rare, Threatened, Endangered Species Study
  Water Fluctuation Study
  Water Quality Study
Preapplication Document FERC Project #2280: *Seneca Pumped Storage Project*, prepared by Natural Resources Consulting Engineers, Nov. 2010
Proposed Study Plan
Revised Scoping Plan
Revised Study Plan
Study Plan Determination
Memorandum of Understanding between New York State Department of Transportation and Seneca Nation of Indians, July 28, 1976.
Nation–State Gaming Compact between the Seneca Nation and the State of New York, August 18, 2002
New York State Department of Transportation Agreement with the Seneca Nation of Indians, Re: Maintenance of Red House Bridge, Dec. 14, 2007
Seneca Nation of Indians' Health Action Group Records
  Press Releases
Tribal Council minutes, 1854–present
Smithsonian Institution
  National Anthropological Archives
    American Indian Chicago Conference Records
    National Congress of American Indian Records
State University of New York, Albany [University at Albany]
  Manley, Henry S., MSS
State University of New York, Buffalo, Charles B. Sears Law Library [University at Buffalo]
  Berman, Howard, Collection
  Seneca Land Claims Records, 1994–2005
    Sullivan, Peter (New York State assistant attorney general)
State University of New York, College at Buffalo

Indian Claims Collection
   Reilly, Paul G., Indian Claims Commission, MSS
State University of New York, Stony Brook
   Javits, Jacob, MSS
St. John Fisher College, Lavery Library, East Rochester, NY
   Decker, George P., MSS
Syracuse University, Bird Library
   Harriman, Averill, MSS
   Moses, Robert, MSS
United States Military Academy, West Point
   Bragdon, John, Cullum File
University of Chicago
   Tax, Sol, MSS
University of Denver, Sturm College of Law Oral History
   Carver, John A., Jr., oral history
University of Kansas, Institute of Politics
   Kemp, Jack, interview
University of Rochester, Rush Rhees Library
   Dewey, Thomas E., MSS
   Keating, Kenneth, MSS
   Parker, Arthur C., MSS
University of Texas, National Humanities Center
   LaFarge, Oliver, MSS
University of Virginia, Miller Center
   Oral histories, Carter administration: Griffin Bell; Stuart Eizenstat; Hamilton
      Jordan; James Schlesinger
   Oral histories, Reagan administration: James A. Baker III; Howard Baker Jr.;
      William P. Clark; Max Friedersdorf
   Oral histories, George H. W. Bush administration: James A. Baker III; William
      P. Barr; Frederick McClure; Richard Thornburgh
Vassar College
   Parrish, Jaspar, MSS
Warren County Historical Society, Warren, PA
   Kinzua Dam Scrapbooks
William J. Clinton Presidential Library
   Kagan, Elena, Collection
   Domestic Policy Council Records

Native Americans (law enforcement)
Wisconsin Historical Society, Madison
    Taylor, Walter, MSS
Yale University, Beinecke Library
    Cohen, Felix, MSS
    Deloria, Vine, Jr., MSS
    Lazarus, Arthur, Jr., MSS
    Wilson, Edmund, MSS
Yale University, Sterling Library
    Collier, John, MSS

INTERVIEWS

A. Conducted by Laurence M. Hauptman

Abrams, Bruce. Feb. 1, 2012, Allegany Indian Reservation.
Abrams, Cornelius, Jr. Sept. 29, 1984, and Mar. 21, 1986, Allegany Indian Reservation.
Abrams, George H. J. Aug. 26, 1983, Allegany Indian Reservation.
Abrams, Rovena. Feb. 23, 2011, Allegany Indian Reservation.
Anderson, Marilyn Jemison. May 4–5, 1977, New Paltz, NY; Sept. 26, 2011, Cattaraugus Indian Reservation.
Batson, Robert. Jan. 15, Mar. 6, 1986, Albany, NY.
Benedict, Chief Ernest. Sept. 10–11, 1982; July 30, 1983; Aug. 1, 2006, Akwesasne Indian Reservation.
Bova, Arlene. Feb. 1, 2012, Allegany Indian Reservation.
Bowen, Duwayne "Duce." Mar. 21, 1986, Allegany Indian Reservation.
Bowen, Merrill. Aug. 26, 1983, and Sept. 28, 1984, Allegany Indian Reservation.
Bray, Ethel Peggy. Aug. 15, 2001, Allegany Indian Reservation.
Bruce, Louis R., Jr. Dec. 11, 1980, and June 30, 1982, Washington, DC.
Charles, (Norma) Ramona. July 21, 1982, and May 14, 1986, Tonawanda Indian Reservation.
Chodos, Laura. Feb. 24, 1986, Albany, NY.
Cook, Adrian. Feb. 24, 1986, Albany, NY.
Crane, Loretta Seneca. Sept. 13, 1990, Washington, DC.
Crotty, Gerald. July 9, 1986, Albany, NY.
Deeghan, Brenda Pierce. Sept. 26, 2011, Allegany Indian Reservation.
Deloria, Vine, Jr. May 4, 1982, New Paltz, NY.
DiMaggio, Fred. Apr. 17, 1986, Albany, NY.

Donovan, James. Apr. 17, 1986, Albany, NY.

Douglas, Marilyn. Aug. 1, 2001, Albany, NY.

Dullea, Henrik. Apr. 18, 1986, Albany, NY.

Fenton, Olive. Oct. 13, 1984, Rensselaerville, NY.

Fenton, William N. Sept. 28, 1977; June 28, 1978; and May 18, 1983, Albany, NY.

Gambill, Jerry (Rarihokwats). Aug. 22, 1984, Ottawa, Ontario.

Hennessy, William. July 9, 1986, Albany, NY.

Heron, George. Sept. 28, 1984, Allegany Indian Reservation.

Heron, Tyler. Aug. 10, 2012, Allegany Indian Reservation.

Hill, Norbert, Sr. Wisconsin Oneida Indian Reservation.

Hill, Rick. Sept. 8, 1982, Syracuse, NY; May 28, 1984, Six Nations Indian Reserve.

Hudacs, John. Mar. 10, 1986, Albany, NY.

Jemison, G. Pete. May 15, 1986, Victor, NY.

Jemison, Jeanne Marie. Aug. 26, 1977, Herndon, VA; Aug. 23, 1978, Tyson's Corners,
    VA; May 2–4, 1978, and July 14–17, 1982, New Paltz, NY; Sept. 8, 1984, and Mar.
    21, Sept. 13, 1986, Cattaraugus Indian Reservation.

Jemison, Rick. Mar. 21, 2012, Cattaraugus Indian Reservation.

John, Calvin "Kelly." May 2, 1987, and May 4, 1997, Allegany Indian Reservation.

John, Hazel Dean. July 16, 1984; Apr. 18, 1986; and Jan. 30, 1987, Albany, NY.

John, Maurice "Mo," Sr. May 30, 2012, telephone interview.

John, Randy. Jan. 31, 2012, Allegany Indian Reservation.

Johnson, Marlene. Aug. 15, 2001, Allegany Indian Reservation; May 16, 2011, Alle-
    gany Indian Reservation.

Kalaijian, Karen. May 7, 1986, Albany, NY.

Kennedy, Fred. Sept. 25, 2011, Dunkirk, NY.

Kennedy, Norma. May 4–5, 1977, New Paltz, NY; and May 15, June 14, 2011, Alle-
    gany Indian Reservation.

Kettle, Francis. July 27, 1977, and June 4, 1978, Cattaraugus Indian Reservation.

Kettle, Wini. May 4–5, 1977, New Paltz, NY; and July 28, 1977, Cattaraugus Indian
    Reservation.

Kimelberg, David. Feb. 1, 2012, Allegany Indian Reservation.

Kimelberg, Michael. Feb. 1, 2010, Allegany Indian Reservation.

Lazarus, Arthur, Jr. July 17, 1982, Buffalo, NY.

Lewis, Anna. June 10, 1983, Albany, NY.

Loret, Jean. Sept. 25, 2011, Dunkirk, NY.

Lyons, Oren. Sept. 8, 1984, Syracuse, NY; May 6, 1985, Old Westbury, NY; and Nov.
    13, 2008, New Paltz, NY.

Mele, Betty. Sept. 25, 2012, Allegany Indian Reservation.

Mele, Robert. Aug. 11, Sept. 27, 2012, Cattaraugus Indian Reservation.

Millar, William. Oct. 24, 1987, Mashantucket Pequot Indian Reservation, Ledyard, CT.

Mladinov, John. Feb. 26, 1986, Albany, NY.

Mohawk, John. Mar. 20–21, 2001, Buffalo, NY.

Moses, Carole. Sept. 28, 1984, and July 18, 2001, Allegany Indian Reservation.

Mt. Pleasant, Chief Edison. Oct. 20–21, 1984, Rome, NY; Nov. 30, 1984, Tuscarora Indian Reservation.

O'Neill, Edward. Jan. 10, 1984, Washington, DC.

Patterson, Elma. Nov. 30, 1984, Lewiston, NY; and Apr. 15, 1972, New Paltz, NY.

Patterson, Chief Kenneth. May 2, 2009, and May 5, 2012, Batavia, NY.

Peterson, Myrtle. Apr. 7, 1978, Cherokee, NC.

Plummer, Genevieve. July 28, 1977, Allegany Indian Reservation.

Porter, Tom. May 5–6, 1982, New Paltz, NY.

Powless, Chief Irving, Jr. Oct. 21, 1984, Rome, NY.

Present, Jess. Mar. 12, 1986, Albany, NY.

Preston, Jack. May 4, 1975, New Paltz, NY.

Redeye, Lana. Aug. 23, 2001, Allegany Indian Reservation.

Rowley, Howard. Mar. 17, 1986, Rochester, NY.

Schindler, Cyrus M., Sr. May 31, 2012, telephone interview.

Schindler, Michael. June 11, 2011, Allegany Indian Reservation.

Schuler, Raymond. June 3, 1986, Albany, NY.

Seneca, Martin, Jr. June 11, 2011, Allegany Indian Reservation.

Seneca, Pauline Lay. June 4, 1978, and July 15–17, 1982, Cattaraugus Indian Reservation.

Shattuck, George. Aug. 25, 1983, Syracuse, NY.

Shenandoah, Chief Leon (Tadodaho). May 15, 1979, Onondaga Indian Reservation.

Soucy, Leo. Mar. 4, 1986, Albany, NY.

Spieler, Cliff. Dec. 10, 1984, Buchanan, NY.

Staub, Dr. Henry. May 4, 1977, New Paltz, NY.

Sundown, Chief Corbett. May 22, 1980, Tonawanda Indian Reservation.

Swamp, Chief Jake. Apr. 25, 1985, New Paltz, NY; and May 6, 1985, Old Westbury, NY.

Taylor, Anita Lillian. June 14, 2011, Allegany Indian Reservation.

Thompson, Jacob. Apr. 15, 1972, May 6, 1976, New Paltz, NY.

Walsh, Daniel. Mar. 13, 1986, Albany, NY.

Watt, Merle, Sr. Feb. 1, 2012, Allegany Indian Reservation.

White, Lincoln. July 1, 1982, Washington, DC.

Whiteing, Jeanne. Feb. 1, 2012, Allegany Indian Reservation.

B. Conducted by Others

Porter, Robert Odawi. Interviewed by Liz Benjamin. *Capital Tonight*, YNN, Aug. 15, 2012.

———. Interviewed by Fred Dicker. *Capital Tonight*, YNN, Jan. 5, 2012.

COURT CASES

Barry E. Snyder, Sr. Doing Business as the Seneca Hawk v. James W. Wetzler [New York State Commissioner of Taxation], 193 A.D.2d 329, 603 N.Y.S. 910 (1993).

California v. Cabazon Band of Mission Indians, 480 U.S. 202 (1987).

Cayuga Indian Nation v. Pataki, 413 F.3d 266 (2d. Circ. 2005).

Cayuga Nation of New York and Seneca-Cayuga Tribe of Oklahoma and United States of America as Plaintiff-Intervenor, 165 F. Supp. 266 (N.D.N.Y., 2001).

Cherokee Nation v. Georgia, 30 U.S. 1 (1831).

Cherokee Tobacco, 78 U.S. 616 (1871).

City of Sherrill v. Oneida Indian Nation, 125 S.Ct. 1478 (2005).

County of Oneida, et al. v. Oneida Indian Nation of New York, 414 U.S. 226 (1985).

Deere, et al. v. St. Lawrence River Power Co., et al., 22 F.2d 851 (1927).

Ex Parte Green, 123 F.2d 862 (1941).

Gregory T. Banner, et al. and the Salamanca Coalition of United Taxpayers v. United States, 44 Fed. Cl. 568 (1999); 238 F.3d 1348 (Ct. App., Fd. Circ., Jan. 29, 2001).

Herzog Bros. Trucking v. [New York State] Tax Commissioner, 69 N.Y. 2d 536 (1987), 487 U.S. 1212 (1988), 72 N.Y. 2d 720 (1988).

In Re New York Indians, 72 U.S. 761 (1866).

Kennedy v. Becker, 241 U.S. 566 (1916).

Lonewolf v. Hitchcock, 187 U.S. 553 (1903).

New York v. Seneca Nation of Indians, 528 U.S. 1073 (2000).

New York Indians v. United States, 40 Ct. Cl. 448 (1905).

New York State v. Seneca Nation of Indians, 528 U.S. 1073 (2000).

[New York State] Department of Taxation and Finance, et al. v. Milhelm Attea and Bros., Inc., et al., 512 U.S. 61 (1994).

Oklahoma Tax Commission v. Citizen Band of Potawatomi Indian Tribe, 498 U.S. 505 (1991).

Oneida Indian Nation of New York v. County of Oneida, et al., 414 U.S. 661 (1974).

People v. Redeye, 358 N.Y. 2d 289 (1974).

Seminole Tribe of Florida v. Butterworth, 658 F.2d 310 (5th Cir. Ct. App., 1981).

Seneca Nation v. Christy, 2 N.Y.S. 546 (Sup. Ct., 1888), affirmed 27 N.E. 275 (N.Y., 1891), appeal dismissed 162 U.S. 208 (1896).

Seneca Nation v. William M. Brucker, et al., 338 F.2d 55 (2d Circ. 1964); 380 U.S. 952 (1965).

Seneca Nation of Indians v. New York, 26 F.Supp. 2d 555 (W.D.N.Y., 1998).

Seneca Nation of Indians v. State of New York, cv-1971-528 (July 24, 1975).

Seneca Nation of Indians v. United States, 12 Ind. Cl. Comm. 552 (1963).

Seneca Nation of Indians v. United States, 39 Ind. Cl. Comm. 355 (1977).

Seneca Nation of Indians v. United States, Tonawanda Seneca Indians v. United States, 20 Ind. Cl. Comm. 177 (1968).

Seneca Nation of Indians v. Wilbur M. Brucker, et al., 360 U.S. 909 (1959); 262 F.2d 27 (1958); 162 F.Supp. 580 (1958).

Seneca Nation of Indians and Tonawanda Band of Senecas (and the United States plaintiff-intervenor) v. State of New York, New York State Thruway, et al., 206 F.Supp. 2d 448 (W.D.N.Y., 2002).

Seneca Nation of Indians and United States of America v. New York, 178 F.3d 959 (2d Circ., 1999).

Seneca Nation of Indians and United States as Plaintiff-Intervenor v. New York, 178 F.3d 95 (2d circ., 1999).

Six Nations v. United States, 173 Ct. Cl. 917 (1965).

Six Nations, et al. v. United States, 12 Ind. Cl. Comm. 86 (1968).

United States v. Cattaraugus County, 67 F.Supp. 294 (W.D.N.Y., 1946); 71 F.Supp. 413 (W.D.N.Y.).

United States v. Elm, 25 Fed. Cas. 1006 (1877).

United States v. Forness, et al. (Salamanca Trust Co., et al., defendant-intervenor), 37 F. Supp. 337 (Feb. 14, 1941); 125 Fed. Rep., 2d Series, 928 (1942).

United States ex. rel. John D. Lynn v. Frederick W. Hamilton, et al., 233 F.685 (W.D.N.Y., 1915).

Winter v. United States, 207 U.S. 564 (1908).

Woodin v. Seeley, 252 N.Y.S. 818 (1931).

FEDERAL, STATE, AND SENECA NATION
GOVERNMENT DOCUMENTS AND PUBLICATIONS

American Indian Policy Review Commission. *Final Report Submitted to Congress, May 17, 1977.* 2 vols. Washington, DC: US Government Printing Office, 1977.

————. Task Force One. *Report on Trust Responsibilities and the Federal–Indian Trust Relationship.* Washington, DC: US Government Printing Office, 1976.

————. Task Force Five. *Report on Indian Education.* Washington, DC: US Government Printing Office, 1976.

————. Task Force Six. *Report on Indian Health.* 2 vols. Washington, DC: US Government Printing Office, 1977.

Austin, Alberta, comp. *Ne´ Ho Niyo´ Dë: Nö´—That's What It Was Like.* 2 vols. Lackawanna, NY: Rebco Enterprises for the Seneca Education Department, 1986 and 1989.

Bardeau, Phyllis E. W. *Definitive Seneca: It's in the Word.* Edited by Jaré Cardinal. Salamanca, NY: Seneca-Iroquois National Museum, 2011.

Cohen, Felix S. *Handbook of Federal Indian Law.* Washington, DC: US Department of the Interior, 1942; reprint, Albuquerque: Univ. of New Mexico Press, 1971.

Donaldson, Thomas, comp. *The Six Nations of New York.* Extra Census Bulletin of the 11th Census of the United States for the Year 1890. Washington, DC: US Census Printing Office, 1892.

Federal Energy Regulatory Commission. *In the Matter of Scoping Document for Kinzua Pumped Storage Project (P-13880-000).* Washington, DC: Federal Regulatory Commission, 2011.

George-Shongo, David, Jr. *Onö´dowa´ga:´ Gano´kyëdoh Nogeh´oweh (Seneca Nation of Indians): The 160 Years of Republican Government.* Allegany Indian Reservation: Seneca Nation of Indians, Archives Department, 2009.

Hoover Commission. *Report on Organization of the Executive Branch of the Government.* New York: n.p., 1949.

Kappler, Charles J., comp. *Indian Affairs: Laws and Treaties.* 5 vols. Washington, DC: US Government Printing Office, 1904–41. Volume 2 has been reprinted as *Indian Treaties, 1778–1883.* New York: Interland, 1972.

Neilan Engineers and Development Counselors International. *Iroquoia: A Practical Action Program for the Recreation–Tourist Development of the Allegany Reservation.* Washington, DC: US Department of Commerce, 1969.

New York State Board of Land Commissioners. *Proceedings of the Commissioners for 1924.* Albany: J. B. Lyon, 1924.

New York State Department of Public Works. *Annual Reports, 1950–1966.* Albany: New York State, 1950–66.

New York State Department of Transportation. *Annual Reports, 1967–2010.* Albany: New York State, 1967–2010.

New York State Governor's Office. *Public Papers of Hugh L. Carey.* 8 vols. New York: New York State, 1982–96.

———. *Public Papers of Malcolm Wilson.* Albany: New York State, 1977.

———. *Public Papers of Nelson A. Rockefeller.* 13 vols. Albany: New York State, 1959–72.

———. *Public Papers of Thomas E. Dewey.* 12 vols. Albany: New York State, 1944–57.

New York State Interdepartmental Committee on Indian Affairs. *Annual Reports, 1959–1974.* Albany: New York State, 1959–74.

New York State Legislature. *Assembly Journal.*

———. *Joint Public Hearing on Indian Land Claim, Casino Gaming, and Tax Agreements.* Syracuse, Mar. 11, 2005. Albany: New York State, 2005.

———. *Report Relative to Indian Affairs, March 4, 1819.* Assembly Doc. no. 90. Albany: New York State, 1819.

———. *Senate Journal.*

———. Joint Legislative Committee on Indian Affairs. *Annual Reports, 1944–1959.* Albany: New York State, 1944–59.

———. Joint Legislative Committee on Indian Affairs. *Minutes of Public Hearing . . . , November 9, 1963.* Albany: New York State, 1963.

———. Joint Legislative Committee on Indians Affairs. *Public Hearing at Akron, New York, Nov. 17, 1961.* Albany: New York State, 1961.

New York State Legislature, Assembly. *Document No. 168, Feb. 8, 1836.* Albany: New York State, 1836.

———. *Report of the Indian Commission to Investigate the Status of the American Indian Residing in the State of New York . . . March 17, 1922.* Albany: New York State, 1922. Transcript in the New York State Library.

———. *Report of the Special Committee to Investigate the Indian Problem of the State of New York. Appointed by the Assembly of 1888.* 2 vols. Assembly Doc. no. 51. Albany: Troy Press, 1889.

———. Standing Committee on Governmental Operations. Subcommittee on Indian Affairs. *Public Hearings, 1970–1971.* Albany: New York State, 1970–71.

———. Standing Committee on Governmental Operations, Subcommittee on Indian Affairs. *Report.* Albany: New York State, 1971.

———. Subcommittee on Indian Affairs. *Public Hearings In Re: State–Indian Relations. Buffalo, May 13, 1993, and Albany, May 25, 1993.* Albany: New York State, 1993. Transcript in the New York State Library.

New York State Legislature, Senate. Standing Committee on Corporations, Authorities, and Commissions. *In the Matter of a Public Hearing to Consider the*

Taxation of Motor Fuels and Cigarettes Sold to Non–Native Americans on Indian Reservations. May 27, 1992. Albany: New York State, 1992. Transcript on file in the New York State Library.

———. Standing Committee on Governmental Operations. Subcommittee on Indian Affairs. *Hearings: Oct. 14, 15, 1970.* Albany: New York State, 1970.

———. Subcommittee on Indian Affairs. *Hearings on State–Indian Relations. Albany, May 25, 1993.* Albany: New York State, 1993. Transcript in the New York State Library.

———. Subcommittee on Indian Affairs. *Hearings on State–Indian Relations. Buffalo and Erie County Public Library, May 13, 1993.* Albany: New York State, 1993. Transcript in the New York State Library.

New York State Office of Indian Affairs. *1991/1992 Annual Report.* Albany: New York State, 1992.

New York State Power Authority. *Annual Reports, 1931–2010.* New York: New York State Power Authority, 1931–2010.

———. *Report, July 18, 1955: Land Acquisition on the American Side for the St. Lawrence Seaway Project.* New York: New York State Power Authority, 1955.

———. *Robert Moses' Open Letter to the Tuscarora Indian Nation, Feb. 11, 1958.* New York: New York Power Authority, 1958.

New York State Racing and Wagering Board. *Oversight of Indian Gaming Activities.* Report 2005-S-45. Albany: New York State, 2005.

New York State Task Force on Casino Gambling. *Report to the Governor, August 30, 1996.* Albany: New York State, 1996.

New York State Thruway Authority. *Annual Report, 1954.* Albany: New York State, 1954.

Nixon, Richard M. *Public Papers of President Richard Nixon, 1970.* Washington, DC: US Government Printing Office, 1970.

O'Callaghan, Edmund B., and Berthold Fernow, eds. *Documents Relative to the Colonial History of the State of New York.* 14 vols. Albany: Weed, Parsons, 1853–57.

Padavan, Frank. *All Gambling All the Time: Turning the Empire State into the Gambling State.* Albany: New York State Legislature, Senate, 2004.

———. *The Dice Are Rolling: Gambling with New York State's Future, January 6, 1997.* Albany: New York State Legislature, Senate, 1997.

———. *Rolling the Dice: Why Casino Gambling Is a Bad Bet for New York State: A Legislative Report.* Parts I and II. Albany: New York State Legislature, Senate, 1994.

President's Commission on Indian Reservation Economies. *Report and Recommendations to the President of the United States*. Washington, DC: US Government Printing Office, 1984.

Reagan, Ronald. *Public Papers of the Presidents: Ronald Reagan*. Washington, DC: US Government Printing Office, 1983.

Regents of the University of the State of New York. *Position Paper No. 22: Native American Education*. Albany: New York State Education Department, 1975.

Seneca Nation of Indians (SNI). *Annual Report for 2006*. Allegany Indian Reservation: SNI, 2006.

———. *Annual Report for 2008*. Allegany Indian Reservation: SNI, 2008.

———. *Seneca Nation of Indians Health Department, 1976–2009*. Allegany Indian Reservation: SNI, 2009.

Taylor, Jonathan B. *The Seneca Nation Economy: Its Foundations, Size, and Impact on New York State and the Western New York Region*. Sarasota, FL: Taylor Policy Group for the Seneca Nation of Indians, 2010.

Townsend, David R., Jr., with the assistance of Ed Byrnes. *Claims Casino: A Report on State–Indian Relations in New York State, August, 1995*. Albany; New York State Legislature, Assembly, 1995.

US Bureau of the Census. *Ninth Census of the United States, 1870*. Washington, DC: US Census Printing Office, 1872.

———. *Seventeenth Census of the United States*. Washington, DC: US Census Printing Office, 1950.

———. *Twenty-third Census of the United States*. Washington, DC: US Census Printing Office, 2010.

US Congress. *Congressional Record*, 1945–2010.

US Congress, House of Representatives. *Conference Report No. 1821: Seneca Indian Nation*. Washington, DC: US Government Printing Office, 1964.

———. *Hearings on H.R. 166: Investigate Indian Affairs, February 2, 1944*. 78th Cong., 2d sess., part 2. Washington, DC: US Government Printing Office, 1944.

———. *House Document No. 300: Hearings: Allegheny River, N.Y. and Pennsylvania, Allegheny Reservoir*. 76th Cong., 1st sess. Washington, DC: US Government Printing Office, 1939.

———. Committee on Appropriations, Subcommittee on Public Works Appropriations. *Hearings on H.R. 7509: Public Works Appropriations for 1958*. 86th Cong., 1st sess. Washington, DC: US Government Printing Office, 1957.

———. Committee on Appropriations, Subcommittee on Public Works Appropriations. *Hearings on H.R. 8090: Public Works Appropriations for 1958*. March

28–May 10, 1957. 2 vols. 85th Cong., 1st sess. Washington, DC: US Government Printing Office, 1957.

———. Committee on Foreign Affairs. *Hearings on H.R. 2498, 11756, 16542, 16547, and 16587: Diversion of Water from the Niagara River, July 15, 1914.* 63rd Cong., 2d sess. Washington, DC: US Government Printing Office, 1914.

———. Committee on Indian Affairs. *Hearings on H.R. 1198 and 1341: Creation of the Indian Claims Commission.* 79th Cong., 1st sess. Washington, DC: US Government Printing Office, 1945.

———. Committee on Interior and Insular Affairs. *Hearings on H.R. 5367: To Provide for the Renegotiation of Certain Leases of the Seneca Nation, September 13, 1990.* 101st Cong., 2d sess. Washington, DC: US Government Printing Office, 1990.

———. Committee on Interior and Insular Affairs. *Hearings on H.R. 6631: Settlement of the Cayuga Indian Land Claims in the State of New York, March 3, 1980.* 96th Cong., 2d sess. Washington, DC: US Government Printing Office, 1980.

———. Committee on Interior and Insular Affairs. *Information on Removal of Restrictions on American Indians.* 88th Cong., 2d sess. Washington, DC: US Government Printing Office, 1964.

———. Committee on Interior and Insular Affairs. *Proceedings, July 27, 1976: Unveiling of a Portrait of the Honorable James A. Haley.* Washington, DC: US Government Printing Office, 1976.

———. Committee on Interior and Insular Affairs. *Report No. 1128: Authorizing Acquisition of and Payment for Flowage Easement and Rights-of-Way within Allegany Indian Reservation. . . .* Washington, DC: US Government Printing Office, 1964.

———. Committee on Interior and Insular Affairs, Subcommittee on Indian Affairs. *Hearings on H.R. 1794, H.R. 3343, and H.R. 7354: Kinzua Dam (Seneca Indian Relocation), May 18–December 10, 1963.* 88th Cong., 1st sess. Washington, DC: US Government Printing Office, 1964.

US Congress, House of Representatives and Senate. *Joint Hearings before the Subcommittee of the Committees on Interior and Insular Affairs . . . Pursuant to H. Con. Res. 108: Termination of Federal Supervision over Certain Tribes of Indians.* 83rd Cong., 1st sess. Washington, DC: US Government Printing Office, 1954.

———. *Joint Hearings before the Subcommittee of the Committees on Interior and Insular Affairs: Termination of Federal Supervision over Certain Tribes of Indians.* Parts 1–12. 83rd Cong., 2d sess. Washington, DC: US Government Printing Office, 1954.

US Congress, Senate. *Indian Education: A National Tragedy—a National Challenge. Senate Report No. 501: Report of the Special Subcommittee on Indian Education, Committee on Labor and Public Welfare.* 91st Cong., 1st sess. Washington, DC: US Government Printing Office, 1969.

———. Committee on Appropriations, Subcommittee on Public Works Appropriations. *Hearings on H.R. 12326: Public Works Appropriations for 1961. February 16–June 16, 1960.* 2 vols. 86th Cong., 2d sess. Washington, DC: US Government Printing Office, 1960.

———. Committee on Appropriations, Subcommittee on Public Works. *Hearings on Public Works Appropriations for 1958.* 85th Cong., 1st sess. Washington, DC: US Government Printing Office, 1957.

———. Committee on Government Operations. *Hearings before Permanent Subcommittee on Investigations. Hearings: Indian Health Care, September 16, 1974.* 93rd Cong., 2d sess. Washington, DC: US Government Printing Office, 1974.

———. Committee on Indian Affairs. *Survey of Conditions of Indian Affairs in the United States.* Partial Report No. 310, 78-1. Serial 10756. Washington, DC: US Government Printing Office, 1943.

———. Committee on Interior and Insular Affairs. *Report No. 969: Authorizing Acquisition and Payment for Flowage Easement and Rights-of-Way over Lands within Allegany Indian Reservation.* . . . Washington, DC: US Government Printing Office, 1964.

———. Committee on Interior and Insular Affairs. *Report No. 1139: Commuting Annuities, Seneca and Six Nations of New York.* Washington, DC: US Government Printing Office, 1948.

———. Committee on Interior and Insular Affairs. *Report No. 1489: Conferring Jurisdiction on Courts of New York over Offenses Committed by Indians.* Washington, DC: US Government Printing Office, 1948.

———. Committee on Interior and Insular Affairs. *Report No. 1836: Conferring Jurisdiction on Courts of New York with Respect to Civil Actions between Indians or to Which Indians Are Parties.* Washington, DC: US Government Printing Office, 1950.

———. Committee on Interior and Insular Affairs, Subcommittee on Indian Affairs. *Hearings on S. 1017 and Related Bills: Indian Self-Determination and Education Program.* Washington, DC: US Government Printing Office, 1973.

———. Committee on Interior and Insular Affairs, Subcommittee on Interior and Insular Affairs. *Hearings on S. 1683, S. 1686, S. 1687: New York Indians, Mar. 9–11, 1948.* Washington, DC: US Government Printing Office, 1948.

———. Committee on Interior and Insular Affairs, Subcommittee on Indian Affairs. *Hearings on S. 1836 and H.R. 1794: Kinzua Dam (Seneca Indian Relocation), March 2, 1964*. 88th Cong., 2d sess. Washington, DC: US Government Printing Office, 1964.

———. Committee on the Post Office and Civil Service. *Hearings on S. Res. 41: Officers and Employees of the Federal Government*. 80th Cong., 1st sess. Washington, DC: US Government Printing Office, 1947.

———. Select Committee on Indian Affairs. *Hearings on S. 2084: Ancient Indian Land Claims*. 97th Cong., 2d sess. Washington, DC: US Government Printing Office, 1982.

———. Select Committee on Indian Affairs. *Hearings on S. 2895: To Provide for the Renegotiation of Certain Leases of the Seneca Nation, September 18, 1990*. 101st Cong., 2d sess. Washington, DC: US Government Printing Office, 1990.

———. Select Committee on Indian Affairs. *Report No. 101-511: Providing for the Renegotiation of Certain Leases of the Seneca Nation and for Other Purposes to Accompany S. 2895, October 8, 1990*. 101st Cong., 2d sess. Washington, DC: US Government Printing Office, 1990.

US Department of Health, Education, and Welfare. Indian Health Service. *The Indian Health Program*. Washington, DC: US Government Printing Office, 1978.

———. Indian Health Service. *Indian Health Program, 1955–1980*. Washington, DC: US Government Printing Office, 1980.

US Department of Health and Human Services. "Substance Use and Substance Use Disorders among American Indians and Alaska Natives." In *NSDUH Report: National Survey on Drug Use and Health* (pamphlet). Washington, DC: US Department of Health and Human Services, Office of Applied Studies, Substance Abuse and Mental Health Services Administration, 2007.

US Department of the Interior. *Indian Health: A Problem and a Challenge*. Washington, DC: US Government Printing Office, 1955.

———. Bureau of Indian Affairs. *BIA Analysis on the Brill Engineering Corporation Proposed Recreation and Industrial Development Plan, Allegany Indian Reservation*. Washington, DC: US Government Printing Office, 1963. Archived at the Seneca-Iroquois National Museum.

———. Bureau of Indian Affairs. *Seneca Indians Who Will Be Affected by the Kinzua Dam Reservoir*. Billings, MT: Missouri River Basin Investigations Project, 1963.

———. Bureau of Reclamation. *Project Data*. Washington, DC: US Government Printing Office, 1961.

———. Bureau of Reclamation. *The Reclamation Program, 1953–1959*. Washington, DC: US Government Printing Office, 1959.

———. Bureau of Reclamation. *Reclamation Project Data—Supplement*. Washington, DC: US Government Printing Office, 1966.

———. Secretary of the Interior. *Annual Reports, 1945–2010*. Washington, DC: US Government Printing Office, 1945–2010.

———. Task Force on Indian Affairs. *Report to the Secretary of the Interior, 1961*. 2 vols. Washington, DC: US Government Printing Office, 1961.

———. Task Force on Indian Economic Development. *Report of the Task Force on Indian Economic Development*. Washington, DC: US Government Printing Office, 1986.

US Indian Claims Commission. *Decisions of the Indian Claims Commission*. Microfiche ed. New York: Clearwater, 1973–78.

———. *Final Report. August 13, 1946–September 30, 1978*. Washington, DC: US Government Printing Office, 1979.

US National Commission on Libraries and Information Science. *Pathways to Excellence: A Report on Improving Library and Information Services for Native American Peoples*. Washington, DC: US National Commission on Libraries and Information Science, 1992.

Whitford, Noble E. *History of the Canal System of the State of New York*. 2 vols. Albany: Brandon Printing for the New York State Engineer and Surveyor Office, 1906.

BOOKS, BOOKLETS, PAMPHLETS, REPORTS

Abler, Thomas S., ed. *Chainbreakers: The Revolutionary War Memoirs of Governor Blacksnake as Told to Benjamin Williams*. Lincoln: Univ. of Nebraska Press, 1989.

———. *Cornplanter: Chief Warrior of the Allegany Senecas*. Syracuse, NY: Syracuse Univ. Press, 2007.

Abourezk, James G. *Advise and Dissent: Memoirs of South Dakota and the U.S. Senate*. Chicago: Lawrence Hill Books, 1989.

Abrams, George H. J. *The Seneca People*. Phoenix: Indian Tribal Series, 1976.

———. *Tribal Museums in America*. Nashville: American Association of State and Local History, 2002.

Aguilar, George W., Sr. *When the Rivers Ran Wild: Indian Traditions on the Mid-Columbia and the Warm Springs Reservation*. Seattle: Univ. of Washington Press, 2005.

Ambler, Marjane. *Breaking the Iron Bonds: Indian Control of Energy Development*. Lawrence: Univ. Press of Kansas, 1990.

American Indian Chicago Conference. *The Declaration of Indian Purpose: The Voice of the American Indian*. Chicago: American Indian Chicago Conference, 1961.

Anderson, Clinton P. *Outsider in the Senate: Senator Clinton P. Anderson's Memoir*. New York: World, 1970.

Atkinson, Brooks. *Tuesdays and Fridays*. New York: Random House, 1963.

Ballon, Hilary, and Kenneth T. Jackson, eds. *Robert Moses and the Modern City: The Transformation of New York*. New York: Norton, 2007.

Barber, Katrine. *Death of Celilo Falls*. Seattle: Univ. of Washington Press, 2005.

Barbour, Hugh, Christopher Densmore, Elizabeth Moger, Nancy Sorel, Alson Van Wagner, and Arthur J. Worrell, eds. *Quaker Crosscurrents: Three Hundred Years of Friends in the New York Yearly Meetings*. Syracuse, NY: Syracuse Univ. Press, 1995.

Barsh, Russel L., and James Youngblood Henderson. *The Road: Indian Tribes and Political Liberty*. Berkeley: Univ. of California Press, 1980.

Barton, Lois. *A Quaker Promise Kept: Philadelphia Friends' Work with the Allegany Seneca, 1795–1960*. Eugene, Ore.: Spencer Butte Press, 1990.

Basso, Keith H. *Wisdom Sits in Places: Landscape and Language among the Western Apache*. Albuquerque: Univ. of New Mexico Press, 1996.

Belknap, Jeremy. *Journal of a Tour from Boston to Oneida, June 1796*. Edited by George Dexter. Cambridge, MA: John Wilson, 1882.

Bilharz, Joy. *The Allegany Senecas and Kinzua Dam: Forced Relocation through Two Generations*. Lincoln: Univ. of Nebraska Press, 1998.

Bingham, Robert W., ed. *Niagara Frontier Miscellany*. Buffalo Historical Society Publications no. 34. Buffalo: Buffalo Historical Society, 1947.

Brandão, Jose Antonio. *"Your Fyre Shall Burn No More": Iroquois Policy toward New France and Its Native Allies to 1701*. Lincoln: Univ. of Nebraska Press, 1997.

Campbell, William W., ed. *The Life and Writings of DeWitt Clinton*. New York: Baker and Scribner, 1949.

Caro, Robert. *The Power Broker: Robert Moses and the Fall of New York*. New York: Random House, 1974.

Castile, George Pierre. *Taking Charge: Native American Self-Determination and Federal Indian Policy, 1975–1993*. Tucson: Univ. of Arizona Press, 2006.

———. *To Show Heart: Native American Self-Determination and Federal Indian Policy, 1960–1975*. Tucson: Univ. of Arizona Press, 1998.

Castile, George Pierre, and Robert Bee, eds. *State and Reservation: New Perspectives on Federal Indian Policy*. Tucson: Univ. of Arizona Press, 1992.

Caswell, Harriet S. *Our Life among the Iroquois Indians*. 1892. With an introduction by Joy Bilharz. Paperback reprint. Lincoln: Univ. of Nebraska Press, 2007.

Cattelino, Jessica R. *High Stakes: Florida Seminole Gaming and Sovereignty*. Durham, NC: Duke Univ. Press, 2008.

Chafe, Wallace L. *Handbook of the Seneca Language*. Albany: New York State Museum and Science Service, 1963.

Clarkin, Thomas. *Federal Indian Policy in the Kennedy and Johnson Administrations, 1961–1969*. Albuquerque: Univ. of New Mexico Press, 2001.

Cobb, Daniel. *Native Activism in Cold War America: The Struggle for Sovereignty*. Lawrence: Univ. Press of Kansas, 2008.

Congdon, Charles E. *Allegany Oxbow: A History of Allegany State Park and the Allegany Reserve of the Seneca Nation*. Little Valley, NY: Straight, 1967.

Cornplanter, Jesse. *Legends of the Longhouse*. New York: Lippincott, 1938.

Cowger, Thomas W. *The National Congress of American Indians: The Founding Years*. Lincoln: Univ. of Nebraska Press, 1999.

Curtin, Jeremiah. *Seneca Indian Myths*. 1922. Paperback reprint. New York: Dover, 2001.

Delafield, Joseph. *The Unfortified Boundary*. Edited by Robert N. MacElroy and Thomas Riggs. New York: privately printed, 1943.

Deloria, Vine, Jr., and Clifford M. Lytle. *American Indians, American Justice*. Austin: Univ. of Texas Press, 1983.

———. *The Nations Within: The Past and Future of American Indian Sovereignty*. New York: Pantheon, 1984.

Deloria, Vine, Jr., and David E. Wilkins. *Tribes, Treaties, and Constitutional Tribulations*. Austin: Univ. of Texas Press, 1999.

Densmore, Christopher. *Red Jacket: Iroquois Diplomat and Orator*. Syracuse, NY: Syracuse Univ. Press, 1999.

Eisenstadt, Peter. *Rochdale Village: Robert Moses, 6000 Families, and New York's Great Experiment in Integrated Housing*. Ithaca, NY: Cornell Univ. Press, 2010.

Engelbrecht, William. *Iroquoia: The Development of a Native World*. Syracuse, NY: Syracuse Univ. Press, 2003.

Fein, Michael R. *Paving the Way: New York Road Building and the American State, 1880–1956*. Lawrence: Univ. Press of Kansas, 2008.

Fenton, William N. *The Great Law and the Longhouse: A Political History of the Iroquois Confederacy*. Norman: Univ. of Oklahoma Press, 1998.

———. *The Iroquois Eagle Dance: An Offshoot of the Calumet Dance*. 1953. Paperback reprint. Syracuse, NY: Syracuse Univ. Press, 1991.

———. *The Little Water Society of the Senecas*. Norman: Univ. of Oklahoma Press, 2002.

————, ed. *Symposium on Local Diversity in Iroquois Culture.* Bureau of American Ethnology Bulletin no. 149. Washington, DC: US Government Printing Office, 1951.

Fenton, William N., and John Gullick, eds. *Symposium on Cherokee and Iroquois Culture.* Bureau of American Ethnology Bulletin no. 180. Washington, DC: Bureau of American Ethnology, 1961.

Ferejohn, John. *Pork Barrel Politics: Rivers and Harbors Legislation, 1947–1968.* Palo Alto, CA: Stanford Univ. Press, 1974.

Fisher, Andrew H. *Shadow Tribe: The Making of Columbia River Indian Identity.* Seattle: Univ. of Washington Press, 2010.

Fixico, Donald L. *The American Indian Mind in a Linear World: American Indian Studies and Traditional Knowledge.* New York: Routledge, 2003.

————. *American Indians in a Modern World.* Lanham, MD: Alta Mira Press, 2008.

————. *The Invasion of Indian Country in the Twentieth Century: American Capitalism and Tribal Natural Resources.* Niwot: Univ. Press of Colorado, 1998.

————. *Rethinking American Indian History.* Albuquerque: Univ. of New Mexico Press, 1997.

————. *Termination and Relocation: Federal Indian Policy, 1945–1960.* Albuquerque: Univ. of New Mexico Press, 1986.

Fortunate Eagle [Nordwall, Adam]. *Heart of the Rock.* Norman: Univ. of Oklahoma Press, 2004.

Ganter, Granville, ed. *The Collected Speeches of Sagoyewatha, or Red Jacket.* Syracuse, NY: Syracuse Univ. Press, 2006.

Garment, Leonard. *Crazy Rhythm: My Journey from Brooklyn, Jazz, and Wall Street to Nixon's White House, Watergate, and Beyond.* New York: Times Books, 1997.

George-Kanentiio, Douglas M. *The Iroquois on Fire.* Lincoln: Univ. of Nebraska Press, 2008.

Gordon-McCutchan, R. C. *The Taos Indians and the Battle for Blue Lake.* Santa Fe: Red Crane Books, 1995.

Graymont, Barbara. *The Iroquois in the American Revolution.* Syracuse, NY: Syracuse Univ. Press, 1972.

Grumet, Robert S., ed. *Journey on the Forbidden Path: Chronicles of a Diplomatic Mission to the Allegheny Country, March–September, 1760.* Philadelphia: American Philosophical Society, 1999.

Hale, Horatio E. *The Iroquois Book of Rites.* 2 vols. Philadelphia: D. G. Brinton, 1883.

Harmon, Alexandra. *Rich Indians: Native People and the Problem of Wealth in American History.* Chapel Hill: Univ. of North Carolina Press, 2010.

Harrington, Michael. *The Other America: Poverty in the United States*. New York: Macmillan, 1962.

Harvard University Project on American Indian Economic Development. *The State of the Native Nations: Conditions under United States Policies of Self-Determination*. New York: Oxford Univ. Press, 2008.

Hauptman, Laurence M. *Conspiracy of Interests: Iroquois Dispossession and the Rise of New York State*. Syracuse, NY: Syracuse Univ. Press, 1999.

———. *Formulating American Indian Policy in New York State, 1970–1986*. Albany: State Univ. of New York Press, 1988.

———. *The Historical Background to the Present Day Seneca Nation–Salamanca Lease Controversy: The First Hundred Years*. Rockefeller Institute of Government Working Paper no. 20. Albany: Rockefeller Institute, 1985. Reprinted in *Iroquois Land Claims*, edited by Christopher Vecsey and William A. Starna, 101–22. Syracuse, NY: Syracuse Univ. Press, 1988.

———. *The Iroquois and the Civil War: From Battlefield to Reservation*. Syracuse, NY: Syracuse Univ. Press, 1993.

———. *The Iroquois and the New Deal*. Syracuse, NY: Syracuse Univ. Press, 1981.

———. *The Iroquois Struggle for Survival: World War II to Red Power*. Syracuse, NY: Syracuse Univ. Press, 1986.

———. *Seven Generations of Iroquois Leadership: The Six Nations since 1800*. Syracuse, NY: Syracuse Univ. Press, 2008.

———. *The Tonawanda Senecas' Heroic Battle against Removal: Conservative Activist Indians*. Albany: State Univ. of New York Press, 2011.

Hauptman, Laurence M., and James Wherry, eds. *The Pequots: The Fall and Rise of an American Indian Nation*. Norman: Univ. of Oklahoma Press, 1990.

Hewitt, J. N. B. *Iroquoian Cosmology*. Part I. Bureau of American Ethnology, 21st Annual Report. Washington, DC: US Government Printing Office, 1899–1900.

———. *Iroquoian Cosmology*. Part II. Bureau of American Ethnology, 21st Annual Report. Washington, DC: Bureau of American Ethnology, 1928.

Hickel, Walter. *Who Owns America?* Englewood Cliffs, NJ: Prentice-Hall, 1971.

Hoover, William N. *Kinzua: From Cornplanter to the Corps*. New York: Universe, 2004.

Hosmer, Brian, ed. *Native Americans and the Legacy of Harry S. Truman*. Kirksvlle, MO: Truman State Univ. Press, 2010.

Hosmer, Brian, and Colleen O'Neill, eds. *Native Pathways: American Indian Culture and Economic Development in the Twentieth Century*. Boulder: Univ. Press of Colorado, 2004.

Jennings, Francis, William N. Fenton, and Mary Druke Becker, eds. *The History and Culture of Iroquois Diplomacy: An Interdisciplinary Guide to the Treaties of the Six Nations and Their League.* Syracuse, NY: Syracuse Univ. Press, 1985.

John, Randy. *The Social Integration of an Elderly Native American Population.* New York: Garland, 1995.

Johnson, Troy R., Joanne Nagel, and Duane Champagne, eds. *American Indian Activism: Alcatraz to the Longest Walk.* Urbana: Univ. of Illinois Press, 1997.

Jordan, Kurt. *The Seneca Restoration, 1715–1754: An Iroquois Local Political Economy.* Gainesville: Univ. Press of Florida, 2008.

Josephy, Alvin M., Jr. *Now That the Buffalo's Gone: A Study of Today's American Indians.* Norman: Univ. of Oklahoma Press, 1982.

————. *Red Power: The American Indians' Fight for Freedom.* New York: McGraw-Hill, 1971.

Kersey, Harry A., Jr. *An Assumption of Sovereignty: Social and Political Transformation among the Florida Seminoles, 1953–1979.* Lincoln: Univ. of Nebraska Press, 2007.

Kersey, Harry A., Jr., and Julian M. Pleasants, eds. *Seminole Voices: Reflections on Their Changing Society, 1970–2000.* Lincoln: Univ. of Nebraska Press, 2010.

Kvasnicka, Robert, and Herman Viola, eds. *The Commissioners of Indian Affairs, 1824–1977.* Lincoln: Univ. of Nebraska Press, 1979.

Lawson, Michael. *Dammed Indians: The Pick-Sloan Plan and the Missouri River Sioux, 1944–1980.* Norman: Univ. of Oklahoma Press, 1982.

————. *Dammed Indians Revisited: The Continuing History of the Pick-Sloan Plan and the Missouri River Sioux.* Pierre: South Dakota State Historical Society, 2010.

Lazarus, Edward. *Black Hills, White Justice: The Sioux Nation versus the United States, 1775 to the Present.* New York: HarperCollins, 1991.

Light, Steven A., and Kathryn R. L. Rand. *Indian Gaming and Tribal Sovereignty.* Lawrence: Univ. Press of Kansas, 2005.

Lilienthal, David E. *TVA: Democracy on the March.* New York: Harper and Row, 1953.

Lubove, Roy. *Twentieth Century Pittsburgh: Government, Business, and Environmental Change.* New York: New Viewpoints, 1969.

Maas, Arthur. *Muddy Waters.* Cambridge, MA: Harvard Univ. Press, 1951.

McCool, Daniel. *Command of the Waters: Iron Triangle, Federal Water Development, and Indian Water.* Berkeley: Univ. of California Press, 1987.

————. *Native Waters: Contemporary Indian Water Settlements and the Second Treaty Era.* Tucson: Univ. of Arizona Press, 2002.

McCraw, Thomas. *Morgan v. Lilienthal: A Feud within TVA*. Chicago: Loyola Univ. Press, 1970.

———. *TVA and the Power Fight, 1933–1939*. Philadelphia: Lippincott, 1971.

McCutcheon, Sean. *Electric Rivers: The Story of the James Bay Project*. Montreal: Black Rose Books, 1991.

McDonald, Michael J., and John Muldowny. *TVA and the Dispossessed: The Resettlement of Population in the Norris Dam Area*. Knoxville: Univ. of Tennessee Press, 1982.

McGeary, M. Nelson. *Pennsylvania Government in Action: Governor Leader's Administration*. Philadelphia: Univ. of Pennsylvania Press, 1982.

Metcalf, R. Warren. *Termination's Legacy: The Discarded Indians of Utah*. Lincoln: Univ. of Nebraska Press, 2002.

[Mohawk, John]. *Basic Call for Consciousness*. Rooseveltown, NY: Akwesasne Notes, 1978.

Momaday, N. Scott. *The Names: A Memoir*. Tucson: Univ. of Arizona Press, 1976.

Morgan, Arthur E. *The Community of the Future and the Future of Community*. Yellow Springs, OH: Community Service, 1957.

———. *Dams and Other Disasters: A Century of the Army Corps of Engineers in Civil Works*. Boston: Porter Sargent, 1971.

———. *The Making of TVA*. Buffalo: Prometheus Books, 1974.

Morgan, Lewis Henry. *League of the Ho-de-no-sau-nee or Iroquois*. 1851. Paperback reprint with an introduction by William N. Fenton. New York: Corinth Books, 1962.

Morse, Edward A., and Ernest P. Goss. *Governing Fortune: Casino Gambling in America*. Ann Arbor: Univ. of Michigan Press, 2007.

Moses, Robert. *Tuscarora Fiction and Fact: A Reply to the Author of "Memoirs of Hecate County" and His Reviewers*. New York: privately printed, 1960.

———. *Working for the People: Promise and Performance in Public Service*. New York: Harper, 1956.

O'Nan, Stewart. *The Circus Fire*. New York: Anchor Books/Random House, 2000.

Parker, Arthur C. *The Life of General Ely S. Parker, Last Sachem of the Iroquois and General Grant's Military Secretary*. Buffalo Historical Society Publications no. 23. Buffalo: Buffalo Historical Society, 1919.

———. *Parker on the Iroquois*. Edited by William N. Fenton. Syracuse, NY: Syracuse Univ. Press, 1968.

———. *Red Jacket*. 1952. Paperback reprint with an introduction by Thomas S. Abler. Lincoln: Univ. of Nebraska Press, 1998.

———. *Seneca Myths and Folk Tales*. 1923. Paperback reprint with an introduction by William N. Fenton. Lincoln: Univ. of Nebraska Press 1989.

Pasquaretta, Paul. *Gambling and Survival in Native North America*. Tucson: Univ. of Arizona Press, 2003.

Pevar, Stephen L. *The Rights of Indians and Tribes*. New York: New York Univ. Press, 2004.

Philadelphia Yearly Meeting of Friends. *The Kinzua Conference: A Practical Solution without Shame*. Philadelphia: Philadelphia Yearly Meeting of Friends, 1961.

Philp, Kenneth R. *Termination Revisited: American Indians on the Trail to Self-Determination, 1933–1953*. Lincoln: Univ. of Nebraska Press, 1999.

Porter, Robert Odawi, ed. *Sovereignty, Colonialism, and the Indigenous Nations*. Durham, NC: Carolina Academic, 2005.

Prucha, Francis Paul. *The Great Father: The United States Government and the American Indians*. 2 vols. Lincoln: Univ. of Nebraska Press, 1984.

Raitz, Karl B., Richard Ulack, and Thomas Leinbach. *Appalachia: A Regional Geography—Land, People, and Development*. Boulder, CO: Westview Press, 1984.

Rector, Chad S. *Federations: The Political Dynamics of Cooperation*. Ithaca, NY: Cornell Univ. Press, 2009.

Richter, Daniel K. *Native Americans' Pennsylvania*. University Park: Pennsylvania Historical Association, 2005.

———. *The Ordeal of the Longhouse: The Peoples of the Iroquois League in the Era of Colonization*. Chapel Hill: Univ. of North Carolina Press, 1992.

Rickard, Chief Clinton. *Fighting Tuscarora: The Autobiography of Chief Clinton Rickard*. Edited by Barbara Graymont. Syracuse, NY: Syracuse Univ. Press, 1973.

Rockefeller-MacArthur, Elizabeth. *American Indian Library Services in Perspective*. Jefferson, NC: McFarland, 1998.

Rose, Mark. *Interstate: Express Highway Politics, 1941–1956*. Lawrence: Regent Press of Kansas, 1979.

Rosen, Deborah A. *American Indians and State Law: Sovereignty, Race, and Citizenship, 1790–1880*. Lincoln: Univ. of Nebraska Press, 2007.

Rosier, Paul C. *Serving Their Country: American Indian Politics and Patriotism in the Twentieth Century*. Cambridge, MA: Harvard Univ. Press, 2009.

Sandstrom, Roy H., ed. *Educating the Educators: A Report of the Institute on "The American Indian Student in Higher Education."* Canton, NY: St. Lawrence Univ. and Xerox Corporation, 1971.

Schwartz, Joel. *The New York Approach: Robert Moses, Urban Liberals, and the Redevelopment of the Inner City*. Columbus: Ohio State Univ. Press, 1993.

Severance, Frank, ed. *Buffalo Historical Publications*. Vol. 6, 2 parts. Buffalo: Buffalo Historical Society, 1906.

Shafer, Jim. *The Allegheny River: Watershed of the Nation*. University Park: Pennsylvania State Univ. Press, 1992.

Shattuck, George C. *The Oneida Land Claims: A Legal History*. Syracuse, NY: Syracuse Univ. Press, 1991.

Shreve, Bradley C. *Red Power Rising: The National Indian Youth Council and the Origins of Native American Activism*. Norman: Univ. of Oklahoma Press, 2011.

Shurts, John. *Indian Reserved Water Rights*. Norman: Univ. of Oklahoma Press, 2000.

Smith, Reed. *State Government in Transition: Reforms of the Leader Administration, 1955–1959*. Philadelphia: Univ. of Pennsylvania Press, 1961.

Smith, Sheryl, and Brian Frehner, eds. *Indians and Energy Exploitation and Opportunity in the Southwest*. Santa Fe: School for Advanced Research, 2010.

Smith, Thomas G. *Green Republican: John Saylor and the Preservation of America's Wilderness*. Pittsburgh: Univ. of Pittsburgh Press, 2006.

Stave, Bruce M. *The New Deal and the Last Hurrah: Pittsburgh Machine Politics*. Pittsburgh: Univ. of Pittsburgh Press, 1970.

Tome, Philip. *Pioneer Life or Thirty Years a Hunter*. 1854. Reprint. Mechanicsburg, PA: Stackpole Books, 2006.

Trigger, Bruce G., and William C. Sturtevant, ed. *Handbook of North American Indians*. Vol. 15: *The Northeast*. Washington, DC: Smithsonian Institution, 1978.

Udall, Stewart L. *The Quiet Crisis*. New York: Holt, Rinehart and Winston, 1963.

Upton, Helen M. *The Everett Report in Historical Perspective: The Indians of New York*. Albany: New York State American Revolution Bicentennial Commission, 1980.

Vecsey, Christopher, and William A. Starna, eds. *Iroquois Land Claims*. Syracuse, NY: Syracuse Univ. Press, 1988.

Wallace, Anthony F. C. *The Death and Rebirth of the Seneca*. New York: Knopf, 1970.
———. *Tuscarora: A History*. Albany: SUNY Press, 2012.

Wallace, Paul A. W. *Indian Paths of Pennsylvania*. Harrisburg: Pennsylvania Historical and Museum Commission, 1965.

Weber, Michael P. *Don't Call Me Boss: David L. Lawrence*. Pittsburgh: Univ. of Pittsburgh Press, 1988.

Wilkins, David E. *American Indian Politics and the American Political System*. 3rd ed. Lanham, MD: Rowman and Littlefield, 2010.

———. *American Indian Sovereignty and the United States Supreme Court: The Masking of Justice.* Austin: Univ. of Texas Press, 1997.

———, ed. *Documents of Native American Political Development, 1500s to 1933.* New York: Oxford Univ. Press, 2009.

Wilkins, David E., and K. Tsianina Lomawaima. *Uneven Ground: American Indian Sovereignty and Federal Law.* Norman: Univ. of Oklahoma Press, 2001.

Wilkinson, Charles F. *Blood Struggle: The Rise of Modern Indian Nations.* New York: Norton, 2005.

Wilson, Edmund. *Apologies to the Iroquois.* 1960. Paperback reprint with an introduction and correspondence by William N. Fenton. Syracuse, NY: Syracuse Univ. Press, 1991.

ARTICLES

Abler, Thomas S. "Friends, Factions, and the Seneca Nation Revolution of 1848." *Niagara Frontier* 21 (Winter 1974): 74–79.

———. "The Kansas Connection: The Seneca Nation and the Iroquois Confederacy Council." In *Extending the Rafters: Interdisciplinary Approaches to Iroquoian Studies,* edited by Michael Foster, Jack Campisi, and Marianne Mithun, 81–93. Albany: State Univ. of New York Press, 1984.

———. "Protestant Missionaries and Native Cultures: Parallel Careers of Asher Wright and Silas T. Rand." *American Indian Quarterly* 26 (Winter 1992): 25–37.

———. "Seneca Moieties and Hereditary Chieftainships: The Early Nineteenth Century Political Organization of an Iroquois Nation." *Ethnohistory* 51 (Summer 2004): 459–88.

Abler, Thomas S., and Elisabeth Tooker. "Seneca." In *North American Indians,* vol. 15: *The Northeast,* edited by Bruce G. Trigger and William C. Sturtevant, 505–17. Washington, DC: Smithsonian Institution, 1978.

Abrams, George H. J. "The Cornplanter Cemetery." *Pennsylvania Archaeologist* 35 (Aug. 1965): 59–73.

———. "Moving the Fire: A Case of Iroquois Ritual Innovation." In *Iroquois Culture, History, and Prehistory: Proceedings of the 1965 Conference on Iroquois Research,* edited by Elisabeth Tooker, 23–24. Albany: New York State Museum, 1967.

Bennett, Robert L. "Building Indian Economies with Land Settlement Funds." *Human Organization* 20 (1961–62): 159–63.

———. "New Era for the American Indian." *Natural History* 76 (Feb. 1967): 6–11.

Berkhofer, Robert F., Jr. "Faith and Factionalism among the Senecas: Theory and Ethnohistory." *Ethnohistory* 12 (1965): 99–112.

Biggs, Bonnie. "Bright Child of Oklahoma: Lotsee Patterson and the Development of Americas Tribal Libraries." *American Indian Culture and Research Journal* 24 (2000): 55–67.

Bird, William A. "Reminiscences of the Boundary Survey between the United States and the British Provinces." In *Buffalo Historical Society Publications*, no. 4, 1–14. Buffalo: Buffalo Historical Society, 1896.

Bray, Ethel. "The Seneca Nation Library." *Bookmark* (Summer 1988): 246–47.

Brown, Ellen C. "Indian Law–State Jurisdiction on Indian Reservations: Effects of Concurrent State and Tribal Taxation on Indian Smokeshops." *Western New England Law Review* 3 (Spring 1981): 715–38.

Coffey, Louis. "Mediated Settlement of a Native American Land Claim." *CPA Journal*, June 2006: 1–6.

Cohn, Benjamin. "History and Anthropology: The State of Play." *Comparative Studies in Society and History* 22 (Apr. 1980): 198–221.

Colombi, Benedict J. "Indigenous Peoples, Large Dams, and Capital-Intensive Energy Development: A View from the Lower Colorado River." In *Indians and Energy Exploitation and Opportunity in the American Southwest*, edited by Sherri Smith and Brian Frehner, 89–109. Santa Fe: School for Advanced Research Press, 2010.

Dean, Robert. "'Dam Building Still Had Some Magic Then': Stewart Udall, the Central Arizona Project, and the Evolution of the Pacific Southwest Water Plan, 1963–1968." *Pacific Historical Review* 66, no. 9 (1997): 81–98.

Deardorff, Merle H. "The Cornplanter Grant in Warren County." *Western Pennsylvania Historical Magazine* 24 (Mar. 1941): 1–22.

Fenton, William N. "A Day on the Allegheny Ox-Bow." *Living Wilderness* 10 (1945): 1–8.

———. "Fishing Drives among the Cornplanter Seneca." *Pennsylvania Archaeologist* 12 (1942): 48–52.

———. "From Longhouse to Ranch-Type House: The Second Housing Revolution of the Seneca Nation." In *Iroquois Culture, History, and Prehistory: Proceedings of the 1965 Conference on Iroquois Research*, edited by Elisabeth Tooker, 3–22. Albany: New York State Museum, 1967.

———. "Locality as a Basic Factor in the Development of Iroquois Social Structure." *Bureau of American Ethnology Bulletin* 149 (1951): 35–54.

———. "Pennsylvania's Remaining Indian Settlement." *Pennsylvania Park News* 44 (1945): 1–2.

———. "Place-Names and Related Activities of the Cornplanter Seneca." *Pennsylvania Archaeologist* 15, no. 1 (1945): 25–29, no. 2 (1945): 42–50, no. 3 (1945): 88–96, no. 4 (1945): 108–18; 16, no. 2 (1946): 42–57.

———, ed. "Seneca Indians by Asher Wright (1859)." *Ethnohistory* 4 (1957): 302–21.

———. "Toward the Gradual Civilization of the Indian Natives: The Missionary and Linguistic Work of Asher Wright (1803–1875) among the Senecas of Western New York." *Proceedings of the American Philosophical Society* 100 (1956): 567–81.

Frohman, L. A., T. D. Doeblin, and F. G. Emorlin. "Diabetes in the Seneca Indians." *Diabetes* 18 (1969): 38–43.

Graymont, Barbara. "New York State Indian Policy after the Revolution." *New York History* 58 (Oct. 1976): 438–74.

Gunther, Gerald. "Governmental Power and New York Indian Lands: A Reassessment of a Persistent Problem of Federal–State Relations." *Buffalo Law Review* 7 (Fall 1958): 1–14.

Harmon, Alexandra, Colleen O'Neill, and Paul C. Rosier. "Interwoven Economic Histories: American Indians in a Capitalist America." *Journal of American History* 98 (Dec. 2011): 698–722.

Hauptman, Laurence M. "Alice Lee Jemison: A Modern 'Mother of the Nation.'" In *Sifters: Native American Women's Lives*, edited by Theda Perdue, 175–86. New York: Oxford Univ. Press, 2001.

———. "The American Indian Federation and the Indian New Deal: A Reinterpretation." *Pacific Historical Review* 52 (Nov. 1983): 378–402.

———. "Beyond Forensic History: Observations Based on a Forty-Year Journey through Iroquois History." *Journal of the West* 49 (Fall 2010): 10–19.

———. "Circle the Wagons: New York State v. the Indians." *Capital Region* (Feb. 1987): 29–31, 52–53.

———. "Compensatory Justice: The Seneca Nation Settlement Act of 1990." *National Forum* 71 (Spring 1991): 31–33.

———. "Ditches, Defense, and Dispossession: The Iroquois and the Rise of the Empire State." *New York History* 79 (Oct. 1998): 325–58.

———. "Finally Acknowledging Native Peoples: American Indian Policies since the Nixon Administration." In *"They Made Us Many Promises": The American*

Indian Experience, 1524 to the Present, edited by Philip Weeks, 210–28. Wheeling, IL: Harlan Davidson, 2002.

———. "General John S. Bragdon, the Office of Public Works Planning, and the Decision to Build Pennsylvania's Kinzua Dam." *Pennsylvania History* 53 (July 1986): 181–200.

———. "'Going off the Reservation': A Memoir." *Public Historian* 25 (Fall 2003): 81–102.

———. "Governor Blacksnake and the Seneca Indian Struggle to Save the Oil Spring Reservation." *Mid-America* 81 (Winter 1999): 51–73.

———. "Jemison, Alice Mae Lee." In *Notable American Women, the Modern Period: A Biographical Dictionary,* 4 vols., edited by Barbara Sicherman, Carol Hurd Green, Ilene Kantrow, and Harriette Walker, 4:379–80. Cambridge, MA: Belknap Press of Harvard Univ. Press, 1980.

———. "On and off State Time: William N. Fenton and the Seneca Indians in Crisis, 1954–1968." *New York History* 93 (Spring 2012): 182–232.

———. "*Seneca Nation v. Christy*: A Background Study." *Buffalo Law Review* 46 (Fall 1998): 947–77.

———. "Senecas and Subdividers: Resistance to Allotment of Indian Lands in New York, 1875–1906." *Prologue: The Journal of the National Archives,* Summer 1977: 105–17.

———. "State's Men, Salvation Seekers, and the Senecas: The Supplemental Treaty of Buffalo Creek, 1842." *New York History* 78 (Jan. 1997): 51–82.

———. "Who Owns Grand Island (Erie County, New York)?" *Oklahoma City University Law Review* 23 (Spring–Summer 1998): 151–74.

Hauptman, Laurence M., and Jack Campisi. "The Voice of Eastern Indians: The American Indian Chicago Conference, 1961, and the Movement for Federal Recognition." *Proceedings of the American Philosophical Society* 132 (Dec. 1988): 316–29.

Heath, Joseph J. "Review of the History of the April 1997 Trade and Commerce Agreement among the Traditional Haudenosaunee Council of Chiefs and New York State and the Impact Thereof on Haudenosaunee Sovereignty." *Buffalo Law Review* 46 (Fall 1998): 1011–40.

Hogan, Thomas E. "City in a Quandary: Salamanca and the Allegany Leases." *New York History* 55 (Jan. 1974): 79–101.

Judkins, Russell. "Diabetes and Perception of Diabetes among Seneca Indians." *New York Journal of Medicine* 78 (July 1978): 1320–23.

Kotlowski, Dean J. "Alcatraz, Wounded Knee, and Beyond: The Nixon–Ford Administrations Respond to Native American Protest." *Pacific Historical Review* 72 (2003): 201–27.

———. "From Backlash to Bingo: Ronald Reagan and Federal Indian Policy." *Pacific Historical Review* 77 (Nov. 2008): 617–52.

Lawrence, Jane. "The Indian Health Service and the Sterilization of Native American Women." *American Indian Quarterly* 24 (Summer 2000): 400–419.

Locklear, Arlinda. "Tribal Land Claims: Before and after Cayuga." *New York State Bar Association Government, Law, and Policy Journal* 8 (Spring 2006): 40–43.

Manley, Henry S. "Buying Buffalo from the Indians." *New York History* 27 (July 1947): 313–29.

———. "Indian Reservation Ownership in New York." *New York State Bar Bulletin* 32 (Apr. 1960): 134–38.

———. "Red Jacket's Last Campaign." *New York History* 31 (Apr. 1950): 149–68.

Miller, Nathan. "Private Enterprise in Inland Navigation: The Mohawk Route Prior to the Erie Canal." *New York History* 31 (Oct. 1950): 398–413.

Mohawk, John C. "Indian Economic Development: An Evolving Concept of Sovereignty." *Buffalo Law Review* 39 (1991): 495–506.

Morgan, Arthur E. "Intelligent Reasonableness and the Utilities: Democratic Decency or Chronic Bitterness." *Vital Speeches* 3 (Feb. 1, 1937): 230–33.

Murphy, Amanda M. "A Tale of Three Sovereigns: The Nebulous Boundaries of the Federal Government, New York State, and the Seneca Nation of Indians Concerning Taxation of Indian Reservation Cigarette Sales to Non-Indians." *Fordham Law Review* 79 (Apr. 2011): 2301–46.

Niemcewicz, Julian Ursyn. "Journey to Niagara, 1805." Edited by J. E. Budka Metchie. *New-York Historical Society Quarterly* 74 (Jan. 1960): 72–113.

Parker, Arthur C. "The White Man Takes Possession, 1783–1842." In *History of the Genesee Country*, 4 vols., edited by Lockwood R. Doty, 1:270–95. Chicago: Clarke, 1925.

Philp, Kenneth R. "Termination; A Legacy of the Indian New Deal." *Western Historical Quarterly* 14 (Apr. 1983): 165–80.

Porter, Robert Odawi. "Decolonizing Indigenous Governance: Observations on Restoring Greater Faith and Legitimacy in the Government of the Seneca Nation." *Kansas Journal of Law and Public Policy* 8 (Winter 1999): 97–141.

———. "The Inapplicability of American Law to the Indian Nations." *Iowa Law Review* 89 (Fall 2004): 1455–595.

———. "Legalizing, Decolonizing, and Modernizing New York State's Indian Law." *Albany Law Review* 63 (1999): 125–200.

———. "Strengthening Tribal Sovereignty through Government Reform: What Are the Issues?" *Kansas Journal of Law and Public Policy* 7 (1997): 72–105.

———. "What Kind of Shared Citizenship Is Actually Possible in a World of Separate Nation-States? Two Peoples, Two Nations: The Meaning of Haudenosaunee Citizenship." *International Studies Review* 7 (Oct. 2005): 512–15.

Pound, Cuthbert W. "Nationals without a Nation: The New York State Tribal Indians." *Columbia Law Review* 22 (Feb. 1922): 97–102.

Purcell, Aaron. "The Engineering of Forever: Arthur E. Morgan, the Seneca Indians, and the Kinzua Dam." *New York History* 78 (July 1997): 309–36.

Rauh, Joseph L., Jr. "The Role of the Leadership Conference on Civil Rights in the Civil Rights Struggle of 1963–1964." In *The Civil Rights Act of 1964: The Passage of the Law That Ended Racial Segregation*, edited by Robert D. Loevy, 49–76. Albany: State Univ. of New York Press, 1997.

Rosenthal, Melissa A. "Where There Is Smoke There Is Fire: New York's Battle to Collect Taxes on Cigarette Sales Made by Indian Retailers to Non-Indians." *Hamline Law Review* 17 (Spring 1994): 507–32.

Rosier, Paul C. "Dam Building and Treaty Breaking: The Kinzua Dam Controversy, 1936–1958." *Pennsylvania Magazine of History and Biography* 119 (Oct. 1995): 345–468.

———. "'They Are Ancestral Homelands': Race, Place, and Politics in Cold War Native America, 1945–1961." *Journal of American History* 92 (Mar. 2006): 1300–326.

Shoemaker, Nancy. "The Rise and Fall of Iroquois Women." *Journal of Women's History* 2 (Winter 1991): 39–57.

Smith, Roland M. "The Politics of Pittsburgh Flood Control, 1908–1936." *Pennsylvania History* 42 (Jan. 1975): 5–24.

———. "The Politics of Pittsburgh Flood Control, 1936–1960." *Pennsylvania History* 44 (Jan. 1977): 3–24.

Smith, Thomas G. "John Kennedy, Stewart Udall, and New Frontier Conservation." *Pacific Historical Review* 49 (Aug. 1985): 329–62.

———. "Voice for Wild and Scenic Rivers: John P. Saylor of Pennsylvania." *Pennsylvania History* 66 (Autumn 1999): 554–79.

Staub, Henry P. "American Indians: New Opportunity for Health Care." *New York State Journal of Medicine* 78 (June 1978): 1137–41.

Staub, Henry P., and Robert Hoekelman. "Health Supervision of Infants on the Cattaraugus Indian Reservation in New York: The Record Is No Better Than in the Big City Slum Areas." *Clinical Pediatrics* 15 (Jan. 1976): 44–52.

Stock, Midge Dean. "Seneca-Iroquois National Museum." In *Encyclopedia of Appalachia*, edited by Rudy Abramson and Jean Haskell, 1507–8. Knoxville: Univ. of Tennessee Press, 2006.

Stull, Donald D. "Reservation Economic Development in the Era of Self-Determination." *American Anthropologist* 92 (Mar. 1990): 206–10.

Tooker, Elizabeth. "The League of the Iroquois: Its History, Politics, and Ritual." In *Handbook of North American Indians*, vol. 15: *The Northeast*, edited by Bruce G. Trigger and William C. Sturtevant, 107–34. Washington, DC: Smithsonian Institution, 1978.

———. "On the Development of the Handsome Lake Religion." *Proceedings of the American Philosophical Society* 133 (1989): 35–50.

———. "On the New Religion of Handsome Lake." *Anthropological Quarterly* 41 (1968): 187–200.

Udall, Stewart. "The State of the Indian Nation—an Introduction." *Arizona Law Review* 10 (Winter 1968): 553–57.

Watkins, Arthur V. "Termination of Federal Supervision: The Removal of Restrictions over Indian Property and Person." *Annals of the American Academy of Political and Social Science* 311 (May 1957): 47–55.

Wilkinson, Charles F., and John M. Volkman. "Judicial Review of Indian Treaty Abrogation: 'As Long as Water Flows, or Grass Grows upon the Earth,' How Long Is That?" *California Law Review* 63 (May 1975): 601–61.

PERIODICALS

Akwesasne Notes
Albany Times Union
Bradford Era (Pennsylvania)
Buffalo Courier-Express
Buffalo News
Cornplanter Descendants Association Newsletter
Current History
Grand Junction Daily Sentinel (Colorado)
Indian Country Today
Indians at Work (US Bureau of Indian Affairs)

Jamestown Post Journal (New York)
Kinzua Planning Newsletter
MacLean's
National Indian Gaming Association Newsletter
New York Law Journal
New York Times
News from Indian Country
O He Yoh Noh (Allegany Indian Reservation)
Olean Times Herald
Oregon Democrat
Pittsburgh Post Gazette
Randolph Register
Rochester Democrat and Chronicle
Salamanca Press, (formerly *Salamanca Republican-Press*)
Sarasota Herald Tribune
Schenectady Gazette
Seneca Nation of Indian's Official Newsletter
Si Wong Geh (Cattaraugus Indian Reservation)
St. Petersburg Times
Syracuse Herald-American
Syracuse Post-Standard
Time
Wall Street Journal
Warren County Observer (Pennsylvania)
Warren Times-Mirror (Pennsylvania)
Washington Post
Wassaja (San Francisco)

DISSERTATIONS AND THESES

Abler, Thomas S. "Factional Dispute and Party Conflict in the Political System of the Seneca Nation (1845–1895): An Ethnohistorical Analysis." PhD diss., Univ. of Toronto, 1969.

Borgia, Melissa E. "An Overview of Language Preservation at Ohi:yo, the Seneca Allegany Territory." PhD diss., Indiana Univ. of Pennsylvania, 2010.

Brant, Roy E. "A Flood Control Dam for the Upper Allegheny River: Forty Years of Controversy." PhD diss., Univ. of Pittsburgh, 1970.

Brown, Dorcas R. "The Reservation Log Houses." MA thesis, State Univ. of New York at Oneonta and New York State Historical Association, 2000.

Cardinal, Jaré R. "Allegheny Be Dammed: The Seneca Nation in Crisis." MA thesis, Bowling Green State Univ., 1987.

Conable, Mary. "A Steady Enemy: The Ogden Land Company and the Seneca Indians." PhD diss., Univ. of Rochester, 1995.

Flad, Harvey. "The City and the Longhouse: A Social Geography of American Indians of Syracuse, New York." PhD diss., Syracuse Univ., 1973.

Hogan, Thomas E. "A History of the Allegany Reservation, 1850–1900." MA thesis, State Univ. of New York at Fredonia, 1974.

Lee, Allen. "The Kinzua Dam Project: A Case Study in the Politics of Flooding." PhD diss., Univ. of Pittsburgh, 1959.

Mt. Pleasant, Alyssa. "After the Whirlwind: Maintaining a Haudenosaunee Place at Buffalo Creek, 1780–1825." PhD diss., Cornell Univ., 2007.

FILM DOCUMENTARIES

Douglas, Ron, dir. *Unseen Tears: The Impact of Native American Residential Boarding Schools in Western New York*. Channels—Stories from the Niagara Frontier by Squeaky Wheels Media Resources. Buffalo: Community Foundation for Greater Buffalo in Cooperation with Native American Community Services of Erie and Niagara Counties, 2009.

Forbes, Allan, dir., with the assistance of George Heron. *Land of Our Ancestors*. Seneca Nation of Indians, 1994.

Gazit, Chana, and David Stewart, dir. *Honorable Nations*. PBS, 1991.

Marzuki, Marcy S. *Indian Warriors: The Untold Story of the Civil War*. History Channel, 2006.

Index

Page numbers in italic indicate photographs, tables, or maps.